6/01

 St. Louis Community College

Forest Park
Florissant Valley
Meramec

Instructional Resources
St. Louis, Missouri

GAYLORD S

Israel
a country study

Federal Research Division
Library of Congress
Edited by
Helen Chapin Metz
Research Completed
December 1988

On the cover: Shield of David—the menorah surrounded by olive branches, the official symbol of Israel

Third Edition; First Printing, 1990.

Library of Congress Cataloging-in-Publication Data

Israel: A Country Study.

Area handbook series, DA Pam 550–25
Research completed December 1988.
Bibliography: pp. 361–386.
Includes index.
1. Israel I. Metz, Helen Chapin, 1928-   . II. Federal Research Division, Library of Congress. III. Area Handbook for Israel. IV. Series: DA Pam 550–25.

DS126.5.I772   1990   90–6119   CIP

Headquarters, Department of the Army
DA Pam 550-25

For sale by the Superintendent of Documents, U.S. Government Printing Office
Washington, D.C. 20402

Foreword

This volume is one in a continuing series of books now being prepared by the Federal Research Division of the Library of Congress under the Country Studies—Area Handbook Program. The last page of this book lists the other published studies.

Most books in the series deal with a particular foreign country, describing and analyzing its political, economic, social, and national security systems and institutions, and examining the interrelationships of those systems and the ways they are shaped by cultural factors. Each study is written by a multidisciplinary team of social scientists. The authors seek to provide a basic understanding of the observed society, striving for a dynamic rather than a static portrayal. Particular attention is devoted to the people who make up the society, their origins, dominant beliefs and values, their common interests and the issues on which they are divided, the nature and extent of their involvement with national institutions, and their attitudes toward each other and toward their social system and political order.

The books represent the analysis of the authors and should not be construed as an expression of an official United States government position, policy, or decision. The authors have sought to adhere to accepted standards of scholarly objectivity. Corrections, additions, and suggestions for changes from readers will be welcomed for use in future editions.

Louis R. Mortimer
Acting Chief
Federal Research Division
Library of Congress
Washington, D.C. 20540

Acknowledgments

The authors wish to acknowledge the contributions of the following individuals who wrote the 1978 edition of *Israel: A Country Study,* which was edited by Richard F. Nyrop: Richard F. Nyrop, Laraine N. Carter, Darrell R. Eglin, Rinn Sup Shinn, and James D. Rudolph. Their work provided the organization and structure of the present volume, as well as portions of the text.

The authors are grateful to individuals in various government agencies and private institutions who gave their time, research materials, and expertise to the production of this book. The authors also wish to thank members of the Federal Research Division staff who contributed directly to the preparation of the manuscript. These people include Thomas Collelo, the substantive reviewer of all the textual material and maps; Richard F. Nyrop, who reviewed all drafts and served as liaison with the sponsoring agency; and Martha E. Hopkins, who managed book editing and production. Noelle B. Beatty, Sharon Costello, Deanna D'Errico, and Evan Raynes edited the chapters. Also involved in preparing the text were editorial assistants Barbara Edgerton and Izella Watson. Catherine Schwartzstein performed final prepublication review. Shirley Kessel compiled the index. Malinda B. Neale of the Library of Congress Composing Unit set the type, under the direction of Peggy Pixley.

Invaluable graphics support was provided by David P. Cabitto, assisted by Sandra K. Ferrell. Carolina E. Forrester reviewed the map drafts and prepared the final maps. Special thanks are owed to Kimberly A. Lord, who designed the cover artwork and the illustrations on the title page of each chapter.

The authors would like to thank Arvies J. Staton, who supplied information on ranks and insignia. Joshua Sinai provided invaluable assistance in the transliteration and translation of Hebrew terms. Finally, the authors acknowledge the generosity of the many individuals and public agencies who allowed their photographs to be used in this study.

Contents

Chapter 4. Government and Politics 177
Joshua Sinai

Preface

Like its predecessor, this study is an attempt to treat in a concise and objective manner the dominant social, political, economic, and military aspects of contemporary Israeli society. Sources of information included scholarly journals and monographs, official reports of governments and international organizations, foreign and domestic newspapers, and numerous periodicals. Chapter bibliographies appear at the end of the book; brief comments on some of the more valuable sources suggested as possible further reading appear at the end of each chapter. Measurements are given in the metric system; a conversion table is provided to assist those readers who are unfamiliar with metric measurements (see table 1, Appendix A).

An effort has been made to limit the use of foreign—mostly Hebrew and Arabic—words and phrases, but a fairly large number were deemed necessary to an understanding of the society. These terms have been defined the first time they appear in a chapter or defined in a Glossary entry. To help readers identify the numerous political groups, Appendix B, Political Parties and Organizations, is provided.

The transliteration of Hebrew words and phrases follows a modified version of the system adopted by the United States Board on Geographic Names and the Permanent Committee on Geographic Names for British Official Use, known as the BGN/PCGN system. The names of people and places of ancient Israel are generally presented as they appear in the Revised Standard Version of the Bible.

A modified version of the BGN/PCGN system for transliterating Arabic was employed. The modification is a significant one, however, entailing as it does the omission of diacritical marks and most hyphens.

Country Profile

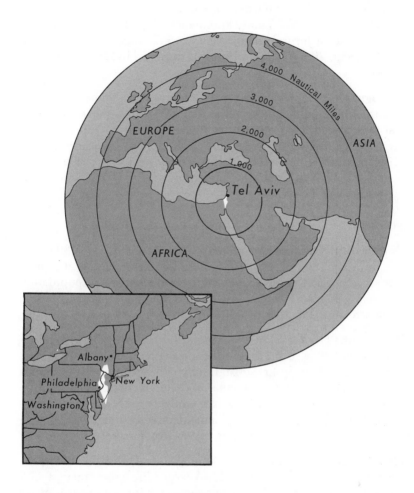

Country

Formal Name: State of Israel

Short Form: Israel

Term for Citizens: Israeli(s)

Capital: Government located in Jerusalem, Israel's officially designated capital. In 1988 United States and most other countries continued to recognize Tel Aviv as capital and to maintain their chanceries there.

Geography

Size: About 20,700 square kilometers. Occupied territories comprise additional 7,477 square kilometers: West Bank, 5,879; Gaza Strip, 378; East Jerusalem, annexed in 1967, annexation reaffirmed in July 1980, 70; and Golan Heights, annexed in December 1981, 1,150.

Topography: Four general areas: coastal plain—fertile, humid, and thickly populated—stretches along Mediterranean Sea; central highlands including Hills of Galilee in north with country's highest elevation at Mt. Meron (1,208 meters), and arid Judean Hills in south; Jordan Rift Valley with lowest point (399 meters below sea level) at Dead Sea; and Negev Desert, which accounts for about half Israel's area.

Society

Population: Officially estimated in October 1987 at 4,389,600, of whom about 82 percent Jews. Population increasing at annual rate of about 1.8 percent, although Arab segment of population increasing at annual rate of about 2.8 percent compared to Jewish population growth rate of 1.3 percent.

Education: High level of education, literacy rate of Jewish population about 90 percent. State education either secular or religious, with independent (but substantially state-supported) religious schools in addition; ratio of secular to religious enrollments approximately 70 to 30. Schools are free and compulsory for students through age fifteen, and are supplemented by scouting, youth movements, and vocational training. Seven universities.

Health: High level of health and medical care, with one of highest physician-patient ratios in world. Average life expectancy of 73.9 for Jewish males and 77.3 for females; 72.0 for non-Jewish males and 75.8 for females. Steadily declining infant mortality rates. Widespread system of public health and broad insurance coverage contribute to eradication and prevention of disease. Many voluntary and charitable organizations, some funded substantially from abroad, involved in health care.

Languages: Hebrew major official language and most widely used in daily life. Arabic, chief language of Arab minority, also official language and may be used in Knesset (parliament) and courts; also spoken by older Sephardim (Oriental Jews—see Glossary). English widely spoken and taught in state schools. Yiddish spoken by older

Ashkenazim (see Glossary) and by ultra-Orthodox. Numerous other languages and dialects spoken by smaller segments of population, reflecting diversity of cultural origins.

Religion: Judaism dominant faith. Substantial Sunni (see Glossary) Muslim (about 77 percent of non-Jewish population) and smaller Christian and Druze (see Glossary) communities also present.

Economy

Gross National Product (GNP): Approximately US$33 billion (US$7,576 per capita) in 1987. Between 1973 and 1983 real GNP growth rate was approximately 2.0 percent per year. Real GNP increased 2.4 percent in 1984, increased 3.7 percent in 1985, increased 3.3 percent in 1986, and increased 5.2 percent in 1987.

Agriculture: Efficient and modern. Irrigation extensive, but all available water resources currently being used. Main products included cereals, fruits, vegetables, poultry, and dairy products. Specialization in high-value produce, partly for export. Imports of grains and meat. Agriculture's share of GNP 5 percent in 1986.

Industry: Contributed 23 percent of GNP and employed 23 percent of labor force in 1986. Major industries included electronics, biotechnology, diamond cutting and polishing, energy, chemicals, rubber, plastics, clothing and textiles, and defense.

Imports: US$9.2 billion in 1986, excluding US$1.1 billion of direct defense imports. Materials for processsing accounted for more than 75 percent of nondefense imports. Bulk of imports from industrialized countries.

Exports: US$6.9 billion in 1986. Metals, machinery, and electronics represented main exports (US$2.2 billion in 1986). Diamonds were next largest export (US$1.9 billion). Main markets in industrial countries.

Balance of Payments: During 1986 Israel had current account surplus of US$1.4 billion. Situation resulted from Economic Stabilization Program adopted in July 1985.

Currency and Exchange Rates: New Israeli shekel introduced September 1985, worth 1,000 of former shekels; 100 agorot (sing., agora—see Glossary) = 1 new Israeli shekel. Average exchange rate 1988 1.6 NIS per US$.

Transportation and Communications

Roads: 13,410 kilometers of roads in 1985, providing relatively dense network.

Railroads: 528 kilometers of state-owned railroads in 1988 linking major centers of Jerusalem, Tel Aviv, Haifa, Beersheba, and Ashdod.

Ports: Haifa most important, handling about 55 percent of foreign trade in 1985, excluding bulk oil transport. Ashdod and Elat (Red Sea) other major cargo ports. Oil terminals at Elat and near Ashqelon; coal terminal at Hadera.

Airports: International airport at Lod; smaller airport at Elat.

Pipelines: Elat to near Ashqelon for crude oil for ongoing shipment; branch leads to Ashdod and Haifa refineries and to consumption centers, including Elat, for petroleum products.

Communications: Modern, developed system with good connections via cable and three ground satellite stations to rest of world. In FY 1986 about 1.9 million telephones. In late 1980s, Israel faced a demand for more telecommunications services than it was able to provide.

Government and Politics

Government: Republic and parliamentary democracy headed by president, titular head of state. Executive power wielded by prime minister and cabinet ministers representing dominant political blocs in Knesset, to which they are collectively responsible. Knesset is unicameral parliament of 120 members elected at-large every four years as a rule by direct secret ballot and under system of proportional representation; voting for party lists rather than individual candidates. Electoral system remains object of political reform. Government system based on no comprehensive written constitution but nine Basic Laws enacted by Knesset. Efforts to introduce constitution delineating principle of separation of powers and establishing supremacy of civil law and secular bill of rights have so far met resistance. Judiciary independent and comprises secular, religious, and military courts. Integrity and performance of governmental system checked by independent and influential ombudsman, Office of the State Comptroller.

Politics: Multiparty system divided into four main categories: left-of-center parties, right-of-center parties, right-wing religious parties, and Arab parties. Inconclusive twelfth Knesset election held in November 1988 repeated pattern of 1984 Knesset elections with neither major party able to form cohesive coalition government without other's equal participation. This resulted in formation of National Unity Government. Long-term electoral trends, however, indicated upswing in support for right-of-center parties.

Administrative Divisions: Divided into six administrative districts and fourteen subdistricts under ultimate jurisdiction of Ministry of Interior. Occupied territories of West Bank and Gaza Strip and annexed Golan Heights administered by Israel Defense Forces.

Foreign Affairs: Foreign policy chiefly influenced by Israel's strategic situation, Palestinian-Israeli conflict, and rejection of Israel by most Arab states. Diplomatic relations established with Egypt following 1979 Egypt-Israel peace treaty, and Israel maintained de facto peaceful relationship with Jordan. General consensus in Israel over terms of 1978 Camp David Accords, but disagreement over principle of exchanging land for peace, particularly over West Bank, and direct negotiations with Palestine Liberation Organization.

National Security

Armed Forces: As of 1987, army 104,000 on active duty, including 88,000 conscripts; navy 8,000, including 3,200 conscripts; air force 39,000, including 7,000 conscripts. Reservists: army 494,000, navy 1,000, air force 50,000. Male conscripts served three years active duty and female conscripts twenty months; annual reserve duty for males thirty to sixty days following active service. Paramilitary groups included Nahal, combining military service with work in agricultural settlements, and Gadna, providing military training at high school level.

Combat Units and Major Equipment: As of 1987, on mobilization, army had eleven divisions composed of thirty-three armored brigades; also nine independent mechanized brigades, three infantry brigades, five paratroop brigades, fifteen artillery brigades. Equipped with 3,900 tanks and 8,000 other armored vehicles. Navy had 100 combat vessels, including 3 submarines, 19 missile attack craft, 40 coastal patrol boats. Three missile corvettes and two submarines on order. Air force had 655 combat aircraft organized into twelve fighter-interceptor squadrons, six fighter squadrons, one reconnaissance squadron. First-line fighters were F–15s, F–16s, and Kfirs.

Equipment Sources: Large domestic defense industry of state-owned and privately owned firms produced aircraft, missiles, small arms, munitions, electronics, and communications gear. Export sales of US$1.2 billion annually exceeded production for domestic use. United States military aid running at US$1.8 billion annually, including fighter aircraft, helicopters, missile boats, and funding for Israeli-manufactured weapons.

Military Budget: US$5.6 billion in Israeli fiscal year 1987; approximately 14 percent of GNP and 25 percent of total government budget.

Police and Intelligence Agencies: As of 1986, Israel Police—20,874, including Border Police of approximately 5,000 and Palestinian Police (1,000). Auxiliary forces included Civil Defense Corps of army reservists (strength unknown) and Civil Guard (approximately 100,000 volunteers). Separate intelligence organizations included Mossad (external), Shin Bet (domestic), and Aman (military).

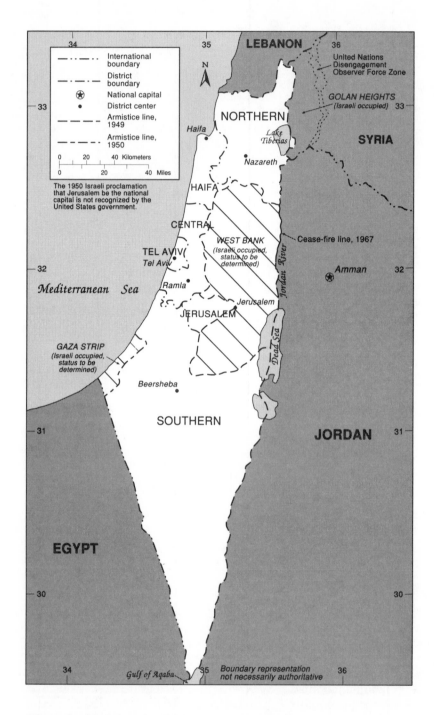

Figure 1. Administrative Divisions, Israel, 1988

Introduction

ISRAEL OBSERVED THE fortieth anniversary of its founding as a state in 1988. Although a young nation in the world community, Israel has been profoundly influenced by Jewish history that dates back to biblical times as well as by the Zionist movement in nineteenth- and twentieth-century Europe. These two strands, frequently in conflict with one another, helped to explain the tensions in Israeli society that existed in the late 1980s. Whereas Orthodox Judaism emphasized the return to the land promised by God to Abraham, secular Zionism stressed the creation of a Jewish nation state.

Zionism historically has taken different forms, and these variations were reflected in twentieth-century Israeli society. The leading type of early Zionism, political Zionism, came out of Western Europe in large measure as a response to the failure of the emancipation of Jews in France in 1791 to produce in the succeeding century the degree of the anticipated reduction in anti-Semitism. Jewish assimilation into West European society was inhibited by the anti-Jewish prejudice resulting from the 1894 trial of Alfred Dreyfus, a French Jewish officer. Theodor Herzl, a Hungarian Jew, in 1896 published a book advocating the creation of a Jewish state to which West European Jews would immigrate, thus solving the Jewish problem. Rather than emphasizing creation of a political entity, cultural Zionism, a product of oppressed East European Jewry, advocated the establishment in Palestine of self-reliant Jewish settlements to create a Hebrew cultural renaissance. Herzl was willing to have the Jewish state located in Uganda but East European Jews insisted on the state's being in Palestine, and after Herzl's death in 1904, the cultural Zionists prevailed. Meanwhile, the need arose for practical implementation of the Zionist dream and Labor Zionism came to the fore, appealing particularly to young Jews who were influenced by socialist movements in Russia and who sought to flee the pogroms in Eastern Europe. Labor Zionism advocated socialism to create an equitable Jewish society and stressed the integration of class and nation. David Ben-Gurion, who came to Palestine in 1906, became a leader of this group, which favored a strong economic basis for achieving political power. Labor Zionism in turn was challenged by the Revisionist Zionism of Vladimir Jabotinsky, a Russian Jew who glorified nationalism and sought to promote Jewish immigration to Palestine and the immediate declaration of Jewish statehood.

The Zionist cause was furthered during World War I by Chaim Weizmann, a British Jewish scientist, skilled in diplomacy, who recognized that Britain would play a major role in the postwar settlement of the Middle East. At that time Britain was seeking the wartime support of the Arabs, and in the October 1915 correspondence between Sharif Husayn of Mecca and Sir Henry McMahon, British high commissioner in Egypt, Britain endorsed Arab postwar independence in an imprecisely defined area that apparently included Palestine. In November 1917, however, Britain committed itself to the Zionist cause by the issuance of the Balfour Declaration, which stated that the British government viewed with favor "the establishment in Palestine of a National Home for the Jewish People," while the "civil and religious rights of existing non-Jewish communities in Palestine" were not to suffer. These two concurrent commitments ultimately proved irreconcilable.

During the succeeding decades until the Holocaust conducted by Nazi Germany during World War II, Jewish immigration to Palestine continued at a fairly steady pace. The Holocaust, in which nearly 6 million Jews lost their lives, gave an impetus to the creation of the state of Israel: thousands of Jews sought to enter Palestine while Britain, as the mandatory power, imposed limits on Jewish immigration to safeguard the indigenous Arab inhabitants. An untenable situation developed, and in 1947 Britain referred the Palestine problem to the United Nations General Assembly. The latter body approved a resolution on November 29, 1947, calling for a complex partition of Palestine into an Arab and a Jewish state. The Arab Higher Committee rejected the resolution, and violence increased. The establishment of the State of Israel was declared on May 14, 1948, and Arab military forces began invading the territory the following day. By January 1949, Israel had gained more territory than had been allotted by the partition; East Jerusalem and the West Bank of the Jordan River remained in Jordanian hands as a result of fighting by the Arab Legion of Transjordan, and the Gaza area remained in Egyptian hands (see fig. 1). Israel held armistice talks with the Arab states concerned in the first half of 1949 and armistice lines were agreed upon, but no formal peace treaties ensued.

Having achieved statehood, the new government faced numerous problems. These included the continued ingathering of Jews from abroad, the provision of housing, education, health and welfare facilities, and employment for the new immigrants; the establishment of all requisite government services as well as expanding the country's infrastructure; the expropriation of Arab lands—including lands left by Arabs who had fled during the 1948 war as well as by Arabs obliged by the government to relocate—so as to provide a livelihood for new immigrants; the establishment of a military government to administer Arab population areas; and the growth of the Israel Defense Forces (IDF) to safeguard national security.

Tensions continued to exist between Israel and its neighbors, and as a result a series of wars occurred: in 1956 in the Suez Canal area; in June 1967, during which Israel captured the Golan Heights, the Sinai Peninsula, the Gaza Strip, East Jerusalem, and the West Bank, adding about 800,000 Palestinian Arabs to its population; and in October 1973, a war that destroyed Israel's image of its invincibility. Israel's poor showing in the early days of the 1973 war led to considerable popular disenchantment with the ruling Labor Party; this declining popularity, combined with the growing number of Oriental Jews who identified more readily with the religious expressions of Menachem Begin than with Labor's socialist policies, contributed to the coming to power of the conservative Likud Bloc in the May 1977 elections.

The rise of Oriental Jews illustrated the changing pattern of ethnicity in the course of Jewish history. In the late nineteenth century, the majority of the Jewish population in Palestine was of Sephardic (Spanish or Portuguese) origin, but by the time the State of Israel was created Ashkenazim (Jews of Central or East European origin) constituted 77 percent of the population. By the mid-1970s, however, as a result of the influx of Oriental Jews from North Africa and the Middle East, the Ashkenazi majority had been reversed, although Ashkenazim still dominated Israel's political, economic, and social structures. Oriental immigrants tended to resent the treatment they had received in transition camps and development towns at the hands of the Labor government that ruled Israel for almost thirty years. Furthermore, Orientals experienced discrimination in housing, education, and employment; they recognized that they constituted a less privileged group in society that came to be known as the "Second Israel."

In addition to the Ashkenazi-Oriental division, Israel has faced a cleavage between religiously observant Orthodox Jews and secular Jews, who constituted a majority of the population. In broad terms, most secular Jews were Zionists who sought in various ways, depending on their conservative, liberal, or socialist political views, to support governmental programs to strengthen Israel economically, politically, and militarily. Jews belonging to religious political parties, however, tended to be concerned with strict observance of religious law, or halakah, and with preserving the purity of Judaism. The latter was reflected in the views of religiously observant

Jews who accepted as Jews only persons born of a Jewish mother and the ultra-Orthodox who considered conversions by Reform or Conservative rabbis as invalid.

A further divisive element in Israeli society concerned the role of minorities: Arab Muslims, Christians, and Druzes. These sectors together constituted approximately 18 percent of Israel's population in late 1989, with a birth rate in each case higher than that of Jews. Israelis in the late 1980s frequently expressed concern over government statistics that indicated that the high birthrate among Arabs in Israel proper (quite apart from the West Bank) had resulted in an Arab population majority in Galilee. They were concerned as well over the comparative youth of the Arab population in comparison with the Jewish population. In general, members of the ethnic minorities were less well off in terms of employment, housing, and education than the average for the Jewish population.

The role of the Arab minority in Israel's economy has historically been controversial. Labor Zionism advocated that all manual labor on kibbutzim and moshavim (see Glossary) be performed by Jewish immigrants themselves. As immigration increased, however, and immigrants had skills needed by the new state in areas other than agriculture, cheap Arab labor came to be used for agricultural and construction purposes. After the occupation of the West Bank and the Gaza Strip in 1967, Arab day laborers became an even more important factor in the Israeli economy, providing as much as 30 percent of the work force in some spheres, and in many instances replacing Oriental Jews who had performed the more menial tasks in Israeli society.

Despite its historical importance in Israel, agriculture has not had major economic significance. For example, in 1985 agriculture provided just over 5 percent of Israel's gross domestic product (GDP—see Glossary) whereas industry contributed almost five times as much. Israel's skilled work force excelled in the industrial sphere, particularly in high-technology areas such as electronics, biotechnology, chemicals, and defense-related industries or in such highly skilled occupations as diamond cutting.

Although Israel had human resources, the lack of capital on the part of many new immigrants after 1948 obliged the government to provide funds for developing the country's infrastructure and for many enterprises. This policy resulted in a quasi-socialist economy in which ownership fell into three broad categories: private, public, and HaHistadrut HaKlalit shel HaOvdim B'Eretz Yisrael (General Federation of Laborers in the Land of Israel) known as Histadrut (see Glossary), the overall trade union organization. Israel depended to a large degree on funds contributed by Jews in the

Diaspora (see Glossary) to provide government services necessary to settle new immigrants and to establish economic ventures that would ensure jobs as well as to maintain the defense establishment at a high level of readiness, in view of Israel's position as a "garrison democracy" surrounded by potential enemies. Despite the inflow of money from Jews in the Diaspora, as a result of large government spending for defense and domestic purposes, Israel has generally been a debtor nation and has relied heavily on grants and loans from the United States. Israel in the early 1980s also had to deal with runaway inflation that reached about 450 percent in fiscal year (FY—see Glossary) 1984. To curb such inflation, the government instituted the Economic Stabilization Program in July 1985 that reduced inflation in 1986 to 20 percent.

By 1987, the Economic Stabilization Program had led to a significant increase in economic activity in Israel. Increased certainty brought about by the Economic Stabilization Program stimulated improved growth in income and productivity. Between July 1985 and May 1988, a cumulative increase in productivity of 10 percent occurred. The 1987 cuts in personal, corporate, and employer tax rates and in employer national insurance contributions stimulated net investment during the same period.

The freezing of public sector employment occasioned by the Economic Stabilization Program began lessening the role of government in the economy and increased the supply of labor available to the business community. However, the outbreak of the *intifadah* (uprising) in December 1987 had an adverse impact on these trends.

The government has played a major role in social and economic life. Even prior to the achievement of statehood in 1948, the country's political leaders belonged primarily to the Labor Party's predecessor, Mapai, which sought to inculcate socialist principles into various aspects of society. Creating effective government under the circumstances prevailing in 1948, however, entailed compromises between the Labor Zionist leadership and the Orthodox religious establishment. These compromises were achieved by creating a framework that lacked a written constitution but relied instead on a number of Basic Laws governing such aspects as the organization of the government, the presidency, the parliament or Knesset, the judiciary, and the army. An uneasy tension continued, however, between religiously observant and secular Jews. For example, in protest against the proposed new Basic Law: Human Rights (and a possible change in the electoral system), which Agudat Israel, a small ultra-Orthodox religious party, believed would have an adverse effect on Orthodox Jews, in early

November 1989 the party left the National Unity Government for two months.

Until 1977 the government operated under a political power system with two dominant parties, Labor and Likud. As a result of the 1977 elections, in which Labor lost control of the government, a multiparty system evolved in which it became necessary for each major party to obtain the support of minor parties in order to govern, or for the two major parties to form a coalition or government of national unity, as occurred in 1984 and 1988. The result of Israel's proportional electoral system, in which voters endorsed national party lists rather than candidates in a given geographic area, has been a stalemate in which the smaller parties, especially the growing right-wing religious parties, have been able to exert disproportionate influence in the formation of governments and on government policies. This situation has led to numerous proposals for electoral reform, which were still being studied in early 1990, but which had a marginal chance of enactment because of the vested interests of the parties involved.

A major factor in Israel's political alignment has been its relations with other countries, particularly those of the West, because of its dependence on financial support from abroad. Although Israel's relations with the United States and Western Europe have generally been good, since late 1987 criticism has grown in the West of Israel's handling of the uprising in the occupied territories of the West Bank and the Gaza Strip. The agreement by the United States in December 1988 to initiate discussions with the Palestine Liberation Organization (PLO) has indicated that United States and Israeli interests may not necessarily be identical. Furthermore, the feeling has increased that the United States should exert greater pressure on Israel to engage in negotiations with the Palestinians and to abandon its "greater Israel" stance, as expressed by Secretary of State James A. Baker on May 22, 1989. In October 1989, Baker proposed a five-point "framework" that involved Israel, the United States, and Egypt to try to advance Prime Minister Yitzhak Shamir's plan for elections in the West Bank and the Gaza Strip. Israel agreed in principle in November but attached two reservations: that the PLO not be involved in the naming of Palestinian delegates and that the discussions be limited to preparations for the elections.

In addition to relations with the West, Israel has sought to expand its economic relations, particularly, with both Third World countries and with Eastern Europe and the Soviet Union, and to influence the latter to allow increased emigration of Jews. The sharp upswing in Soviet Jewish immigration to Israel—approximately

2,000 persons in November 1989 and 3,700 in December, with a continued influx in mid-January 1990 at the rate of more than 1,000 persons per week—led to an announcement that Israel would resettle 100,000 Soviet Jews over the following three years. The cost was estimated at US$2 billion, much of which Israel hoped to raise in the United States. This influx aroused considerable concern on the part of Palestinian Arabs, who feared many Soviet Jews would settle in the West Bank.

Israel's relations with neighboring states have been uneven. Egyptian president Anwar as Sadat's historic visit to Jerusalem in November 1977 led to the Camp David Accords in September 1978 and ultimately to the signing of a peace treaty and the return of the Sinai Peninsula to Egypt. In 1989 Egypt began to play an increasingly prominent role as mediator between Israel and the Palestinians, particularly as reflected in President Husni Mubarak's ten-point peace proposals in July. The PLO accepted the points in principle, and the Israel Labor Party considered them a viable basis for negotiations.

Tensions continued along Israel's northern border with Lebanon because of incursions into Israel by Palestinian guerrillas based in Lebanon. These raids led to Israel's invasion of Lebanon (known in Israel as Operation Peace for Galilee) in June 1982, the siege of Beirut, the Israeli occupation of southern Lebanon, and withdrawal to the armistice line in June 1985. As a result, relations with factions in Lebanon and relations with Syria remained tense in early 1990, whereas Israeli relations with Jordan had ended in cooperation agreements concerning the West Bank; such agreements were canceled by King Hussein's disclaimer on July 31, 1989, of Jordanian involvement in the West Bank.

Israel's relationship with its neighbors must be understood in the context of its overriding concern for preserving its national security. Israel saw itself as existing alone, beleaguered in a sea of Arabs. Accordingly, it has developed various security principles: such as anticipating a potential extensive threat from every Arab state, needing strategic depth of terrain for defensive purposes, or, lacking that, needing an Israeli deterrent that could take a conventional or nuclear form, and the necessity to make clear to neighboring states, particularly Syria, actions that Israel would consider potential causes for war. Another security principle was Israeli autonomy in decision making concerning military actions while the country concurrently relied on the United States for military matériel. (United States military aid to Israel averaged US$1.8 billion annually in the mid- and late 1980s; other United States government aid from 1985 onward brought the total to more than US$3 billion annually).

Because of its national security concerns, the IDF, primarily a citizen army, has played a leading role in Israeli society. With exceptions granted to Orthodox individuals for religious reasons, men and women have an obligation to perform military service, a factor that has acted to equalize and educate Israel's heterogeneous Jewish population. Although Israel operates on the principle of civilian control of defense matters, a number of the country's leaders have risen to political prominence on retiring from the military, such as Moshe Dayan, Yitzhak Rabin, Ezer Weizman, and Ariel Sharon. The key national role of the IDF and its pursuit of the most up-to-date military matériel, although costly, have benefited the economy. Defense-related industries are a significant employer, and, through military equipment sales, also serve as a leading source of foreign currency. Israel has excelled in arms production and has developed weapons used by the United States and other countries.

The IDF has not only served in a traditional military capacity in the wars in which Israel has been engaged since 1948. Since 1967 it also has exercised military government functions in the West Bank and the Gaza Strip. This role has proved particularly onerous for Israeli citizen soldiers once the *intifadah* began in December 1987.

The *intifadah* has probably had a greater impact on the lives of both Palestinians and Israelis than any other event in recent years. For Palestinians in the West Bank and the Gaza Strip, the uprising has created a new younger generation of leadership, a sense of self-reliance, and an ability to transcend religious, political, economic, and social differences in forming a common front against the Israeli occupation. In so doing, Palestinians have organized themselves into local popular committees (coordinated at the top by the Unified National Command of the Uprising) to handle such matters as education, food cultivation and distribution, medical care, and communications. Committee membership remained secret, as such membership was declared a prison offense in August 1988. Observers have commented that the committees were reliably considered to include representatives of various political factions within the PLO and some of its more radical offshoots, as well as communists and members of the Muslim fundamentalist Islamic Resistance Movement, known as Hamas. Israeli authorities initially endorsed Hamas in the hope that it would draw Arabs from the PLO (Hamas was given time on Israeli television in the November 1988 elections), but as it became more powerful, especially in the Gaza Strip, Israel outlawed Hamas, Islamic Jihad (Holy War), and Hizballah (Party of God), which were radical Muslim groups, in June 1989, setting jail terms of ten years for members. The PLO itself had been banned earlier in the occupied territories.

Various restrictions and punishments have been imposed from time to time and in different locations on West Bank and Gaza Strip residents since the *intifadah* began. Among actions taken against Palestinians in the West Bank was the outlawing of professional unions of doctors, lawyers, and engineers in August 1988. Universities in the West Bank and the Gaza Strip have been closed since October 1987. Schools in the West Bank were closed for more than six months in 1988 and, after reopening in December 1988, were again closed one month later; schools were open for only three months in 1989. Instruction in homes or elsewhere was punishable by imprisonment. Extended curfews have been instituted, often requiring people's confinement to their houses. (For example, the approximately 130,000 Palestinian inhabitants of Nabulus experienced an eleven-day curfew in February 1989, during which United Nations Relief and Works Agency for Palestine Refugees in the Near East trucks bearing food were forbidden to enter the city). Water, electricity, and telephone service have been cut, and periodically Palestinian workers have been refused permission to enter Israel to work. By the end of 1989, at least 244 houses had been destroyed, affecting almost 2,000 persons. Beatings and shootings had resulted in 795 deaths and more than 45,000 injuries by the end of 1989. Approximately 48,000 Palestinians had been arrested and imprisoned since the uprising began through December 1989. Administrative detention without charge, originally for a period of six months and increased in August 1989 to twelve months, was imposed on about 7,900 Palestinians, and 61 Palestinians had been deported from Israel by the end of 1989. These restrictions were documented in detail in the United States Department of State's Country Reports on Human Rights Practices and the statistics of Al Haq (Law in the Service of Man), a Ram Allah-based human rights organization. Countermeasures instituted by Palestinians have included demonstrations, boycotts of Israeli products, refusal to pay taxes (resulting in the case of Bayt Sahur, near Bethlehem, in September 1989 of extended twenty-four-hour curfews and the seizure of property in lieu of taxes), strikes and intermittent closings of shops, stonethrowing, and some terrorist acts including the use of fire bombs, and the killing of about 150 Palestinians considered Israeli collaborators.

Both Palestinians and foreign observers saw the *intifadah* as having had a profound effect on the PLO. In the opinion of many observers, the PLO had previously sought to minimize the role of Palestinians in the occupied territories so as to maintain its own control of the Palestinian movement. The coordinated activities of the young Palestinian leadership in the West Bank and the Gaza Strip since the uprising have obliged the PLO to relinquish its sole leadership. The PLO has been compelled to support solutions for the Palestinian problem that it had previously opposed but which were favored by residents of the occupied territories, namely an international conference to resolve the Palestine issue and a two-state solution. The uprising brought pressure on the Palestine National Council, which included representatives of Palestinians throughout the world, to bury its differences and to provide psychological support to Palestinians within the occupied territories by announcing the creation of a Palestinian state in mid-November 1988.

The *intifadah* has also had a substantial impact on Israelis because of the escalation of violence. Israeli settlers in the West Bank have taken the law into their own hands on numerous occasions, shooting and killing Palestinians. In the course of the *intifadah*, 44 Israelis had been killed by the end of 1989, and, according to Israeli government statistics, more than 2,000 Israelis had been injured. The uprising has also affected Israeli Arabs, many of whom have experienced a greater sense of identity with their Palestinian brothers and sisters. Evidence is lacking, however, of acts of violence by Israeli Arabs against Israeli authorities, something that many Israelis had anticipated.

The cost to Israel of quelling the uprising has been calculated by the United States government at US$132 million per month, not counting the loss in revenues from production and from tourism—the latter dropped 40 percent but were beginning to rise again in late 1989. The violence has not occurred without protest by Israelis. Many of the soldiers of the IDF, for example, have found particularly distasteful the use of force on civilians, especially on young children, women, and the elderly, and have complained to government leaders such as Prime Minister Shamir. The liberal Israeli movement Peace Now organized a large-scale peace demonstration that involved Israelis and Palestinians as well as about 1,400 foreign peace activists on December 30, 1989, in Jerusalem; more than 15,000 persons formed a human chain around the city.

Many Israelis have expressed concern about the effects of the violence on Israel's democratic institutions as well as on Israel's image in the world community. A number of Israeli leaders have publicly advocated a political rather than a military settlement of the uprising. As early as the spring of 1988, a group of retired generals, primarily members of the Labor Party, organized the Council for Peace and Security, maintaining that continued occupation of the West Bank and the Gaza Strip was actually harmful to Israel's security, and that Israel should rely on the IDF rather than the occupied territories for its security. The Jaffee Center for Strategic Studies of Tel Aviv University, a think tank composed of high-level political and military figures, in a study conducted by Aryeh Shalev, retired former military governor of the West Bank, concluded in December 1989 that Israel's repressive measures had actually fueled the uprising. Among individuals who have spoken out are former Foreign Minister Abba Eban, who endorsed chief of staff Lieutenant General Dan Shomron's view that the *intifadah* cannot be solved "because it is a matter of nationalism." To this Eban added, "You cannot fight a people with an army." Eban maintained that the PLO could not endanger Israel because Israel had "540,000 soldiers, 3,800 tanks, 682 fighter-bombers, thousands of artillery units, and a remarkable electronic capacity." Observers have pointed out that Israel's launching on September 19, 1988, of the Ofeq-1 experimental satellite provided it with a military intelligence potential that reduced the need for territorial holdings. In September 1989, Israel launched Ofeq-2, a ballistic missile that further demonstrated Israel's military response capabilities.

Both Eban and Ezer Weizman, minister of science and technology in the 1988 National Unity Government, favored talking with the PLO, as did General Mordechai Gur, also a Labor cabinet member, former military intelligence chief General Yehoshafat Harkabi, and several other generals. The Jaffee Center for Strategic Studies, in its early March 1989 report, *Israel's Options for Peace*, supported talks with the PLO. In fact, informal contacts between Israelis and PLO members had already occurred, although such meetings were a criminal offense for Israelis. On February 23, 1989, PLO chief Yasir Arafat met in Cairo with fifteen Israeli journalists. In early March, several Knesset members met PLO officials in New York at a conference sponsored by Columbia University. In other instances, Egyptians, Americans, and West Bank Palestinians have served as intermediaries in bringing Israelis and PLO officials together. In October 1989, however, Abie Nathan, a leading Israeli peace activist, was sentenced to six months' imprisonment for meeting PLO members, and in early January 1990, Ezer Weizman was forced out of the inner cabinet for meeting with PLO figures. The families of Israeli prisoners of war, however, were authorized in December 1989 to contact the PLO to seek the prisoners' release.

In addition to the pressures exerted by the *intifadah*, the reason for the greater willingness to talk to the PLO has been a perception that the PLO has followed a more moderate policy than in the past. For example, in December 1988, Arafat explicitly met

United States conditions for discussions with the PLO by announcing the acceptance of United Nations Security Council Resolutions 242 and 338, which indicated recognition of the State of Israel, and by renouncing the use of terrorism.

The majority of the government of Israel in January 1990, however, continued to oppose talks with the PLO. For example, on January 19, 1989, Minister of Defense Rabin proposed that Palestinians end the *intifadah* in exchange for an opportunity to elect local leaders who would negotiate with the Israeli government. The plan, which made no mention of the PLO, was presented to Faisal Husayni, head of the Arab Studies Center in Jerusalem and a West Bank Palestinian leader, just after his release from prison on January 28. Minister of Industry and Trade Sharon in February 1989 sharply denounced any talks with the PLO. In mid-April, Prime Minister Shamir stated that he would not withdraw Israeli troops from the West Bank and the Gaza Strip to facilitate free Palestinian elections in those areas, nor would he allow international observers of such elections. In late April, Rabin asserted that any PLO candidate in Palestinian elections would be imprisoned.

Despite such indications of an apparent negative attitude toward facilitating peace negotiations, on May 14, 1989, Shamir announced a twenty-point cabinet-approved peace plan, which he had aired privately with President George Bush during his May visit to Washington. The basic principles of the plan stated that Israel wished to continue the Camp David peace process; it opposed the creation of an additional Palestinian state in the Gaza Strip or the West Bank (by implication Jordan was considered already to be a Palestinian state); it would not negotiate with the PLO; and there would be "no change in the status of Judea, Samaria, and the Gaza district, unless in accord with the basic program of the government." Israel proposed free elections in the occupied territories, which were to be preceded by a "calming of the violence" (the plan did not specifically set forth an end to the uprising as a precondition for elections, as Sharon had wished); elections were to choose representatives to negotiate the interim stage of self-rule, which was set at five years to test coexistence and cooperation. No later than three years after the interim period began, negotiations were to start for a final solution; negotiations for the first stage were to be between Israelis and Palestinians, with Jordan and Egypt participating if they wished; for the second stage, Jordan would also participate and Egypt if it desired. In the interim period, Israel would be responsible for security, foreign affairs, and matters relating to Israeli citizens in the occupied territories. The plan made no mention of voting rights for the approximately 140,000 Arab residents of East Jerusalem, which Israel occupied in 1967. In countering Israeli criticism of the plan, Shamir restated his commitment not to yield "an inch of territory."

Such an intransigent position also characterized those Israeli West Bank settlers whose vigilante tactics have created problems not only for Palestinians but also for the IDF in the occupied territories. In late May 1989, West Bank military commander Major General Amran Mitzna begged a visiting Knesset committee to help "stop the settlers' incitement against the Israel Defense Forces." The settlers were provoked by the army's interference with their "reprisal raids" on Palestinians. The substantial reduction in IDF forces in the West Bank, following a January 1989 reduction in the defense appropriation (variously reported as US$67 or US$165 million) was followed by increased settler violence. Concurrently, the IDF has reduced the number of days of annual service to be performed by reservists from sixty (the number set after the uprising began—it was thirty before the *intifadah*) to forty-five, as a direct economy measure and to minimize the impact on the Israeli economy of lengthy reserve service.

The serious problems facing the Israeli economy have fallen to Minister of Finance Shimon Peres, who, as Labor Party head, served as prime minister in the previous National Unity Government. The need to remedy the serious deficits incurred by the kibbutzim and the industries operated by the Histadrut, both areas of the economy associated with the Labor Party, were considered a major reason for Peres's having been named minister of finance in the new 1988 government. Observers have commented that Peres made a slow start in addressing the rising inflation rate, which was nearing 23 percent in 1989; the growing unemployment, which amounted to more than 9 percent; and the budget deficits. In late December, Peres announced a 5 percent devaluation of the new Israeli shekel (for value of the shekel—see Glossary) and a week later, when unveiling the new budget on January 1, a further 8 percent devaluation. Budget cuts of US$550 million were made in addition to government savings of US$220 million by reducing food and gasoline subsidies. The government also announced plans to dismiss thousands of civil servants and to cut cost-of-living increases for all workers. These components were collectively designed to revive the economy and to stimulate exports. The Israeli public, however, was understandably critical of these harsh measures, which made Peres personally unpopular and decreased the possibility of his being able to force an early election to overturn the Likud-led National Unity Government.

Israel in January 1990, therefore, faced a difficult future. Economically, the country was undergoing stringent budgetary limitations that affected all Israelis. Politically and militarily, it confronted the ongoing *intifadah* and the question of its willingness to talk to the PLO and to consider giving up land for peace, or its continued use of the IDF to repress the Palestinian uprising in the occupied territories. Militarily, it faced a possible threat from its enemy Syria as well as from the battle-tested army of Iraq. Politically, Israel was challenged by the growing strength of right-wing religious and religio-nationalist parties and the need for electoral reform to create a more effective system of government. Socially and religiously, the country faced the issue of reconciling the views of Orthodox Jews with those of secular Jews, considered by most observers as a more serious problem than differences between Oriental Jews and Ashkenazim. Any Israeli government confronting such challenges was indeed called upon to exercise the proverbial wisdom of Solomon.

January 25, 1990

*   *   *

The major event since the above was written was the fall on March 15 of the government of Likud prime minister Yitzhak Shamir on a no-confidence vote over his refusal to accept the United States proposal for discussions between Israelis and Palestinians to initiate steps toward an Israeli-Arab peace plan. (Minister of Commerce and Industry Ariel Sharon had resigned from the coalition government on February 18 after the Likud central committee moved toward approving such a dialogue). The fall of the government, which was the first time that the Knesset had dissolved a government, was preceded by Shamir's firing of Deputy Prime Minister Shimon Peres on March 13, leading to the resignation of all other Labor Party ministers in the National Unity Government. The no-confidence vote resulted from a last-minute decision by Shas, a small ultra-Orthodox Sephardic party, to abstain from voting, giving Labor and its allies a sixty to fifty-five majority in the Knesset. On March 20, President Chaim Herzog asked Peres to form a government; despite five-week efforts to achieve a coalition, Peres notified Herzog on April 26 that he was unable to do so. This process again was a first—the first time in forty-two years that a prime minister candidate designated by a president had failed to put together a government. On April 27 the mandate for forming a government was given to Shamir, who as of early May was still negotiating. Should this attempt fail, new elections will be required, but the composition of the Knesset will probably not change significantly in such an election.

Meanwhile, the negotiations conducted by both major parties involved bargaining and significant material and policy commitments to tiny fringe parties, particularly the religious parties, that were out of proportion to their strength. As a result, Israelis have become increasingly disenchanted with their electoral system. On April 7 a demonstration for electoral reform drew approximately 100,000 Israelis, the largest number since the 1982 demonstration protesting Israel's invasion of Lebanon. More than 70,000 people signed a petition, endorsed by President Herzog, calling for the direct election of the prime minister and members of the Knesset so as to eliminate the disproportionate influence of small parties. Moreover, on April 9 an Israeli public opinion poll revealed that 80 percent of Israelis favored changing the electoral system.

The situation was further complicated by the Israeli response to Secretary of State Baker's statement on March 1 that the United States would back Israel's request for a US$400 million loan to construct housing for Soviet Jewish immigrants only if Israel stopped establishing settlements in the West Bank and the Gaza Strip. The Israeli government stated that this condition was the first time that the United States government had linked American aid to the way that Israel spent its own money. In a March 3 news conference, President Bush included East Jerusalem in the category of territory occupied by Israel, saying that the United States government opposed new Jewish immigrants being settled there (an estimated 115,000 Jews and 140,000 Palestinian Arabs lived in East Jerusalem as of March). Prime Minister Shamir announced on March 5 that new Jewish neighborhoods of East Jerusalem would be expanded as rapidly as possible to settle Soviet Jews—7,300 Soviet Jews arrived in March and 10,500 in April.

On April 18, Shamir appointed Michael Dekel, a Likud advocate of settlements, to oversee the groundbreaking for four new settlements in the occupied territories of the West Bank and the Gaza Strip and to try to buy residential property in the Armenian Quarter of the Old City of Jerusalem for Jewish occupancy. This action was made possible by the absence from the government of Labor Party ministers, who had been opposing various settlement activities. Government sponsorship of Jewish settlement in Jerusalem, although initially denied, included a grant of US$1.8 million to a group of 150 persons, consisting of Jewish religious students and their families, to rent through a third party St. John's Hospice in the Christian Quarter of the Old City, which they occupied on

April 12, the eve of Good Friday. This incident caused an uproar among Christian Palestinians and led to the protest closing of Christian churches in Jerusalem for one day on April 27—the first time in 800 years that the Church of the Holy Sepulcher had been closed. Jerusalem Mayor Teddy Kollek testified in court opposing the settlement on the grounds that it would damage Israel's international reputation, harm public order in the Christian Quarter, and disrupt the delicate and established ethnic balance of Jerusalem. The Supreme Court announced on April 26 that it upheld the eviction of the settlers by May 1.

In other developments, the European Community threatened sanctions against Israel unless the government allowed the reopening of Palestinian institutions of higher education in the West Bank and the Gaza Strip, which had been closed since October 1987. In reply, Israel stated on February 26 that it would allow sixteen community colleges and vocational institutions, serving approximately 18,000 Palestinian students, to reopen in stages on unspecified dates.

Iraq's president Saddam Husayn, who was extremely fearful of an Israeli strike against Iraq, on April 2 threatened that Iraq would use chemical weapons against Israel if it attacked. This threat outraged the world community and was followed on April 3 by Israel's launch of a new three-stage rocket earth satellite into a surveillance orbit.

Meanwhile, the *intifadah* continued. The Palestine Center for Human Rights reported on March 19 that 878 Palestinian fatalities had occurred up to that date. The Israeli human rights body stated on April 3 that thirty Palestinians had been killed by Israeli army gunfire in the first quarter of 1990, whereas Palestinians had killed thirty-five of their number as suspected Israeli collaborators over the same period. Israel announced on February 18 a 15 percent reduction in the defense budget for 1990–91, together with a reduced number of service days for reservists, caused by the financial costs of the uprising. No end to the *intifadah* appeared in sight, with well-informed Israeli sources suggesting that the uprising had strengthened the convictions of Israelis on both sides: those favoring territorial maximalism and those advocating compromise. The difference was thought to be a greater realism, with maximalists feeling that the territories could be retained only by removing a number of Palestinians from the West Bank and the Gaza Strip, and compromisers recognizing that negotiations with the PLO would require significant concessions.

May 2, 1990   Helen Chapin Metz

Chapter 1. Historical Setting

A Jew wearing a tasseled cap or simlah,
shown on the Black Obelisk of Shalmaneser III (r. 859–825 B.C.)

ON MAY 14, 1948, in the city of Tel Aviv, David Ben-Gurion proclaimed the Declaration of the Establishment of the State of Israel. The introductory paragraph affirmed that "Eretz Yisrael (the Land of Israel) was the birthplace of the Jewish people. Here they first attained statehood, created cultural values of national and universal significance, and gave the world the eternal Book of Books." The issuance of the proclamation was signaled by the ritual blowing of the shofar (ram's-horn trumpet) and was followed by the recitation of the biblical verse (Lev. 25:10): "Proclaim liberty throughout the land and to all the inhabitants thereof." The same verse is inscribed on the American Liberty Bell in Independence Hall in Philadelphia.

The reestablishment of the Jewish nation-state in Palestine has been the pivotal event in contemporary Jewish history. After nearly two millennia of exile, the Jewish people were brought together in their ancient homeland. Despite the ancient attachments of Jews to biblical Israel, the modern state of Israel is more deeply rooted in nineteenth- and twentieth-century European history than it is in the Bible. Thus, although Zionism—the movement to establish a national Jewish entity—is rooted in the messianic impulse of traditional Judaism and claims a right to Palestine based on God's promise to Abraham, the vast majority of Zionists are secularists.

For nearly 2,000 years following the destruction of the Second Temple in A.D. 70, the attachment of the Jewish Diaspora (see Glossary) to the Holy Land was more spiritual then physical. The idea of an ingathering of the exiles and a wholesale return to the Holy Land, although frequently expressed in the liturgy, was never seriously considered or acted upon. Throughout most of the exilic experience, the Jewish nation connoted the world Jewish community that was bound by the powerful moral and ethical ethos of the Jewish religion. The lack of a state was seen by many as a virtue, for it ensured that Judaism would not be corrupted by the exigencies of statehood. Despite frequent outbreaks of anti-Semitism, Jewish communities survived and in many cases thrived as enclosed communities managed by a clerical elite in strict accordance with Jewish law.

Zionism called for a revolt against the old established order of religious orthodoxy (see Origins of Zionism, this ch.). It repudiated nearly 2,000 years of Diaspora existence, claiming that the Judaism of the Exile, devoid of its national component, had rendered the

Jews a defenseless pariah people. As such, Zionism is the most radical attempt in Jewish history to escape the confines of traditional Judaism. The new order from which Zionism sprang and to which the movement aspired was nineteenth-century liberalism: the age of reason, emancipation, and rising nationalism.

Before Napoleon emancipated French Jewry in 1791, continental and Central European Jews had been forced to reside in designated Jewish ''ghettos'' apart from the non-Jewish community. Emancipation enabled many Jews to leave the confines of the ghetto and to attain unprecedented success in business, banking, the arts, medicine, and other professions. This led to the assimilation of many Jews into non-Jewish European society. The concomitant rise of ethnically based nationalisms, however, precluded Jewish participation in the political leadership of most of the states where they had settled. Political Zionism was born out of the frustrated hopes of emancipated European Jewry. Political Zionists aspired to establish a Jewish state far from Europe but modeled after the postemancipation European state.

In Eastern Europe, where the bulk of world Jewry lived, any hope of emancipation ended with the assassination of the reform-minded Tsar Alexander II in 1881. The pogroms that ensued led many Russian Jews to emigrate to the United States, while others joined the communist and socialist movements seeking to overthrow the tsarist regime and a much smaller number sought to establish a Jewish state in Palestine. Zionism in its East European context evolved out of a Jewish identity crisis; Jews were rapidly abandoning religious orthodoxy, but were unable to participate as equal citizens in the countries where they lived. This was the beginning of cultural Zionism, which more than political Zionism attached great importance to the economic and cultural content of the new state.

The most important Zionist movement in Palestine was Labor Zionism, which developed after 1903. Influenced by the Bolsheviks, the Labor movement led by David Ben-Gurion created a highly centralized Jewish economic infrastructure that enabled the Jewish population of Palestine (the Yishuv—see Glossary) to absorb waves of new immigrants and to confront successfully the growing Arab and British opposition during the period of the British Mandate (1920–48). Following independence in May 1948, Ben-Gurion's Labor Zionism would guide Israel through the first thirty years of statehood.

The advent of Zionism and the eventual establishment of the State of Israel posed anew a dilemma that has confronted Jews and Judaism since ancient times: how to reconcile the moral imperatives of the Jewish religion with the power politics and military force necessary to maintain a nation-state. The military and political exigencies of statehood frequently compromised Judaism's transcendent moral code. In the period before the Exile, abuses of state power set in rapidly after the conquests of Joshua, in the reign of Solomon in both the northern and southern kingdoms, under the Hasmoneans, and under Herod the Great.

In the twentieth century, the Holocaust transformed Zionism from an ideal to an urgent necessity for which the Yishuv and world Jewry were willing to sacrifice much. From that time on, the bulk of world Jewry would view Jewish survival in terms of a Jewish state in Palestine, a goal finally achieved by the creation of the state of Israel in 1948. The Nazi annihilation of 6 million Jews, on whose behalf the West proved unwilling to intervene, and the hostility of Israel's Arab neighbors, some of which systematically evicted their Jewish communities, later combined to create a sense of siege among many Israelis. As a result, the modern State of Israel throughout its brief history has given security priority over the country's other needs and has considerably expanded over time its concept of its legitimate security needs. Thus, for reasons of security Israel has justified the dispossession of hundreds of thousands of Palestinian Arabs, the limited rights granted its Arab citizens, and harsh raids against bordering Arab states that harbored Palestinian guerrillas who had repeatedly threatened Israel.

The June 1967 War was an important turning point in the history of Israel (see 1967 and Afterward, this ch.). The ease of victory and the reunification of Jerusalem spurred a growing religio-nationalist movement. Whereas Labor Zionism was a secular movement that sought to sow the land within the Green Line (see Glossary), the new Israeli nationalists, led by Gush Emunim and Rabbi Moshe Levinger, called for Jewish settlement in all of Eretz Yisrael. The June 1967 War also brought under Israel's control the Sinai Peninsula, the Golan Heights (see Glossary), the West Bank (see Glossary), the Gaza Strip (see Glossary), and East Jerusalem. From the beginning, control of Jerusalem was a nonnegotiable item for Israel. The Gaza Strip and especially the West Bank, however, posed a serious demographic problem that continued to fester in the late 1980s.

In contrast to the euphoria that erupted in June 1967, the heavy losses suffered in the October 1973 War ushered in a period of uncertainty. Israel's unpreparedness in the early stages of the war discredited the ruling Labor Party, which also suffered from a rash of corruption charges. Moreover, the demographic growth of Oriental Jews (Jews of African or Asian origin), a large number of whom felt alienated from Labor's blend of socialist Zionism, tilted the electoral balance for the first time in Israel's history away from the Labor Party (see Jewish Ethnic Groups, ch. 2). In the May 1977 elections Menachem Begin's Likud Bloc unseated Labor.

The early years of the Begin era were dominated by the historic peace initiative of President Anwar as Sadat of Egypt. His trip to Jerusalem in November 1977 and the subsequent signing of the Camp David Accords and the Treaty of Peace between Egypt and Israel ended hostilities between Israel and the largest and militarily strongest Arab country. The proposed Palestinian autonomy laid out in the Camp David Accords never came to fruition because of a combination of Begin's limited view of autonomy—he viewed the West Bank as an integral part of the State of Israel—and because of the refusal of the other Arab states and the Palestinians to participate in the peace process. As a result, violence in the occupied territories increased dramatically in the late 1970s and early 1980s.

Following Likud's victory in the 1981 elections, Begin and his new minister of defense, Ariel Sharon, pursued a harder line toward the Arabs in the territories. After numerous attempts to quell the rising tide of Palestinian nationalism failed, Begin, on the advice of Sharon and Chief of Staff General Rafael Eitan, decided to destroy the Palestine Liberation Organization (PLO) major base of operations in Lebanon. On June 6, 1982, Israeli troops crossed the border into Lebanon initiating Operation Peace for Galilee. This was the first war in Israel's history that lacked wide public support.

Ancient Israel

The history of the evolving relationship between God and the Jewish people set forth in the the Hebrew Bible—the five books of the Torah (see Glossary), *neviim* (prophets), and *ketuvim* (writings)—known to Christians as the Old Testament, begins with myths. The stories of creation, the temptation and sin of the first humans, their expulsion from an idyllic sanctuary, the flood, and other folkloric events have analogies with other early societies. With the appearance of Abraham, however, the biblical stories introduce a new idea—that of a single tribal God. Over the course of several centuries, this notion evolved into humanity's first complete monotheism. Abraham looms large in the traditions of the Jewish people and the foundation of their religion. Whether Jews by birth or by conversion, each male Jew is viewed as "a son of Abraham."

It was with Abraham that God, known as Yahweh, made a covenant, promising to protect Abraham and his descendants, to wage wars on their behalf, and to obtain for them the land of

*Muslim mosque above the Cave of Machpela, the traditional
burial place of the Jewish patriarchs, in Hebron, occupied West Bank
Courtesy* Palestine Perspectives

Canaan, an area roughly approximate to modern Israel and the
occupied West Bank (in another part of the Torah, God pledges
to Abraham's descendants "the land from the river of Egypt to
the great river, the river Euphrates," an area much larger than
historic Canaan). In exchange, the ancient Hebrews were bound
individually and collectively to follow the ethical precepts and rituals
laid down by God.

Canaan, the land promised to Abraham and his descendants,
was a narrow strip, 130 kilometers wide, bounded by the Mediterranean Sea to the west, the Arabian Desert to the east, Egypt to
the south, and Mesopotamia to the north. Situated between the
great Mesopotamian and Egyptian cultures, Canaan served as a
burgeoning trading center for caravans between the Nile Valley
and the Euphrates and as a cultural entrepôt. The clash of cultures and the diverse commercial activities gave Canaan a dynamic
spiritual and material creativity. Prior to the emergence of Abraham, however, Egyptian and Mesopotamian hostility, continuous
invasions of hostile peoples, and Canaan's varied topography had
resulted in frequent fighting and general instability.

In the last quarter of the second millennium B.C., the collapse
of the Hittite Empire to the north, and the decline of Egyptian power

7

to the south at a time when the Assyrians had not yet become a major force set the stage for the emergence of the Hebrews. As early as the latter part of the third millennium B.C., invasions from the east significantly disrupted Middle Eastern society. The people who moved from Mesopotamia to the Mediterranean spoke western Semitic languages of which Hebrew is one. The term *Hebrew* apparently came from the word *habiru* (also *hapiru* or *apiru*), a term that was common to the Canaanites and many of their neighbors. The word was used to designate a social class of wanderers and seminomads who lived on the margins of, and remained separate from, sedentary settlements. Abraham was the leader of one of these immigrant *habiru* groups. He is depicted as a wealthy seminomad who possessed large flocks of sheep, goats, and cattle, and enough retainers to mount small military expeditions.

The Canaanite chieftains urged Abraham to settle and join with them. Abraham remained in the land, but when it came time to select a wife for his and Sarah's son Isaac, the wife was obtained from their relatives living in Haran, near Urfa in modern Turkey. This endogamous practice was repeated by Isaac's son Jacob, who became known as Israel because he had wrestled with God (Gen. 32:28).

During Jacob-Israel's lifetime the Hebrews completely severed their links with the peoples of the north and east and his followers began to think of themselves as permanently linked to Canaan. By his two wives, Leah and Rachel, and their two serving maids, Bilhah and Zilpah, Israel fathered twelve sons, the progenitors of the twelve tribes of Israel, the "children of Israel." The term *Jew* derives from the name of one of the tribes, Judah, which was not only one of the largest and most powerful of the tribes but also the tribe that produced David and from which, according to biblical prophecy and postbiblical legend, a messiah will emerge.

Some time late in the sixteenth or early in the fifteenth century B.C., Jacob's family—numbering about 150 people—migrated to Egypt to escape the drought and famine in Canaan. Beginning in the third millennium B.C. large numbers of western Semites had migrated to Egypt, usually drawn by the richness of the Nile Valley. They came seeking trade, work, or escape from hunger, and sometimes they came as slaves. The period of Egyptian oppression that drove the Israelites to revolt and escape probably occurred during the reign of Ramses II (1304–1237 B.C.). Most scholars believe that the Exodus itself took place under his successor Merneptah. A victory stela dated 1220 B.C. relates a battle fought with the Israelites beyond Sinai in Canaan. Taken together with other evidence, it is believed that the Exodus occurred in the thirteenth century B.C. and had been completed by about 1225 B.C.

The Book of Exodus describes in detail the conditions of slavery of the Jews in Egypt and their escape from bondage. The Exodus episode is a pivotal event in Jewish history. The liberation of a slave people from a powerful pharaoh—the first such successful revolt in recorded antiquity—through divine intervention tied successive generations of Hebrews (Jews) to Yahweh. The scale of the revolt and the subsequent sojourn in Sinai created a self-awareness among the Hebrews that they were a separate people sharing a common destiny. Moreover, the giving of the Law to Moses at Mount Sinai set down a moral framework that has guided the Jewish people throughout their history. The Mosaic Code, which includes the Ten Commandments and a wide body of other laws derived from the Torah, not only proclaimed the unity of God but also set forth the revolutionary idea that all men, because they were created in God's image, were equal. Thus, the Hebrews believed that they were to be a people guided by a moral order that transcended the temporal power and wealth of the day.

The conquest of Canaan under the generalship of Joshua took place over several decades. The biblical account depicts a primitive, outnumbered confederation of tribes slowly conquering pieces of territory from a sedentary, relatively advanced people who lived in walled cities and towns. For a long time the various tribes of Israel controlled the higher, less desirable lands, and only with the advent of David did the kingdoms of Israel and Judah come into being with a capital in Jerusalem.

Prior to the emergence of David, the Hebrew tribes, as portrayed in the last three chapters of the Book of Judges, were fighting among themselves when the Philistines (whence the term *Palestine*) appeared on the coast and pushed eastward. The Philistines were a warlike people possessing iron weapons and organized with great discipline under a feudal-military aristocracy. Around 1050 B.C., having exterminated the coastal Canaanites, they began a large-scale movement against the interior hill country, now mainly occupied by the Israelites. To unify the people in the face of the Philistine threat, the prophet Samuel anointed the guerrilla captain Saul as the first king of the Israelites. Only one year after his coronation, however, the Philistines destroyed the new royal army at Mount Gilboa, near Bet Shean, southeast of the Plain of Yizreel (also known as the Plain of Jezreel and the Plain of Esdraelon), killing Saul and his son Jonathan.

Facing imminent peril, the leadership of the Israelites passed to David, a shepherd turned mercenary who had served Saul but also trained under the Philistines. Although David was destined to be the most successful king in Jewish history, his kingdom initially was not a unified nation but two separate national entities, each of which had a separate contract with him personally. King David, a military and political genius, successfully united the north and south under his rule, soundly defeated the Philistines, and expanded the borders of his kingdom, conquering Ammon, Moab, Edom, Zobah (also seen as Aram-Zobah), and even Damascus (also seen as Aram-Damascus) in the far northeast (see fig. 2). His success was caused by many factors: the establishment of a powerful professional army that quelled tribal unrest, a regional power vacuum (Egyptian power was on the wane and Assyria and Babylon to the east had not yet matured), his control over the great regional trade routes, and his establishment of economic and cultural contacts with the rich Phoenician city of Tyre. Of major significance, David conquered from the Jebusites the city of Jerusalem, which controlled the main interior north-south route. He then brought the Ark of the Covenant, the most holy relic the Israelites possessed and the symbol of their unity, into the newly constituted "City of David," which would serve as the center of his united kingdom.

Despite reigning over an impressive kingdom, David was not an absolute monarch in the manner of other rulers of his day. He believed that ultimate authority rested not with any king but with God. Throughout his thirty-three-year reign, he never built a grandiose temple associated with his royal line, thus avoiding the creation of a royal temple-state. His successor and son Solomon, however, was of a different ilk. He was less attached to the spiritual aspects of Judaism and more interested in creating sumptuous palaces and monuments. To carry out his large-scale construction projects, Solomon introduced corvées, or forced labor; these were applied to Canaanite areas and to the northern part of the kingdom but not to Judah in the south. He also imposed a burdensome tax system. Finally, and most egregious to the northern tribes of Israel, Solomon ensured that the Temple in Jerusalem and its priestly caste, both of which were under his authority, established religious belief and practice for the entire nation. Thus, Solomon moved away from the austere spirituality founded by Moses in the desert toward the pagan cultures of the Mediterranean Coast and Nile Valley.

When Solomon died in 925 or 926 B.C., the northerners refused to recognize his successor Rehoboam. Subsequently the north broke away and was ruled by the House of Omri. The northern kingdom of Israel, more populous than the south, possessing more fertile land and closer to the trading centers of the time, flourished until it was completely destroyed and its ten tribes sent into permanent exile by the Assyrians between 740 and 721 B.C. The destruction of the north had a sobering effect on the south. The prophet Isaiah eloquently proclaimed that rather than power and wealth, social justice and adherence to the will of God should be the focus of the Israelites.

At the end of the sixth century B.C., the Assyrian Empire collapsed and the Babylonians under Nebuchadnezzar besieged the city of Jerusalem, captured the king, and ended the first commonwealth. Even before the first Exile, the prophet Jeremiah had stated that the Israelites did not need a state to carry out the mission given to them by God. After the Exile, Ezekiel voiced a similar belief: what mattered was not states and empires, for they would perish through God's power, but man.

From the time of the destruction of the First Temple in 586 B.C., the majority of Jews have lived outside the Holy Land. Lacking a state and scattered among the peoples of the Near East, the Jews needed to find alternative methods to preserve their special identity. They turned to the laws and rituals of their faith, which became unifying elements holding the community together. Thus, circumcision, sabbath observance, festivals, dietary laws, and laws of cleanliness became especially important.

In the middle of the sixth century B.C., the Persian emperor Cyrus the Great defeated the Babylonians and permitted the Jews to return to their homeland "to rebuild the house of the Lord." The majority of Jews, however, preferred to remain in the Diaspora, especially in Babylon, which would become a great center of Jewish culture for 1,500 years. During this period Ezra, the great codifier of the laws, compiled the Torah from the vast literature of history, politics, and religion that the Jews had accumulated. The written record depicting the relationship between God and the Jewish people contained in the Torah became the focal point of Judaism.

Hellenism and the Roman Conquest

In 332 B.C., Alexander the Great of Macedon destroyed the Persian Empire but largely ignored Judah. After Alexander's death, his generals divided—and subsequently fought over—his empire. In 301 B.C., Ptolemy I took direct control of the Jewish homeland, but he made no serious effort to interfere in its religious affairs. Ptolemy's successors were in turn supplanted by the Seleucids, and in 175 B.C. Antiochus IV seized power. He launched a campaign to crush Judaism, and in 167 B.C. he sacked the Temple.

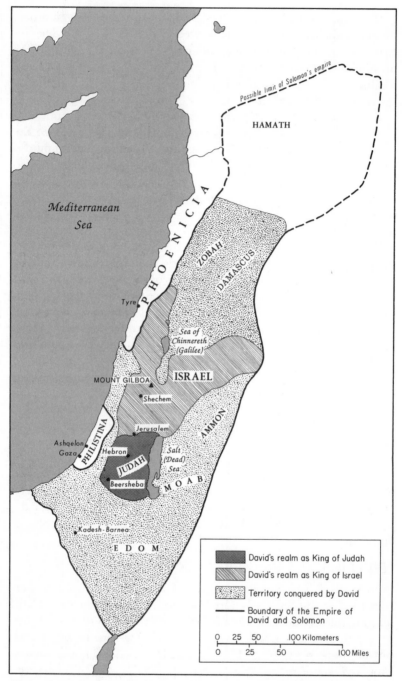

Figure 2. Land of Israel During the Reigns of David and Solomon

The violation of the Second Temple, which had been built about 520–515 B.C., provoked a successful Jewish rebellion under the generalship of Judas (Judah) Maccabaeus. In 140 B.C. the Hasmonean Dynasty began under the leadership of Simon Maccabaeus, who served as ruler, high priest, and commander in chief. Simon, who was assassinated a few years later, formalized what Judas had begun, the establishment of a theocracy, something not found in any biblical text.

Despite priestly rule, Jewish society became Hellenized except in its generally staunch adherence to monotheism. Although rural life was relatively unchanged, cities such as Jerusalem rapidly adopted the Greek language, sponsored games and sports, and in more subtle ways adopted and absorbed the culture of the Hellenes. Even the high priests bore such names as Jason and Menelaus. Biblical scholars have identified extensive Greek influence in the drafting of commentaries and interpolations of ancient texts during and after the Greek period. The most obvious influence of the Hellenistic period can be discerned in the early literature of the new faith, Christianity.

Under the Hasmonean Dynasty, Judah became comparable in extent and power to the ancient Davidic dominion. Internal political and religious discord ran high, however, especially between the Pharisees, who interpreted the written law by adding a wealth of oral law, and the Sadducees, an aristocratic priestly class who called for strict adherence to the written law. In 64 B.C., dynastic contenders for the throne appealed for support to Pompey, who was then establishing Roman power in Asia. The next year Roman legions seized Jerusalem, and Pompey installed one of the contenders for the throne as high priest, but without the title of king. Eighty years of independent Jewish sovereignty ended, and the period of Roman dominion began.

In the subsequent period of Roman wars, Herod was confirmed by the Roman Senate as king of Judah in 37 B.C. and reigned until his death in 4 B.C. Nominally independent, Judah was actually in bondage to Rome, and the land was formally annexed in 6 B.C. as part of the province of Syria Palestina. Rome did, however, grant the Jews religious autonomy and some judicial and legislative rights through the Sanhedrin. The Sanhedrin, which traces its origins to a council of elders established under Persian rule (333 B.C. to 165 B.C.) was the highest Jewish legal and religious body under Rome. The Great Sanhedrin, located on the Temple Mount in Jerusalem, supervised smaller local Sanhedrins and was the final authority on many important religious, political, and legal issues, such as declaring war, trying a high priest, and supervising certain rituals. Scholars have sharply debated the structure and composition of the Sanhedrin. The Jewish historian Josephus and the New Testament present the Sanhedrin as a political and judicial council whereas the Talmud (see Glossary) describes it as a religious, legislative body headed by a court of seventy-one sages. Another view holds that there were two separate Sanhedrins. The political Sanhedrin was composed primarily of the priestly Sadducee aristocracy and was charged by the Roman procurator with responsibility for civil order, specifically in matters involving imperial directives. The religious Sanhedrin of the Pharisees was concerned with religious law and doctrine, which the Romans disregarded as long as civil order was not threatened. Foremost among the Pharisee leaders of the time were the noted teachers, Hillel and Shammai.

Chafing under foreign rule, a Jewish nationalist movement of the fanatical sect known as the Zealots challenged Roman control in A.D. 66. After a protracted siege begun by Vespasian, the Roman commander in Judah, but completed under his son Titus in A.D. 70, Jerusalem and the Second Temple were seized and destroyed by the Roman legions. The last Zealot survivors perished in A.D. 73 at the mountain fortress of Massada, about fifty-six kilometers southwest of Jerusalem above the western shore of the Dead Sea.

During the siege of Jerusalem, Rabbi Yohanan Ben-Zakki received Vespasian's permission to withdraw to the town of Yibna (also seen as Jabneh) on the coastal plain, about twenty-four kilometers southwest of present-day Tel Aviv. There an academic center or academy was set up and became the central religious authority; its jurisdiction was recognized by Jews in Palestine and beyond. Roman rule, nevertheless, continued. Emperor Hadrian (A.D. 117–38) endeavored to establish cultural uniformity and issued several repressive edicts, including one against circumcision.

The edicts sparked the Bar-Kochba Rebellion of 132–35, which was crushed by the Romans. Hadrian then closed the Academy at Yibna, and prohibited both the study of the Torah and the observance of the Jewish way of life derived from it. Judah was included in Syria Palestina, Jerusalem was renamed Aelia Capitolina, and Jews were forbidden to come within sight of the city. Once a year on the anniversary of the destruction of the Temple, controlled entry was permitted, allowing Jews to mourn at a remaining fragment on the Temple site, the Western Wall, which became known as the Wailing Wall. The Diaspora, which had begun with the Babylonian captivity in the sixth century B.C.,and which had resumed early in the Hellenistic period, now involved most Jews in an exodus from what they continued to view as the land promised to them as the descendants of Abraham.

Following the destruction of the Temple in 70 A.D., and especially after the suppression of the Bar-Kochba Rebellion in 135 A.D., religio-nationalist aspects of Judaism were supplanted by a growing intellectual-spiritual trend. Lacking a state, the survival of the Jewish people was dependent on study and observance of the written law, the Torah. To maintain the integrity and cohesiveness of the community, the Torah was enlarged into a coherent system of moral theology and community law. The rabbi and the synagogue became the normative institutions of Judaism, which thereafter was essentially a congregationalist faith.

The focus on study led to the compilation of the Talmud, an immense commentary on the Torah that thoroughly analyzed the application of Jewish law to the day-to-day life of the Jewish community. The complexity of argument and analysis contained in the Palestinian Talmud (100–425 A.D.) and the more authoritative Babylonian Talmud (completed around 500) reflected the high level of intellectual maturity attained by the various schools of Jewish learning. This inward-looking intellectualism, along with a rigid adherence to the laws and rituals of Judaism, maintained the separateness of the Jewish people, enabling them to survive the exilic experience despite the lure of conversion and frequent outbreaks of anti-Semitism.

Palestine Between the Romans and Modern Times

As a geographic unit, Palestine extended from the Mediterranean on the west to the Arabian Desert on the east and from the lower Litani River in the north to the Gaza Valley in the south. It was named after the Philistines, who occupied the southern coastal region in the twelfth century B.C. The name Philistia was used in the second century A.D. to designate Syria Palestina, which formed the southern third of the Roman province of Syria.

Emperor Constantine (ca. 280–337) shifted his capital from Rome to Constantinople in 330 and made Christianity the official religion. With Constantine's conversion to Christianity, a new era of prosperity came to Palestine, which attracted a flood of pilgrims from all over the empire. Upon partition of the Roman Empire in 395, Palestine passed under eastern control. The scholarly Jewish communities in Galilee continued with varying fortunes under Byzantine rule and dominant Christian influence until the Arab-Muslim conquest of A.D. 638. The period included, however, strong Jewish support of the briefly successful Persian invasion of 610–14.

The Arab caliph, Umar, designated Jerusalem as the third holiest place in Islam, second only to Mecca and Medina. Under the Umayyads, based in Damascus, the Dome of the Rock was erected in 691 on the site of the Temple of Solomon, which was also the alleged nocturnal resting place of the Prophet Muhammad on his journey to heaven. It is the earliest Muslim monument still extant. Close to the shrine, to the south, the Al Aqsa Mosque was built. The Umayyad caliph, Umar II (717-720), imposed humiliating restrictions on his non-Muslim subjects that led many to convert to Islam. These conversions, in addition to a steady tribal flow from the desert, changed the religious character of the inhabitants of Palestine from Christian to Muslim. Under the Abbasids the process of Islamization gained added momentum as a result of further restrictions imposed on non-Muslims by Harun ar Rashid (786–809) and more particularly by Al Mutawakkil (847-61).

The Abbasids were followed by the Fatimids who faced frequent attacks from Qarmatians, Seljuks, and Byzantines, and periodic beduin opposition. Palestine was reduced to a battlefield. In 1071 the Seljuks captured Jerusalem. The Fatimids recaptured the city in 1098, only to deliver it a year later to a new enemy, the Crusaders of Western Europe. In 1100 the Crusaders established the Latin Kingdom of Jerusalem, which remained until the famous Muslim general Salah ad Din (Saladin) defeated them at the decisive Battle of Hattin in 1187. The Crusaders were not completely evicted from Palestine, however, until 1291 when they were driven out of Acre. The fourteenth and fifteenth centuries were a "dark age" for Palestine as a result of Mamluk misrule and the spread of several epidemics. The Mamluks were slave-soldiers who established a dynasty that ruled Egypt and Syria, which included Palestine, from 1250 to 1516.

In 1516 the Ottoman Turks, led by Sultan Selim I, routed the Mamluks, and Palestine began four centuries under Ottoman domination. Under the Ottomans, Palestine continued to be linked administratively to Damascus until 1830, when it was placed under Sidon, then under Acre, then once again under Damascus. In 1887-88 the local governmental units of the Ottoman Empire were finally settled, and Palestine was divided into the administrative divisions (sing., *mutasarrifiyah*) of Nabulus and Acre, both of which were linked with the *vilayet* (largest Ottoman administrative division, similar to a province) of Beirut and the autonomous *mutasarrifiyah* of Jerusalem, which dealt directly with Constantinople.

For the first three centuries of Ottoman rule, Palestine was relatively insulated from outside influences. At the end of the eighteenth century, Napoleon's abortive attempt to establish a Middle

East empire led to increased Western involvement in Palestine. The trend toward Western influence accelerated during the nine years (1831–40) that the Egyptian viceroy Muhammad Ali and his son Ibrahim ruled Palestine. The Ottomans returned to power in 1840 with the help of the British, Austrians, and Russians. For the remainder of the nineteenth century, Palestine, despite the growth of Christian missionary schools and the establishment of European consulates, remained a mainly rural, poor but self-sufficient, introverted society. Demographically its population was overwhelmingly Arab, mainly Muslim, but with an important Christian merchant and professional class residing in the cities. The Jewish population of Palestine before 1880 consisted of fewer than 25,000 people, two-thirds of whom lived in Jerusalem where they made up half the population (and from 1890 on more than half the population). These were Orthodox Jews (see Glossary), many of whom had immigrated to Palestine simply to be buried in the Holy Land, and who had no real political interest in establishing a Jewish entity. They were supported by alms given by world Jewry.

Origins of Zionism

The major event that led to the growth of the Zionist movement was the emancipation of Jews in France (1791), followed shortly thereafter by their emancipation in the rest of continental and Central Europe. After having lived for centuries in the confines of Jewish ghettos, Jews living in Western and Central Europe now had a powerful incentive to enter mainstream European society. Jews, who had previously been confined to petty trade and to banking, rapidly rose in academia, medicine, the arts, journalism, and other professions. The accelerated assimilation of Jews into European society radically altered the nature of relations between Jews and non-Jews. On the one hand, Jews had to reconcile traditional Judaism, which for nearly 2,000 years prior to emancipation had developed structures designed to maintain the integrity and separateness of Jewish community life, with a powerful secular culture in which they were now able to participate. On the other hand, many non-Jews, who prior to the emancipation had had little or no contact with Jews, increasingly saw the Jew as an economic threat. The rapid success of many Jews fueled this resentment.

The rise of ethnically based nationalism in the mid-nineteenth century gave birth to yet another form of anti-Semitism. Before the mid-nineteenth century, European anti-Semitism was based mainly on Christian antipathies toward Jews because of their refusal to convert to Christianity. As a result, an individual Jew could usually avoid persecution by converting, as many did over the

17

Temple Mount in Jerusalem with the Dome of the Rock,
a Muslim holy place, as seen from Mount Scopus
Courtesy Les Vogel

centuries. The emergence of ethnically based nationalism, however, radically changed the status of the Jew in European society. The majority gentile population saw Jews as a separate people who could never be full participants in the nation's history.

The vast majority of Jews in Western and Central Europe responded by seeking even deeper assimilation into European culture and a secularization of Judaism. A minority, who believed that greater assimilation would not alter the hostility of non-Jews, adopted Zionism. According to this view, the Jew would remain an outsider in European society regardless of the liberalism of the age because Jews lacked a state of their own. Jewish statelessness, then, was the root cause of anti-Semitism. The Zionists sought to solve the Jewish problem by creating a Jewish entity outside Europe but modeled after the European nation-state. After more then half a century of emancipation, West European Jewry had become distanced from both the ritual and culture of traditional Judaism. Thus, Zionism in its West European Jewish context envisioned a purely political solution to the Jewish problem: a state of Jews rather than a Jewish state.

For the bulk of European Jewry, however, who resided in Eastern Europe's Pale of Settlement (see Glossary)—on the western fringe of the Russian Empire, between the Baltic and the Black seas—there was no emancipation. East European Jewry had lived for centuries in *kehilot* (sing., *kehilah*), semiautonomous Jewish municipal corporations that were supported by wealthy Jews. Life in the *kehilot* was governed by a powerful caste of learned religious scholars who strictly enforced adherence to the Jewish legal code. Many Jews found the parochial conformity enforced by the *kehilot* leadership onerous. As a result, liberal stirring unleashed by the emancipation in the West had an unsettling effect upon the *kehilot* in the East.

By the early nineteenth century, not only was *kehilot* life resented but the tsarist regimes were becoming increasingly absolute. In 1825 Tsar Nicholas I, attempting to centralize control of the empire and Russify its peoples, enacted oppressive measures against the Jews; he drafted a large number of under-age Jews for military service, forced Jews out of their traditional occupations, such as the liquor trade, and generally repressed the *kehilot*. Facing severe economic hardship and social upheaval, tens of thousands of Jews migrated to the cities, especially Odessa on the Russian coast. In their new urban environments, the restless and highly literate Jews clamored for the liberalization of tsarist rule.

In 1855 the prospects for Russian Jewry appeared to improve significantly when the relatively liberal-minded Tsar Alexander II ascended the throne. Alexander II ended the practice of drafting

Jewish youth into the military and granted Jews access, albeit limited, to Russian education institutions and various professions previously closed to them. Consequently, a thriving class of Jewish intellectuals, the *maskalim* (enlightened), emerged in cities like Odessa, just as they had in Western Europe and Central Europe after emancipation. The *maskalim* believed that Tsar Alexander II was ushering in a new age of Russian liberalism which, as in the West, would eventually lead to the emancipation of Russian Jewry.

The hopes of the *maskalim* and of Russian Jewry in general, however, were misplaced. Alexander II was assassinated in 1881, and a severe pogrom ensued that devastated Jewish communities throughout the Pale of Settlement. The new Tsar, Alexander III, enacted oppressive policies against the Jews and denied police protection to those Jews who remained in the countryside. As a result, a floodtide of impoverished Jews entered the cities where they joined various movements that sought to overthrow the tsar.

The openly anti-Semitic policies pursued by the new tsar and the popularity of these policies among large segments of the non-Jewish population posed serious political, economic, and spiritual dilemmas for Russian Jewry. On the economic level, the tsar's anti-Semitic policies severely limited Jewish economic opportunities and undermined the livelihood of the Jewish masses. Many impoverished East European Jews, therefore, emigrated from the Russian Empire. Between 1881 and 1914, an estimated 2.5 million Jews left the empire, 2 million of whom settled in the United States.

For many Jews, especially the *maskalim,* however, the pogroms and the anti-Semitism of the new tsar not only meant economic hardship and physical suffering but also a deep spiritual malaise. Before 1881, they had been abandoning the strict confines of the *kehilot* en masse and rebelling against religious orthodoxy, anxiously waiting for the expected emancipation to reach Russia. The 1881 pogroms and their aftermath shattered not only the faith of the *maskalim* in the inevitable liberalization of tsarist Russia but also their belief that the non-Jewish Russian intellectual would take an active role in opposing anti-Semitism. Most of the Russian intelligentsia were either silent during the pogroms or actually supported them. Having lost their faith in God and in the inevitable spread of liberalism, large numbers of Russian Jews were forced to seek new solutions. Many flocked to the revolutionary socialist and communist movements opposing the tsar, while others became involved with the Bund (see Glossary), a cultural society that sought to establish a Yiddish (see Glossary) cultural renaissance within Russia.

A smaller but growing number of Jews were attracted to the ancient but newly formulated notion of reconstituting a Jewish nation-state in Palestine. Zionism as it evolved in Eastern Europe, unlike Zionism in the West, dealt not only with the plight of Jews but with the crisis of Judaism. Thus, despite its secularism, East European Zionism remained attached to the Jewish biblical home in Palestine. It also was imbued with the radical socialist fervor challenging the tsarist regime.

Zionism's reformulation of traditional Judaism was deeply resented by Orthodox Jews, especially the Hasidim (sing., Hasid—see Glossary). Most Orthodox Jews rejected the notion of a return to the promised land before the appearance of the Messiah. They viewed Zionism as a secular European creation that aspired to change the focus of Judaism from devotion to Jewish law and religious ritual to the establishment of a Jewish nation-state.

Zionist Precursors

The impulse and development of Zionism was almost exclusively the work of Ashkenazim—Jews of European origin; few Sephardim (see Glossary) were directly engaged in the movement in its formative years. (In 1900 about 9.5 million of the world's 10.5 million Jews were Ashkenazim, and about 5.2 million of the Ashkenazim lived in the Pale of Settlement.)

The first writings in what later came to be known as Zionism appeared in the mid-1800s. In 1840 the Jews of Eastern Europe and the Balkans had been aroused by rumors that the messianic era was at hand. Various writers, most prominently Rabbi Judah Alkalai and Rabbi Zevi Hirsch Kalisher but including many others, were impressed by the nationalist fervor of Europe that was creating new nation-states and by the resurgence of messianic expectations among Jews. Kalisher wrote that Jewish nationalism was directly akin to other nationalist movements and was the logical continuation of the Jewish enlightenment that had begun in France in 1791 when Jews were granted civil liberties. Alkalai consciously altered his expectations from a miraculous messianic salvation to a redemption by human effort that would pave the way for the arrival of the Messiah. Both authors urged the development of Jewish national unity, and Kalisher in particular foresaw the ingathering to Palestine of many of the world's Jews as part of the process of emancipation.

Another important early Zionist was Moses Hess, a German Jew and socialist comrade of Karl Marx. In his book *Rome and Jerusalem,* published in 1862, Hess called for the establishment of a Jewish socialist commonwealth in Palestine. He was one of the first

Desert west of the Dead Sea in the occupied West Bank
Courtesy Les Vogel
The Jordan River in northern Israel, east of Bet Shean
Courtesy Les Vogel

Jewish thinkers to see that emancipation would ultimately exacerbate anti-Semitism in Europe. He concluded that the only solution to the Jewish problem was the establishment of a national Jewish society managed by a Jewish proletariat. Although his synthesis of socialism and Jewish nationalism would later become an integral part of the Labor Zionist movement, during his lifetime the prosperity of European Jewry lessened the appeal of his work.

Political Zionism

Political Zionism was emancipated West European Jewry's response to the pervasiveness of anti-Semitism and to the failure of the enlightenment to alter the status of the Jew. Its objective was the establishment of a Jewish homeland in any available territory—not necessarily in Palestine—through cooperation with the Great Powers. Political Zionists viewed the "Jewish problem" through the eyes of enlightenment rationalism and believed that European powers would support a Jewish national existence outside Europe because it would rid them of the Jewish problem. These Zionists believed that Jews would come en masse to the new entity, which would be a secular nation modeled after the postemancipation European state.

The first Jew to articulate a political Zionist platform was not a West European but a Russian physician residing in Odessa. A year after the 1881 pogroms, Leo Pinsker, reflecting the disappointment of other Jewish *maskalim*, wrote in a pamphlet entitled *Auto-Emancipation* that anti-Semitism was a modern phenomenon, beyond the reach of any future triumphs of "humanity and enlightenment." Therefore Jews must organize themselves to find their own national home wherever possible, not necessarily in their ancestral home in the Holy Land. Pinsker's work attracted the attention of Hibbat Tziyyon (Lovers of Zion), an organization devoted to Hebrew education and national revival. Ignoring Pinsker's indifference toward the Holy Land, members of Hibbat Tziyyon took up his call for a territorial solution to the Jewish problem. Pinsker, who became leader of the movement, obtained funds from the wealthy Jewish philanthropist, Baron Edmond de Rothschild—who was not a Zionist—to support Jewish agricultural settlement in Palestine at Rishon LeZiyyon, south of Tel Aviv, and Zikhron Yaaqov, south of Haifa. Although the numbers were meager—only 10,000 settlers by 1891—especially when compared to the large number of Jews who emigrated to the United States, the First Aliyah (1882–1903), or immigration, was important because it established a Jewish bridgehead in Palestine espousing political objectives.

The impetus to the founding of a Zionist organization with specific goals was provided by Theodor Herzl. Born in Budapest on May 2, 1860, Herzl grew up in an environment of assimilation. He was educated in Vienna as a lawyer but instead became a journalist and playwright. By the early 1890s, he had achieved some recognition in Vienna and other major European cities. Until that time, he had only been identified peripherally with Jewish culture and politics. He was unfamiliar with earlier Zionist writings, and he noted in his diary that he would not have written his book had he known the contents of Pinsker's *Auto-Emancipation.*

While working as Paris correspondent for a Viennese newspaper, Herzl became aware of the pervasiveness of anti-Semitism in French society. He saw that emancipation rather than dissipating anti-Semitism had exacerbated popular animosity toward the Jews. The tearing down of the ghetto walls placed Jews in competition with non-Jews. Moreover, the newly liberated Jew was blamed by much of non-Jewish French society for the socioeconomic upheaval caused by both emancipation and accelerated industrialization.

The turning point in Herzl's thinking on the Jewish question occurred during the 1894 Paris trial of Alfred Dreyfus, a Jewish officer in the French army, on charges of treason (the sale of military secrets to Germany). Dreyfus was convicted, and although he was eventually cleared, his career was ruined. The trial and later exoneration sharply divided French society and unleashed widespread anti-Semitic demonstrations and riots throughout France. To Herzl's shock and dismay, many members of the French intellectual, social, and political elites—precisely those elements of society into which the upwardly mobile emancipated Jews wished to be assimilated—were the most vitriolic in their anti-Semitic stance.

The Dreyfus affair proved for Herzl, as the 1881 pogroms had for Pinsker, that Jews would always be an alien element in the societies in which they resided as long as they remained stateless. He believed that even if Jewish separateness in religion and social custom were to disappear, the Jews would continue to be treated as outsiders.

Herzl put forth his solution to the Jewish problem in *Der Judenstaat* (The Jewish State) published in 1896. He called for the establishment of a Jewish state in any available territory to which the majority of European Jewry would immigrate. The new state would be modeled after the postemancipation European state. Thus, it would be secular in nature, granting no special place to the Hebrew language, Judaism, or to the ancient Jewish homeland in Palestine.

Another important element contained in Herzl's concept of a Jewish state was the enlightenment faith that all men—including anti-Semites—are basically rational and will work for goals that they perceive to be in their best interest. He was convinced, therefore, that the enlightened nations of Europe would support the Zionist cause to rid their domains of the problem-creating Jews. Consequently, Herzl actively sought international recognition and the cooperation of the Great Powers in creating a Jewish state.

Herzl's ideas were not original, his belief that the Great Powers would cooperate in the Zionist enterprise was naive, and his indifference to the final location of the Jewish state was far removed from the desires of the bulk of the Jewish people residing in the Pale of Settlement. What he accomplished, however, was to cultivate the first seeds of the Zionist movement and to bestow upon the movement a mantle of legitimacy. His stature as a respected Western journalist and his meetings with the pope, princes of Europe, the German kaiser, and other world figures, although not successful, propelled the movement into the international arena. Herzl sparked the hopes and aspirations of the mass of East European Jewry living under Russian oppression. It was the oppressed Jewish masses of the Pale, however—with whom Herzl, the assimilated bourgeois of the West, had so little in common—who absorbed his message most deeply.

In 1897 Herzl convened the First Zionist Congress in Basel, Switzerland. The first congress adopted the goal: "To create for the Jewish people a home in Palestine secured by Public Law." The World Zionist Organization (WZO—see Glossary) was founded to work toward this goal, and arrangements were made for future congresses. The WZO established a general council, a central executive, and a congress, which was held every year or two. It developed member societies worldwide, continued to encourage settlement in Palestine, registered a bank in London, and established the Jewish National Fund (Keren Kayemet) to buy land in Palestine. The First Zionist Congress was vital to the future development of Zionism, not only because it established an institutional framework for Zionism but also because it came to symbolize for many Jews a new national identity, the first such identity since the destruction of the Second Temple in A.D. 70.

Cultural Zionism

The counterpoint to Herzl's political Zionism was provided by Asher Ginsberg, better known by his pen name Ahad HaAm (One of the People). Ahad HaAm, who was the son of a Hasidic rabbi, was typical of the Russian *maskalim*. In 1886, at the age of thirty, he moved to Odessa with the vague hope of modernizing Judaism. His views on Zionism were rooted in the changing nature of Jewish communal life in Eastern Europe. Ahad HaAm realized that a new meaning to Jewish life would have to be found for the younger generation of East European Jews who were revolting against traditional Jewish practice. Whereas Jews in the West could participate in and benefit from a secular culture, Jews in the East were oppressed. While Herzl focused on the plight of Jews alone, Ahad HaAm was also interested in the plight of Judaism, which could no longer be contained within the limits of traditional religion.

Ahad HaAm's solution was cultural Zionism: the establishment in Palestine of small settlements aimed at reviving the Jewish spirit and culture in the modern world. In the cultural Zionist vision, a small number of Jewish cadres well versed in Jewish culture and speaking Hebrew would settle in Palestine. Ahad HaAm believed that by settling in that ancient land, religious Jews would replace their metaphysical attachment to the Holy Land with a new Hebrew cultural renaissance. Palestine and the Hebrew language were important not because of their religious significance but because they had been an integral part of the Jewish people's history and cultural heritage.

Inherent in the cultural Zionism espoused by Ahad HaAm was a deep mistrust of the gentile world. Ahad HaAm rejected Herzl's notion that the nations of the world would encourage Jews to move and establish a Jewish state. He believed that only through Jewish self-reliance and careful preparation would the Zionist enterprise succeed. Although Ahad HaAm's concept of a vanguard cultural elite establishing a foothold in Palestine was quixotic, his idea of piecemeal settlement in Palestine and the establishment of a Zionist infrastructure became an integral part of the Zionist movement.

The ascendancy of Ahad HaAm's cultural Zionism and its emphasis on practical settlement in Eretz Yisrael climaxed at the Sixth Zionist Congress in 1903. After an initial discussion of settlement in the Sinai Peninsula, which was opposed by Egypt, Herzl came to the congress apparently willing to consider, as a temporary shelter, a British proposal for an autonomous Jewish entity in East Africa. The Uganda Plan, as it was called, was vehemently rejected by East European Zionists who, as before, insisted on the ancient political identity with Palestine. Exhausted, Herzl died of pneumonia in 1904, and from that time on the mantle of Zionism was carried by the cultural Zionists led by Ahad HaAm and his close colleague, Chaim Weizmann. They took over the WZO, increased support for Hibbat Tziyyon, and sought Jewish settlement in Palestine as a prerequisite to international support for a Jewish state.

Labor Zionism

The defeat of Herzl's Uganda Plan ensured that the fate of the Zionist project would ultimately be determined in Palestine. In Palestine the Zionist movement had to devise a practical settlement plan that would ensure its economic viability in the face of extremely harsh conditions. Neither Herzl's political Zionism nor Ahad HaAm's cultural Zionism articulated a practical plan for settlement in Palestine. Another major challenge facing the fledgling movement was how to appeal to the increasing number of young Jews who were joining the growing socialist and communist movements in Russia. To meet these challenges, Labor Zionism emerged as the dominant force in the Zionist movement.

The intellectual founders of Labor Zionism were Nachman Syrkin and Ber Borochov. They inspired the founding of Poalei Tziyyon (Workers of Zion, see Appendix B)—the first Labor Zionist party, which grew quickly from 1906 until the start of World War I. The concepts of Labor Zionism first emerged as criticisms of the Rothschild-supported settlements of the First Aliyah. Both Borochov and Syrkin believed that the Rothschild settlements, organized on purely capitalist terms and therefore hiring Arab labor, would undermine the Jewish enterprise. Syrkin called for Jewish settlement based on socialist modes of organization: the accumulation of capital managed by a central Jewish organization and employment of Jewish laborers only. He believed that "anti-Semitism was the result of unequal distribution of power in society. As long as society is based on might, and as long as the Jew is weak, anti-Semitism will exist." Thus, he reasoned, the Jews needed a material base for their social existence—a state and political power.

Ber Borochov's contribution to Labor Zionism was his synthesis of the concepts of class and nation. In his most famous essay, entitled *Nationalism and Class Struggle,* Borochov showed how the nation, in this case the Jewish nation, was the best institution through which to conduct the class struggle. According to Borochov, only through the establishment of a Jewish society controlling its own economic infrastructure could Jews be integrated into the revolutionary process. His synthesis of Marxism and Zionism attracted many Russian Jews caught up in the revolutionary fervor of the Bolshevik movement.

Another important Labor Zionist and the first actually to reside in Palestine was Aaron David Gordon. Gordon believed that only by physical labor and by returning to the land could the Jewish people achieve national salvation in Palestine. Gordon became a folk hero to the early Zionists by coming to Palestine in 1905 at a relatively advanced age—forty-seven—and assiduously working the land. He and his political party, HaPoel HaTzair (The Young Worker), were a major force behind the movement to collectivize Jewish settlements in Palestine. The first kibbutz was begun by Gordon and his followers at Deganya in eastern Galilee.

Before Gordon's arrival, the major theorists of Labor Zionism had never set foot in Palestine. Zionism in its theoretical formulations only took practical effect with the coming to Palestine of the Second Aliyah. Between 1904 and 1914, approximately 40,000 Jews immigrated to Palestine in response to the pogroms that followed the attempted Russian revolution of 1905. By the end of the Second Aliyah, the Jewish population of Palestine stood at about 85,000, or 12 percent of the total population. The members of the Second Aliyah, unlike the settlers of the first, were dedicated socialists set on establishing Jewish settlement in Palestine along socialist lines. They undertook a number of measures aimed at establishing an autonomous Jewish presence in Palestine, such as employing only Jewish labor, encouraging the widespread use of Hebrew, and forming the first Jewish self-defense organization, HaShomer (The Watchmen).

The future leadership cadre of the state of Israel emerged out of the Second Aliyah. The most important leader of this group and the first prime minister of Israel was David Ben-Gurion (*ben,* son of—see Glossary). Ben-Gurion, who arrived in Palestine in 1906, believed that economic power was a prerequisite of political power. He foresaw that the fate of Zionist settlement in Palestine depended on the creation of a strong Jewish economy. This aim, he believed, could only be accomplished through the creation of a Hebrew-speaking working class and a highly centralized Jewish economic structure. Beginning in the 1920s, he set out to create the immense institutional framework for a Jewish workers' state in Palestine.

Revisionist Zionism

Labor Zionism, although by far the largest organization in the Yishuv (the prestate Jewish community in Palestine), did not go unchallenged. The largest and most vocal opposition came from a Russian-born Jewish intellectual residing in Odessa, Vladimir Jabotinsky. Jabotinsky was both a renowned writer and the first military hero of the Zionist revival; he was commander of the Jewish Legion. While residing in Italy, Jabotinsky became attached to the notions of romantic nationalism espoused by the great Italian nationalist Giuseppe Garibaldi. Like Garibaldi, Jabotinsky viewed nationalism as the highest value to which humans can aspire. He called for massive Jewish immigration to Palestine and the immediate declaration of Jewish statehood in all of biblical Palestine. He viewed the world in Machiavellian terms: military and political power ultimately determine the fate of peoples and nations. Therefore, he called for the establishment of a well-armed Jewish self-defense organization.

Jabotinsky sharply criticized Ben-Gurion's single-minded focus on creating a Jewish working-class movement, which he felt distracted the Zionist movement from the real issue at hand, Jewish statehood. He gained wide popularity in Poland, where his criticisms of socialism and his calls for Jewish self-defense appealed to a Jewish community of small entrepreneurs hounded as a result of anti-Semitism.

Events in Palestine, 1908–48

Arab Nationalism

Before the Second Aliyah, the indigenous Arab population of Palestine had worked for and generally cooperated with the small number of Jewish settlements. The increased Jewish presence and the different policies of the new settlers of the Second Aliyah aroused Arab hostility. The increasing tension between Jewish settler and Arab peasant did not, however, lead to the establishment of Arab nationalist organizations. In the Ottoman-controlled Arab lands the Arab masses were bound by family, tribal, and Islamic ties; the concepts of nationalism and nation-state were viewed as alien Western categories. Thus, an imbalance evolved between the highly organized and nationalistic settlers of the Second Aliyah and the indigenous Arab population, who lacked the organizational sophistication of the Zionists.

There were, however, small groups of Western-educated Arab intellectuals and military officers who formed nationalist organizations demanding greater local autonomy. The primary moving force behind this nascent Arab nationalist movement was the Committee of Union and Progress, a loose umbrella organization of officers and officials within the Ottoman Empire in opposition to the policies of Sultan Abdul Hamid. The removal of Sultan Abdul Hamid by the Committee of Union and Progress in 1908 was widely supported by both Arab nationalists and Zionists. The committee's program of constitutional reform and promised autonomy aroused hope of independence on the part of various nationalities throughout the Ottoman Empire.

After 1908, however, it quickly became clear to Zionists and Arabs alike that the nationalism of Abdul Hamid's successors was Turkish nationalism, bent on Turkification of the Ottoman domain

A street in the
Old City of Jerusalem
Courtesy Les Vogel

Damascus Gate leading to
the Old City of Jerusalem
Courtesy Les Vogel

rather than granting local autonomy. In response, Arab intellectuals in Beirut and Damascus formed clandestine political societies, such as the Ottoman Decentralization Party, based in Cairo; Al Ahd (The Covenant Society), formed primarily by army officers in 1914; and Al Fatat (The Young Arabs), formed by students in 1911. The Arab nationalism espoused by these groups lacked support, however, among the Arab masses.

World War I: Diplomacy and Intrigue

On the eve of World War I, the anticipated break-up of the enfeebled Ottoman Empire raised hopes among both Zionists and Arab nationalists. The Zionists hoped to attain support from one of the Great Powers for increased Jewish immigration and eventual sovereignty in Palestine, whereas the Arab nationalists wanted an independent Arab state covering all the Ottoman Arab domains. From a purely demographic standpoint, the Zionist argument was not very strong—in 1914 they comprised only 12 percent of the total population of Palestine. The nationalist ideal, however, was weak among the Arabs, and even among articulate Arabs competing visions of Arab nationalism—Islamic, pan-Arab, and statism—inhibited coordinated efforts to achieve independence.

A major asset to Zionism was that its chief spokesman, Chaim Weizmann, was an astute statesman and a scientist widely respected in Britain and he was well versed in European diplomacy. Weizmann understood better than the Arab leaders at the time that the future map of the Middle East would be determined less by the desires of its inhabitants than by Great Power rivalries, European strategic thinking, and domestic British politics. Britain, in possession of the Suez Canal and playing a dominant role in India and Egypt, attached great strategic importance to the region. British Middle East policy, however, espoused conflicting objectives, and as a result London became involved in three distinct and contradictory negotiations concerning the fate of the region.

The earliest British discussions of the Middle East question revolved around Sharif Husayn ibn Ali, scion of the Hashimite (also seen as Hashemite) family that claimed descent from the Prophet and acted as the traditional guardians of Islam's most holy sites of Mecca and Medina in the Arabian province of Hijaz. In February 1914, Amir Abdullah, son of Sharif Husayn, went to Cairo to visit Lord Kitchener, British agent and consul general in Egypt, where he inquired about the possibility of British support should his father stage a revolt against Turkey. Turkey and Germany were not yet formally allied, and Germany and Britain were not yet at war; Kitchener's reply was, therefore, noncommittal.

Shortly after the outbreak of World War I in August 1914, Kitchener was recalled to London as secretary of state for war. By 1915, as British military fortunes in the Middle East deteriorated, Kitchener saw the usefulness of transferring the Islamic caliphate— the caliph, or successor to the Prophet Muhammad, was the traditional leader of the Islamic world—to an Arab candidate indebted to Britain, and he energetically sought Arab support for the war against Turkey. In Cairo Sir Henry McMahon, the first British high commissioner in Egypt, conducted an extensive correspondence from July 1915 to January 1916 with Husayn, two of whose sons—Abdullah, later king of Jordan, and Faysal, later king of Syria (ejected by the French in 1920) and of Iraq (1921–33)—were to figure prominently in subsequent events.

In a letter to McMahon enclosed with a letter dated July 14, 1915, from Abdullah, Husayn specified an area for Arab independence under the "Sharifian Arab Government" consisting of the Arabian Peninsula (except Aden) and the Fertile Crescent of Palestine, Lebanon, Syria, and Iraq. In his letter of October 24, 1915, to Husayn, McMahon, on behalf of the British government, declared British support for postwar Arab independence, subject to certain reservations and exclusions of territory not entirely Arab or concerning which Britain was not free "to act without detriment to the interests of her ally, France." The territories assessed by the British as not purely Arab included: "The districts of Mersin and Alexandretta, and portions of Syria lying to the west of the districts of Damascus, Homs, Hama, and Aleppo." As with the later Balfour Declaration, the exact meaning was not clear, although Arab spokesmen since then have usually maintained that Palestine was within the pledged area of independence. Although the Husayn-McMahon correspondence was not legally binding on either side, on June 5, 1916, Husayn launched the Arab Revolt against Turkey and in October declared himself "King of the Arabs."

While Husayn and McMahon corresponded over the fate of the Middle East, the British were conducting negotiations with the French over the same territory. Following the British military defeat at the Dardanelles in 1915, the Foreign Office sought a new offensive in the Middle East, which it thought could only be carried out by reassuring the French of Britain's intentions in the region. In February 1916, the Sykes-Picot Agreement (officially the "Asia Minor Agreement") was signed, which, contrary to the contents of the Husayn-McMahon correspondence, proposed to partition the Middle East into French and British zones of control and interest. Under the Sykes-Picot Agreement, Palestine was to be administered by an international "condominium" of the British, French, and Russians (also signatories to the agreement).

The final British pledge, and the one that formally committed the British to the Zionist cause, was the Balfour Declaration of November 1917. Before the emergence of David Lloyd George as prime minister and Arthur James Balfour as foreign secretary in December 1916, the Liberal Herbert Asquith government had viewed a Jewish entity in Palestine as detrimental to British strategic aims in the Middle East. Lloyd George and his Tory supporters, however, saw British control over Palestine as much more attractive than the proposed British-French condominium. Since the Sykes-Picot Agreement, Palestine had taken on increased strategic importance because of its proximity to the Suez Canal, where the British garrison had reached 300,000 men, and because of a planned British attack on Ottoman Syria originating from Egypt. Lloyd George was determined, as early as March 1917, that Palestine should become British and that he would rely on its conquest by British troops to obtain the abrogation of the Sykes-Picot Agreement.

In the new British strategic thinking, the Zionists appeared as a potential ally capable of safeguarding British imperial interests in the region. Furthermore, as British war prospects dimmed throughout 1917, the War Cabinet calculated that supporting a Jewish entity in Palestine would mobilize America's influential Jewish community to support United States intervention in the war and sway the large number of Jewish Bolsheviks who participated in the 1917 Bolshevik Revolution to keep Russia in the war. Fears were also voiced in the Foreign Office that if Britain did not come out in favor of a Jewish entity in Palestine the Germans would preempt them. Finally, both Lloyd George and Balfour were devout churchgoers who attached great religious significance to the proposed reinstatement of the Jews in their ancient homeland.

The negotiations for a Jewish entity were carried out by Weizmann, who greatly impressed Balfour and maintained important links with the British media. In support of the Zionist cause, his protracted and skillful negotiations with the Foreign Office were climaxed on November 2, 1917, by the letter from the foreign secretary to Lord Rothschild, which became known as the Balfour Declaration. This document declared the British government's "sympathy with Jewish Zionist aspirations," viewed with favor "the establishment in Palestine of a National Home for the Jewish People," and announced an intent to facilitate the achievement of this objective. The letter added the provision of "it being clearly understood that nothing shall be done which may prejudice the civil and religious rights of existing non-Jewish communities in Palestine or the rights and political status enjoyed by Jews in any other country.''

The Balfour Declaration radically changed the status of the Zionist movement. It promised support from a major world power and gave the Zionists international recognition. Zionism was transformed by the British pledge from a quixotic dream into a legitimate and achievable undertaking. For these reasons, the Balfour Declaration was widely criticized throughout the Arab world, and especially in Palestine, as contrary to the spirit of British pledges contained in the Husayn-McMahon correspondence. The wording of the document itself, although painstakingly devised, was interpreted differently by different people, according to their interests. Ultimately, it was found to contain two incompatible undertakings: establishment in Palestine of a national home for the Jews and preservation of the rights of existing non-Jewish communities, i.e., the Arabs. The incompatibility sharpened over the succeeding years and became irreconcilable.

On December 9, 1917, five weeks after the Balfour Declaration, British troops led by General Sir Edmund Allenby took Jerusalem from the Turks; Turkish forces in Syria were subsequently defeated; an armistice was concluded with Turkey on October 31, 1918; and all of Palestine came under British military rule. British policy in the Arab lands of the now moribund Ottoman Empire was guided by a need to reduce military commitments, hold down expenditures, prevent a renewal of Turkish hegemony in the region, and safeguard Britain's strategic interest in the Suez Canal. The conflicting promises issued between 1915 and 1918 complicated the attainment of these objectives.

Between January 1919 and January 1920, the Allied Powers met in Paris to negotiate peace treaties with the Central Powers. At the conference, Amir Faysal, representing the Arabs, and Weizmann, representing the Zionists, presented their cases. Although Weizmann and Faysal reached a separate agreement on January 3, 1919, pledging the two parties to cordial cooperation, the latter wrote a proviso on the document in Arabic that his signature was tied to Allied war pledges regarding Arab independence. Since these pledges were not fulfilled to Arab satisfaction after the war, most Arab leaders and spokesmen have not considered the Faysal-Weizmann agreement as binding.

The conferees faced the nearly impossible task of finding a compromise between the generally accepted idea of self-determination, wartime promises, and plans for a division of the spoils. They ultimately decided upon a mandate system whose details were laid out at the San Remo Conference of April 1920. The terms of the British Mandate were approved by the League of Nations Council on July 24, 1922, although they were technically not official until September 29, 1923. The United States was not a member of the League of Nations, but a joint resolution of the United States Congress on June 30, 1922, endorsed the concept of the Jewish national home.

The Mandate's terms recognized the "historical connection of the Jewish people with Palestine," called upon the mandatory power to "secure establishment of the Jewish National Home," and recognized "an appropriate Jewish agency" for advice and cooperation to that end. The WZO, which was specifically recognized as the appropriate vehicle, formally established the Jewish Agency (see Glossary) in 1929. Jewish immigration was to be facilitated, while ensuring that the "rights and position of other sections of the population are not prejudiced." English, Arabic, and Hebrew were all to be official languages. At the San Remo Conference, the French also were assured of a mandate over Syria. They drove Faysal out of Damascus in the summer; the British provided him with a throne in Iraq a year later. In March 1921, Winston Churchill, then colonial secretary, established Abdullah as ruler of Transjordan under a separate British mandate.

To the WZO, which by 1921 had a worldwide membership of about 770,000, the recognition in the Mandate was seen as a welcome first step. Although not all Zionists and not all Jews were committed at that time to conversion of the Jewish national home into a separate political state, this conversion became firm Zionist policy during the next twenty-five years. The patterns developed during these years strongly influenced the State of Israel proclaimed in 1948.

Arab spokesmen, such as Husayn and his sons, opposed the Mandate's terms because the Covenant of the League of Nations had endorsed popular determination and thereby, they maintained, supported the cause of the Arab majority in Palestine. Further, the covenant specifically declared that all other obligations and understandings inconsistent with it were abrogated. Therefore, Arab argument held that both the Balfour Declaration and the Sykes-Picot Agreement were null and void. Arab leaders particularly objected to the Mandate's numerous references to the "Jewish community," whereas the Arab people, then constituting about 88 percent of the Palestinian population, were acknowledged only as "the other sections."

Prior to the Paris Peace Conference, Palestinian Arab nationalists had worked for a Greater Syria (see Glossary) under Faysal.

The British military occupation authority in Palestine, fearing an Arab rebellion, published an Anglo-French Joint Declaration, issued after the armistice with Turkey in November 1918, which called for self-determination for the indigenous people of the region. By the end of 1919, the British had withdrawn from Syria (exclusive of Palestine), but the French had not yet entered (except in Lebanon) and Faysal had not been explicitly repudiated by Britain. In March 1920, a General Syrian Congress meeting in Damascus elected Faysal king of a united Syria, which included Palestine. This raised the hope of the Palestinian Arab population that the Balfour Declaration would be rescinded, setting off a feverish series of demonstrations in Palestine in the spring of 1920. From April 4 to 8, Arab rioters attacked the Jewish quarter of Jerusalem. Faysal's ouster by the French in the summer of 1920 led to further rioting in Jaffa (contemporary Yafo) as a large number of Palestinian Arabs who had been with Faysal returned to Palestine to fight against the establishment of a Jewish nation.

The end of Faysal's Greater Syria experiment and the application of the mandate system, which artificially carved up the Arab East into new nation-states, had a profound effect on the history of the region in general and Palestine in particular. The mandate system created an identity crisis among Arab nationalists that led to the growth of competing nationalisms: Arab versus Islamic versus the more parochial nationalisms of the newly created states. It also created a serious legitimacy problem for the new Arab elites, whose authority ultimately rested with their European benefactors. The combination of narrowly based leadership and the emergence of competing nationalisms stymied the Arab response to the Zionist challenge in Palestine.

To British authorities, burdened with heavy responsibilities and commitments after World War I, the objective of the Mandate administration was peaceful accommodation and development of Palestine by Arabs and Jews under British control. Sir Herbert Samuels, the first high commissioner of Palestine, was responsible for keeping some semblance of order between the two antagonistic communities. In pursuit of this goal, Samuels, a Jew, was guided by two contradictory principles: liberalism and Zionism. He called for open Jewish immigration and land acquisition, which enabled thousands of highly committed and well-trained socialist Zionists to enter Palestine between 1919 and 1923. The Third Aliyah, as it was called, made important contributions to the development of Jewish agriculture, especially collective farming. Samuels, however, also promised representative institutions, which, if they had emerged in the 1920s, would have had as their first objective the curtailment of Jewish immigration. According to the census of 1922, the Jews numbered only 84,000, or 11 percent of the population of Palestine. The Zionists, moreover, could not openly oppose the establishment of democratic structures, which was clearly in accordance with the Covenant of the League of Nations and the mandatory system.

The Arabs of Palestine, however, believing that participation in Mandate-sanctioned institutions would signify their acquiescence to the Mandate and thus to the Balfour Declaration, refused to participate. As a result, Samuels's proposals for a legislative council, an advisory council, and an Arab agency envisioned as similar to the Jewish Agency, were all rejected by the Arabs. After the collapse of the bid for representative institutions, any possibility of joint consultation between the two communities ended.

The Arab Community During the Mandate

The British Mandate and the intensification of Jewish settlement in Palestine significantly altered Palestinian leadership structures and transformed the socioeconomic base of Palestinian Arab society. First, British policy in Palestine, as elsewhere in the Middle East, was based on patronage. This policy entailed granting wide powers to a small group of competing traditional elites whose authority would depend upon the British high commissioner. In Palestine, Samuels granted the most important posts to two competing families, the Husaynis (also seen as Husseinis) and the Nashashibis. Of the two clans, the Husaynis were given the most powerful posts, many of which had no precedent under Ottoman rule. In 1921 Samuels appointed Hajj Amin al Husayni, an ardent anti-Zionist and a major figure behind the April 1920 riots, as mufti (chief Muslim religious jurist) of Jerusalem. In 1922 he augmented Hajj Amin's power by appointing him president of the newly constituted Supreme Muslim Council (SMC), which was given wide powers over the disbursement of funds from religious endowments, fees, and the like.

By heading the SMC, Hajj Amin controlled a vast patronage network, giving him power over a large constituency. This new patronage system competed with and threatened the traditional family-clan and Islamic ties that existed under the Ottoman Empire. Traditional Arab elites hailing from other locales, such as Hebron and Haifa, resented the monopoly of power of the British-supported Jerusalem-based elite. Furthermore, as an agricultural depression pushed many Arabs westward into the coastal cities, a new urban-based elite emerged that challenged the Nashashibis and Husaynis.

A building on Jaffa Road in the New City of Jerusalem Courtesy Les Vogel

Tension between members of Arab elites was exacerbated because Hajj Amin, who was not an elected official, increasingly attempted to dictate Palestinian politics. The competition between the major families and the increased use of the Zionist threat as a political tool in interelite struggles placed a premium on extremism. Hajj Amin frequently incited his followers against the Nashashibis by referring to the latter as Zionist collaborators. As a result, Palestinian leadership during the Mandate was fragmented and unable to develop a coherent policy to deal with the growing Zionist movement.

The other major transformation in Palestinian Arab society during the Mandate concerned the issue of land ownership. During the years of Ottoman rule, the question of private property rights was never fully articulated. The tenuous nature of private property rights enabled the Zionist movement to acquire large tracts of land that had been Arab owned. The sale of land to Jewish settlers, which occurred even during the most intense phases of the Palestinian Revolt, reflected the lack of national cohesion and institutional structure that might have enabled the Palestinian Arabs to withstand the lure of quick profits. Instead, when increased Jewish land purchases caused property prices to spiral, both the Arab landowning class and absentee landlords, many of whom resided outside Palestine, were quick to sell for unprecedented profits. In the 1930s, when Palestine was beset by a severe economic depression, large

39

numbers of Arab peasants, unable to pay either their Arab land-lords or taxes to the government, sold their land. The British did not intervene in the land purchases mainly because they needed the influx of Jewish capital to pay for Jewish social services and to maintain the Jewish economy.

The Jewish Community under the Mandate

The greatest asset brought by the Zionists settling Palestine was their organizational acumen, which allowed for the institutionali-zation of the movement despite deep ideological cleavages. The WZO established an executive office in Palestine, thus implement-ing the language of the Mandate prescribing such an agency. In August 1929, the formalized Jewish Agency was established with a council, administrative committee, and executive. Each of these bodies consisted of an equal number of Zionist and nominally non-Zionist Jews. The president of the WZO was, however, ex officio president of the agency. Thereafter, the WZO continued to con-duct external diplomatic, informational, and cultural activities, and the operational Jewish Agency took over fundraising, activities in Palestine, and local relations with the British Mandate Authority (administered by the colonial secretary). In time, the World Zionist Organization and the Jewish Agency became two different names for virtually the same organization.

Other landmark developments by the WZO and the Jewish Agency under the Mandate included creation of the Asefat Haniv-harim (Elected Assembly—see Glossary) and the Vaad Leumi (National Council) in 1920 to promote religious, educational, and welfare services; establishment of the chief rabbinate in 1921; cen-tralized Zionist control of the Hebrew school system in 1919, open-ing of the Technion (Israel Institute of Technology) in Haifa in 1924, and dedication of the Hebrew University of Jerusalem in 1925; and continued acquisition of land—largely via purchases by the Jewish National Fund—increasing from 60,120 hectares in 1922 to about 155,140 hectares in 1939, and the concurrent growth of Jewish urban and village centers.

The architect of the centralized organizational structure that dominated the Yishuv throughout the Mandate and afterward was Ben-Gurion. To achieve a centralized Jewish economic infrastruc-ture in Palestine, he set out to form a large-scale organized Jewish labor movement including both urban and agricultural laborers. In 1919 he founded the first united Labor Zionist party, Ahdut HaAvodah (Unity of Labor), which included Poalei Tziyyon and affiliated socialist groups. This achievement was followed in 1920 by the formation of the Histadrut, or HaHistadrut HaKlalit shel HaOvdim B'Eretz Yisrael (General Federation of Laborers in the Land of Israel).

The Histadrut was the linchpin of Ben-Gurion's reorganization of the Yishuv. He designed the Histadrut to form a tightly controlled autonomous Jewish economic state within the Palestinian economy. It functioned as much more than a traditional labor union, providing the Yishuv with social services and security, setting up training centers, helping absorb new immigrants, and instructing them in Hebrew. Its membership was all-inclusive: any Jewish laborer was entitled to belong and to obtain shares in the organization's assets. It established a general fund supported by workers' dues that provided all members with social services previously provided by individual political parties. The Histadrut also set up Hevrat HaOvdim (Society of Workers) to fund and manage large-scale agricultural and industrial enterprises. Within a year of its establishment in 1921, Hevrat HaOvdim had set up Tenuvah, the agriculture marketing cooperative; Bank HaPoalim, the workers' bank; and Soleh Boneh, the construction firm. Originally established by Ahdut HaAvodah after the Arab riots in 1920, the Haganah under the Histadrut rapidly became the major Jewish defense force (see Historical Background, ch. 5).

From the beginning, Ben-Gurion and Ahdut HaAvodah dominated the Histadrut and through it the Yishuv. As secretary general of the Histadrut, Ben-Gurion oversaw the development of the Jewish economy and defense forces in the Yishuv. This centralized control enabled the Yishuv to endure both severe economic hardship and frequent skirmishes with the Arabs and British in the late 1920s. The resilience of the Histadrut in the face of economic depression enabled Ben-Gurion to consolidate his control over the Yishuv. In 1929 many private entrepreneurs were forced to look to Ahdut HaAvodah to pull them through hard economic times. In 1930 Ahdut HaAvodah was powerful enough to absorb its old ideological rival, HaPoel HaTzair. They merged to form Mifleget Poalei Eretz Yisrael (better known by its acronym Mapai), which would dominate political life of the State of Israel for the next two generations (see Multiparty System, ch. 4).

The hegemony of Ben-Gurion's Labor Zionism in the Yishuv did not go unchallenged. The other major contenders for power were the Revisionist Zionists led by Vladimir Jabotinsky, who espoused a more liberal economic structure and a more zealous defense policy than the Labor movement. Jabotinsky, who had become a hero to the Yishuv because of his role in the defense of the Jews of Jerusalem during the riots of April 1920, believed that there was an inherent conflict between Zionist objectives and the aspirations of Palestinian Arabs. He called for the establishment of a strong Jewish military force capable of compelling the Arabs to accept Zionist claims to Palestine. Jabotinsky also thought that Ben-Gurion's focus on building a socialist Jewish economy in Palestine needlessly diverted the Zionist movement from its true goal: the establishment of a Jewish state in Palestine.

The appeal of Revisionist Zionism grew between 1924 and 1930 as a result of an influx of Polish immigrants and the escalating conflict with the Arabs. In the mid-1920s, a political and economic crisis in Poland and the Johnson-Lodge Immigration Act passed by the United States Congress, which curtailed mass immigration to America, spurred Polish-Jewish immigration to Israel. Between 1924 and 1931, approximately 80,000 Jews arrived in Palestine from Central Europe. The Fourth Aliyah, as it was called, differed from previous waves of Jewish immigration. The new Polish immigrants, unlike the Bolshevik-minded immigrants of the Second Aliyah, were primarily petty merchants and small-time industrialists with their own capital to invest. Not attracted to the Labor Party's collective settlements, they migrated to the cities where they established the first semblance of an industrialized urban Jewish economy in Palestine. Within five years, the Jewish populations of Jerusalem and Haifa doubled, and the city of Tel Aviv emerged. These new immigrants disdained the socialism of the Histadrut and increasingly identified with the laissez-faire economics espoused by Jabotinsky.

Another reason for Jabotinsky's increasing appeal was the escalation of Jewish-Arab violence. Jabotinsky's belief in the inevitable conflict between Jews and Arabs and his call for the establishment of an ''iron wall'' that would force the Arabs to accept Zionism were vindicated in the minds of many Jews after a confrontation over Jewish access to the Wailing Wall in August 1929 turned into a violent Arab attack on Jews in Hebron and Jerusalem. By the time the fighting ended, 133 Jews had been killed and 339 wounded. The causes of the disturbances were varied: an inter-Palestinian power struggle, a significant cutback in British military presence in Palestine, and a more conciliatory posture by the new British authorities toward the Arab position.

The inability of the Haganah to protect Jewish civilians during the 1929 riots led Jewish Polish immigrants who supported Jabotinsky to break away from the Labor-dominated Haganah. They were members of Betar, an activist Zionist movement founded in 1923 in Riga, Latvia, under the influence of Jabotinsky. The first Betar congress met at Danzig in 1931 and elected Jabotinsky as its leader. In 1937, a group of Haganah members left the organization in protest against its "defensive" orientation and joined forces with Betar to set up a new and more militant armed underground organization, known as the Irgun. The formal name of the Irgun was the Irgun Zvai Leumi (National Military Organization), sometimes also called by the acronym, Etzel, from the initial letters of the Hebrew name. The more extreme terrorist group, known to the British as the Stern Gang, split off from the Irgun in 1939. The Stern Gang was formally known as the Lohamei Herut Israel (Fighters for Israel's Freedom), sometimes identified by the acronym Lehi (see Glossary). Betar (which later formed a nucleus for Herut—see Appendix B) and Irgun rejected the Histadrut/ Haganah doctrine of *havlaga* (self-restraint) and favored retaliation.

Although the 1929 riots intensified the Labor-Revisionist split over the tactics necessary to attain Jewish sovereignty in Palestine, their respective visions of the indigenous Arab population coalesced. Ben-Gurion, like Jabotinsky, came to realize that the conflict between Arab and Jewish nationalisms was irreconcilable and therefore that the Yishuv needed to prepare for an eventual military confrontation with the Arabs. He differed with Jabotinsky, however, on the need to make tactical compromises in the short term to attain Jewish statehood at a more propitious time. Whereas Jabotinsky adamantly put forth maximalist demands, such as the immediate proclamation of statehood in all of historic Palestine—on both banks of the Jordan River—Ben-Gurion operated within the confines of the Mandate. He understood better than Jabotinsky that timing was the key to the Zionist enterprise in Palestine. The Yishuv in the 1930s lacked the necessary military or economic power to carry out Jabotinsky's vision in the face of Arab and British opposition.

Another development resulting from the 1929 riots was the growing animosity between the British Mandate Authority and the Yishuv. The inactivity of the British while Arab bands were attacking Jewish settlers strengthened Zionist anti-British forces. Following the riots, the British set up the Shaw Commission to determine the cause of the disturbances. The commission report, dated March 30, 1930, refrained from blaming either community but focused on Arab apprehensions about Jewish labor practices and land purchases. The commission's allegations were investigated by an agrarian expert, Sir John Hope Simpson, who concluded that about 30 percent of the Arab population was already landless and that the amount of land remaining in Arab hands would be insufficient to divide among their offspring. This led to the Passfield White Paper (October 1930), which recommended that Jewish immigration be stopped if it prevented Arabs from obtaining employment and that Jewish land purchases be curtailed.

Although the Passfield White Paper was publicly repudiated by Prime Minister Ramsay MacDonald in 1931, it served to alienate further the Yishuv from the British.

The year 1929 also saw the beginning of a severe economic crisis in Germany that launched the rise of Adolf Hitler. Although both Germany and Austria had long histories of anti-Semitism, the genocide policies preached by Hitler were unprecedented. When in January 1930 he became chancellor of the Reich, a massive wave of mostly German Jewish immigration to Palestine ensued. Recorded Jewish immigration was 37,000 in 1933, 45,000 in 1934, and an all-time record for the Yishuv of 61,000 in 1935. In addition, the British estimated that a total of 40,000 Jews had entered Palestine without legal certificates during the period from 1920 to 1939. Between 1929, the year of the Wailing Wall disturbances, and 1936, the year the Palestinian Revolt began, the Jewish population of Palestine increased from 170,000 or 17 percent of the population, to 400,000, or approximately 31 percent of the total. The immigration of thousands of German Jews accelerated the pace of industrialization and made the concept of a Jewish state in Palestine a more formidable reality.

The Palestinian Revolt, 1936-39

By 1936 the increase in Jewish immigration and land acquisition, the growing power of Hajj Amin al Husayni, and general Arab frustration at the continuation of European rule, radicalized increasing numbers of Palestinian Arabs. Thus, in April 1936 an Arab attack on a Jewish bus led to a series of incidents that escalated into a major Palestinian rebellion. An Arab Higher Committee (AHC), a loose coalition of recently formed Arab political parties, was created. It declared a national strike in support of three basic demands: cessation of Jewish immigration, an end to all further land sales to the Jews, and the establishment of an Arab national government.

The intensity of the Palestinian Revolt, at a time when Britain was preparing for the possibility of another world war, led the British to reorient their policy in Palestine. As war with Germany became imminent, Britain's dependence on Middle Eastern oil, and therefore the need for Arab goodwill, loomed increasingly large in its strategic thinking. Jewish leverage in the Foreign Office, on the other hand, had waned; the pro-Zionists, Balfour and Samuels, had left the Foreign Office and the new administration was not inclined toward the Zionist position. Furthermore, the Jews had little choice but to support Britain against Nazi Germany. Thus, Britain's commitment to a Jewish homeland in Palestine dissipated, and the Mandate authorities pursued a policy of appeasement with respect to the Arabs.

Britain's policy change in Palestine was not, however, easily implemented. Since the 1917 Balfour Declaration, successive British governments had supported (or at least not rejected) a Jewish national home in Palestine. The Mandate itself was premised on that pledge. By the mid-1930s, the Yishuv had grown to about 400,000, and the Jewish economic and political structures in Palestine were well ensconced. The extent of the Jewish presence and the rapidly deteriorating fate of European Jewry meant that the British would have an extremely difficult time extricating themselves from the Balfour Declaration. Furthermore, the existing Palestinian leadership, dominated by Hajj Amin al Husayni, was unwilling to grant members of the Jewish community citizenship or to guarantee their safety if a new Arab entity were to emerge. Thus, for the British the real options were to impose partition, to pull out and leave the Jews and Arabs to fight it out, or to stay and improvise.

In 1937 the British, working with their regional Arab allies, Amir Abdullah of Transjordan, King Ghazi of Iraq, and King Abdul Aziz ibn Saud of Saudi Arabia, mediated an end to the revolt with the AHC. A Royal Commission on Palestine (known as the Peel Commission) was immediately dispatched to Palestine. Its report, issued in July 1937, described the Arab and Zionist positions and the British obligation to each as irreconcilable and the existing Mandate as unworkable. It recommended partition of Palestine into Jewish and Arab states, with a retained British Mandate over Nazareth, Bethlehem, and Jerusalem and a corridor from Jerusalem to the coast (see fig. 3).

In 1937 the Twentieth Zionist Congress rejected the proposed boundaries but agreed in principle to partition. Palestinian Arab nationalists rejected any kind of partition. The British government approved the idea of partition and sent a technical team to make a detailed plan. This group, the Woodhead Commission, reversed the Peel Commission's findings and reported in November 1937 that partition was impracticable; this view in its turn was accepted. The Palestinian Revolt broke out again in the autumn of 1937. The British put down the revolt using harsh measures, shutting down the AHC and deporting many Palestinian Arab leaders.

With their leadership residing outside Palestine, the Arabs were unable to match the Zionists' highly sophisticated organization. Another outcome of the Palestinian Revolt was the involvement of the Arab states as advocates of the Palestinian Arabs. Whereas Britain had previously tended to deal with its commitments in

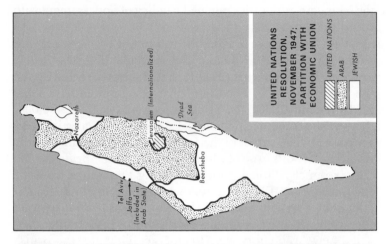

UNITED NATIONS RESOLUTION, NOVEMBER 1947; PARTITION WITH ECONOMIC UNION

UNITED NATIONS
ARAB
JEWISH

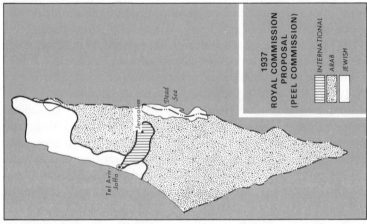

1937 ROYAL COMMISSION PROPOSAL (PEEL COMMISSION)

INTERNATIONAL
ARAB
JEWISH

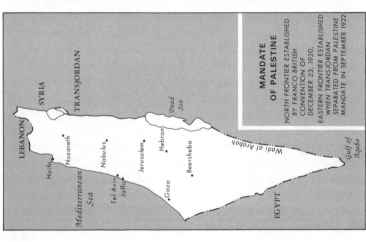

MANDATE OF PALESTINE

NORTH FRONTIER ESTABLISHED BY FRANCO-BRITISH CONVENTION OF DECEMBER 23, 1920.
EASTERN FRONTIER ESTABLISHED WHEN TRANSJORDAN SEPARATED FROM PALESTINE MANDATE IN SEPTEMBER 1922

Figure 3. Palestine during the Mandate and Two of the Partition Proposals

Palestine as separate from its commitments elsewhere in the Middle East, by 1939 pan-Arab pressure carried increasing weight in London.

In the Yishuv, the Palestinian Revolt reinforced the already firm belief in the need for a strong Jewish defense network. Finally, the Arab agricultural boycott that began in 1936 forced the Jewish economy into even greater self-sufficiency.

World War II and Zionism

In May 1939, the British published a White Paper that marked the end of its commitment to the Jews under the Balfour Declaration. It provided for the establishment of a Palestinian (Arab) state within ten years and the appointment of Palestinian ministers to begin taking over the government as soon as "peace and order" were restored to Palestine; 75,000 Jews would be allowed into Palestine over the next five years, after which all immigration would be subject to Arab consent; all further land sales would be severely restricted. The 1939 White Paper met a mixed Arab reception and was rejected by the AHC. The Jewish Agency rejected it emphatically, branding it as a total repudiation of Balfour and Mandate obligations. In September 1939, at the outset of World War II, Ben-Gurion, then chairman of the Jewish Agency, declared: "We shall fight the war against Hitler as if there were no White Paper, and we shall fight the White Paper as if there were no war."

Ben-Gurion's statement of 1939 set the tone for Jewish Agency policy and operations during World War II. In May 1940, however, when Winston Churchill, a longtime Zionist sympathizer, became prime minister, it appeared that the 1939 White Paper might be rescinded. A brief period of close British-Jewish military cooperation ensued, and there was talk (which never came to fruition) of establishing a Jewish division within the British Army. The British trained Jewish commando units, the first elements of the famous Palmach (Pelugot Mahatz—Shock Forces—see Glossary)—the strategic reserve of the Haganah—and they also gave Jewish volunteers intensive training in sabotage, demolition, and partisan warfare. Ironically, this training proved indispensable in the Yishuv's efforts after the war to force the British to withdraw from Palestine.

The entry of Italy into the war in May 1940, which brought the war closer to the Middle East, convinced Churchill and his military advisers that the immigration provisions of the White Paper needed to be enforced so as not to antagonize the Arabs. Thus, the British strictly enforced the immigration limits at a time when European Jewry sought desperately to reach the shores of Palestine.

Despite rising British-Jewish tensions, thousands of Jewish volunteers served in the British army, and on September 14, 1944, the Jewish Brigade was established.

The event that did the most to turn the Zionist movement against Churchill's Britain was the *Struma* affair. The *Struma*, a ship carrying Jewish refugees from Romania, was denied entry into Palestine, after which the ship sank in the Black Sea leaving all but two of its passengers dead. In the aftermath of the loss of the *Struma* in April 1942, young Menachem Begin, then a soldier in the Polish army-in-exile, first came to Palestine. Begin was a disciple of Jabotinsky, but he rejected Jabotinsky's pro-British sympathies. Upon entering Palestine, Begin immediately set out to draw together the whole underground, including Lehi, in preparation for a Jewish war of liberation against the British.

By 1943 as news regarding Nazi persecution of Jews in Europe increased, the Irgun and Stern Gang stepped up harassment of British forces in an attempt to obtain unrestricted Jewish immigration. In November 1944, Lord Moyne, the British minister-resident in Cairo and a close personal friend of Churchill, was assassinated by Lehi. Lord Moyne's assassination alienated the British prime minister, who until then had supported a Jewish national home in Palestine. Subsequently, no British government considered setting up a Jewish state in Palestine. The assassination also led the Jewish Agency's clandestine military arm, Haganah, to cooperate with the British against the Irgun.

Another result of the anti-Zionist trend in British policy was the Yishuv's increasing reliance on the United States. In May 1942, Zionist policy and objectives were clarified at a conference of Zionist parties held at the Biltmore Hotel in New York City. This conference was called at the initiative of Ben-Gurion, who had come to solicit the support of American Jews. Ben-Gurion was determined to seek a resolution that Jewish immigration to Palestine and the establishment of a Jewish state would proceed despite British opposition. Weizmann, who objected to the idea of severing ties with Britain, was outflanked at the conference. The Biltmore Program adopted at the conference and approved by the Zionist General Council in November 1942 called for unlimited Jewish immigration to Palestine and control of immigration by the Jewish commonwealth, the word *commonwealth* thus replacing *homeland.*

The Holocaust

The impact of the Holocaust on world Jewry, either on contemporaries of the horror or on succeeding generations, cannot be exaggerated. The scope of Hitler's genocidal efforts can be quickly summarized. In 1939 about 10 million of the estimated 16 million Jews in the world lived in Europe. By 1945 almost 6 million had been killed, most of them in the nineteen main concentration camps. Of prewar Czechoslovakia's 281,000 Jews, about 4,000 survived. Before the German conquest and occupation, the Jewish population of Greece was estimated to be between 65,000 and 72,000; about 2,000 survived. Only 5,000 of Austria's prewar Jewish community of 70,000 escaped. In addition, an estimated 4.6 million Jews were killed in Poland and in those areas of the Soviet Union seized and occupied by the Germans.

The magnitude of the Holocaust cast a deep gloom over the Jewish people and tormented the spirit of Judaism. The faith of observant Jews was shaken, and the hope of the assimilationists smashed. Not only had 6 million Jews perished, but the Allies, who by 1944 could have easily disrupted the operation of the death camps, did nothing. In this spiritual vacuum, Zionism alone emerged as a viable Jewish response to this demonic anti-Semitism. Zionist thinkers since the days of Pinsker had made dire predictions concerning the fate of European Jewry. For much of world Jewry that had suffered centuries of persecution, Zionism and its call for a Jewish national home and for the radical transformation of the Jew from passive victim to self-sufficient citizen residing in his own homeland became the only possible positive response to the Holocaust. Zionism unified the Jewish people, entered deeply into the Jewish spirit, and became an integral part of Jewish identity and religious experience.

Prelude to Statehood

The British position in Palestine at the end of World War II was becoming increasingly untenable. Hundreds of thousands of Jewish Holocaust survivors temporarily housed in displaced persons camps in Europe were clamoring to be settled in Palestine. The fate of these refugees aroused international public opinion against British policy. Moreover, the administration of President Harry S Truman, feeling morally bound to help the Jewish refugees and exhorted by a large and vocal Jewish community, pressured Britain to change its course in Palestine. Postwar Britain depended on American economic aid to reconstruct its war-torn economy. Furthermore, Britain's staying power in its old colonial holdings was waning; in 1947 British rule in India came to an end and Britain informed Washington that London could no longer carry the military burden of strengthening Greece and Turkey against communist encroachment.

In May 1946, the Anglo-American Committee of Inquiry unanimously declared its opposition to the White Paper of 1939 and proposed, among other recommendations, that the immigration to Palestine of 100,000 European Jews be authorized at once. The British Mandate Authority rejected the proposal, stating that such immigration was impossible while armed organizations in Palestine—both Arab and Jewish—were fighting the authority and disrupting public order.

Despite American, Jewish, and international pressure and the recommendations of the Anglo-American Committee of Inquiry, the new Labour Party government of Prime Minister Clement Atlee and his foreign minister, Ernest Bevin, continued to enforce the policy articulated in the White Paper. British adamancy on immigration radicalized the Yishuv. Under Ben-Gurion's direction, the Jewish Agency decided in October 1945 to unite with Jewish dissident groups in a combined rebellion against the British administration in Palestine. The combined Jewish resistance movement organized illegal immigration and kidnapping of British officials in Palestine and sabotaged the British infrastructure in Palestine. In response Bevin ordered a crackdown on the Haganah and arrested many of its leaders. While the British concentrated their efforts on the Haganah, the Irgun and Lehi carried out terrorist attacks against British forces, the most spectacular of which was the bombing of the King David Hotel in Jerusalem in July 1946. The latter event led Ben-Gurion to sever his relationship with the Irgun and Lehi.

By 1947 Palestine was a major trouble spot in the British Empire, requiring some 100,000 troops and a huge maintenance budget. On February 18, 1947, Bevin informed the House of Commons of the government's decision to present the Palestine problem to the United Nations (UN). On May 15, 1947, a special session of the UN General Assembly established the United Nations Special Committee on Palestine (UNSCOP), consisting of eleven members. The UNSCOP reported on August 31 that a majority of its members supported a geographically complex system of partition into separate Arab and Jewish states, a special international status for Jerusalem, and an economic union linking the three members. Backed by both the United States and the Soviet Union, the plan was adopted after two months of intense deliberations as the UN General Assembly Resolution of November 29, 1947. Although considering the plan defective in terms of their expectations from the League of Nations Mandate twenty-five years earlier, the Zionist General Council stated willingness in principle to accept partition. The League of Arab States (Arab League) Council, meeting in

December 1947, said it would take whatever measures were required to prevent implementation of the resolution.

Despite the passage of the UN partition plan, the situation in Palestine in early 1948 did not look auspicious for the Yishuv. When the AHC rejected the plan immediately after its passage and called for a general strike, violence between Arabs and Jews mounted. Many Jewish centers, including Jerusalem, were besieged by the Arabs. In January 1948, President Truman, warned by the United States Department of State that a Jewish state was not viable, reversed himself on the issue of Palestine, agreeing to postpone partition and to transfer the Mandate to a trusteeship council. Moreover, the British forces in Palestine sided with the Arabs and attempted to thwart the Yishuv's attempts to arm itself.

In mid-March the Yishuv's military prospects changed dramatically after receiving the first clandestine shipment of heavy arms from Czechoslovakia. The Haganah went on the offensive and, in a series of operations carried out from early April until mid-May, successfully consolidated and created communications links with those Jewish settlements designated by the UN to become the Jewish state. In the meantime, Weizmann convinced Truman to reverse himself and pledge his support for the proposed Jewish state. In April 1948, the Palestinian Arab community panicked after Begin's Irgun killed 250 Arab civilians at the village of Dayr Yasin near Jerusalem. The news of Dayr Yasin precipitated a flight of the Arab population from areas with large Jewish populations.

On May 14, 1948, David Ben-Gurion proclaimed the establishment of the State of Israel. On the following day Britain relinquished the Mandate at 6:00 P.M. and the United States announced de facto recognition of Israel. Soviet recognition was accorded on May 18; by April 1949, fifty-three nations, including Britain, had extended recognition. In May 1949, the UN General Assembly, on recommendation of the Security Council, admitted Israel to the UN.

Meanwhile, Arab military forces began their invasion of Israel on May 15. Initially these forces consisted of approximately 8,000 to 10,000 Egyptians, 2,000 to 4,000 Iraqis, 4,000 to 5,000 Transjordanians, 3,000 to 4,000 Syrians, 1,000 to 2,000 Lebanese, and smaller numbers of Saudi Arabian and Yemeni troops, about 25,000 in all. Israeli forces composed of the Haganah, such irregular units as the Irgun and the Stern Gang, and women's auxiliaries numbered 35,000 or more. By October 14, Arab forces deployed in the war zones had increased to about 55,000, including not more than 5,000 irregulars of Hajj Amin al Husayni's Palestine Liberation Force. The Israeli military forces had increased to approximately 100,000. Except for the British-trained Arab Legion of Transjordan, Arab units were largely ill-trained and inexperienced. Israeli forces, usually operating with interior lines of communication, included an estimated 20,000 to 25,000 European World War II veterans.

By January 1949, Jewish forces held the area that was to define Israel's territory until June 1967, an area that was significantly larger than the area designated by the UN partition plan. The part of Palestine remaining in Arab hands was limited to that held by the Arab Legion of Transjordan and the Gaza area held by Egypt at the cessation of hostilities. The area held by the Arab Legion was subsequently annexed by Jordan and is commonly referred to as the West Bank (see Glossary). Jerusalem was divided. The Old City, the Western Wall and the site of Solomon's Temple, upon which stands the Muslim mosque called the Dome of the Rock, remained in Jordanian hands; the New City lay on the Israeli side of the line. Although the West Bank remained under Jordanian suzerainty until 1967, only two countries—Britain and Pakistan—granted de jure recognition of the annexation.

Early in the conflict, on May 29, 1948, the UN Security Council established the Truce Commission headed by a UN mediator, Swedish diplomat Folke Bernadotte, who was assassinated in Jerusalem on September 17, 1948. He was succeeded by Ralph Bunche, an American, as acting mediator. The commission, which later evolved into the United Nations Truce Supervision Organization-Palestine (UNTSOP), attempted to devise new settlement plans and arranged the truces of June 11–July 8 and July 19–October 14, 1948. Armistice talks were initiated with Egypt in January 1949, and an armistice agreement was concluded with Egypt on February 24, with Lebanon on March 23, with Transjordan on April 3, and with Syria on July 20. Iraq did not enter into an armistice agreement but withdrew its forces after turning over its positions to Transjordanian units.

Problems of the New State, 1948–67

Etatism

The War of Independence was the most costly war Israel has fought; more than 6,000 Jewish fighters and civilians died. At the war's end in 1949, the fledgling state was burdened with a number of difficult problems. These included reacting to the absorption of hundreds of thousands of new immigrants and to a festering refugee problem on its borders, maintaining a defense against a hostile and numerically superior Arab world, keeping a war-torn economy afloat, and managing foreign policy alignments. Faced with such intractable problems, Ben-Gurion sought to ensure a fluid transition from existing prestate institutions to the new state apparatus. He announced the formation of a Provisional Council of State, actually a transformed executive committee of the Jewish Agency with himself as prime minister. Weizmann became president of the council, although Ben-Gurion was careful to make the presidency a distinctly ceremonial position. The provisional government would hold elections no later than October 1948 for the Constituent Assembly to draw up a formal constitution. The proposed constitution was never ratified, however, and on February 16, 1949 the Constituent Assembly became Israel's first parliament or Knesset (see Glossary).

A key element of Ben-Gurion's etatism was the integration of Israel's independent military forces into a unified military structure. On May 28, 1948, Ben-Gurion's provisional government created the Israel Defense Forces (IDF), the Hebrew name of which, Zvah Haganah Le Yisrael, is commonly abbreviated to Zahal, and prohibited maintenance of any other armed force. This proclamation was challenged by the Irgun, which sailed the *Altalena,* a ship carrying arms, into Tel Aviv harbor. Ben-Gurion ordered Haganah troops to fire on the ship, which was set aflame on the beach in Tel Aviv. With the two camps on the verge of civil war, Begin, the leader of the Irgun, ordered his troops not to fire on the Haganah. Although the *Altalena* affair unified the IDF, it remained a bitter memory for Begin and the Irgun. Begin subsequently converted his armed movement into a political party, the Herut (or Freedom Movement). By January 1949, Ben-Gurion had also dissolved the Palmach, the strike force of the Haganah.

Ingathering of the Exiles

The first legislative act of the Provisional Council of State was the Law and Administrative Ordinance of 1948 that declared null and void the restrictions on Jewish immigration imposed by British authorities. In July 1950, the Knesset passed the Law of Return (see Glossary), which stated that "Every Jew has the right to come to this country as an *olah* (new immigrant)."

In 1939 the British Mandate Authority had estimated that about 445,000 out of 1.5 million residents of the Mandate were Jews. Israeli officials estimated that as of May 15, 1948, about 650,000 Jews lived in the area scheduled to become Israel under the November 1947 UN partition proposal. Between May 1948 and December 31, 1951, approximately 684,000 Jewish immigrants entered the new state, thus providing a Jewish majority in the region for the first time in the modern era. The largest single group of immigrants consisted of Jews from Eastern Europe; more than 300,000 people came from refugee and displaced persons camps.

The highly organized state structure created by Ben-Gurion and the old guard Mapai leadership served the Yishuv well in the prestate era, but was ill prepared for the massive influx of non-European refugees that flooded into the new state in its first years of existence. Between 1948 and 1952 about 300,000 Sephardic immigrants came to Israel. Aside from 120,000 highly educated Iraqi Jews and 10,000 Egyptian Jews, the majority of new immigrants (55,000 Turkish Jews, 40,000 Iranian Jews, 55,000 Yemeni Jews, and thousands more from Jewish enclaves in Afghanistan, the Caucasus, and Cochin in southwest India) were poorly educated, impoverished, and culturally very different from the country's dominant European culture. They were religious Jews who had worked primarily in petty trade, while the ruling Ashkenazim of the Labor Party were secular socialists. As a result, the Ashkenazim-dominated kibbutz movement spurned them, and Mapai leadership as a whole viewed the new immigrants as "raw material" for their socialist program (see Jewish Ethnic Groups, ch. 2).

In the late 1950s, a new flood of 400,000 mainly undereducated Moroccan, Algerian, Tunisian, and Egyptian Jews immigrated to Israel following Israel's Sinai Campaign (see 1956 War, ch. 5). The total addition to Israel's population during the first twelve years of statehood was about 1.2 million, and at least two-thirds of the newcomers were of Sephardic extraction. By 1961 the Sephardic portion of the Jewish population was about 45 percent, or approximately 800,000 people. By the end of the first decade, about four-fifths of the Sephardic population lived in the large towns, mostly development towns, and cities where they became workers in an economy dominated by Ashkenazim.

Israeli Arabs, Arab Land, and Arab Refugees

Events immediately before and during the War of Independence and during the first years of independence remain, so far as those events involved the Arab residents of Palestine, matters of bitter and emotional dispute. Palestinian Arab refugees insist that they were driven out of their homeland by Jewish terrorists and regular Jewish military forces; the government of Israel asserts that the invading Arab forces urged the Palestinian Arabs to leave their houses temporarily to avoid the perils of the war that would end the Jewish intrusion into Arab lands. Forty years after the event, advocates of Arabs or Jews continue to present and believe diametrically opposed descriptions of those events.

According to British Mandate Authority population figures in 1947, there were about 1.3 million Arabs in all of Palestine. Between 700,000 and 900,000 of the Arabs lived in the region eventually bounded by the 1949 Armistice line, the so-called Green Line. By the time the fighting stopped, there were only about 170,000 Arabs left in the new State of Israel. By the summer of 1949, about 750,000 Palestinian Arabs were living in squalid refugee camps, set up virtually overnight in territories adjacent to Israel's borders. About 300,000 lived in the Gaza Strip, which was occupied by the Egyptian army. Another 450,000 became unwelcome residents of the West Bank of the Jordan, recently occupied by the Arab Legion of Transjordan.

The Arabs who remained inside post-1948 Israel became citizens of the Jewish state. They had voting rights equal to the state's Jewish community, and according to Israel's Declaration of Independence were guaranteed social and political equality. Because Israel's parliament has never passed a constitution, however, Arab rights in the Jewish state have remained precarious (see Minority Groups, ch. 2; Arab Parties, ch. 4). Israel's Arab residents were seen both by Jewish Israelis and by themselves as aliens in a foreign country. They had been waging war since the 1920s against Zionism and could not be expected to accept enthusiastically residence in the Jewish state. The institutions of the new state were designed to facilitate the growth of the Jewish nation, which in many instances entailed a perceived infringement upon Arab rights. Thus, Arab land was confiscated to make way for Jewish immigrants, the Hebrew language and Judaism predominated over Arabic and Islam, foreign economic aid poured into the Jewish economy while Arab agriculture and business received only meager assistance, and Israeli security concerns severely restricted the Arabs' freedom of movement.

After independence the areas in which 90 percent of the Arabs lived were placed under military government. This system and the assignment of almost unfettered powers to military governors were based on the Defense (Emergency) Regulations promulgated by the British Mandate Authority in 1945. Using the 1945 regulations as a legal base, the government created three areas or zones to be ruled by the Ministry of Defense. The most important was the Northern Area, also known as the Galilee Area, the locale of about two-thirds of the Arab population. The second critical area was the so-called Little Triangle, located between the villages of Et Tira and Et Taiyiba near the border with Jordan (then Transjordan).

The third area included much of the Negev Desert, the region traversed by the previously apolitical nomadic beduins.

The most salient feature of military government was restriction of movement. Article 125 of the Defense (Emergency) Regulations empowered military governors to declare any specified area "off-limits" to those having no written authorization. The area was then declared a security zone and thus closed to Israeli Arabs who lacked written permission either from the army chief of staff or the minister of defense. Under these provisions, 93 out of 104 Arab villages in Israel were constituted as closed areas out of which no one could move without a military permit. In these areas, official acts of military governors were, with rare exceptions, not subject to review by the civil courts. Individuals could be arrested and imprisoned on unspecified charges, and private property was subject to search and seizure without warrant. Furthermore, the physical expulsion of individuals or groups from the state was not subject to review by the civil courts.

Another land expropriation measure evolved from the Defense (Emergency) Regulations, which were passed in 1949 and renewed annually until 1972 when the legislation was allowed to lapse. Under this law, the Ministry of Defense could, subject to approval by an appropriate committee of the Knesset, create security zones in all or part of what was designated as the "protected zone," an area that included lands adjacent to Israel's borders and other specified areas. According to Sabri Jiryis, an Arab political economist who based his work exclusively on Israeli government sources, the defense minister used this law to categorize "almost half of Galilee, all of the Triangle, an area near the Gaza Strip, and another along the Jerusalem-Jaffa railway line near Batir as security zones." A clause of the law provided that permanent as well as temporary residents could be required to leave the zone and that the individual expelled had four days within which to appeal the eviction notice to an appeals committee. The decisions of these committees were not subject to review or appeal by a civil court.

Yet another measure enacted by the Knesset in 1949 was the Emergency Regulations (Cultivation of Waste Lands) Ordinance. One use of this law was to transfer to kibbutzim or other Jewish settlements land in the security zones that was lying fallow because the owner of the land or other property was not allowed to enter the zone as a result of national security legislation. The 1949 law provided that such land transfers were valid only for a period of two years and eleven months, but subsequent amending legislation extended the validity of the transfers for the duration of the state of emergency.

Another common procedure was for the military government to seize up to 40 percent of the land in a given region—the maximum allowed for national security reasons—and to transfer the land to a new kibbutz or moshav (see Glossary). Between 1948 and 1953, about 370 new Jewish settlements were built, and an estimated 350 of the settlements were established on what was termed abandoned Arab property.

The property of the Arabs who were refugees outside the state and the property expropriated from the Arabs who remained in Israel became a major asset to the new state. According to Don Peretz, an American scholar, by 1954 "more than one-third of Israel's Jewish population lived on absentee property, and nearly a third of the new immigrants (250,000 people) settled in the urban areas abandoned by Arabs." The fleeing Arabs emptied thriving cities such as Jaffa, Acre (Akko), Lydda (Lod), and Ramla, plus "338 towns and villages and large parts of 94 other cities and towns, containing nearly a quarter of all the buildings in Israel."

To the Israeli Arabs, one of the more devastating aspects of the loss of their property was their knowledge that the loss was legally irreversible. The early Zionist settlers—particularly those of the Second Aliyah—adopted a rigid policy that land purchased or in any way acquired by a Jewish organization or individual could never again be sold, leased, or rented to a non-Jew. The policy went so far as to preclude the use of non-Jewish labor on the land. This policy was carried over into the new state. At independence the State of Israel succeeded to the "state lands" of the British Mandate Authority, which had "inherited" the lands held by the government of the Ottoman Empire. The Jewish National Fund was the operating and controlling agency of the Land Development Authority and ensured that land once held by Jews—either individually or by the "sovereign state of the Jewish people"—did not revert to non-Jews. This denied Israel's non-Jewish, mostly Arab, population access to about 95 percent of the land.

The Emergence of the IDF

In February 1950, the Israeli government had discreetly negotiated a draft treaty with King Abdullah of Transjordan, including a five-year nonaggression pact, open borders, and free access to the port of Haifa. In April Abdullah annexed the West Bank and East Jerusalem, thus creating the united Hashemite Kingdom of Jordan. Ben-Gurion acquiesced because he thought this would mean an end to independent claims on Israeli territory and material claims on confiscated Arab territory. Abdullah, however, was assassinated in July 1951. Moreover, Israel was boycotted by all its Arab neighbors, and from the end of 1951 the Suez Canal and the Strait of Tiran (at the southern end of the Gulf of Aqaba, where it opens into the Red Sea) were closed to Israeli shipping.

Surrounded by enemies and having to integrate thousands of immigrants into the new state, Ben-Gurion attempted to make the IDF the new unifying symbol of the fledgling state. He realized that the socialism of the Histadrut was ill suited to solving the problems facing the new state. Above all, Israel needed a unity of purpose, which in Ben-Gurion's thinking could only be provided by a strong army that would defend the country against its enemies and help assimilate its culturally diverse immigrants. Thus, Ben-Gurion added to the socialist ethos of the Histadrut and kibbutz movements an aggressive Israeli nationalism spearheaded by the IDF. To carry out this new orientation, he cultivated a "new guard" Mapai leadership headed by dynamic young General Moshe Dayan and technocrat Shimon Peres. Throughout the 1950s and early 1960s the Dayan-Peres supporters in Mapai and the "old guard" Labor establishment would compete for power (see Multiparty System, ch. 4).

In November 1953, Ben-Gurion tendered his resignation, and the less militaristic Moshe Sharett took over as prime minister. Under Sharett's weaker leadership, the conflict between the old-guard Mapai leadership and Ben-Gurion's new technocratic elite festered openly. This led to a major scandal in the Labor Party called the Lavon affair. Defense Minister Pinchas Lavon, an important figure in the old guard, had authorized intelligence chief Benjamin Gibly to launch Israeli spy rings in Cairo and Alexandria in an attempt to embarrass Egyptian president Gamal Abdul Nasser. The Egyptians, however, caught and later executed the spies, and the affair proved to be a major embarrassment to the Israeli government. The commission authorized to investigate the affair became embroiled in a test of strength between the young military establishment—including Dayan and Peres—and the Mapai old guard, whose support Lavon solicited.

In February 1955, Ben-Gurion returned to the Ministry of Defense, and with the malleable Sharett still as prime minister was able to promote his hard-line defense policy. This position resulted in a number of raids against the Egyptians in response to attacks on Israeli settlements originating from Egyptian-held territory. Subsequently, Ben-Gurion was restored to leadership of the Mapai government. At this time, his biggest concern was the rising power of Nasser. By October 1955, Nasser had signed an agreement to buy arms from the Soviet Union and Czechoslovakia, while President Dwight D. Eisenhower refused to supply Israel with weapons.

Old city gate of Jaffa,
outside Tel Aviv
Courtesy Les Vogel

Ben-Gurion sought to inflict a mortal blow on the Egyptian regime. Because Nasser threatened Western interests in the Suez Canal, Ben-Gurion entered into secret talks with Britain and France about the possibility of Israel striking at the Sinai Peninsula, while Britain and France moved in on the Suez Canal, ostensibly to help protect Western shipping from combat. In late October, the IDF routed the Egyptian army at Gaza and after a week pushed to the Gidi and Mitla passes. On November 5, 1956, the French and British took over the Suez Canal area. After intense pressure from the Eisenhower administration, which was worried about the threat of Soviet military involvement, the European powers acceded to a cease-fire.

In March 1957, Israeli troops were forced to withdraw. The war served to spur Ben-Gurion's drive toward greater militarization. Although Israel was forced to withdraw from Sinai, Ben-Gurion deemed the war a success: the raids from Gaza ceased, UN peace-keeping forces separated Egypt and Israel, greater cooperation with France led to more arms sales to Israel and the building of a nuclear reactor, and, most important, the army's near-perfect performance vindicated his view on the centrality of the IDF.

1967 and Afterward

By the spring of 1967, Nasser's waning prestige, escalating Syrian-Israeli tensions, and the emergence of Levi Eshkol as prime minister set the stage for the third Arab-Israeli war. Throughout the 1950s and early 1960s, Nasser was the fulcrum of Arab politics. Nasser's success, however, was shortlived; his union with Syria fell apart, a revolutionary government in Iraq proved to be a competitor for power, and Egypt became embroiled in a debilitating civil war in Yemen. After 1964, when Israel began diverting waters (of the Jordan River) originating in the Golan Heights for its new National Water Carrier, Syria built its own diverting facility, which the IDF frequently attacked. Finally, in 1963, Ben-Gurion stepped down and the more cautious Levi Eshkol became prime minister, giving the impression that Israel would be less willing to engage the Arab world in hostilities.

On April 6, 1967, Israeli jet fighters shot down six Syrian planes over the Golan Heights, which led to a further escalation of Israeli-Syrian tensions. The Soviet Union, wanting to involve Egypt as a deterrent to an Israeli initiative against Syria, misinformed Nasser on May 13 that the Israelis were planning to attack Syria on May 17 and that they had already concentrated eleven to thirteen brigades on the Syrian border for this purpose. In response Nasser put his armed forces in a state of maximum alert, sent combat troops into Sinai, notified UN Secretary General U Thant of his decision "to terminate the existence of the United Nations Emergency Force (UNEF) on United Arab Republic (UAR) soil and in the Gaza Strip," and announced the closure of the Strait of Tiran.

The Eshkol government, to avoid the international pressure that forced Israel to retreat in 1956, sent Foreign Minister Abba Eban to Europe and the United States to convince Western leaders to pressure Nasser into reversing his course. In Israel, Eshkol's diplomatic waiting game and Nasser's threatening rhetoric created a somber mood. To reassure the public, Moshe Dayan, the hero of the 1956 Sinai Campaign, was appointed minister of defense and a National Unity Government was formed, which for the first time included Begin's Herut Party, the dominant element in Gahal.

The actual fighting was over almost before it began; the Israeli Air Corps on June 5 destroyed nearly the entire Egyptian Air Force on the ground. King Hussein of Jordan, misinformed by Nasser about Egyptian losses, authorized Jordanian artillery to fire on Jerusalem. Subsequently, both the Jordanians in the east and the Syrians in the north were quickly defeated.

The June 1967 War was a watershed event in the history of Israel and the Middle East. After only six days of fighting, Israel had radically altered the political map of the region. By June 13, Israeli forces had captured the Golan Heights from Syria, Sinai and the Gaza Strip from Egypt, and all of Jerusalem and the West Bank from Jordan. The new territories more than doubled the size of pre-1967 Israel, placing under Israel's control more than 1 million Palestinian Arabs. In Israel, the ease of the victory, the expansion of the state's territory, and the reuniting of Jerusalem, the holiest place in Judaism, permanently altered political discourse. In the Arab camp, the war significantly weakened Nasserism, and led to the emergence of the Palestine Liberation Organization (PLO) as the leading representative of the Palestinian people and effective player in Arab politics.

The heroic performance of the IDF and especially the capture of Jerusalem unleashed a wave of religious nationalism throughout Israel. The war was widely viewed in Israel as a vindication of political Zionism; the defenseless Jew of the *shtetl* (the typical Jewish town or village of the Pale of Settlement), oppressed by the tsar and slaughtered by the Nazis, had become the courageous soldier of the IDF, who in the face of Arab hostility and superpower apathy had won a miraculous victory. After 2,000 years of exile, the Jews now possessed all of historic Palestine, including a united Jerusalem. The secular messianism that had been Zionism's creed since its formation in the late 1800s was now supplanted by a religious-territorial messianism whose major objective was securing the unity of Eretz Yisrael. In the process, the ethos of Labor Zionism, which had been on the decline throughout the 1960s, was overshadowed.

In the midst of the nationalist euphoria that followed the war, talk of exchanging newly captured territories for peace had little public appeal. The Eshkol government followed a two-track policy with respect to the territories, which would be continued under future Labor governments: on the one hand, it stated a willingness to negotiate, while on the other, it laid plans to create Jewish settlements in the disputed territories. Thus, immediately following the war, Eshkol issued a statement that he was willing to negotiate "everything" for a full peace, which would include free passage through the Suez Canal and the Strait of Tiran and a solution to the refugee problem in the context of regional cooperation. This was followed in November 1967 by his acceptance of UN Security Council Resolution 242, which called for "withdrawal of Israeli armed forces from territories occupied in the recent conflict" in exchange for Arab acceptance of Israel. Concurrently, on September 24, Eshkol's government announced plans for the resettlement of the Old City of Jerusalem, of the Etzion Bloc—kibbutzim on the Bethlehem-Hebron road wiped out by Palestinians in the war of 1948—and for kibbutzim in the northern sector of the Golan Heights. Plans were also unveiled for new neighborhoods around

Jerusalem, near the old buildings of Hebrew University, and near the Hadassah Hospital on Mount Scopus.

The Arab states, however, rejected outright any negotiations with the Jewish state. At Khartoum, Sudan, in the summer of 1967, the Arab states unanimously adopted their famous "three nos": no peace with Israel, no recognition of Israel, no negotiation with Israel concerning any Palestinian territory. The stridency of the Khartoum resolution, however, masked important changes that the June 1967 War caused in inter-Arab politics. At Khartoum, Nasser pledged to stop destabilizing the region and launching acerbic propaganda attacks against the Persian Gulf monarchies in exchange for badly needed economic assistance. This meant that Egypt, along with the other Arab states, would focus on consolidating power at home and on pressing economic problems rather than on revolutionary unity schemes. After 1967 Arab regimes increasingly viewed Israel and the Palestinian problem not as the key to revolutionary change of the Arab state system, but in terms of how they affected domestic political stability. The Palestinians, who since the late 1940s had looked to the Arab countries to defeat Israel and regain their homeland, were radicalized by the 1967 defeat. The PLO—an umbrella organization of Palestinian resistance groups led by Yasir Arafat's Al Fatah—moved to the forefront of Arab resistance against Israel. Recruits and money poured in, and throughout 1968 Palestinian guerrillas launched a number of border raids on Israel that added to the organization's popularity. The fedayeen (Arab guerrillas) attacks brought large-scale Israeli retaliation, which the Arab states were not capable of counteracting. The tension between Arab states' interests and the more revolutionary aspirations of the Palestinian resistance foreshadowed a major inter-Arab political conflict.

The War of Attrition

The tarnished legitimacy of the Arab states following the June 1967 War was especially poignant in Egypt. Israeli troops were situated on the east bank of the Suez Canal, the canal was closed to shipping, and Israel was occupying a large piece of Egyptian territory. Nasser responded by maintaining a constant state of military activity along the canal—the so-called War of Attrition—between February 1969 and August 1970. Given the wide disparity in the populations of Israel and Egypt, Israel could not long tolerate trading casualties with the Egyptians. The Israeli government, now led by Golda Meir, pursued a policy of "asymmetrical response"—retaliation on a scale far exceeding any individual attack.

As the tension along the Egyptian border continued to heat, United States secretary of state William Rogers proposed a new peace plan. In effect, the Rogers Plan was an interpretation of UN Security Council Resolution 242; it called for the international frontier between Egypt and Israel to be the secure and recognized border between the two countries. There would be "a formal state of peace between the two, negotiations on Gaza and Sharm ash Shaykh, and demilitarized zones." In November Israel rejected the offer, and in January 1970 Israeli fighter planes made their first deep penetration into Egypt.

Following the Israeli attack, Nasser went to Moscow requesting advanced surface-to-air missiles (SAMs) and other military equipment. After some wavering, the Kremlin committed itself to modernizing and retraining the Egyptian military. Egypt's new Soviet-made arsenal threatened to alter the regional military balance with Israel. The tension in Israeli-Soviet relations escalated in July 1970, when Israeli fighter planes shot down four Egyptian planes flown by Soviet pilots about thirty kilometers west of the canal. Fearing Soviet retaliation, and uncertain of American support, Israel in August accepted a cease-fire and the application of Resolution 242.

Following the June 1967 War, the PLO established in Jordan its major base of operations for the war against Israel. Throughout the late 1960s, a cycle of Palestinian guerrilla attacks followed by Israeli retaliatory raids against Jordan caused much damage to Jordan. In September 1970, after militant factions of the PLO (who previously had stated that "the road to Tel Aviv lies through Amman") hijacked four foreign planes and forced them to land in Jordan, King Hussein decided it was time to act. Throughout September the Jordanian military launched an attack to push the PLO out of Jordan. Jordan's attack on the PLO led to an escalation of Syrian-Israeli tensions. It was widely believed in Washington that deployment of Israeli troops along the Jordan River had deterred a large-scale Syrian invasion of Jordan. As a result, President Richard M. Nixon increasingly viewed Israel as an important strategic asset, and the Rogers Plan was allowed to die.

While negotiating a cease-fire to the conflict in Jordan, Nasser died of a heart attack. The new Egyptian president, Anwar as Sadat, quickly realized, just as Nasser had toward the end of his life, that Egypt's acute economic and social problems were more pressing than the conflict with Israel. Sadat believed that by making peace with Israel Egypt could reduce its huge defense burden and obtain desperately needed American financial assistance. He realized, however, that before some type of arrangement with Israel could be reached, Egypt would have to regain the territory lost to Israel in the June 1967 War. To achieve these ends, Sadat launched a diplomatic initiative as early as 1971, aimed at exchanging territory for peace. On February 4, 1971, he told the Egyptian parliament:

> that if Israel withdrew her forces in Sinai to the passes I would be willing to reopen the Suez Canal; to have my forces cross to the east bank . . . to make a solemn declaration of a cease-fire; to restore diplomatic relations with the United States and to sign a peace agreement with Israel through the efforts of Dr. Jarring, the representative of the Secretary General of the United Nations.

Sadat's peace initiative, similar to the Rogers Plan, was not warmly received in Israel. Prime Minister Golda Meir stated unequivocally that Israel would never return to the prewar borders. She also commissioned the establishment of a settlement on occupied Egyptian territory at Yamit, near the Gaza Strip. Her rejection of the Egyptian offer reflected the hawkish but also complacent politico-military strategy that had guided Israeli policy after the June 1967 War. Advised by Minister of Defense General Moshe Dayan and ambassador to Washington General Yitzhak Rabin, the Meir government held that the IDF's preponderance of power, the disarray of the Arab world, and the large buffer provided by Sinai, the West Bank, and the Golan Heights would deter the Arab states from launching an attack against Israel. Therefore, the Israeli government perceived no compelling reason to trade territory for peace. This view had wide Israeli public support as a result of a growing settler movement in the occupied territories, a spate of Arab terrorist attacks that hardened public opinion against compromise with the Arabs, and the widespread feeling that the Arab states were incapable of launching a successful attack on Israel. Israel's complacency concerning an Arab attack was bolstered in July 1972 by Sadat's surprise announcement that he was expelling most Soviet military advisers.

The October 1973 War

The Meir government's rejection of Sadat's peace overtures convinced the Egyptian president that to alter the status quo and gain needed legitimacy at home he must initiate a war with limited objectives. On Yom Kippur, the Jewish Day of Atonement, October 6, 1973, Syria and Egypt launched a surprise attack against Israel. In the south, waves of Egyptian infantrymen crossed the Suez Canal and overran the defense of the much touted Bar-Lev Line. In the north, Syrian forces outnumbering the Israeli defenders

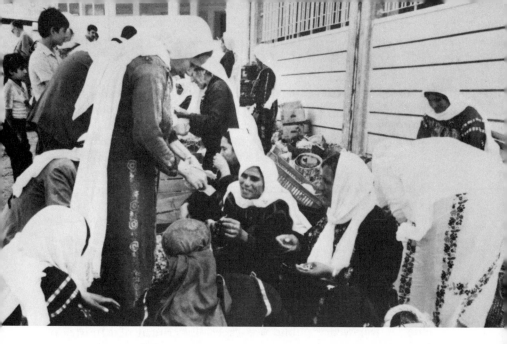

*Palestinian women in traditional dress selling produce
at an outdoor market in the occupied West Bank*
Courtesy Palestine Perspectives

(1,100 Syrian tanks against 157 Israeli tanks) reached the outer
perimeter of the Golan Heights overlooking the Hula Basin. In
the first few days of the war, Israeli counterattacks failed, Israel
suffered hundreds of casualties, and lost nearly 150 planes. Finally,
on October 10 the tide of the war turned; the Syrians were driven
out of all territories conquered by them at the beginning of the war
and on the following day Israeli forces advanced into Syria proper,
about twenty kilometers from the outskirts of Damascus. The Soviet
Union responded by making massive airlifts to Damascus and
Cairo, which were matched by equally large United States airlifts
to Israel. In the south, an Egyptian offensive into Sinai was repelled,
and Israeli forces led by General Ariel Sharon crossed the canal
to surround the Egyptian Third Army. At the urgent request of
the Soviet Union, United States Secretary of State Henry Kissinger
went to Moscow to negotiate a cease-fire arrangement. This arrangement found expression in UN Security Council Resolution 338, which called for a cease-fire to be in place within twelve
hours, for the implementation of Resolution 242, and for "negotiations between the parties concerned under appropriate auspices
aimed at establishing a just and durable peace in the Middle East."
Following Kissinger's return to Washington, the Soviets announced
that Israel had broken the terms of the cease-fire and was threatening

to destroy the besieged Egyptian Third Army. Soviet leader Leonid Brezhnev informed Nixon that if the siege were not lifted the Soviet Union would take unilateral steps. The United States pressured Israel, and the final cease-fire took effect on October 25.

The October 1973 War had a devastating effect on Israel. More than 6,000 troops had been killed or wounded in eighteen days of fighting. The loss of equipment and the decline of production and exports as a consequence of mobilization came to nearly US$7 billion, the equivalent of Israel's gross national product (GNP—see Glossary) for an entire year. Most important, the image of an invincible Israel that had prevailed since the June 1967 War was destroyed forever. Whereas the June 1967 War had given Israel in general and the declining Labor Party in particular a badly needed morale booster, the events of October 1973 shook the country's self-confidence and cast a shadow over the competence of the Labor elite. A war-weary public was especially critical of Minister of Defense Dayan, who nonetheless escaped criticism in the report of the Agranat Commission, a body established after the war to determine responsibility for Israel's military unpreparedness.

Israel's vulnerability during the war led to another important development: its increasing dependence on United States military, economic, and diplomatic aid. The war set off a spiraling regional arms race in which Israel was hard pressed to match the Arab states, which were enriched by skyrocketing world oil prices. The vastly improved Arab arsenals forced Israel to spend increasingly on defense, straining its already strapped economy. The emergence of Arab oil as a political weapon further isolated Israel in the world community. The Arab oil boycott that accompanied the war and the subsequent quadrupling of world oil prices dramatized the West's dependence on Arab oil production. Evidence of this dependence was reflected, for example, in the denial of permission during the fighting for United States transport planes carrying weapons to Israel to land anywhere in Europe except Portugal.

The dominant personality in the postwar settlement period was Kissinger. Kissinger believed that the combination of Israel's increased dependence on the United States and Sadat's desire to portray the war as an Egyptian victory and regain Sinai allowed for an American-brokered settlement. The key to this diplomatic strategy was that only Washington could induce a vulnerable Israel to exchange territories for peace in the south.

The first direct Israeli-Egyptian talks following the war were held at Kilometer 101 on the Cairo-Suez road. They dealt with stabilizing the cease-fire and supplying Egypt's surrounded Third Army. Following these talks, Kissinger began his highly publicized "shuttle

diplomacy,'' moving between Jerusalem and the Arab capitals trying to work out an agreement. In January 1974, Kissinger, along
with Sadat and Dayan, devised the First Sinai Disengagement
Agreement, which called for thinning out forces in the Suez Canal
zone and restoring the UN buffer zone. The published plan was
accompanied by private (but leaked) assurances from the United
States to Israel that Egypt would not interfere with Israeli freedom
of navigation in the Red Sea and that UN forces would not be withdrawn without the consent of both sides. Following the signing of
this agreement, Kissinger shuttled between Damascus and Jerusalem, finally attaining an agreement that called for Israel to withdraw from its forward positions in the Golan Heights, including
the return of the Syrian town of Al Qunaytirah. The evacuated
zone was to be demilitarized and monitored by a UN Disengagement Observer Force (UNDOF).

After the signing of the Israeli-Syrian Disengagement Agreement
in June 1974, the public mood in Israel shifted against concessions.
In part, Israel's hardened stance was a reaction to the 1974 Arab
summit in Rabat, Morocco. At that summit, both Syria and Egypt
supported a resolution recognizing the PLO as the sole representative of the Palestinian people. The Israeli public viewed the
PLO as a terrorist organization bent on destroying the Jewish
state. Throughout 1974 Palestinian terrorism increased; in the summer alone there were attacks in Qiryat Shemona, Maalot, and
Jerusalem.

Another important factor underlying Israel's firmer stance was
an internal political struggle in the newly elected government of
Yitzhak Rabin. Rabin had narrowly defeated his chief rival Shimon
Peres in bitterly fought internal Labor Party elections in late December 1973. Peres, who was appointed minister of defense, forced
Israel into a less flexible posture by blocking any concessions proposed by Rabin. In addition, the issuing of the Agranat Commission report and the return from the front of reservists mobilized
for the war further fueled public clamor for a stronger defense
posture.

In Washington, President Gerald R. Ford, facing a recalcitrant
Israel and under pressure from the pro-Israel lobby, decided to
sweeten the offer to Israel. The United States pledged to provide
Israel US$2 billion in financial aid, to drop the idea of an interim
withdrawal in the West Bank, and to accept that only cosmetic
changes could be expected in the Second Syrian-Israeli Disengagement Agreement. In addition, in a special secret memorandum
Israel received a pledge that the United States would not deal with
the PLO as long as the PLO failed to recognize Israel's right to

exist and failed to accept Security Council Resolution 242. In September 1975, Israel signed the Second Sinai Disengagement Agreement, which called for Israel to withdraw from the Sinai passes, leaving them as a demilitarized zone monitored by American technicians and the UNEF.

The Decline of the Labor Party

Even before the October 1973 War, the Labor Party was hampered by internal dissension, persistent allegations of corruption, ambiguities and contradictions in its political platform, and by the disaffection of Oriental Jews (see Oriental Jews, this ch.). Labor's failure to prepare the country for the war further alienated a large segment of the electorate.

Despite Labor's commitment to exchange occupied territories for peace, successive Labor governments beginning soon after the June 1967 War established settlements in the territories and refrained from dismantling illegal settlements, such as those established in 1968 at Qiryat Arba in Hebron by Rabbi Moshe Levinger and others set up by the extremist settler movement Gush Emunim. By 1976 more than thirty settlements had been established on the West Bank.

Another contradiction in Labor's political platform concerned Jerusalem. All Labor governments have proclaimed that Jerusalem will always remain the undivided capital of Israel. In effect, this stance precludes the peace for territories formula contained in Resolution 242 because neither Jordan nor the Palestinians would be likely to accept any agreement by which Jerusalem remained in Israeli hands.

The post-1973 Labor Party estrangement from the Israeli public intensified throughout 1976 as the party was hit with a barrage of corruption charges that struck at the highest echelons. Rabin's minister of housing, who was under investigation for alleged abuses during his time as director general of the Histadrut Housing Authority, committed suicide in January 1977. At the same time, the governor of the Bank of Israel, who had been nominated by Rabin, was sentenced to jail for taking bribes and evading taxes, and the director general of the Ministry of Housing was apprehended in various extortion schemes. Finally, and most egregious, Rabin himself was caught lying about money illegally kept in a bank account in the United States.

Israel's growing defense budget (about 35 to 40 percent of GNP), along with rising world oil prices, also created chaos in the Israeli economy. Inflation was running at 40 to 50 percent annually, wages were falling, and citizen accumulation of so-called black money (unreported income) was rampant. The worsening economic situation led to greater income disparities between the Ashkenazim, who dominated the higher echelons of government, the military, and business, and the majority Oriental population, which was primarily employed in low paying blue-collar jobs.

Oriental Jews

By the mid-1970s, economic grievances, corruption, and the perceived haughtiness of the Labor elite led to a major shift in the voting patterns of Oriental Jews (those of African or Asian origin). During the first twenty years of Israel's existence, Oriental Jews voted for the Labor Party mainly because the Histadrut, the Jewish Agency, and other state institutions on which they as new immigrants depended were dominated by Labor. But even during the early years of the state, Labor's ideological blend of secular-socialist Zionism conflicted sharply with the Oriental Jews' cultural heritage, which tended to be more religious and oriented toward a free market economy. As Oriental Jews became more integrated into Israeli society, especially after the June 1967 War, resentment of Labor's cultural, political, and economic hegemony increased. Most unacceptable to the Oriental Jews was the hypocrisy of Labor slogans that continued to espouse egalitarianism while Ashkenazim monopolized the political and economic reins of power.

Despite Labor's frequent references to closing the Ashkenazi-Oriental socioeconomic gap, the disparity of incomes between the two groups actually widened. Between 1968 and 1971, Minister of Finance Pinchas Sapir's program of encouraging foreign investment and subsidizing private investment led to an economic boom; GNP grew at 7 percent per year. Given the persistent dominance of Labor institutions in the economy, however, this economic growth was not evenly distributed. The kibbutzim, moshavim, and Histadrut enterprises, along with private defense and housing contractors, enriched themselves, while the majority of Oriental Jews, lacking connections with the ruling Labor elite, saw their position deteriorate. Furthermore, while Oriental Jews remained for the most part in the urban slums, the government provided new European immigrants with generous loans and new housing. This dissatisfaction led to the growth of the first Oriental protest movement—the Black Panthers—based in the Jerusalem slums in early 1971.

Oriental Jews, many of whom were forced to leave their homes in the Arab states, also supported tougher measures against Israeli Arabs and neighboring Arab states than the policies pursued by Labor. Their ill feelings were buttressed by the widely held perception that the establishment of an independent Palestinian entity would oblige Oriental Jews to accept the menial jobs performed by Arab laborers, as they had in the early years of the state.

The Begin Era

In the May 1977 elections, the Labor Party's dominance of Israeli politics ended. The Likud Bloc—an alliance of Begin's Herut Party, the Liberal Party, and other smaller parties formed in the aftermath of the October 1973 War—formed a ruling coalition government for the first time in Israel's history. Likud gained forty-three seats, Labor dropped to thirty-two seats, down by nineteen from the 1973 figure. Likud's supporters consisted of disaffected middle-class elements alienated by the series of scandals, many new immigrants from the Soviet Union, and large numbers of defecting Oriental Jews. Begin appealed to many because he was viewed as incorruptible and untarnished by scandal. He was a strong leader who did not equivocate about his plans for a strong Israel (which he believed included the occupied territories), or about his willingness to stand up to the Arabs or even the superpowers if Israel's needs demanded. Begin also attracted some veteran Labor Zionists for whom his focus on Jewish settlement and self-reliance was reminiscent of an earlier unadulterated Labor Zionism.

Begin's vision of Israel and its role in the region was deeply rooted in the Revisionist platform with which he had been associated since the days of Jabotinsky. He strongly advocated Israeli sovereignty over all of Eretz Yisrael, which in his view included Jerusalem and the West Bank, but not Sinai.

The Peace Process

The international climate at the time of Begin's rise to power in May 1977 leaned strongly toward some type of superpower-sanctioned settlement to the Arab-Israeli dispute. New United States president Jimmy Carter and Soviet leader Brezhnev both advocated a comprehensive Arab-Israeli settlement that would include autonomy for the Palestinians. On October 1, 1977, in preparation for a reconvened Geneva conference, the United States and the Soviet Union issued a joint statement committing themselves to a comprehensive settlement incorporating all parties concerned and all questions.

Nevertheless, the idea of a Geneva conference on the Middle East was actively opposed and eventually defeated by a constellation of Israeli, Egyptian, and powerful private American interests. Begin proclaimed that he would never accept the authority of an international forum to dictate how Israel should deal with its

Arrival of Egyptian President Anwar as Sadat
at Ben-Gurion Airport, Lod, near Tel Aviv, November 21, 1977
Courtesy Embassy of Israel, Washington

territory, especially because, aside from Washington, the Israelis would lack allies at such a meeting. Inside the United States, the Jewish lobby and anti-Soviet political groups vehemently opposed the Geneva conference idea. Sadat also opposed a Geneva conference, seeing it as a way for Syria, supported by the Soviet Union, to gain leverage in an Arab-Israeli settlement. Sadat realized that if an international conference were held, Egypt's recovery of Sinai, which was his primary objective in dealing with Israel, would be secondary to the Palestinian issue and the return of the Golan Heights to Syria.

To stave off an international conference and to save Egypt's rapidly collapsing economy, Sadat made the boldest of diplomatic moves: he offered to address the Knesset. Begin consented, and in November 1977 Sadat made his historic journey to Jerusalem, opening a new era in Egyptian-Israeli relations. Although Sadat expressed his commitment to the settlement of the Palestinian issue and to that issue's centrality in Arab-Israeli relations, his main interest remained Israel's return of Egyptian territory. Begin's acceptance of the Egyptian initiative was based on the premise that Sinai, but not the West Bank, was negotiable. He foresaw that exchanging Sinai for a peace treaty with Egypt would remove Egypt from the Arab-Israeli military balance and relieve pressure on Israel

71

to make territorial concessions on the West Bank. President Carter, who had been a major advocate of a Geneva conference, was forced by the momentum of Sadat's initiative to drop the international conference idea. Subsequently, he played a crucial role in facilitating an Egyptian-Israeli peace settlement.

Following nearly a year of stalled negotiations, Begin, Sadat, and Carter met at Camp David near Washington, D.C., for two weeks in September 1978. The crux of the problem at Camp David was that Begin, the old-time Revisionist who had opposed territorial concessions to the Arabs for so many years, was reluctant to dismantle existing Sinai settlements. Finally, on September 17 he consented, and the Camp David Accords were signed. On the following day, Begin obtained Knesset approval of the accords.

The Camp David Accords consisted of two agreements: one dealt with the future of the West Bank and the other with the return of Sinai. The sections on the West Bank were vague and open to various interpretations. They called for Egypt, Israel, Jordan, and "the representatives of the Palestinian people to negotiate about the future of the West Bank and Gaza." A five-year period of "transitional autonomy" was called for "to ensure a peaceful and orderly transfer of authority." The agreement also called for peace talks between Israel and its other Arab neighbors, namely Syria. The other part of the accords was more specific. It provided for "the full exercise of Egyptian sovereignty up to the internationally recognized border," as well as for the Israeli right of free passage through the Strait of Tiran and the Suez Canal. The agreements were accompanied by letters. A letter from Begin to Carter promised that the removal of settlers from Sinai would be put to Knesset vote. A letter from Sadat to Carter stated that if the settlers were not withdrawn from Sinai, there would be no peace treaty between Egypt and Israel. It was also understood that to make the agreement more palatable the United States would significantly increase aid to both countries.

Begin's limited view of Palestinian autonomy in the West Bank became apparent almost immediately after the agreement known as the Treaty of Peace Between Egypt and Israel was signed in March 1979. The following month his government approved two new settlements between Ram Allah and Nabulus. The military government established civilian regional councils for the Jewish settlements. Finally, and most provocative, autonomy plans were prepared in which Israel would keep exclusive control over the West Bank's water, communications, roads, public order, and immigration.

In effect, the acceleration of settlements, the growth of an increasingly militaristic Jewish settler movement, and Israel's stated desire to retain complete control over resources in the territories precluded the participation in the peace process of either moderate Palestinians, such as the newly formed National Guidance Committee composed of West Bank mayors (the PLO refused from the beginning to participate in the peace process) or King Hussein of Jordan. No Arab leader could accept Begin's truncated version of autonomy. Hussein, who had initially withheld judgment on the accords, joined hands with the Arab radicals in a meeting in Baghdad that denounced the Camp David Accords and the peace treaty and ostracized Egypt. Sadat protested Israeli actions in the occupied territories, but he was unwilling to change his course for fear that doing so would leave Sinai permanently in Israeli hands. President Carter objected to the new settlements but was unable to force the Begin government to change its settlement policy. Although ambassadors were exchanged; commercial, trade, and cultural ties were established; and Sinai was returned in May 1982, relations between Israel and Egypt remained chilly.

The Occupied Territories

During the June 1967 War, about 1.1 million Palestinian Arabs living in the West Bank, Gaza Strip, and East Jerusalem came under Israeli rule. Immediately after the war, East Jerusalem was occupied and reunited with the rest of Israel's capital. Its Arab inhabitants—about 67,000 after the war—became citizens of Israel with the same rights as other Israeli Arabs. The West Bank, ruled by Jordan since 1948, was economically underdeveloped but possessed a relatively efficient administrative infrastructure. Its 750,000 people consisted of a settled population and refugees from Israel who had fled during the 1948 War. Both the refugees and the settled population were Jordanian citizens, free to work in Jordan. Most of the leading urban families and virtually all the rural clans had cooperated with Hussein. The Gaza Strip, on the other hand, was seething with discontent when Israeli forces arrived in 1967. Its 1967 population of 350,000—the highest population density in the world at the time—had been under Egyptian rule, but the inhabitants were not accepted as Egyptian citizens or allowed to travel to Egypt proper. As a result they were unable to find work outside the camps and were almost completely dependent on the UN Relief and Works Agency (UNRWA) for Palestine Refugees in the Near East. In the Gaza Strip, Israel implemented harsh security measures to quell widespread unrest and root out the growing resistance movement.

Labor's settlement policy in the occupied territories was based on a plan formulated during the summer of 1965 by Yigal Allon, deputy prime minister of the Eshkol government. The plan, primarily dictated by security concerns, called for rural and urban settlements to be erected in a sparsely Arab-populated strip twelve to fifteen kilometers wide along the western bank of the Jordan River and the western shores of the Dead Sea. Labor governments sought to interfere as little as possible in the day-to-day lives of the Arab inhabitants. Political and social arrangements were, as much as possible, kept under Jordanian or pro-Jordanian control, the currency remained the Jordanian dinar, the application of Jordanian law continued, and a revised Jordanian curriculum was used in the schools.

Another aspect of Labor's occupation policies was the integration of the territories into the Israeli economy. By the mid-1970s, Arabs from Israel and the territories provided nearly one-quarter of Israel's factory labor and half the workers in construction and service industries. Moreover, the territories became an important market for Israeli domestic production; by 1975 about 16 percent of all Israeli exports were sold in the territories.

The final element of Labor's occupation policies was economic and social modernization. This included the mechanization of agriculture, the spread of television, and vast improvements in education and health care. This led to a marked increase in GNP, which grew by 14.5 percent annually between 1968 and 1973 in the West Bank and 19.4 percent annually in Gaza. As a result, the traditional elites, who had cooperated with Hussein during the years of Jordanian rule, were challenged by a younger, better educated, and more radical elite that was growing increasingly impatient with the Israeli occupation and the older generation's complacency. In the spring of 1976, Minister of Defense Shimon Peres held West Bank municipal elections, hoping to bolster the declining power of the old guard Palestinian leadership. Peres wrongly calculated that the PLO would boycott the elections. Instead, pro-PLO candidates won in every major town except Bethlehem.

Israel's settlement policy in the occupied territories changed in 1977 with the coming to power of Begin. Whereas Labor's policies had been guided primarily by security concerns, Begin espoused a deep ideological attachment to the territories. He viewed the Jewish right of settlement in the occupied territories as fulfilling biblical prophecy and therefore not a matter for either the Arabs or the international community to accept or reject. Begin's messianic designs on the territories were supported by the rapid growth of religio-nationalist groups, such as Gush Emunim, which established settlements in heavily populated Arab areas.

The increase in Jewish settlements and the radicalization of the settlers created an explosive situation. When in May 1980 six students of a Hebron yeshiva, a Jewish religious school, were killed by Arab gunfire, a chain of violence was set off that included a government crackdown on Hebron and the expulsion of three leaders of the Hebron Arab community. West Bank Jewish settlers increasingly took the law into their own hands; they were widely believed to be responsible for car-bomb attacks on the mayors of Ram Allah and Nabulus.

Begin's policies toward the occupied territories became increasingly annexationist following the Likud victory in the 1981 parliamentary elections. He viewed the Likud's victory, which surprised many observers, as a mandate to pursue a more aggressive policy in the territories. After the election, he appointed the hawkish Ariel Sharon as minister of defense, replacing the more moderate Ezer Weizman, who had resigned in protest against Begin's settlement policy. In November 1981, Sharon installed a civilian administration in the West Bank headed by Menachem Milson. Milson immediately set out to stifle rapidly growing Palestinian nationalist sentiments; he deposed pro-PLO mayors, dissolved the mayors' National Guidance Committee, and shut two Arab newspapers and Bir Zeit University.

While Milson was working to quell Palestinian nationalism in the territories, the Begin regime accelerated the pace of settlements by providing low-interest mortgages and other economic benefits to prospective settlers. This action induced a number of secular Jews, who were not part of Gush Emunim, to settle in the territories, further consolidating Israel's hold on the area. Moreover, Israel established large military bases and extensive road, electricity, and water networks in the occupied territories.

In November 1981, Milson established village leagues in the West Bank consisting of pro-Jordanian Palestinians to counter the PLO's growing strength there. The leadership of the village leagues had a limited base of support, however, especially because the growth of Jewish settlements had adversely affected Arab villagers. The failure of the Village League Plan, the escalating violence in the occupied territories, in addition to increased PLO attacks against northern Israeli settlements, and Syria's unwillingness to respond when the Knesset extended Israeli law to the occupied Golan Heights in December 1981 convinced Begin and Sharon of the need to intervene militarily in southern Lebanon.

Israeli Action in Lebanon, 1978–82

The precarious sectarian balance prevailing in Lebanon has presented Israeli policy makers with opportunities and risks. Lebanon's Christian Maronites, who under French tutelage occupied the most important political and economic posts in the country, were, like Israeli Jews, a minority among the region's Muslim majority. As early as 1954, Ben-Gurion had proposed that Israel support the establishment in part of Lebanon of a Maronite-dominated Christian ministate that would ally itself with Israel. During the Lebanese Civil War (1975–76), then Prime Minister Rabin reportedly invested US$150 million in equipping and training the Maronite Phalange Party's militia.

The instability of Lebanon's sectarian balance, however, enabled hostile states or groups to use Lebanon as a staging ground for attacks against Israel. The PLO, following its expulsion from Jordan in September 1970, set up its major base of operations in southern Lebanon from which it attacked northern Israel. The number and size of PLO operations in the south accelerated throughout the late 1970s as central authority deteriorated and Lebanon became a battleground of warring militias. In March 1978, following a fedayeen attack, originating in Lebanon, on the Tel Aviv-Haifa road that killed thirty-seven people, Israel launched Operation Litani, a massive military offensive that resulted in Israeli occupation of southern Lebanon up to the Litani River. By June Prime Minister Begin, under intense American pressure, withdrew Israeli forces, which were replaced by a UN Interim Force in Lebanon (UNIFIL). The withdrawal of Israeli troops without having removed the PLO from its bases in southern Lebanon became a major embarrassment to the Begin government.

By the spring of 1981, Bashir Jumayyil (also cited as Gemayel) emerged as the Maronite strong man and major Israeli ally in Lebanon. Having ruthlessly eliminated his Maronite rivals, he was attempting to extend his authority to other Lebanese Christian sects. In late 1980 and early 1981, he extended the protection of his Maronite militia to the Greek Orthodox inhabitants of Zahlah, in eastern Lebanon. Syrian president Hafiz al Assad considered Zahlah, which was located near the Beirut-Damascus road, a stronghold that was strategically important to Syria. In April 1981, Syrian forces bombed and besieged Zahlah, ousting the Phalangists, the Maronite group loyal to Jumayyil, from the city. In response to the defeat of its major Lebanese ally, Israeli aircraft destroyed two Syrian helicopters over Lebanon, prompting Assad to move Soviet-made SAMs into Lebanon. Israel threatened to destroy the missiles but was dissuaded from doing so by the administration of President Ronald Reagan. In the end, the Zahlah crisis, like the Litani Operation, badly tarnished the image of the Begin government, which had come to power in 1977 espousing a hard-line security policy.

In June 1981, Israel held Knesset elections that focused on the Likud's failure to stop the PLO buildup in southern Lebanon or to remove Syrian missile batteries from the Biqa (Bekaa) Valley in eastern Lebanon. To remove a potential nuclear threat and also to bolster its public image, the IDF launched a successful attack on the French-built Iraqi Osiraq (acronym for Osiris-Iraq) nuclear reactor three weeks before the elections. Begin interpreted widespread public approval of the attack as a mandate for a more aggressive policy in Lebanon. The Likud also rallied a large number of undecided voters by reducing import duties on luxury goods, enabling Israeli consumers to go on an unprecedented buying spree that would later result in spiraling inflation. Although Labor regained an additional fifteen seats over its poor showing in 1977 when it won only thirty-two seats, it was unable to prevail over Likud.

Begin's perception that the Israeli public supported a more active defense posture influenced the composition of his 1981 postelection cabinet. His new minister of defense, Ariel Sharon, was unquestionably an Israeli war hero of longstanding; he had played an important role in the 1956, 1967, and 1973 wars and was widely respected as a brilliant military tactician. Sharon, however, was also feared as a military man with political ambitions, one who was ignorant of political protocol and who was known to make precipitous moves. Aligned with Sharon was chief of staff General Rafael Eitan who also advocated an aggressive Israeli defense posture. Because Begin was not a military man, Israel's defense policy was increasingly decided by the minister of defense and the chief of staff. The combination of wide discretionary powers granted Sharon and Eitan over Israeli military strategy, the PLO's menacing growth in southern Lebanon, and the existence of Syrian SAMs in the Biqa Valley pointed to imminent Syrian-PLO-Israeli hostilities.

In July 1981, Israel responded to PLO rocket attacks on northern Israeli settlements by bombing PLO encampments in southern Lebanon. United States envoy Philip Habib eventually negotiated a shaky cease-fire that was monitored by UNIFIL.

Another factor that influenced Israel's decision to take action in Lebanon was the disarray of the Arab world throughout the early 1980s. The unanimity shown by the Arab states in Baghdad in condemning Sadat's separate peace with Israel soon dissipated. The 1979 Iranian Islamic Revolution, the outbreak of the Iran-Iraq War in September 1980, and the December 1980 Soviet invasion of Afghanistan badly divided the Arab world. The hard-line countries, Syria and Libya, supported Iran, and the moderate countries, Jordan, Saudi Arabia, and the Gulf states, supported Iraq. Moreover, Syrian president Assad's regime, dominated by the minority Alawi Muslim sect, was confronted with growing domestic opposition from the Muslim Brotherhood, which Assad violently quelled in February 1982 by besieging the city of Hamah. Finally, early United States opposition to an invasion of Lebanon appeared to have weakened, following Israel's final withdrawal from Sinai in May 1982.

Israel's incursion into Lebanon, called Operation Peace for Galilee, was launched in early June 1982. After an attack on Israel's ambassador in London carried out by the Abu Nidal group but blamed on the PLO, Israeli troops marched into southern Lebanon. On the afternoon of June 4 the Israeli air force bombed a sports stadium in Beirut, said to be used for ammunition storage by the PLO. The PLO responded by shelling Israeli towns in Galilee. On June 5, the government of Israel formally accused the PLO of breaking the cease-fire. At 11 A.M. on June 6, Israeli ground forces crossed the border into Lebanon. The stated goals of the operation were to free northern Israel from PLO rocket attacks by creating a forty-kilometer-wide security zone in southern Lebanon and by signing a peace treaty with Lebanon (see 1982 Invasion of Lebanon, ch. 5).

The June 1982 invasion of Lebanon was the first war fought by the IDF without a domestic consensus. Unlike the 1948, 1967, and 1973 wars, the Israeli public did not view Operation Peace for Galilee as essential to the survival of the Jewish state. By the early 1980s—less than forty years after its establishment—Israel had attained a military prowess unmatched in the region. The architects of the 1982 invasion, Ariel Sharon and Rafael Eitan, sought to use Israel's military strength to create a more favorable regional political setting. This strategy included weakening the PLO and supporting the rise to power in Lebanon of Israel's Christian allies. The attempt to impose a military solution to the intractable Palestinian problem and to force political change in Lebanon failed. The PLO, although defeated militarily, remained an important political force, and Bashir Jumayyil, Israel's major ally in Lebanon, was killed shortly after becoming president. Inside Israel, a mounting death toll caused sharp criticism by a war-weary public of the war and of the Likud government.

*   *   *

The literature on the cultural, political, and religious history of Israel is immense. The works noted here and those listed in the bibliography include easily available English-language materials that are valuable futher reading not only for the serious student but also for the interested layperson.

For a comprehensive and very detailed view of Jewish history see the eighteen-volume work by Salo W. Baron and *A History of the Jewish People,* edited by H.H. Ben Sasson. Another valuable source covering all aspects of Jewish history is the *Encyclopaedia Judaica;* a condensed history of the Jews is contained in the sixteen volumes of the Israel Pocket Library. Paul Johnson's *A History of the Jews* provides a more recent overview.

A valuable summary of the origins of Zionism is set forth in Arthur Hertzberg's introduction to *The Zionist Idea: A Historical Analysis and Reader.* David Vital's books, *The Origins of Zionism* and *Zionism: The Formative Years,* offer scholarly accounts of the history of Zionism. More recent works on Zionism include Shlomo Avineri's *The Making of Modern Zionism* and Bernard Avishai's *The Tragedy of Zionism.*

The most comprehensive history of the modern State of Israel is Howard Morley Sachar's two-volume *A History of Israel.* Two other reliable general histories of Israel are Noah Lucas's *The Modern History of Israel* and *The Siege* by Connor Cruise O'Brien. A solid account of Israel's wars is provided by Chaim Herzog's *The Arab-Israeli Wars.*

Five classics covering the pre-state era are Neville Mandel's *The Arabs and Zionism Before World War I,* J.C. Hurewitz's *The Struggle for Palestine,* Christopher Sykes's *Crossroads to Israel,* George Antonius's *The Arab Awakening,* and Michael J. Cohen's *Palestine: Retreat from the Mandate: The Making of British Policy, 1936–1945.* New Revisionist accounts of the crucial years 1948–49 are contained in Tom Segev's *1949: The First Israelis,* Simha Flapan's *The Birth of Israel: Myths and Realities,* and Benny Morris's *The Birth of the Palestinian Refugee Problem.*

The most authoritative source on Israel's settlement policy in the occupied territories is Meron Benvenisti's *The West Bank and Gaza Data Project.* Two seminal works on Arabs in Israel are Sammy Smooha's *Israel: Pluralism and Conflict* and Sabri Jiryis's *The Arabs in Israel.* The best accounts of Israel's incursion into Lebanon are Itamar Rabinovich's *The War for Lebanon, 1970–1983* and Zeev Schiff and Ehud Yaari's *Israel's War in Lebanon.* (For further information and complete citations, see Bibliography.)

Chapter 2. The Society and Its Environment

Moroccan Jewish immigrant and Sephardic rabbi

THE SOCIETY OF MODERN ISRAEL has diverse sources, but the majority of these sources stem ultimately from Judaism and the modern political movement called Zionism. Crystallizing in the late nineteenth century as a response to both the repression of Jews in Eastern Europe and the non-Jewish European nationalist movements of the time, Zionism called for the reversal of the Jewish dispersion (Diaspora) and the "ingathering of the exiles" to their biblical homeland. Although only small numbers of Jews had resided in Palestine since the destruction of the Second Temple by the Romans in A.D. 70, the "new Yishuv" (as opposed to the "old Yishuv" consisting of traditional Orthodox Jewish residents), or prestate Jewish community in Palestine, dates from 1882 and the arrival from Russia of a group called Hibbat Tziyyon (Lovers of Zion), intent on settling the land as part of its fulfillment of the Zionist ideal.

As a nationalist movement, Zionism largely succeeded: much of the Jewish Diaspora was dissolved, and the people were integrated into the population of the State of Israel—a self-consciously modern Jewish state. Along with this political achievement, a cultural achievement of equal, if not greater, importance took place. Hebrew, the ancient biblical language, was revived and became the modern spoken and written vernacular. The revival of Hebrew linked the new Jewish state to its Middle Eastern past and helped to unify the people of the new state by providing them with a common tongue that transcended the diversity of languages the immigrants brought with them.

Despite these political and cultural achievements—achievements that Israeli sociologist S.N. Eisenstadt sees as comprising "the Jewish re-entry into history"—modern Israeli society is still beset by problems, some of them profound. Among these are problems found in all industrial and economically differentiated social systems, including stratification by socioeconomic class, differential prestige attached to various occupations or professions, barriers to social mobility, and different qualities of life in urban centers, towns, and rural localities. For example, there are significant differences between the quality of life in the so-called development towns and the rural localities known as kibbutzim (sing., kibbutz—see Glossary) and moshavim (sing., moshav), respectively collective and cooperative settlements that are strongly socialist and Zionist in history and character.

Other social problems that Israel faces are unique to its own society and culture. The role that traditional Judaism should play in the modern state is a major source of controversy. The tension between religious and secular influences pervades all aspects of society. For example, religious practices influence the education system, the way ethnic groups are dealt with, how political debate is conducted, and there is no civil marriage in Israel.

The division between the Ashkenazim (Jews of European or American origin) and Oriental Jews (Jews of African or Asian origin) is another serious problem. This divisiveness results from the extreme cultural diversity in the migratory streams that brought Jewish immigrants to Israel between the late nineteenth century and the late 1980s. Already-settled members of the receiving society have had difficulty absorbing immigrants whose cultures differ so greatly from their own and from each other. Adding further to cultural disharmony is the problem of the place of non-Jews in the Jewish state. In Israel non-Jews are primarily Arabs (who are mostly Muslims, but also Christians and Druzes); a small number are non-Arab Muslims (such as the Circassians) or Christians (such as the Armenian residents of Jerusalem). Jewish Israelis also distinguish between Arabs who reside within the pre-June 1967 War boundaries of Israel and Arabs who live in the West Bank, the Golan Heights, and the Gaza Strip—the latter group is perceived as having no loyalty to the state.

The rift between Arabs and Jews in Israel is, of course, related to Israel's position in the contemporary Middle East. By Israeli count, the 1982 invasion of Lebanon was the fifth major Arab-Israeli war since 1948. This does not count smaller military actions or larger, more celebrated military actions, such as the Entebbe raid of July 1976. American political scientist Bernard Reich has written that "Israel is perhaps unique among states in having hostile neighbors on all of its borders, with the exception, since 1979, of Egypt." He adds that this fact has dominated all aspects of Israeli life since 1948, when the state was established and was invaded by Arab armies. It might be noted that security concerns were a striking feature of life (especially after 1929 and Arab violence against Jews) in the Yishuv as well. To the tension caused by cleavages between Oriental and Ashkenazi Jews, between the religious and the secularists, and between Jews and non-Jews must be added the profound social and psychological stress of living in a society at war with, and feeling itself to be under siege by, its neighbors. Many Israelis would also cite the special stress of having to serve as soldiers in areas regarded by Arab inhabitants as "occupied territories," a situation characterized, especially since December 1987, by increasing civil disobedience and violence.

Geography

Israel is located at the eastern end of the Mediterranean Sea. It is bounded on the north by Lebanon, on the northeast by Syria, on the east and southeast by Jordan, on the southwest by Egypt, and on the west by the Mediterranean Sea (see fig. 1). Before June 1967, the area composing Israel (resulting from the armistice lines of 1949 and 1950) was about 20,700 square kilometers, which included 445 square kilometers of inland water. Thus Israel was roughly the size of the state of New Jersey, stretching 424 kilometers from north to south. Its width ranged from 114 kilometers to, at its narrowest point, 10 kilometers. The area added to Israel after the June 1967 War, consisting of occupied territories (the West Bank—see Glossary—and the Gaza Strip) and annexed territories (East Jerusalem and the Golan Heights) totaled an additional 7,477 square kilometers. The areas comprised the West Bank, 5,879 kilometers; the Gaza Strip, 378; East Jerusalem, 70; and the Golan Heights, 1,150.

Topography

The country is divided into four regions: the coastal plain, the central hills, the Jordan Rift Valley, and the Negev Desert (see fig. 4). The Mediterranean coastal plain stretches from the Lebanese border in the north to Gaza in the south, interrupted only by Cape Carmel at Haifa Bay. It is about forty kilometers wide at Gaza and narrows toward the north to about five kilometers at the Lebanese border. The region is fertile and humid (historically malarial) and is known for its citrus and viniculture. The plain is traversed by several short streams, of which only two, the Yarqon and Qishon, have permanent water flows.

East of the coastal plain lies the central highland region. In the north of this region lie the mountains and hills of Upper Galilee and Lower Galilee; farther to the south are the Samarian Hills with numerous small, fertile valleys; and south of Jerusalem are the mainly barren hills of Judea. The central highlands average 610 meters in height and reach their highest elevation at Mount Meron, at 1,208 meters, in Galilee near Zefat (Safad). Several valleys cut across the highlands roughly from east to west; the largest is the Yizreel or Jezreel Valley (also known as the Plain of Esdraelon), which stretches forty-eight kilometers from Haifa southeast to the valley of the Jordan River, and is nineteen kilometers across at its widest point.

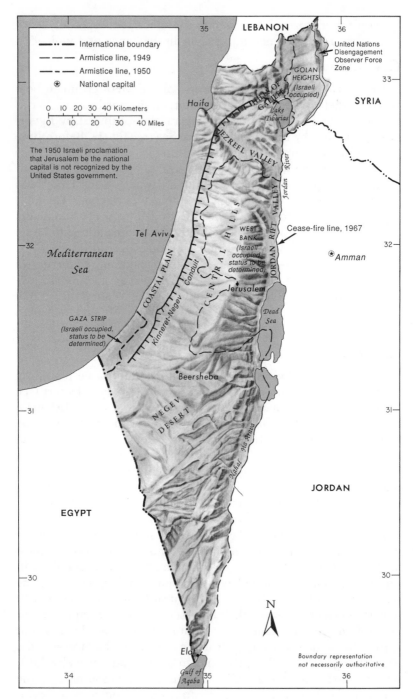

International boundary
Armistice line, 1949
Armistice line, 1950
⊛ National capital

| 0 | 10 | 20 | 30 | 40 Kilometers |
| 0 | 10 | 20 | 30 | 40 Miles |

The 1950 Israeli proclamation that Jerusalem be the national capital is not recognized by the United States government.

LEBANON

United Nations Disengagement Observer Force Zone

GOLAN HEIGHTS *(Israeli occupied)*

SYRIA

Haifa

HILLS OF GALILEE

Lake Tiberias

JEZREEL VALLEY

Jordan River

Tel Aviv

CENTRAL HILLS

WEST BANK *(Israeli occupied, status to be determined)*

JORDAN RIFT VALLEY

Cease-fire line, 1967

⊛ Amman

Mediterranean Sea

COASTAL PLAIN

Kinneret-Negev Conduit

Jerusalem

Dead Sea

GAZA STRIP *(Israeli occupied, status to be determined)*

Beersheba

NEGEV DESERT

Nahal Ha-Arava

JORDAN

EGYPT

N

Elat

Gulf of Aqaba

Boundary representation not necessarily authoritative

Figure 4. Topography and Drainage

East of the central highlands lies the Jordan Rift Valley, which is a small part of the 6,500-kilometer-long Syrian-East African Rift. In Israel the Rift Valley is dominated by the Jordan River, Lake Tiberias (known also as the Sea of Galilee and to Israelis as Lake Kinneret), and the Dead Sea. The Jordan, Israel's largest river (322 kilometers long), originates in the Dan, Baniyas, and Hasbani rivers near Mount Hermon in the Anti-Lebanon Mountains and flows south through the drained Hula Basin into the freshwater Lake Tiberias. Lake Tiberias is 165 square kilometers in size and, depending on the season and rainfall, is at about 213 meters below sea level. With a capacity estimated at 3 billion cubic meters, it serves as the principal reservoir of the National Water Carrier (also known as the Kinneret-Negev Conduit). The Jordan River continues its course from the southern end of Lake Tiberias (forming the boundary between the West Bank and Jordan) to its terminus in the highly saline Dead Sea. The Dead Sea is 1,020 square kilometers in size and, at 399 meters below sea level, is the lowest point in the world. South of the Dead Sea, the Rift Valley continues in the Nahal HaArava (Wadi al Arabah in Arabic), which has no permanent water flow, for 170 kilometers to the Gulf of Aqaba.

The Negev Desert comprises approximately 12,000 square kilometers, more than half of Israel's total land area. Geographically it is an extension of the Sinai Desert, forming a rough triangle with its base in the north near Beersheba (also seen as Beersheva), the Dead Sea, and the southern Judean Hills, and it has its apex in the southern tip of the country at Elat. Topographically, it parallels the other regions of the country, with lowlands in the west, hills in the central portion, and the Nahal HaArava as its eastern border.

Climate

Israel has a Mediterranean climate characterized by long, hot, dry summers and short, cool, rainy winters, as modified locally by altitude and latitude. The climate is determined by Israel's location between the subtropical aridity characteristic of Egypt and the subtropical humidity of the Levant or eastern Mediterranean. January is the coldest month, with temperatures from 5°C to 10°C, and August is the hottest month at 18°C to 38°C. About 70 percent of the average rainfall in the country falls between November and March; June through August are often rainless. Rainfall is unevenly distributed, decreasing sharply as one moves southward. In the extreme south, rainfall averages less than 100 millimeters annually; in the north, average annual rainfall is 1,128 millimeters. Rainfall varies from season to season and from year to year, particularly in the Negev Desert. Precipitation is often concentrated in violent storms, causing erosion and flooding. During January and February, it may take the form of snow at the higher elevations of the central highlands, including Jerusalem. The areas of the country most cultivated are those that receive more than 300 millimeters of rainfall annually; about one-third of the country is cultivable.

Population

At the end of October 1987, according to the Central Bureau of Statistics, the population of Israel was 4,389,600, of which 3,601,200 (82 percent) were Jews. About 27 percent of the world's Jews lived in Israel. About 605,765 (13.8 percent) of the population of Israel were Muslims, 100,960 (2.3 percent) were Christians, and about 74,623 (1.7 percent) were Druzes and others. At the end of 1986 the population was growing at a rate of 1.3 percent for Jews, 3.0 percent for Muslims, 1.5 percent for Christians, and 2.8 percent for Druzes and others.

In 1986 the median age of the Israeli population was 25.4. Differences among segments of the population, among Jews and Muslim Arabs in particular, were striking. The non-Jewish population was much younger; in 1986 its median age was 16.8, that of Jews was 27.6. The Jewish population was skewed toward the upper and lower extremes of age, as compared with the non-Jewish age distribution. This skewing resulted from large-scale Jewish immigration, especially the immigration that accompanied the formation of the state in 1948. Many of these immigrants were older individuals; moreover, most of the younger immigrants were single and did not marry and raise families until after their settlement. This circumstance accounts in part for the relatively small percentage of the Jewish population in the twenty to thirty-five-year-old age-group (see fig. 5).

With regard to minorities, Muslim Arabs clearly predominated over Christians, Druzes, and others. In 1986 Muslims accounted for 77 percent of the non-Jewish Israeli population. Together with the Druzes, who resembled them closely in demographic terms, they had the highest rate of growth, with all the associated indicators (family size, fertility rate, etc.). Christian Arabs in 1986 were demographically more similar to Israeli Jews than to Muslims or Druzes (see fig. 6).

The Jewish Israeli population differed also in country of origin; the population included African-Asian and European-American Jews, and native-born Israelis, or sabras (see Glossary). In the oldest age-groups, those of European-American provenance, called "Ashkenazim," predominated, reflecting the population of the pre-1948 era. By the early 1970s, the number of Israelis of African-Asian origin outnumbered European or American Jews. In Israel, immigrants from African and Asian countries were called either Orientals, from the Hebrew Edot Mizrah (communities of the East), or Sephardim (see Jewish Ethnic Groups, this ch.), from an older and different usage. It was not until 1975 that the sabras outnumbered immigrants (see fig. 7).

Understanding the importance of aliyah (pl., aliyot—see Glossary), as immigration to Israel is called in Hebrew, is crucial to understanding much about Israeli society, from its demography to its ethnic composition. Aliyah has historical, ideological, and political ramifications. Ideologically, aliyah was one of the central constituents of the Zionist goal of ingathering of the exiles. Historically and politically, aliyah accounted for most of the growth in the Jewish population before and just after the advent of the state. For example, between 1922 and 1948 the Jewish population in Palestine grew at an annual average rate of 9 percent. Of this growth, 75 percent was due to immigration. By contrast, in the same period, the Arab population grew at an average annual rate of 2.75 percent—almost all as a result of natural increase. Between 1948 and 1960, immigration still accounted for 69 percent of the annual average growth rate of 8.6 percent. A significant group entering Israel since 1965 has been Soviet Jews, of whom approximately 174,000 immigrated between 1965 and 1986. In the most recent period for which data existed in 1988, the period from 1983 through 1986, immigration contributed only a little more than 6 percent to a much diminished average annual growth rate of 1.5 percent (see table 2, Appendix A).

The practical political aspects of declining aliyot are important in comparing the Jewish and non-Jewish population growth rates; one must also consider emigration of Jews from Israel, called *yerida,* a term with pejorative connotations in Hebrew. It is estimated that from 400,000 to 500,000 Israelis emigrated between 1948 and 1986. Emigration is a politically sensitive topic, and statistical estimates of its magnitude vary greatly. To take one possible index, the Central Bureau of Statistics noted that of the more than 466,000 Israeli residents who went abroad for any period of time in 1980, about 19,200 had not returned by the end of 1986. Continued emigration combined with falling immigration, together with unequal natural population growth rates of Jews and Arabs, mean that by the year 2010, assuming medium projections of Arab and Jewish fertility, the proportion of the Jewish population within Israel's pre-1967 borders would decrease to 75 percent. If the occupied territories in the West Bank and Gaza Strip were to be annexed, by

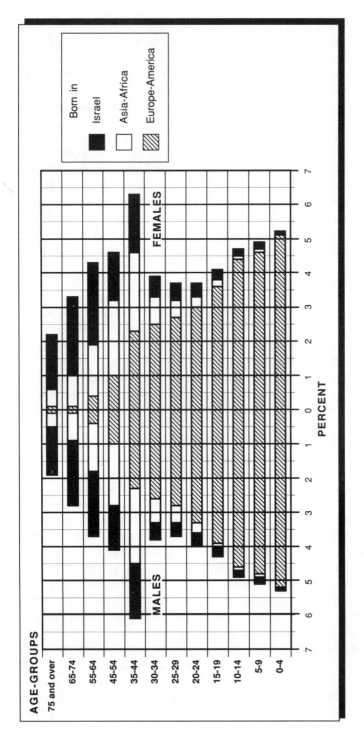

Source: Based on information from Israel, Central Bureau of Statistics, *Statistical Abstract of Israel, 1987,* No. 38, Jerusalem, 1987, 74–75.

Figure 5. Jewish Population Distribution by Age, Sex, and Origin, 1986

2010 Jews would become a clear minority in the state, comprising approximately 45 percent of the total population.

These demographic facts have affected population and family planning policies in Israel, but as of 1988 no consistent course of action had emerged. Until the mid-1960s, Israel followed a policy favoring large families, and family planning was not a priority. In the early 1970s, as a result of unrest among Oriental Jews, the Labor government under Golda Meir decided to support family planning as a way of reducing the size of Oriental Jewish families and narrowing the socioeconomic gap between them and Ashkenazim. Nevertheless, most family planning consisted, unsatisfactorily to most people concerned with the issue, of abortions performed under a liberal abortion law that was opposed bitterly by Orthodox Jews for religious reasons. (Orthodox Jews managed to restrict the criteria for performing abortions after Menachem Begin came to power in 1977.) Thus, because Jews feared being demographically overtaken by Arabs and because of potent opposition by Orthodox Jews, the development of a coherent family-planning policy was stymied. In the late 1980s, Israel's policies on family planning remained largely contradictory.

The dispersal of the population has been a matter of concern throughout the existence of the state. In 1986 the average population density in Israel was 199 persons per square kilometer, with densities much higher in the cities (close to 6,000 persons per square kilometer in the Tel Aviv District in 1986) and considerably lower in the very arid regions of the south. The population continues to be overwhelmingly urban. Almost 90 percent resides in urban localities, more than one-third of the total in the three largest cities (in order of population), Jerusalem, Tel Aviv, and Haifa. Since 1948, despite calls throughout the 1960s to "Judaize" Galilee, the population has been shifting southward. Still, as of 1988, almost two-thirds of the population was concentrated on the Mediterranean coast between Haifa and Ashdod.

In the mid-1950s, in an effort both to disperse the population from the coast and settle the large numbers of immigrants coming from Middle Eastern and North African countries, so-called development towns were planned and built over the next fifteen years. They were settled primarily by Oriental Jews, or Sephardim (see Glossary) and through the years they have often been arenas of unrest and protest among ethnic groups. In 1986, about 77 percent of rural Jews lived in kibbutzim and moshavim; still, these two rather striking Israeli social institutions attracted a very small percentage (3.5 percent and 4.4 percent, respectively) of the total Jewish population.

91

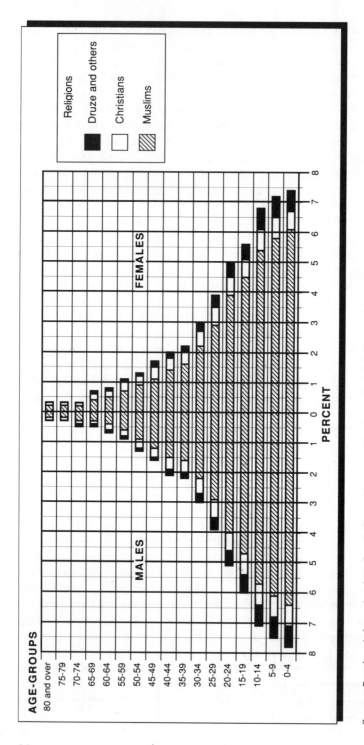

Source: Based on information from Israel, Central Bureau of Statistics, *Statistical Abstract of Israel, 1987*, No. 38, Jerusalem, 1987, 67.

Figure 6. Non-Jewish Population Distribution by Age, Sex, and Religion, 1986

The changing distribution of population was more pronounced among Arabs. Whereas 75 percent of the Arabs lived in rural localities in 1948, less than 30 percent did by 1983. This pattern was not entirely because of internal migration to urban areas, but rather resulted from the urbanization of larger Arab villages. For example, in 1950 the Arab locality of Et Taiyiba near Nabulus had 5,100 residents; by 1986 its population had risen to 19,000. Israeli Arabs were concentrated in central and western Galilee, around the city of Nazareth, and in the city of Jaffa (Yafo in Hebrew), northeast of Tel Aviv. Arabs resided also in Acre (Akko in Hebrew), Lydda (Lod in Hebrew), Ramla, Haifa, and near Beersheba. They constituted the majority in East Jerusalem, annexed after the June 1967 War.

According to the Central Bureau of Statistics, at the end of 1986 about 51,200 Jews resided in the the West Bank occupied territories (called Judea and Samaria by Jewish Israelis), and an additional 2,100 resided in the Gaza Strip (these figures represented 1.4 percent and 0.1 percent, respectively, of the 1986 Jewish population of Israel). They lived in 122 localities in both areas, including 4 cities, 10 kibbutzim, 31 moshavim, and 77 "other rural localities." This last category included more than fifty localities of a kind called *yishuv kehilati*, a nonagricultural cooperative settlement, a form new to Israel. Such settlements were associated especially with Amana, the settlement arm of Gush Emunim, and developed in the mid-1970s especially to enhance Jewish presence in the West Bank. According to the Central Bureau of Statistics, in 1985 about 7,094, and in 1986 approximately 5,160, Jews settled in the occupied territories. Some did so for religious and nationalistic reasons, but many more were motivated by the high costs of housing inside Israel, combined with economic incentives offered by the Likud governments of the late 1970s and early 1980s to those who settled in the West Bank.

The Central Bureau of Statistics estimated the 1986 Arab population of the West Bank to be 836,000, and that of Gaza to be 545,000, for a total population of close to 1.4 million. In 1986 the population increased at a rate of 2.5 percent for the West Bank and 3.4 percent for Gaza—among the highest annual rates attained during the Israeli occupation.

Social Structure

The social structure of contemporary Israel has been shaped by a variety of forces and circumstances. Israel inherited some institutions and customs from the Ottomans and some from the British mandatory rule over Palestine. Zionists who strove to build the

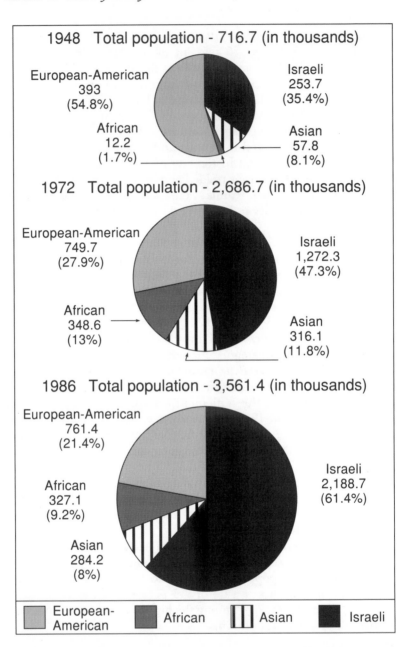

1948 Total population - 716.7 (in thousands)

European-American
393
(54.8%)

Israeli
253.7
(35.4%)

African
12.2
(1.7%)

Asian
57.8
(8.1%)

1972 Total population - 2,686.7 (in thousands)

European-American
749.7
(27.9%)

Israeli
1,272.3
(47.3%)

African
348.6
(13%)

Asian
316.1
(11.8%)

1986 Total population - 3,561.4 (in thousands)

European-American
761.4
(21.4%)

Israeli
2,188.7
(61.4%)

African
327.1
(9.2%)

Asian
284.2
(8%)

European-American   African   Asian   Israeli

Source: Based on information from Israel, Central Bureau of Statistics, *Statistical Abstract of Israel, 1987*, No. 38, Jerusalem, 1987, 73.

Figure 7. Analysis of Jewish Population Distribution by Origin, 1948, 1972, and 1986

Yishuv under Ottoman and British rule (see Origins of Zionism, ch. 1) also wielded influence. Immigration patterns have altered the social structure radically at different times. From 1882 to 1948, Israel received many immigrants from Eastern Europe and Central Europe. Following independence, huge numbers of Middle Eastern, North African, and Asian Jews came to the new state and altered its dominant Ashkenazi cast. Another shaping force was the presence of non-Jews in the Jewish state—a growing Arab minority within the pre-1967 borders of Israel and an absolute majority in the territories held under military occupation since the June 1967 War. Finally, among the most important forces shaping contemporary Israeli society is religion.

Varieties of Israeli Judaism

As the references to "Orthodox Zionists," "Orthodox non-Zionists," and "Orthodox anti-Zionists" indicate, Judaism is not a monolithic cultural entity in contemporary Israel. Furthermore, an understanding of religious categories in American Judaism is not sufficient for understanding Israeli Judaism. Israelis religiously categorize themselves first as *dati,* that is, "religiously" observant Jews or *lo dati,* "not religiously" observant Jews. One who is religious strictly follows halakah, that is, adheres to the totality of rabbinic law. One who is not religious is not a strict follower of rabbinic law; however, the category can be further subdivided into agnostic or atheistic secularists, on the one hand, and individuals who are committed to Judaism in principle, on the other. The latter group calls itself "traditionalist" (*mesoratim*).

Many Oriental Jews, especially in the second generation since immigration, are traditionalists, expressing this commitment in observance of folk customs such as ethnic festivals and pilgrimages. This group is important because, although members may not vote directly for religious political parties, they respond positively to religious symbols used politically by a number of parties; for example, the idea of the Jewish people's right to a greater, biblical land of Israel as divinely ordained.

Orthodox Judaism

Within the Orthodox or *dati* category one can distinguish between the ultra-Orthodox or *haredi,* and the "modern" or "neo-Orthodox." At the very extreme, the ultra-Orthodox consists of groups such as the Neturei Karta, a small fringe group of anti-Zionist extremists, who reject Israel and view it as a heretical entity. They want nothing to do with the state and live in enclaves (Mea Shearim in Jerusalem and towns such as Bene Beraq), where they shut out the secular modern world as much as possible. Nevertheless, among the ultra-Orthodox one can also count some of the adherents of the Agudat Israel Party, who accept the state, although not its messianic pretensions, and work within many of its institutions. These adherents are exempt from compulsory military service and do not volunteer for police work, yet they demand that the state protect their way of life, a political arrangement known as the "preservation of the status quo" (see The Role of Judaism, this ch.). In practice, they live in the same neighborhoods as the more extreme *haredi* and maintain their own schools, rabbinical courts, charitable institutions, and so on. The state has not only committed itself to protecting the separate institutions of different Orthodox Jewish groups but also, especially since 1977, to their financial subvention.

The modern or neo-Orthodox are those who, while scrupulously adhering to halakah, have not cut themselves off from society at large. They are oriented to the same ideological goals as many of the secularists, and they share the basic commitment to Israel as a Zionist state. Furthermore, they participate fully in all the major institutions of the state, including the Israel Defense Forces (IDF). This group is also referred to as "Orthodox Zionists." They have been represented historically by a number of political parties or coalitions, and have been the driving force behind many of the extraparliamentary social, political, and Jewish terrorist movements that have characterized Israeli society since the June 1967 War (see Extraparliamentary Religio-nationalist Movements, ch. 4). Most Orthodox Zionists have been "ultra-hawkish" and irredentist in orientation; Gush Emunim, the Bloc of the Faithful, is the most prominent of these groups. A minority of other Zionist groups, for example, Oz Veshalom, an Orthodox Zionist movement that is the religious counterpart to Peace Now, has been more moderate.

Relations between the ultra-Orthodox and the neo-Orthodox have been complicated and not always cordial. Nevertheless, the neo-Orthodox have tended to look to the ultra-Orthodox for legitimacy on religious matters, and the ultra-Orthodox have managed to maintain their virtual monopoly on the training and certification of rabbis (including neo-Orthodox ones) in Israel. (The neo-Orthodox university, Bar-Ilan, as part of the parliamentary legislation that enabled it, was prohibited from ordaining rabbis.) Thus ultra-Orthodoxy has an aura of ultimate authenticity, a special connection to tradition that has been difficult for others to overcome. Even a staunch secularist such as David Ben-Gurion lamented during a confrontation that the ultra-Orthodox "look like

our grandfathers. How can you slap your grandfather into jail, even
if he throws stones at you?''

Non-Orthodox Judaism

The American denominations of Conservative Jews (see Glossary) and Reform Jews (see Glossary), although they have enrolled
between them the vast majority of affiliated American Jews, have
achieved a very modest presence in Israel. Neither Reform nor Conservative rabbinical ordination is recognized by the Israeli Chief
Rabbinate; thus, these rabbis are generally forbidden to perform
weddings or authorize divorces. (In the mid-1980s a few Conservative rabbis were granted the right, on an ad hoc basis, to perform weddings.) In the early 1980s, there were twelve Reform
congregations in Israel and about 900 members—almost 90 percent of whom were born outside the country. During the same
period there were more than twenty Conservative congregations
with more than 1,500 members; only about 14 percent were native-born Israelis (and, as in the case of Reform, the great majority
of these were of Ashkenazi descent).

Although both Reform and Conservative movements dated their
presence in Israel to the 1930s, they experienced real growth, the
Conservative movement in particular, only in the late 1960s to
mid-1970s. During this period, relatively large numbers of American Jews immigrated—more than 36,000 between 1968 and 1975.
Nevertheless, the opposition of the Israeli Orthodox establishment
to recognizing Conservative and (particularly) Reform Judaism as
legitimate was strong, and it continued to be unwilling to share
power and patronage with these movements. Neither of the newer
movements has attracted native-born Israelis in significant numbers. The importance of the non-Orthodox movements in Israel
in the late 1980s mainly reflects the influence they have wielded
in the American and West European Diaspora.

The Role of Judaism

In 1988 two-thirds to three-quarters of Jewish Israelis were not
religious or Orthodox in observance or practice. Among the minority of the religious who were the most extreme in their adherence
to Judaism—the *haredi*—the very existence of Israel as a self-proclaimed Jewish state was anathema because Israel is for them
(ironically, as it is for many Arabs) a wholly illegitimate entity.
Given these facts—the large number of secular Israelis, and the
sometimes fierce denunciation of the state by a small number of
the most religious extremists—one might expect Judaism to play
a modest role in Israeli society and culture. But the opposite

is true; traditional Judaism has been playing a more dominant role since the late 1960s and affecting more of the political and economic dimensions of everyday life (see Prospects for Electoral Reform, ch. 4).

The relation between Judaism and the Jewish state has always been ambivalent and fraught with paradox. In the nineteenth century, Zionism often competed with Orthodox Judaism for the hearts and minds of young Jews, and enmity existed between Orthodox Jews of Eastern Europe and the Zionists (and those residing in Palestine in the late nineteenth and early twentieth centuries). Orthodox Jews resented the dominantly secular nature of Jewish nationalism (for example, the desire to turn the holy tongue of Hebrew into an instrument of everyday discourse), whereas the Zionists derogated the other-worldly passivity of Orthodox Jews. Among the most extreme Orthodox Jews, the Zionist movement was deemed heretical because it sought to ''force the End of Days'' and preempt the hand of God in restoring the Jewish people to their Holy Land before the Messiah's advent.

Nevertheless, for all its secular trappings, Zionism as an ideology was also profoundly tied to Jewish tradition—as its commitment to the revival of the Jews' biblical language, and, indeed, its commitment to settle for nothing less than a Jewish home in biblical Palestine indicate. Thus, secular Zionism and religious Judaism are inextricably linked, and hence the conceptual ambivalence and paradoxes of enmity and attraction.

In any case, conceptual difficulties have been suspended by world events: the violence of the pogroms in Eastern Europe throughout the nineteenth and early twentieth centuries, and the Holocaust carried out by Nazi Germany, in which approximately 6 million Jews were killed, nearly destroying Central and East European Jewry in the 1930s and 1940s. In the face of such suffering—and especially after the magnitude of the Holocaust became known—Orthodox and non-Orthodox Jews devised ways to work together in Palestine despite their fundamental differences. When the advent of the state was followed immediately by invasion and lasting Arab hostility, this cooperative modus vivendi in the face of a common enemy continued.

The spearheads of cooperation on the Orthodox side were the so-called religious Zionists, who were able to reconcile their nationalism with their piety. Following Rabbi A.I. Kook (1865–1935), the first Ashkenazi chief rabbi of Palestine, many believed that Zionism and Zionists, however secular, were nonetheless instruments of God who were engaged in divinely inspired work. On a more pragmatic level, under leadership such as that of Rabbi

I.J. Reines (1839–1915), the religious, like the secularists, organized in political parties, such as the Mizrahi Party (see Religious Parties, ch. 4). They were joined in the political arena by the non-Zionist Orthodox, organized as the Agudat Israel Party. Although Agudat Israel was originally opposed to the idea of a Jewish state, it came to accept the rationale for it in a hostile gentile world (especially after the Central and East European centers of Orthodoxy were destroyed in the Holocaust). Because Orthodox Jews, like secularists, were organized in political parties, from an early date they participated—the religious Zionists more directly than the religious non-Zionists—in the central institutions of the Yishuv and, later, the State of Israel. Indeed, since 1977 and the coming to power of Menachem Begin's Likud, Orthodox Jews have been increasingly vocal in their desire not just to participate in but also to shape—reshape, if need be—the central institutions of Israeli society.

Judaism, Civil Religion, and the "New Zionism"

All varieties of Judaism—ultra-Orthodoxy, neo-Orthodoxy, the Reform and Conservative forms—together counted as their formal adherents only a minority of Jewish Israelis. Yet religion was a potent force, and increasingly so, in Israeli society. Traditional Judaism has exerted its influence in Israel in three important ways. First, traditional Judaism has influenced political and judicial legislation and state institutions, which have been championed by the various Orthodox political parties and enshrined in the "preservation of the status quo" arrangements through the years. Second, religion has exerted influence through the symbols and practices of traditional Judaism that literally pervade everyday life. Saturday is the sabbath (Shabbat—see Glossary), the official day of rest for Jews (although the majority do not attend synagogue), and most enterprises are closed. Jewish holidays also affect school curricula, programming on radio and television, features in the newspapers, and so on. Traditionalists, who extol halakah even if they do not observe all rabbinic law, also observe many folk customs. Through the years, much of the folk religion has taken on an Oriental-Jewish flavor, reflecting in part the demographic preponderance of Oriental Jews since the 1970s. Such customs include ethnic festivals such as the Moroccan *mimouna* (an annual festival of Moroccan Jews, originally a minor holiday in Morocco, which has become in Israel a major celebration of Moroccan Jewish ethnic identity) and family pilgrimages to the tombs of Jewish holy men. The latter have become country-wide events. Traditional Judaism has influenced Israeli society in yet a third way: Israel's political elite has selectively co-opted symbols and practices of traditional Judaism in an attempt to promote nationalism and social integration. In this way traditional Judaism, or some aspects of it, becomes part of the political culture of the Jewish state, and aspects of traditional Judaism are then enlisted in what some analysts have called the "civil religion" of Jewish society. Thus, Judaism speaks to Israelis who may themselves be nonreligious, indeed even secularist.

Of all the manifestations of religion in Israel, civil religion has undergone the most profound changes through the years, specifically becoming more religious—in the sense of incorporating more traditional, Orthodox-like Judaism. In the prestate period, the civil religion of Jewish society was generally socialist, that is, Labor Zionism. Labor Zionists were hostile to much of traditional Jewish life, to the concept of exile, and to what they viewed as the cultural obscurantism of traditional Jews. They actively rejected Orthodoxy in religion and considered it to be a key reason for the inertia and lack of modernity of exiled Jews. Labor Zionists sought to reconstitute a revolutionary new form of Jewish person in a radically new kind of society.

After 1948, however, new problems faced Israeli society—not only military and economic problems, but also the massive immigration of Jews and their assimilation. First came the remnants of East and Central European Jewry from the detention and displaced-persons camps; then came Jews from Africa and Asia (see Ingathering of the Exiles, ch. 1). Social integration and solidarity were essential to successful assimilation, yet Labor Zionism neither appealed to nor united many sectors of the new society. Throughout the 1950s and early 1960s—roughly the period of Ben-Gurion's preeminence—a civil religion was fashioned by some factions of the political elite (led by Ben-Gurion himself), which sought to stress the new Israeli state as the object of ultimate value.

Israelis have called this the period of *mamlakhtiyut* or statism. The Jewish Bible was the key text and symbol, and secular youths studied parts of it as the Jewish nation's history and cultural heritage. Religious holidays, such as Hanukkah and Passover, or Pesach, were reinterpreted to emphasize nationalist and liberation themes, and Independence Day was promoted as a holiday of stature equal to the old religious holidays. The archaeology of the Holy Land, particularly during the Israelite (post-Joshua) period, became a national obsession, first because of the discovery of the Dead Sea Scrolls and later because of Yigal Yadin's excavations at Massada (a site of fierce Jewish resistance to the Romans after the fall of Jerusalem in 70 A.D.). At the same time, the two thousand years of Jewish history that followed the Roman destruction of Jerusalem, Jewish cultural life in the various diasporas (Ashkenazi as well as Sephardi), and Jewish religion of the postbiblical eras (rabbinic Judaism, exemplified in the Talmud—see Glossary) were rejected or ignored.

For many reasons, the statist focus of Israeli civil religion did not continue after the June 1967 War. These reasons ranged from the greater traditionalism and piety of the Oriental immigrants, who were never satisfactorily engaged by the more limited scope of statism; to the exhaustion of the Labor Alignment, which, after the October 1973 War, had sought to embody socialist Zionism and Israeli modern statism as a manifestation of its own identity and agenda; to the rise of Begin's Likud Bloc with its populist appeals to ethnic traditionalism and an irredentist territorial program as a challenge to Labor Zionism's fading hegemony. Begin and his Likud championed a new civil religion to embody *its* identity and agenda. This new right-wing civil religion affirmed traditional Judaism and denigrated modernistic secularism—the reverse of the earlier civil religion. Unlike the statist version of Ben-Gurion's time, which focused on the Bible and pre-exilic Jewish history, the new civil religion was permeated by symbols from the whole of Jewish history. It gave special emphasis, however, to the Holocaust as a sign of the ultimate isolation of the Jewish people and the enduring hostility of the gentile world.

The new civil religion (which in its more political guise some have called the New Zionism) has brought traditional Judaism back to a position in the Jewish state very different from that which it occupied twenty, forty, or eighty years ago. After the June 1967 War, the New Zionists linked up with the revitalized and transformed neo-Orthodox—young, self-assured religious Jews who have self-consciously connected retention and Jewish settlement of the West Bank, the biblical Judea and Samaria, with the Messiah's advent. The rise of messianic right-wing politics gave birth in the mid-1970s to the irredentist, extraparliamentary movement Gush Emunim, which in turn led to the Jewish terrorist underground of the 1980s (see Jewish Terrorist Organizations, ch. 5). When the underground was uncovered and broken by Israeli security in April 1984, it had already carried out several attacks on Arabs, including, it was thought, Arab mayors, in the West Bank and was planning to destroy the Dome of the Rock mosque in Jerusalem. Even before the June 1967 War, however, Orthodox Judaism had been able to exert influence on Israeli society simply because its religious institutions were so historically entrenched in the society.

101

Religious Institutions

The basis of all religious institutions in Israel dates back to the Ottoman Empire (1402–1921) and its system of confessional group autonomy called the millet system. Under the millet, each religious group was allowed limited independence in running its own community under a recognized (usually religious) leader who represented the community politically to the imperial authorities. Matters of law relating to personal status—marriage, divorce, inheritance, legitimacy of children—were also left to community control, so long as they did not involve a Muslim, in which case the sharia (Islamic law) courts took precedence.

The Jewish community in Ottoman Palestine was represented by its chief rabbi, called the Hakham Rashi or Rishon Le Tziyyon (the First in Zion), who was a Sephardi. The Orthodox Ashkenazim in Ottoman Palestine, who never formed a unified community, resented Sephardi preeminence. The secular European Jews who began to arrive in large numbers after 1882 ignored the constraints of the millet system and the standing of the chief rabbi and his council as best they could.

Under their League of Nations Mandate over Palestine, the British retained this system of religious courts (the Jewish Agency became the political representative of the Yishuv as a whole). In recognition of the growing numerical preponderance of Ashkenazim, however, the British recommended the formation of a joint chief rabbinate, one Sephardi and one Ashkenazi, and a joint chief rabbinical council. This system was implemented in 1921, together with a hierarchical court structure composed of local courts, regional appellate courts, and the joint Supreme Rabbinical Court in Jerusalem. After Israel's independence—even with the establishment of autonomous secular and military judiciaries—this system of rabbinical courts prevailed. An addition to the system was a Ministry of Religious Affairs under the control of the religious political party that sat in coalition to form the government, originally Mizrahi and later the National Religious Party (see The Judicial System; Multiparty System, ch. 4).

In 1988, in addition to the two chief rabbis and their Chief Rabbinical Council, local chief rabbis were based in the larger cities (again, generally two, one Ashkenazi and one Sephardi) and on local religious councils. These councils (under the Ministry of Religious Affairs) functioned as administrative bodies and provided religious services. They supervised dietary laws (*kashrut*) in public institutions, inspected slaughterhouses, maintained ritual baths, and supported synagogues—about 5,000 of them—and their

A Druze elder
Courtesy Embassy of Israel,
Washington

Samaritan priest and
followers on a
holy day of sacrifice
Courtesy Les Vogel

103

officials. They also registered marriages and divorces, that is, legal matters of personal status that came under their jurisdiction.

Israel's Proclamation of Independence guarantees freedom of religion for all groups within the society. Thus, the Ministry of Religious Affairs also supervised and supported the local religious councils and religious courts of the non-Jewish population: Christian, Druze, and Muslim. As in Ottoman times, the autonomy of the confessional groups is maintained in matters of religion and personal status, although all courts are subject to the jurisdiction of the (secular) Supreme Court. (This was true technically even of Jewish rabbinical courts, but outright confrontation or imposition of secular appellate review was, in fact, avoided.) Among Christians, the Greek Catholic, Greek Orthodox, Latin, Maronite, and Arab Anglican groups operated their own courts. In 1962 a separate system of Druze courts was established. Sunni Muslim (see Glossary) judges (*qadis*) presided over courts that followed sharia.

The Ministry of Religious Affairs also exerted control over Muslim religious endowments (*waqfs*), and for this reason has been a political presence in Muslim communities. The ministry traditionally was a portfolio held by the National Religious Party, which at times also controlled the Arab departments in the Ministry of Interior and the Ministry of Social Welfare. This helped to account for the otherwise paradoxical fact that some Arabs—8.2 percent of voters in 1973—supported the neo-Orthodox, Zionist, Nationalist Religious Party in elections.

Besides Christian, Muslim, and Druze courts, there was yet another system of Orthodox Jewish courts that ran parallel to, and independently of, the rabbinate courts. These courts served the ultra-Orthodox (non-Zionist Agudat Israel as well as anti-Zionist Neturei Karta and other groups) because the ultra-Orthodox had never accepted the authority or even the legitimacy of the official, state-sponsored (pro-Zionist, neo-Orthodox) rabbinate and the Ministry of Religious Affairs. In place of the rabbinate and rabbinical council, Agudat Israel and the community it represented were guided by a Council of Torah Sages, which functioned also as the highest rabbinical court for the ultra-Orthodox. The members of this council represent the pinnacle of religious learning (rather than political connections, as was alleged for the rabbinate) in the ultra-Orthodox community. The council also oversaw for its community inspectors of *kashrut,* ritual slaughterers, ritual baths, and schools—all independent of the rabbinate and the Ministry of Religious Affairs.

In 1983 this state of affairs was even further complicated when the former Sephardi chief rabbi, Ovadia Yoseph, angry at not being reelected to this post, withdrew from the rabbinate to set up his own Sephardic ultra-Orthodox council and political party, called Shas (an acronym for Sephardic Torah Guardians). Shas ran successfully in the 1983 Jerusalem municipal elections, winning three of twenty-one seats, and later in the national Knesset (parliament) elections in 1984, where it cut deeply into Agudat Israel's hold on ultra-Orthodox Oriental voters. Shas won four seats in 1984, Agudat Israel only two (see Religious Parties, ch. 4). In this context, Shas's importance lay in the fact that it split the Oriental ultra-Orthodox from Ashkenazi domination under Agudat Israel, adding yet another institutionalized variety of Israeli traditional Judaism to an already complicated mix.

The practical result of all these separate and semiautonomous judiciaries based on religious grounds was that, for a large area of law dealing with matters of personal status, there was no civil code or judiciary that applied to all Israeli citizens. Marriages, divorces, adoptions, wills, and inheritance were all matters for adjudication by Christian clerics, Muslim *qadis,* or *dayanim* (sing., *dayan;* Jewish religious judge). An essential practical difficulty was that, in strictly legal terms, marriages across confessional lines were problematic. Another result was that citizens found themselves under the jurisdiction of religious authorities even if they were themselves secular. This situation has posed the greatest problem for the Jewish majority, not only because most Jewish Israelis are neither religiously observant nor Orthodox, but also because the hegemony of Orthodox halakah has from time to time forced the raising of issues of fundamental concern to modern Israel. Foremost among these has been the issue of "Who is a Jew?" in the Jewish state.

The "Who Is a Jew?" Controversy

The predominance of halakah and religious courts in adjudicating matters of personal status—and for that matter, the privileged position of the Orthodox minority in Israeli society—date back to arrangements worked out between the Orthodox and Labor Zionists on the eve of statehood. In June 1947, the executive committee of Agudat Israel received a letter from Ben-Gurion, then chairman of the executive committee of the Jewish Agency, who was the predominant political leader of the Yishuv. Ben-Gurion, wishing to have the support of all sectors of the Yishuv in the dire struggle he knew was soon to come, asked Agudat Israel to join the coalition that would constitute the first government of the State of Israel. In return for Agudat Israel's support, Ben-Gurion offered a set of guarantees relating to traditional Judaism's place in the new society. These guarantees formalized the customary arrangements that had developed in Ottoman times and continued through the British Mandate; hence they came to be known as agreements for the "preservation of the status quo."

The core of the status quo agreements focused on the following areas: the Jewish Shabbat, Saturday, would be the official day of rest for all Jews; public transportation would not operate nationwide on Shabbat and religious holidays, although localities would remain free to run local transportation systems; *kashrut* would be maintained in all public institutions; the existing religious school system would remain separate from the secular one but would receive funding from the state; and rabbinical courts applying halakah would decide matters of personal status (see Education, this ch.). Both Agudat Israel and the Zionist Orthodox party, Mizrahi (later the National Religious Party), accepted the agreements and joined the first elected government of Israel in 1949.

Ben-Gurion's concern that a more-or-less united Israel confront its enemies was answered by the status quo arrangement. But this arrangement—particularly the educational and judicial aspects—also set the stage for conflict between Orthodox and secular Jewish Israelis. This conflict became quickly apparent in the wake of the first flood of Jewish immigration to the new state and as a direct result of one of the first laws passed by the new Knesset, the Law of Return.

The Law of Return, passed in 1950, guaranteed to all Jews the right to immigrate to Israel. Along with the Nationality Law (1952), which granted Israeli citizenship to people (including non-Jews) who lived in the country prior to 1948, the Law of Return also extended to Jewish immigrants (unless they specifically deferred citizenship or renounced it) immediate Israeli citizenship. Non-Jewish immigrants could acquire citizenship through a slower process of naturalization.

The problem of what constitutes Jewish "nationality" (*leom*) was essentially new. Before the modern era, one was a Jew (in the eyes of Jews and gentiles alike) by religious criteria; to renounce the religion meant renouncing one's membership in the community. In modern nation-states membership (citizenship) and religion were formally and, it was hoped, conceptually independent: one could be a British, French, or American citizen of the "Jewish persuasion." But the modern State of Israel presented special opportunities to Jews—the right to settle in the country and claim Israeli citizenship as a right, in Ben-Gurion's words, "inherent in being a Jew." With these opportunities have come problems, both formal and conceptual, about the definition of "a Jew."

A halakic definition is available: a Jew is one who is born of a Jewish mother or who converts according to the halakah. The traditional criteria thus consist of biology (descent) and religion. In a sense, biology dominates religion, because, according to halakah, someone remains a Jew if born of a Jewish mother, even if he or she converts to another religion, although such a person is referred to as "one who has destroyed himself."

Another problem is that of defining "nationality." Such an issue is of concern to a modern state and its minister of interior. Moreover, a modern state is interested in the nationality question as part of the determination of citizenship, with all its associated rights and duties. The Orthodox, however, are less concerned with nationality as a guide to citizenship and more concerned with nationality as it determines proper marriage partners, with the attendant legitimacy of children. In Orthodox Judaism an illegitimate child (*mamzer;* pl., *mamzerim*) is severely limited in the range of permissible marriage partners; the children of *mamzerim* are ("even to the tenth generation," according to Deuteronomy 23:2) themselves illegitimate. Furthermore, a woman who has not been divorced according to halakah will have *mamzerim* as the children of subsequent marriages. Rabbis would never knowingly sanctify the marriage of improper or forbidden partners, nor would such improper unions hold up in rabbinical courts. For the Orthodox, therefore, to know, as assuredly as one can, the status of a potential marriage partner as a "full and proper" Jew is crucial. Any doubts, even in principle, would have the effect of dividing the Jewish community into endogamous groups, that is, groups that would marry only within the confines of assurance against bastardy (*mamzerut*). This threat of sundering the "whole Jewish community" into mutually nonintermarrying segments has been used by the Orthodox to great effect.

Against this background one can understand much of the "Who is a Jew?" question and the vehemence with which positions have been taken. In 1958 the Bureau of the Registration of Inhabitants, under the minister of interior (from a left-of-center party), was directed to register individuals and issue identity cards that had separate categories under nationality and religion, according to the "good faith" declaration of the individual. Thus a non-Jewish mother could declare herself or her children to be Jewish and would be so registered. The rabbinate and the religious political parties were incensed, especially after they were told that population registry and identity cards were civil matters and need never affect marriages and divorces, which, under the status quo arrangements, would continue to fall under the jurisdiction of rabbinical courts.

Orthodox Jews reasoned that if they had to deal with questions of Jewish nationality in a modern society, they could not allow nationality to be separated from religion in the Jewish state. The National Religious Party precipitated a cabinet crisis, and Prime Minister Ben-Gurion responded by forming a committee of Jewish ''sages'' (including non-Orthodox Diaspora scholars) to study the question.

The response of the scholars—even the non-Orthodox ones—was that it was premature to define who was a Jew in such a way that religion and nationality were separate. If not born of a Jewish mother, then a person must undergo a conversion to the Jewish faith to become a Jew. On the basis of this agreement, as well as Ben-Gurion's own political considerations, a new minister of interior from the National Religious Party, which rejoined the government, was appointed. In 1960 the new minister redirected the Bureau of the Registration of Inhabitants to define a Jew by administrative fiat as ''a person born of a Jewish mother who does not belong to another religion, or one who has converted in accordance with religious law.'' This definition, advanced by an Orthodox minister, is not strictly halakic, since an apostate is still a Jew according to halakah but not according to this definition. Such was the criterion used to deny automatic Israeli citizenship to Brother Daniel, a Carmelite monk who was born Oswald Rufeisen, a Jew, but who converted to Christianity and then tried to claim citizenship under the Law of Return. The Supreme Court in 1962 upheld the ministry's definition, since according to the ''commonsense'' definition of who is a Jew of the ''average'' Israeli, ''a Christian cannot be a Jew.'' (Brother Daniel later acquired Israeli citizenship through naturalization.)

The ''Who is a Jew?'' question still vexes the Knesset and the Supreme Court, and it has brought Orthodox and secular Israelis into sharp conflict. Sometimes, as in the Brother Daniel case, the issue has arisen as individuals tested the directives in terms of their own predicament. In 1968 Benjamin Shalit, an officer in the Israeli navy who was married to a non-Jewish naturalized Israeli citizen, sought to register his children as ''Jewish'' under the nationality category, but to leave the category under religion blank. This would have the effect of separating religion from nationality but not violate the ''commonsense'' notion that one cannot be an adherent of another religion (as was Brother Daniel) and still be Jewish. Shalit was claiming *no* religion for his children. The citizenship of the children was never in question: they were Israelis. What was at stake was their nationality.

The court's first response was to ask the government to drop the nationality category from registration lists; the government declined, ostensibly for security reasons. Finally, after the 1969 national elections, the court ruled by a five-to-four majority in 1970 that Shalit could register his children as "Jews" by nationality with no religion—invalidating the directives of 1960. Orthodox Jews rose up in defiance; Prime Minister Golda Meir backed down, and in 1970, after fierce debate, the Knesset passed an amendment to the Law of Return that revalidated and legalized the 1960 administrative directive; thus: a Jew is one "born to a Jewish mother, or who has become converted to Judaism, and who is not a member of another religion." What the Orthodox did not win, at this time, was the proviso that the conversion to Judaism must have been carried out in conformance with halakah. Thus the status of conversions carried out by Reform or Conservative rabbis in the Diaspora remained in question in the eyes of the religious minority in Israel.

Another way in which the "Who is a Jew?" issue arose involved the status of entire communities. Among these were the Karaites (a schismatic Jewish sect of the eighth century that rejected the legitimacy of rabbinic law), the Bene Yisrael (Jews from near Bombay, India, who immigrated in large numbers in the 1950s), and from the 1970s onward, Jews from Ethiopia—Falashas. The controversy arose over the fitness of these Jews, according to halakic criteria, for intermarriage with other Jews—not over whether they were Jews. The question was whether, because of their isolation (Bene Israel or Falashas) or schismatic deviance (the Karaites), their ignorance or improper observance of halakic rules had not rendered them essentially communities of *mamzerim*, fit only to marry each other or (according to halakah) Jewish proselytes.

These community-level disputes have had different outcomes: the Orthodox Jewish authorities have not relented on the Karaites, who were doctrinal opponents of rabbinic law, despite pleas to bring them fully into the fold. The Karaites thus remained, according to halakah, a separate community for purposes of marriage. Young Karaites sometimes concealed their affiliation to "pass" in the larger Jewish Israeli society, where they were in all ways indistinguishable. In the mid-1960s, the Orthodox backed down on the Bene Yisrael, changing the rabbinate's special caution against them in the registration of marriages between Jewish ethnic groups to a general caution. The Ethiopian Falashas, among the newest additions to the Israeli Jewish mix, still faced some uncertainty in the 1980s—again, not so much in terms of their Jewishness, which was accepted, but with respect to marriage to other Jews.

Halakah provides many other stipulations and constraints on proper marriages and divorces. Among others these include the biblical levirate, whereby a childless widow must first obtain the ritual release of her brother-in-law before she may remarry; laws restricting the marriage of Cohens, the priestly caste of Israelites, who today have few corporate functions but whose putative individual members are recognized; and laws governing the status of *agunot* (sing., *aguna*), married women "abandoned" by their husbands whose remarriage is disallowed until the man files a proper bill of divorce or until his death can be halakically established. This last law has made it difficult for women married to soldiers listed as "missing in action" to remarry within halakah, because the requisite two witnesses to their husband's death (or other admissible evidence) are not always forthcoming. People involved in such hardship cases can get married outside Israel, but then the status of their children, in the eyes of halakah, is tainted. Although such cases arouse the sympathy of Orthodox Jews, the principle followed is that halakah, being divine and eternal, cannot be modified.

It is in regard to the principles of the divinity and immutability of halakah that Orthodoxy opposes Conservative and Reform Judaism. Conservative Judaism affirms the divinity of halakah, but questions its immutability. Reform Judaism denies the authority of both principles. Because of these views and their control over the religious establishment, Orthodox Jews have been able to keep rabbis of either persuasion from establishing full legitimacy in Israel. But because the majority of Jews in the Western democracies, if they are affiliated at all, are affiliated with Reform or Conservative congregations, and because of the high intermarriage rates, as of 1988 Orthodox Jews have been unable publicly to invalidate Reform or Conservative conversions to Judaism under the Law of Return by amending the law again to stipulate specific conformance with halakah as the sole mode of conversion. Yet many new immigrants (and some long-time residents) whose status is in doubt have undergone Orthodox conversions—often added onto their previous Reform or Conservative ones—once resident in Israel.

The Orthodox-Secular Cleavage

As has been seen, Israeli Judaism in the late 1980s exerted its influence on society through a complex interplay of ethnicity, halakah, and political and ideological ferment—as well as through the notions of Israeli Jewish citizenship, nationality, security, and sovereignty. In part because of the institutionalization of the status quo arrangements of the late 1940s and early 1950s, in part because of the disproportionate power available to small (religious)

The Wailing Wall on the Temple Mount, Jerusalem
Courtesy Jean E. Tucker
Blowing of the Shofar during Rosh Hashanah, Jewish New Year
Courtesy Embassy of Israel, Washington

political parties in the Israeli parliamentary system, traditional Judaism both pervades and structures much of everyday life (see Multiparty System, ch. 4). Because many of the Orthodox of various persuasions view the status quo as the baseline from which to advance, they are accused by many secular Israelis of trying to impose additional cultural controls and religious structures. As an example of Orthodox pressures, when Begin formed his first coalition government in 1977, the religious parties took advantage of this change in the political status quo to push for changes in the religious status quo as well. Thirty-five of the forty-three clauses in the 1977 multiparty coalition agreement submitted to the Knesset dealt with religious questions.

Since the early 1970s, neo-Orthodox youths have been more assertive and less defensive in their religious observance—a charge leveled against their elders in the 1950s and 1960s. The "knitted skullcap generation" of the post-June 1967 War era has in some ways replaced the Labor Zionist kibbutzniks of a former era as the pioneering vanguard of Israeli society. Meanwhile, the ultra-Orthodox in 1988 were as willing as ever to challenge secular authorities, on the streets and with violence if need be, to protect their prerogatives and to preserve the special character of their enclave communities.

The results of these trends have been twofold: a growing traditionalization of Israeli society in terms of religion, and the sharpening of conflict between the extremist Orthodox and their sympathizers and the secularists who oppose the Orthodox Jews and their agendas. Despite the sharp rift, a sort of modus vivendi has emerged, which is what the status quo agreements intended. But the status quo itself has not been stable or stagnant; on the contrary it has been dynamic, gradually shifting toward religion.

Jewish Ethnic Groups

The division of Jewish Israelis into ethnic groups is primarily a legacy of the cultural diversity and far-flung nature of the Jewish Diaspora: it is said that Jews have come to modern Israel from 103 countries and speak more than 70 different languages. As in the United States, the immigrants of yesterday became the ethnic groups of today. But Jewish ethnicity troubles many Israelis, and since the late 1950s it has sometimes been viewed as Israel's major social problem.

There are two principal sources of concern. First, in a rather utopian way, Zionism was supposed to bring about the dissolution of the Diaspora and the reconstitution of world Jewry into a single, unified Jewish people. The persistence of cultural diversity—

Jewish ethnicity in a Jewish state—was simply inconceivable. Second, the socialist Labor Zionists assumed that the Jewish society of Israel would be egalitarian, free of the class divisions that plagued Europe. Instead, along with the growing, industrializing economy came the usual divisions of class, stratification, and socioeconomic inequality. These class divisions seemed to coincide with ethnic divisions: certain kinds of ethnic groups were overrepresented in the lowest classes. For utopian thinkers, the persistence of Jewish ethnic groups was troubling enough; their stratification into a class structure was unthinkable.

The Ashkenazi-Oriental Distinction

The two dominant Jewish ethnic groups in Israel are the Ashkenazim (the term comes from the old Hebrew word for Germany), which now includes Jews from northern and eastern Europe (and, later, their descendants from America); and Sephardim (the term comes from the old Hebrew word for Spain), which now includes Jews of Mediterranean, Balkan, Aegean, and Middle Eastern lands. There are differences in ritual and liturgy between these two groups, but both sides have always recognized the validity and authority of the other's rabbinical courts and rulings. Nor, throughout the centuries, were scholars or notables from either branch totally isolated from the other. In some countries, Italy for example, communities representing both groups lived together. Originally, Ashkenazi meant one who spoke Yiddish, a dialect of German, in everyday life and Sephardi meant one who spoke Ladino (see Glossary), a dialect of Castilian Spanish. Although this narrow understanding of Sephardim is still retained at times, in Israeli colloquial usage, Sephardim include Jews who speak (or whose fathers or grandfathers spoke) dialects of Arabic, Berber, or Persian as well. In this extended sense of Sephardim, they are now also referred to as the Edot Mizrah, "the communities of the East," or in English as "Oriental Jews."

Whereas the Ashkenazi-Sephardi division is a very old one, the Ashkenazi-Oriental division is new to Israel. The term "Oriental" refers specifically to Israelis of African or Asian origin. This geographical distinction has developed over the years into a euphemism for talking about the poor, underprivileged, or educationally disadvantaged (those "in need of fostering," in the Hebrew phrase). Some social scientists as well as some Sephardi activists have seen a sort of self-fulfilling prophecy in this classification. Many Sephardim will not refer to themselves as Orientals.

The heterogenous nature of the Oriental segment of Israeli Jewry is sometimes lost when someone speaks of "the" Oriental community, or collects census data (as does the Central Bureau of Statistics) on the basis of the "continent of origin" ("Europe-America versus Africa-Asia") of its citizens and residents. The category "Oriental" includes Jews from Moroccan and Yemeni backgrounds—to take only two examples that span the range of the Arabic-speaking world. These two communities see themselves, and are seen by other Israelis—particularly Ashkenazim—very differently. Yemenis enjoy a positive self-image, and they are likewise viewed positively by other Israelis; the Moroccans' self-image has been more ambivalent, and they are often viewed by others as instigators of violence and crime. Although this image has become something of a stereotype, Moroccan Jews did instigate acts of violence against the Labor Party in the 1981 elections, and statistically their communities have tended to have a high crime rate. In a similar way, Iraqi, Iranian, and Kurdish Jewish ethnic groups all differ from one another in matters of self-perception and perception by other Israelis. They differ also according to such indices as income (for example, Iraqis are more concentrated in the middle class, Kurds in the lower classes), orientation to tradition (Yemenis are probably the most religious of all non-Ashkenazi groups, Iranians are relatively secular), and so on. These differences are likely to continue, moreover, as marriage statistics in the 1980s indicate a higher rate of endogamy among members of Oriental ethnic groups, as compared to the Ashkenazim. As an ethnic group in the 1980s, Ashkenazim have become much more culturally homogeneous than the Orientals.

The Second Israel

Before 1882 Sephardim or Oriental Jews were the majority, about 60 percent, of the Jewish population in Palestine. Although Oriental Jews did immigrate between this period and that of the British Mandate—more than 15,000 came from Yemen and Aden Protectorate between 1919 and 1948—they were a minority, about 10 percent of all immigrants. Thus, by 1948 Ashkenazim accounted for 77 percent of the population of the new State of Israel. But this was to change quickly in the period of mass migration that followed the establishment of the state. Between 1948 and 1951 Oriental immigrants accounted for 49 percent of all immigrants; in the Jewish calendar year 1952-53 they comprised 70 percent, and from 1954 to 1957 (following the Sinai Campaign and turbulence in North Africa), African-born Jews, the majority from Morocco, constituted 63 percent of all immigrants. By 1958 almost the entire Jewish populations of Yemen, Aden, Libya, and Iraq had immigrated.

The new state was barely equipped, and had few of the resources needed, to handle this influx. The immigrants were housed in tented "transition camps" (*maabarot;* sing., *maabara);* and then directed, often without their approval, to some cooperative settlement (immigrants' moshav) or one of the new development towns. In both cases, authorities wanted to disperse the Jewish population from the coast and place the immigrants in economically productive (especially agricultural or light industrial) settings. The results were village or town settlements that were peripherally located, ethnically homogeneous or nearly homogeneous, and the poorest settlements in the nation.

The lack of resources, however, was not the only obstacle to the successful integration of the Oriental immigrants. Although their intentions were noble, in practice the Ashkenazim viewed their Oriental brethren as primitive—if not quite savage—representatives of "stone age Judaism," according to one extreme phrase. Paternalism and arrogance went hand in hand; the socialist Labor Zionists, in particular, had little use for the Orientals' reverence for the traditional Jewish criteria of accomplishment and rectitude: learnedness and religious piety. In the transition camps and the new settlements, the old elite of the Oriental communities lost their status and with it, often, their self-respect. The wealthy among them had been obliged to leave most of their wealth behind; besides, more often than not, they had been merchants or engaged in some "bourgeois" profession held in low esteem by the Labor Zionists. The rabbis and learned men among them fared no better with the secular Zionists but they were often patronized as well by representatives of the Ashkenazi religious parties, who respected their piety but evinced little respect for the scholarly accomplishments of rabbinical authorities who did not discourse in Yiddish. The religious and secular political parties knew, however, that the immigrants represented votes, and so, despite their patronizing attitudes, at times they courted them for support. In the early years, the leftist predecessor parties to the Labor Party even tried adding religious education to their transition camp schools as a way of enrolling Orientals.

The transition camps were largely eliminated within a decade; a few became development towns. But the stresses and strains of immigrant absorption had taken their toll, and in July 1959 rioting broke out in Wadi Salib, a slum area in Haifa inhabited mostly by Moroccan Jews. The rioters spread to Haifa's commercial area, damaging stores and automobiles. It was the first violence of its kind in Israel, and it led to disturbances in other towns as the summer progressed. Israelis were now acutely aware of the ethnic problem, and soon afterward many began to speak of Israel Shniya, the "Second Israel," in discussing the socioeconomic gaps that separated the two segments of society. In the early 1970s, violent protests again erupted, as second-generation Orientals (mostly Moroccans), organized as the "Black Panthers" (named to great effect after the American Black protest group of the same period) confronted the Ashkenazi "establishment," demanding equality of opportunity in housing, education, and employment. Prime Minister Meir infuriated them even more by calling them "not nice boys."

This remark underscored the perception of many Orientals that when they protested against Israel's establishment they were largely protesting against the Labor Party and its leaders. Many Orientals came to see the Labor Party as being unresponsive to their needs, and many also blamed Labor for the indignities of the transition camps. These were legacies that contributed to Labor's fall from power in 1977; but, in fact, Oriental voters were turning away from Labor and toward Herut, Menachem Begin's party, as early as the 1965 national elections.

The Oriental protest movements, however, were never separatist. On the contrary, they expressed the intense desire of the Oriental communities for integration—to be closer to the centers of power and to share in the rewards of centrality. For example, some of the Black Panthers were protesting against their exclusion from service in the IDF, the result in most cases of previous criminal convictions. This desire was also reflected in the Orientals' turn to Labor's opposition, Herut and later Likud, as a means of penetrating power centers from which they felt excluded—by supporting the establishment of new ones.

Ethnicity and Social Class

The Orientals' electoral rejection of Labor and embrace of Likud can thus be seen as the political part of a larger attempt to try to lessen the socioeconomic gaps that have separated these two broad segments of Israel's Jewry. The gaps are reflected in the close correlation between Israel's class structure and its ethnic divisions along several critical dimensions, among them educational achievement, occupational structure, housing, and income.

In education, the proportion of Orientals in junior high schools and high schools has risen through the years, but in the late 1980s a gap remained. For example, in 1975 the median years of schooling for Ashkenazim was 9.8, compared with 7.1 for Orientals. In 1986, although both groups enjoyed increased schooling, the median for Ashkenazim was 12.2 years, compared with 10.4 for

Oriental Jews. Despite the expansion of higher education in Israel after the June 1967 War, Orientals lagged considerably behind Ashkenazim in their presence in institutions of higher education. In the 1984–85 school year, only 14 percent of university degree recipients were of Oriental heritage, up from 10.6 percent a decade earlier.

In terms of occupational structures, Oriental Jews were still overrepresented in the blue-collar occupations. In 1982, for example, 36.6 percent of Oriental immigrants and 34.5 percent of second-generation Orientals were employed in the blue-collar sector. Among Ashkenazim, 25.2 percent of the immigrant generation, and 13 percent of the next (sabra or native-born) generation were employed in the blue-collar sector. Among professional and technical workers, the proportion for Orientals rose from 9 percent in the immigrant generation to 12 percent in the sabra generation, clearly some improvement. Nevertheless, in the same occupations among Ashkenazim, professional and technical employment rose from 15.5 percent in the immigrant to 24.7 percent in the Ashkenazi sabra generation. In the sciences and academia, the gap has remained much larger, in generational terms.

As a result of differential income levels and larger families, Orientals have lagged behind Ashkenazim in housing. In 1984 Ashkenazi households averaged 3.1 persons per room, as compared with 4.5 per room in Oriental households. In 1984 the income of the average Oriental family was 78 percent of that of the average Ashkenazi family—the same proportion as it had been in 1946, and down 4 percent from what it was in 1975. Studies of the regional distribution of income indicated that development towns, most with large Oriental populations, ranked well below the national average in income. Data comparing the period 1975–76 with that of 1979–80, however, indicated a significant improvement in Oriental income status. In this period, there was a decrease in the proportion of Oriental Jews defined as "poor" (having incomes in the lowest 10 percent of the population). These data on education, occupation, and income indicate that although Oriental Jews have made progress over the years, the gaps separating them from Ashkenazim have not been significantly reduced. Moreover, these gaps have not been closing under Likud governments any more quickly or substantively than they had been under Labor.

The close correlation between ethnicity and socioeconomic class in Israel remains the main axis along which the Ashkenazi-Oriental cleavage is drawn. The "hardening" of ethnicity into social class— what some analysts have referred to as the formation of Israeli "ethnoclasses"—represents, with the Orthodox-secular division, the most serious cleavage that divides the Jewish society of Israel from within. In Israel's class structure in the late 1980s, the upper classes were predominantly Ashkenazi and the lower classes predominantly Oriental. Mobility has been most evident in the movement, even though gradual, by Orientals into the large middle class.

Those Sephardim, however, who do rise to the middle class are unlikely to think of themselves as Orientals. They identify more with Ashkenazi patterns—in family size, age at termination of childbearing, nature of leisure activities, and the like. Upwardly mobile Orientals loosen their ties with their own ethnic groups, and for them the term "Oriental" is reserved for the poor or underprivileged. This phenomenon has been seen by some as a sort of co-optation of upwardly mobile Orientals by Ashkenazi Israelis. Oriental upward mobility has strengthened the correlation for those who do not rise in class between Oriental ethnicity and low class standing. This correlation has led some analysts to speak of Oriental cultural patterns as essentially the culture of a particular stratum of society, the "Israeli working class." To some extent, too, Oriental culture patterns mitigate the integrationist effect of Ashkenazi-Oriental "intermarriage," estimated at nearly 30 percent for women of Oriental heritage who have nine or more years of schooling.

The social manifestations of this rift, however, have been more evident in the political arena than in the economic. Since the mid-1970s, Orientals have comprised a numerical majority of the Jewish population. Thus far, the beneficiaries of this majority have been political parties, often religious ones and typically right-of-center, that have ranged themselves in opposition to Labor. The height of Ashkenazi-Oriental ethnic tensions occurred in the national elections of the 1980s—especially 1981—in which anti-Labor sentiment was expressed, sometimes with violence, as anti-Ashkenazi sentiment. That Orientals supported in those elections the Likud Bloc led by Menachem Begin, himself an Ashkenazi from Poland, whose ultranationalist oratory served to inflame the violence, was a paradox that troubled few in Israel at the time. More troubling to many Israelis were the violence and anti-Ashkenazi overtones of the opposition to the peace demonstrations that were organized by Israeli doves in the wake of the 1982 Israeli invasion of Lebanon, and, from the doves' side, the imputation of "anti-democratic" tendencies, en masse, to the Orientals.

Some commentators have referred to these recent crystallizations as the "new Oriental ethnicity." Unlike the Oriental ethnicity of the 1970s, it has been less concerned with promoting festivals,

An Arab village scene in the occupied West Bank
Courtesy Palestine Perspectives

pilgrimages, and other cultural events, and more explicitly focused on political power. In the 1980s, self-consciously Oriental minor political parties have reentered the political arena, the first serious and successful ones since the Yishuv and early years of the state.

To some extent, the new ethnicity dovetailed with the new civil religion, the new Zionism, in its positive orientation to traditional Judaism and its negative orientation to the modern secularism of Labor Zionism. In this sense, the new ethnicity has contributed to the traditionalization of Israeli society. But the two movements are not identical. As a group, for example, Oriental Jews—although they are hawkish on the question of the occupied territories—have been less committed than many ultranationalist Ashkenazim to the settlement of the West Bank. The primary reason has been that Orientals see such costly efforts as draining resources into new settlements at the expense of solving serious housing problems in the cities and development towns of pre-1967 Israel.

Around issues such as the Jewish settlement of the West Bank can be seen the complicated interplay of ethnicity, religion, politics, and social class interests in contemporary Israeli society. In the late 1980s, the Ashkenazi-Oriental distinction continued to be colored by all these factors. Both Israeli and foreign observers believed that the Ashkenazi-Oriental rift would remain salient for many years, partly because it was a source of social tensions in Israel and partly because it was a lightning rod for them.

Minority Groups

The non-Jewish—almost entirely Arab—population of Israel in the mid-1980s comprised 18 percent of the total population (these figures refer to Arabs resident within the pre-1967 borders of Israel). More than three-fourths were Sunni (see Glossary) Muslims. Among Muslim Arabs the beduins, concentrated in the Negev, were culturally and administratively distinctive. They numbered about 29,000, divided among about forty tribally based factions. There were approximately 2,500 (non-Arab) Sunni Muslim Circassians, concentrated in two small villages in Galilee. Among non-Muslim Arabs were Christians of various affiliations: Greek Orthodox, Greek Catholics, Roman Catholics, Anglicans, and Protestants of different sects; the Greek Orthodox community being the largest of the Christian groups. In addition, there were Armenians who belonged to several Christian churches (see also Population, this ch.).

Another tiny minority group was that of the Samaritans, of whom about 500 remained in Israel in the late 1980s. The Samaritans are thought to be descendants of the Jews who lived in the area at the time of the Exile in Babylon beginning in 722 B.C. and who intermarried with the local inhabitants. Their religion resembles the form of ancient Judaism.

In addition, Israel contained a small number of adherents of Bahaism, an offshoot of Shia Islam. They are followers of Mirza Husayn Ali, known as Baha Ullah (the glory of God), who claimed leadership of a community founded by an Iranian spiritual leader known as the Bab (the way), in the 1850s, after the Bab was executed as a heretic. Bahais have a syncretistic faith that incorporates elements of Islam, Christianity, and universal ethical principles. Their governing body, the Universal House of Justice, which consists of elected representatives from various national spiritual assemblies, acts as supreme administrative, legislative, and judicial body for Bahais, and is located in Haifa.

As a result of a high birth rate and improved health and sanitation conditions, the total number of Israeli Arabs in 1988 (exclusive of those in the West Bank and Gaza Strip) was about equal to (and was expected soon to surpass) what it was in 1947 Palestine under the British Mandate. During and immediately after Israel's War of Independence, approximately 600,000 Arabs left the country of their own volition or were expelled; most went to Jordan's West Bank or the Gaza Strip, and some to Lebanon and the Persian Gulf states. In 1948 many had expected to return to their homes (or to take over abandoned Jewish property) in the wake of victorious Arab armies. Instead, they have come to constitute the Palestinian diaspora, whose disposition has proved fateful to the history of many states in the modern Middle East.

Israel's Arabs are guaranteed equal religious and civil rights with Jews under the Declaration of the Establishment of the State of Israel. They have voted in national elections and sent members to the Knesset since 1949; following the 1984 elections, seven Arabs sat in the Knesset. Nevertheless, until the end of 1966, Israel's Arabs lived under a military jurisdiction that severely limited their physical mobility and ranges of permissible political expression. They have also lost much land to the Israeli government, a good deal of it expropriated by the army for "security purposes," but much more turned over to Jewish settlements in attempts to increase the Jewish presence in northern and western Galilee, the centers of Arab population.

In social and economic terms, the state has sought to dominate its Arab minority by encouraging dependence. This aim has been achieved, for example, by providing funding for the separate Arab (Muslim, Christian, and Druze) school systems, as well as access to Jewish institutions of higher learning, and by providing funding for health facilities, religious institutions, and courts. Many of these institutions have encouraged the maintenance of Arab spheres of interaction segregated from Jewish ones. But the real dependency has resulted from the integration of Arab labor into Israel's economy. This has entailed an acute deemphasis on agriculture (abetted by government expropriations of arable land) and a funneling of labor into industry, especially construction, and into services. Under the British Mandate, for example, about two-thirds of all Arabs worked in agriculture. By 1955, this figure dropped to 50 percent of Arab labor employed in the agricultural sector, 36 percent in industry and construction, and almost 14 percent in services. By the early 1980s, less than 12 percent were engaged in agriculture, 45 percent in industry and construction, and close to 43 percent in the service sector. Along with this proletarianization of Arab labor—the loss of its agrarian base—has come the urbanization of its population. In 1948 less than one-fourth of the Arab population lived in cities or towns; by the 1980s more than two-thirds did.

Yet another way in which the government has related to its Arab minorities has been by encouraging internal segmentation, primarily along religious lines, in the Arab communities. Thus Muslims, Christians, and Druzes have been differentially treated. (So have the beduins, who are Muslims but are culturally distinctive as pastoralists from Muslim Arab village and town dwellers; and so have the Circassians, who although Muslims are not Arabs. Like Christians, beduins may volunteer for service in the army, and some do; like the Druzes, Circassians are conscripted.) Differential treatment almost always has favored Christians and Druzes over Muslims; at least this has been the semi-official "policy." Some ethnographic and sociological studies of Arab villages, however, indicate that other Israeli policies have had the effect of weakening the Christian and Druze position and strengthening that of Arab Muslims.

In the past, Christian dominance, for example, was based on the control of agrarian resources in villages. The dismantling of the agrarian bases of the Arab economy and the proletarianization of Arab labor led to Arab dependence on the Jewish economy. But it did so at the expense of the wealth, and thus the political standing, of Christians. Similarly, the building and support of village and town schools open to all created an educated (and underemployed) Muslim cadre whose intellectual energies have tended to flow into antiestablishment politics.

The Druzes

The case of the Druzes is a special one. The Druzes belong to an eleventh century offshoot of Shia (see Glossary) Islam, which originated in Egypt. They soon migrated northward, settling first along the western slopes of Mount Hermon, and thence westward into the Shuf Mountains of Lebanon, south to Galilee and Mount Carmel, and east into Syria. In 1988 there were approximately 318,000 Druzes in Syria and 182,000 in Lebanon. Including the Druze population of the Golan Heights, annexed by Israel in December 1981, there were about 72,000 Druzes in Israel. This number represented a large increase from the 1948 population of about 13,000. Besides the Golan Heights, in the late 1980s Druzes lived in seventeen villages in Galilee and around Mount Carmel. Of these, nine were all Druze and the rest mixed, mostly with Christian Arabs. Less than 10 percent of Druzes in Israel lived in cities— compared to more than 60 percent of Christians.

The Druze religion is known mainly for being shrouded in secrecy, even from large groups of Druzes themselves, the *juhhal*, uninitiated or "ignorant ones." The *uqqal*, the "wise," or initiated, undergo periods of initiation, each signaling an increased mastery of the mysteries of the faith. Although there is a formal separation between religious and political leadership, the wise ones (particularly the *ajawid*, or excellent, among them) have traditionally

The Church of All Nations
and a Russian Orthodox
church, both near the Garden
of Gethsemane, Jerusalem
Courtesy Jean E. Tucker

Haifa, with a view
of the Bahai Temple
Courtesy Les Vogel

123

wielded considerable political influence. The religion is fiercely monotheistic and includes an elaborate doctrine of the reincarnation and transmigration of souls. It shares with Shia Islam the doctrine of practicing *taqiya,* the art of dissimulation in hostile environments. In the past this practice meant seeming to worship in the manner of the conqueror or dominant group, without apostasy. In more recent times, some observers note, it has meant being loyal to the state in which they reside, including serving in its army.

Because the Druze religion was considered schismatic to Islam, even to Shia Islam, Druzes occasionally suffered discrimination and persecution at the hands of Muslims and, like other Middle Eastern dissidents, inhabited marginal or easily defensible areas: mountain slopes and intermontane valleys. Because the Druzes have long enjoyed a reputation for military prowess and good soldiery, they have often not suffered discrimination or persecutions lightly or without responding in kind. Whether because of the desire to settle old scores, or because the doctrine of *taqiya* can be stretched in this direction, Druzes have been remarkable in being a non-Jewish, Arabic-speaking group that has supported the Jewish state, both in the late Mandate period and since Israel's independence through service of Druze young men in the IDF and the paramilitary Border Police. About 175 Druzes have been killed in action, including a large proportion of that number in the 1982 invasion of Lebanon.

Jewish Israelis have recognized this service and sought to reward it. Druze villages had military supervision and restrictions lifted from them about four years before other Arab areas. Since 1977 there has been a Druze member of the Knesset from the right-of-center Likud, and under Labor they have served in highly visible positions such as that of presidential adviser on minority affairs and, at one time, the Israeli consul in New York City. In 1962 Israeli authorities recognized "Druze" as a separate nationality on internal identification cards—previously Druzes were differentiated only under *dat,* religion; their nationality was Arab. Although authorities assured Druzes that recognition as a separate nationality would enhance their most favored status, some analysts and younger Druzes have viewed the identification as an attempt to drive a wedge between them and other Arabs.

Many among the younger generation of Druzes have been partly radicalized in their politics—for a number of reasons. First, the favored status accorded the Druzes has not significantly helped them materially. Druzes have been among the least affluent of all groups in Israel, the number receiving higher education has been low, and few Druzes could be found in top professional or technical positions.

Even those who have made the army their career have complained of severe limitations in promotions. Second, Israeli actions against Druzes in the occupied and then annexed Golan Heights troubled their coreligionists in Israel. Particularly troublesome was the 1982 invasion of Lebanon. During this invasion, Israeli soldiers, as allies of the Lebanese Christians, were opposed by Druzes of the Shuf Mountains. Pitched battles or military encounters between the IDF and the Lebanese Druzes were avoided. Nevertheless, the Lebanese Christian Maronites have been among the Druzes' most bitter enemies, and many Druzes serving in the IDF were killed or wounded in Lebanon. This was a particularly difficult time for Jewish-Druze relations, one from which they had not fully recovered in 1988.

The Arab-Jewish Cleavage

The case of the Druzes highlights the peculiar problem of non-Jews, even demonstrably loyal ones, in the Jewish state. Both conceptually and pragmatically, the cleavage between Arabs and Jews is much more profound and perhaps unbridgeable than the one between Orthodox and secular Jews, or that between Ashkenazim and Oriental Jews. There has been an inherent tension between evolving an authentic Israeli national identity centered on the age-old religious character of Judaism and forging an egalitarian socioeconomic system open to all citizens. Reconciling the place of non-Jews within the Jewish state has been a particular problem. These problems have been characterized with special lucidity and frankness by the Israeli-American political scientist, Daniel Elazar:

> The views of Israeli Jews regarding the Arabs in their midst are hardly monolithic, but whatever their character, all flow out of a common wish and a general ambivalence. The common wish of virtually all Jews is that the Arabs simply would go away (and vice versa, it may be added). It is possible to get many Israelis to articulate this wish when they are pushed to do so, but needless to say, its very unreality means that it is rarely articulated, and, if articulated by a few extremists, such as Meir Kahane, it is rapidly dismissed from consideration by the vast majority. Yet it should be noted at the outset, because for Israeli Jews, every other option, no matter which they choose, is clearly a poor second.

It is against this background that the Israeli settlement policies of the West Bank and Gaza must be understood. To annex these areas would be to add almost 1.5 million Arabs to the non-Jewish population of the Jewish state—hardly a way to make the problem "simply go away." Until late 1987, Israeli planners had proceeded to build infrastructure in the West Bank as though operating under the premise that two totally separate socioeconomic systems—one Arab, the other Jewish—would exist side by side. Alternatively, the Arab sector was hardly mentioned—as if it did not exist. Still, West Bank Arab labor has been significantly absorbed into the larger Israeli economy; the situation recalls the experience of Arabs in pre-1967 Israel.

The violent protests that began in the Gaza Strip and the West Bank in December 1987 may well change this sort of thinking (see Palestinian Uprising, December 1987– , ch. 5). For example, it has been argued by some analysts that the West Bank (as Judea and Samaria) had already become part of a "cognitive map" for a generation of Jewish Israelis born after the June 1967 War. In light of this analysis, some have noted that security efforts begun in April 1988 to close off the West Bank, thereby keeping journalists (among others) out and, Israelis hope, violent Palestinians in, have already had the unintended effect of reviving the old Green Line (see Glossary). Israeli Arabs living within the old Green Line have also been affected by events on the West Bank and Gaza— events that might prove fateful for Israel.

Between 1948 and 1967 Israeli Arabs were effectively isolated from the rest of the Arab world. They were viewed by other Arabs as, at worst, collaborators, and, at best, hostages. After the Israeli occupation of the West Bank and Gaza and the economic integration of its Arab population into Israel, social intercourse between Israeli Arabs and West Bank and Gaza Palestinians increased. Among other things, this contact has done much to raise the political consciousness of Israeli Arabs and strengthen their sense of Palestinian identity. In this sense, in the minds of many Jewish Israelis the dismantling of the old Green Line and the movement of Jewish settlers to fulfill their religio-nationalistic aspirations in biblical Judea and Samaria has been a double-edged sword. Along the way, the nationalist aspirations of Israeli Arabs have been invigorated as well.

Renewed political activity among Israeli Arabs was already evident when, in 1976, March 30 was proclaimed Land Day as a protest against Israeli expropriations of Arab lands. Several Arabs were shot by authorities during a demonstration, and since then Land Day has become a major event for expressing Israeli Arab political discontent, and for testing its organizational potential. Since early 1988, the political energies of Israeli Arabs have also been focused on expressing solidarity with their West Bank and Gazan brothers and sisters, who themselves have pursued more violent confrontations with Israeli authorities. It seems less and less likely that an unproblematic Israeli Arab identity will develop and that the Israeli Arabs will become, as Israeli Jews had once hoped, "proud Arabs and loyal Israelis." In the late 1980s, it was more relevant to speak of the Palestinization of Israel's Arab minorities.

Distinctive Social Institutions

Israeli society in the late 1980s continued to be characterized by a number of distinctive institutions. Some, like the Histadrut, were legacies of the socialist aspects of Labor Zionism, with its commitments to the socioeconomic reconfiguration of the Jewish people and the establishment of an egalitarian and industrial nation-state society. Others, like the kibbutz and moshav, stemmed from these values but combined them with the practical problems posed by the need to pioneer and settle the land. Still others—the *ulpan* (Hebrew school for immigrants) or the *merkaz klita* (absorption center)—arose from the need to settle and integrate large numbers of Jewish immigrants from diverse lands and cultures.

The Histadrut

The Histadrut (short for HaHistadrut HaKlalit shel HaOvdim B'Eretz Yisrael—The General Federation of Laborers in the Land of Israel) was founded in December 1920 as the primary representative of Jewish labor in Palestine; it has accepted Arabs as full members since 1969. When founded the Histadrut claimed 4,500 members; in the 1985 Histadrut elections more than 1.5 million members were eligible to vote.

Much more than a labor union, the Histadrut was also, next to the government itself, the second largest employer in Israel, through its many cooperative economic enterprises—in industry, building trades, banking, insurance, transportation, travel agencies, dairy cooperatives, and so on—organized under Hevrat HaOvdim, the Histadrut's holding company (see Overview of the 1948–72 Period, ch. 3). The Histadrut also operated pension and social service programs, the most important of which was Kupat Holim (the Sick Fund), the largest provider of health care to Israelis (see Health, this ch.). The Histadrut published *Davar,* a liberal Hebrew daily newspaper, and owned Am Oved, a major publishing house. In addition, the collective and cooperative agricultural settlements—kibbutzim and moshavim—founded by the Labor-Zionist parties belonged to Histadrut, which marketed their products through its various cooperatives. The dual character of the Histadrut, as both the largest trade union federation in the country and the second largest employer, has sometimes led to difficulties with both the government and labor. A long doctors' strike in the summer of 1983, for example, caused much rancor.

Kibbutz and Moshav

The first kibbutz, Deganya, near the Sea of Galilee, was founded in 1910. In addition to the two largest kibbutz federations, HaKibbutz HaMeuhad (the United Kibbutz Movement) and HaKibbutz HaArtzi (the Kibbutz of the Land), there were in 1988 a number of small movements including the agricultural collective settlements of the religious HaKibbutz HaDati, affiliated with the labor wing of the National Religious Party. In 1986 there were 125,700 residents of about 265 kibbutzim, divided among five kibbutz federations. The kibbutz is a collective settlement, originally devoted solely to agriculture, but since the late 1960s, it has included industrial concerns, too. Founded by ardent socialists, kibbutzim are characterized by the collectivization of labor and capital: the means of production, consumption, and distribution are communally owned and controlled, with considerable emphasis on participatory democracy in the operation of kibbutzim. Education and, in some federations, the rearing of children in age-graded dormitories, are communal as well.

Until the 1980s, the kibbutz and its residents played a larger-than-life role in Israeli society. Kibbutzim embodied the courageous and selfless pioneer who settled the most difficult and dangerous areas to claim them for the Jewish state. They sent the highest proportion of young men to elite units of the army and its officers' corps, and later to positions of responsibility in the Histadrut and the government. If there were a sociopolitical elite in Israel (not an economic one, because members of the kibbutz lived with simplicity), it came from the kibbutzim.

This highly positive image no longer held in 1988 for a number of reasons. First, the kibbutz was to a large extent a victim of its own successes. Its economic success raised the standard of living of the average member into the solid middle or upper middle class. It is difficult to conceive of a rural village with air-conditioned housing, a well-equipped clinic, a large auditorium, and an olympic-sized swimming-pool as a pioneer outpost. Second, the economic success and the expansion of the kibbutz economy has forced it to go outside the community to hire labor—a direct contradiction of its earliest canons. Third, the membership of kibbutzim has been overwhelmingly Ashkenazi. Often the labor hired, if not Arab, consisted of Oriental Jews who resided in development towns near the kibbutz. Oriental Jews complained that the only time they saw members of kibbutzim as near equals was when the members came to town just before national elections to lobby the Orientals for votes for the left-of-center parties aligned with the kibbutzim. The turn of the mass of the Israeli electorate to the right wing was both a reflection and a cause of the loss of social prestige for the kibbutz, which has suffered a relative loss of influence in the centers of power in Israel. Nevertheless, the kibbutzim still contributed to Israel's economy and sociopolitical elite out of proportion to their number.

The first moshav was established in the Jezreel, or Yizreel, Valley (Emeq Yizreel is also seen as the Valley of Esdraelon in English) in 1921. In 1986 about 156,700 Israelis lived and worked on 448 moshavim, the great majority divided among eight federations. There are two types of moshavim, the more numerous (405) moshavim *ovdim,* and the moshavim *shitufim.* The former relies on cooperative purchasing of supplies and marketing of produce; the family or household is, however, the basic unit of production and consumption. The moshav *shitufi* form is closer to the collectivity of the kibbutz: although consumption is family- or household-based, production and marketing are collective. Unlike the moshavim *ovdim,* land is not allotted to households or individuals, but is collectively worked.

Because the moshav form retained the family as the center of social life and eschewed bold experiments with communal child-rearing or equality of the sexes, it was much more attractive to traditional Oriental immigrants in the 1950s and early 1960s than was the more communally radical kibbutz. For this reason, the kibbutz has remained basically an Ashkenazi institution, whereas the moshav has not. On the contrary, the so-called immigrants' moshav (moshav *olim*) was one of the most used and successful forms of absorption and integration of Oriental immigrants, and it allowed them a much steadier ascent into the middle class than did life in some development towns.

Like the kibbutzim, moshavim since 1967 have relied increasingly on outside—particularly Arab—labor. Financial instabilities in the early 1980s have hit many moshavim hard, as has the problem of absorbing all the children who might wish to remain in the community. By the late 1980s, more and more moshav members were employed in nonagricultural sectors outside the community, so that some moshavim were coming to resemble suburban or exurban villages whose residents commute to work. In general moshavim never enjoyed the elite status accorded to kibbutzim; correspondingly they have not suffered a decline in prestige in the 1970s and 1980s.

The Ulpan *and* Merkaz Klita

Immigration has always been a serious Israeli concern, as evidenced by the ministerial rank given to the chief official in charge of immigration and the absorption of immigrants. Various institutions and programs have helped integrate immigrants into Israeli society. Perhaps the most ubiquitous is the *ulpan* (pl., *ulpanim*—see Glossary), or intensive Hebrew language school. Some *ulpanim* were funded by municipalities, others by the Ministry of Education and Culture, the Ministry of Immigrant Absorption, or the Jewish Agency. Because they were heavily subsidized, *ulpanim* were free or charged only nominal fees to new immigrants. Some were residential, offering dormitory-like accommodations with board. They were mainly intended for single immigrants and offered half-day instruction in a course that lasted six months. The municipal *ulpanim* offered less intensive night classes. Many kibbutzim also ran *ulpanim,* which combined half-day language instruction with a half day's labor on the kibbutz. In the late 1970s, when immigration to Israel was high, about 23,000 individuals were enrolled in some sort of *ulpan.*

The *merkaz klita,* or absorption center, was developed in the late 1960s to accommodate the increased immigration that occurred between 1969 and 1975 of relatively well-off and educated Jews from the West, particularly from the United States. These centers combined the *ulpan* with long-term (often exceeding one year) accommodation for families. With representatives of all the major ministries ideally on hand or on call, these centers were supposed to cushion the entry of the new immigrant into Israeli society. They were a far cry from the often squalid transition camps of the 1950s, a fact that did not go unnoticed by many Oriental Jews. In the late 1970s, at the height of immigration from the United States, there were more than twenty-five absorption centers housing almost 4,000 new immigrants. Taking all the forms of such immigrant-absorption institutions together—centers, hostels (for families without children) and residential *ulpanim*—almost 10,000 persons were living in some form of them in early 1976. As of 1988 the occupancy had declined, as had Western immigration to Israel.

Education

Education in Israel has been characterized historically by the same social and cultural cleavages separating the Orthodox from the secular and Arabs from Jews. In addition, because of residential patterns and concentrations—of Orientals in development towns, for example—or because of ''tracking'' of one sort or another, critics

Campus of Hebrew University, Jerusalem
Courtesy Les Vogel

have charged that education has been functionally divided by an Ashkenazi-Oriental distinction, as well.

Before 1948 there were in the Jewish sector alone four different, recognized educational systems or "trends," each supported and used by political parties and movements or interest groups. As part of the prestate status quo agreements between Ben-Gurion and the Orthodox, this educational segregation, favored by the Orthodox, was to be protected and supported by the state. This system proved unwieldy and was the source of intense conflict and competition, especially as large numbers of immigrants arrived between 1948 and 1953. The different parties fought over the immigrants for their votes and over the immigrants' children for the chance to socialize them and thus secure their own political future. This conflict precipitated several parliamentary crises, and in 1953 resulted in reform legislation—the State Education Law—which reduced the number of trends to two: a state-supported religious trend and a state-supported secular trend. In reality, however, there were still a few systems outside the two trends that nevertheless enjoyed state subsidies: schools run by the various kibbutz federations and traditional religious schools, yeshivot (sing., yeshiva—see Glossary), devoted to the study of the Talmud, run by the ultra-Orthodox Agudat Israel and others. In the 1986–87 school year, about 6 percent of all Jewish primary school students were enrolled in yeshivot, about 22 percent in state religious primary schools, and about 72 percent in state secular primary schools. These figures remained constant throughout secondary education as well. Throughout this period and in 1988, Arab education was separately administered by the Ministry of Education and Culture and was divided by emphases on Muslim, Christian, or Druze subjects (see table 3, Appendix A).

Israeli youth were required to attend at least ten years of school, in addition to preschool. The education system was structured in four levels. Preschool was available to children between the ages of three and six; it was obligatory from age five. Primary education ran from grades one through six; grades seven, eight, and nine were handled in intermediate or junior high schools. Secondary education comprised grades ten through twelve. Secondary schools were of three main types: the general academic high school, which prepared students to take the national matriculation examination, passage of which was necessary to enter university; vocational high schools; and agricultural high schools. The latter two schools offered diplomas that allowed holders to continue in technical or engineering fields at the postsecondary level but did not lead to the matriculation exam. The Ministry of Labor and the Ministry of Agriculture shared with the Ministry of Education and Culture some responsibilities for curriculum and support of vocational and agricultural schools. Education through the intermediate school level was free. Before 1978 tuition was charged in secondary schools, and many argued that this discriminated against the poor, especially Orientals. A January 1984 reform imposed a reduced monthly fee of approximately US$10 in secondary schools.

Israeli education has often been at the center of social and ideological controversy. In the late 1950s and early 1960s, sociological surveys indicated that youth attending the state secular system were both ignorant of and insufficiently attached to "traditional Jewish values," which included a sense of kinship with Diaspora Jewry. A Jewish Consciousness Program was then hastily implemented, but results were considered mixed. Most observers of Israeli education believed that the events of the June 1967 War, and the subsequent trauma of the October 1973 War, from which followed the increasing political isolation of Israel, did more than any curriculum to reinstill a sense of Jewish national identity in Israeli youth.

Meanwhile, in the 1960s the state religious system, particularly at the high school level, underwent its own transformation, which many analysts considered to have had far-reaching effects on Israeli society. The state religious system has always included a high proportion of Oriental students from traditional homes. Middle class Ashkenazim began to complain of the "leveling effects" the Orientals were having, and more specifically of the teachers (who were accused of not being pious enough) and the curriculum (criticized for giving insufficient attention to the study of the Talmud).

In response to this dissatisfaction, activists from the youth organization of the National Religious Party, the Bene Akiva (Sons of Rabbi Akiva), in the 1960s fashioned an alternative religious high school system, in which academic and religious standards were much higher than in the usual state religious high school. This alternative form soon attracted many middle class, Ashkenazi youth from the older state religious high schools. In addition to having a more rigorous academic curriculum, the new system was also strongly ultranationalistic, as reflected in the form known as the yeshiva *hesder,* which combined the traditional values of the European talmudic academy with a commitment, on the part of its students, to serve in the IDF. These institutions have turned out a generation of self-assured religious youth who are not apologetic about their piety—something they accused their elders of being. Israelis referred to them as the "knitted skullcap generation," after their characteristic headgear (as distinguished from the solid black cloth or silk skullcaps of the ultra-Orthodox). Over the years, they have been more aggressive than their elders in trying to extend Orthodox Judaism's political influence in the society at large as well as within the territorial boundaries of the Jewish state. Many of these graduates have been instrumental in shaping the New Zionism.

Arab education in Israel followed the same pattern as Jewish education, with students learning about Jewish history, heroes, and the like, but education is in Arabic. Arab education in East Jerusalem and the West Bank followed the Jordanian curriculm and students sat for Jordanian examinations; the textbooks used, however, had to be approved by Israeli authorities. After the outbreak of the *intifadah* (uprising) in December 1987, frequent school closings occurred so that students attended school only infrequently (see The Palestinian Uprising, December 1987– , ch. 5).

Higher Education

In the late 1980s, seven universities existed in Israel: the Technion (Israel Institute for Technology, founded in 1912); the Hebrew University (1925); Tel Aviv University (begun in 1935, functioning fully since 1956); Bar-Ilan University (1955); Haifa University (1963); Ben-Gurion University of the Negev (1965); and the postgraduate Weizmann Institute of Technology (1934). Higher education in Israel has grown tremendously since independence: in the 1948–49 academic year a total of 1,635 students attended degree-granting institutions, whereas in 1986–87 the figure was 67,160. In terms of enrollments, the largest institution was Tel Aviv University (19,400 students in 1986–87), followed by Hebrew University (16,870), Bar-Ilan (9,480), the Technion (9,090), Haifa (6,550), Ben-Gurion University (5,200), and the Weizmann Institute (570).

Israeli universities have not been isolated from the larger problems of society. High inflation and budget cutbacks have hit them severely since the late 1970s; many observers have expressed fear of a potential ''brain-drain'' as talented academics, unable to find suitable employment in Israel, emigrate. There have been repeated calls to increase the number of Israelis of Oriental background in colleges and universities, at the same time that charges of ''compromised standards'' have been advanced. The university campuses have also been centers of political activity among all shades of the political spectrum in Israel, including Arab students.

Youth Movements and Organizations

During the Yishuv period and in the early 1950s, youth movements associated with political parties were important institutions of political education and socialization. Affiliated branches even existed in the European and American diasporas. They were training grounds for future members, and especially for the future elite, of the parties. Each party of any size had one: Mapam (the original Labor-oriented youth movement was HaShomer HaTzair—see Appendix B), Herut (Betar—see Appendix B), National Religious Party (Bene Akiva), as well as the Histadrut and other organizations. The fate of these youth movements over the years has reflected the broader changes that have occurred in Israeli society. The relatively apolitical and nonideological Boy Scout organization has grown; left-of-center movements have not. The Bene Akiva, on the other hand, has also grown, more than threefold since 1960. In the late 1980s, it enrolled more than 30,000 Israeli religious youths, who make up a large part of the ''knitted skullcaps.'' The Bene Akiva has acted as a training ground for many of the young extremist and right-wing Orthodox political activists who have gained prominence since the June 1967 War.

Health

In part as a legacy of the socialist thrusts of Labor Zionism, Israelis enjoy a widely available health care system. The major

Housing built in the 1950s and 1960s for immigrants
Courtesy Les Vogel
Geometric designs characterize housing
in Ramot Allon, East Jerusalem

135

complaints of the population have focused on the heavy bureaucratization of health care. In general, the health of the population compares favorably with West European standards, and the decrease in rates of infectious diseases has been very marked. The highest incidences of disease in 1986 were bacillary dysentery, 162 per 100,000, and viral hepatitis, 75 per 100,000. There were reportedly forty-three cases in Israel of acquired immune deficiency syndrome, or AIDS, by the end of September 1987.

In both Arab and Jewish populations, control of sanitation also has improved markedly since the the mid-1950s. Still, health care delivery has been better developed for the Jewish sector than for the Arab sector. In 1985 the life expectancy of Jewish men and women was 73.9 and 77.3 years, respectively; for non-Jews the figures were 72.0 (men) and 75.8 (women). Among Jews, in 1986 the live birth rate per 1,000 was 21.2, the death rate 7.5. Among Muslims the live birth rate per 1,000 was 33.8, the death rate 3.4. The average number of children a woman may have during her lifetime was 2.83 for Jews and 4.63 for Muslims. The infant mortality rate was 9.6 for Jews and 18.0 for Muslims (see table 4, Appendix A).

The Ministry of Health, the principal public health agency in the country, functioned as the supreme body for licensing medical, dental, nursing, pharmaceutical, and paramedical professions, as well as for implementing all health-related legislation passed by the Knesset. It also functioned when no other nongovernmental agency was present. This fact was important in Israel because in 1985–86 the sick funds contributed almost 45 percent of the national expenditure on health; in comparison, the government contributed only some 22 percent. Kupat Holim, the largest sick fund, was affiliated with the Histadrut and was supported by almost two-thirds of the Histadrut's membership dues. As the largest medical insurance carrier in Israel, the Histadrut fund covered about 70 percent of the population (Arabs included). Another 20 percent was covered by the sick funds of other organizations, which means that in general the Israeli population was well protected by health care coverage. Further evidence of the availability of health care was the ratio of physicians to the general population; in the 1970s it was more than 1 to 400, one of the highest in the world.

Welfare

The Ministry of Social Welfare began its work in June 1948, carrying on the mission of the Social Welfare Department established in 1931 under the Mandate. The National Insurance Act of 1953 and the Social Welfare Service Law, passed by the Knesset in 1958, authorized a broad range of welfare programs, including old age and survivors' pensions, maternity insurance, workers' compensation provisions, and special allowances for large families. Retirement age was seventy for men and sixty-five for women, but persons were eligible for some benefits five years before retirement age. The Histadrut was also a principal provider of pensions and a supplier of insurance. In addition, there were a number of voluntary agencies, many funded by Diaspora Jewry, that contributed significantly to the social welfare of Israelis.

Special subventionary programs, including low-interest loans, subsidized housing, and rent or mortgage relief, were available to new immigrants after 1967 through the Ministry of Immigrant Absorption and the World Zionist Organization. At times these programs have been criticized by native-born Israelis or long-time settlers in the lower income brackets, especially for benefiting relatively well-to-do immigrants from the West. Even more controversial have been benefit programs designed to aid returning Israeli emigrants readjust to life in Israel.

* * *

Of the numerous books on Israeli society, Michael Wolffsohn's *Israel, Polity, Society and Economy, 1882–1986* is a veritable compendium of demographic information and social indicators. *Israel: Building a New Society,* by Daniel Elazar is lucidly written and closely argued. Sammy Smooha's *Israel: Pluralism and Conflict* explains the major social rifts discussed in this chapter and contains useful statistical information in detailed appendices. More concise, and focused upon the post-Begin era, is Peter Grose's *A Changing Israel.* For two views of Israel by Israelis, see Amos Elon's *The Israelis: Founders and Sons* and Amos Oz's *In the Land of Israel.* Finally, the *Political Dictionary of the State of Israel,* edited by Susan Hattis Rolef, contains many valuable entries on aspects of Israeli society and politics.

On religion in Israel, the most comprehensive treatment remains S.Z. Abramov's *Perpetual Dilemma: Jewish Religion in the Jewish State.* More analytical is *Religion and Politics in Israel* by Charles S. Liebman and Eliezer Don-Yehiya. Their civil religion thesis is developed at greater length in *Civil Religion in Israel.* Also recommended is an article by Shlomo Deshen, ''Israeli Judaism: Introduction to the Major Patterns,'' in the *International Journal of Middle East Studies.*

On the waves of Oriental immigration and the settlement of Oriental Jews, see *Nation-Building and Community in Israel* by Dorothy Willner. A series of anthropological studies covers this period especially well. These include *Cave Dwellers and Citrus Growers,* by Harvey Goldberg; *Immigrants from India in Israel,* by Gilbert Kushner; and *The Dual Heritage: Immigrants from the Atlas Mountains in an Israeli Village,* by Moshe Shokeid. Myron J. Aronoff's *Frontiertown: The Politics of Community Building in Israel* is a study of a development town in the same period. Also recommended is *The Predicament of Homecoming,* by Shlomo Deshen and Moshe Shokeid. The best book on Oriental ethnicity is the collection edited by Alex Weingrod, *Studies in Israeli Ethnicity: After the Ingathering.* On more recent immigration, see *American Immigrants in Israel: Social Identities and Change,* by Kevin Avruch; for a comparison of American with Soviet immigrants, see Zvi Gitelman's *Becoming Israelis: Political Resocialization of Soviet and American Immigrants.*

A critical study of Israeli education in a development town may be found in *Power, Poverty, and Education* by Arnold Lewis. The classic study of a kibbutz is Melford E. Spiro's *Kibbutz: Venture in Utopia.* On Israeli Arabs, the most comprehensive and balanced study is Ian Lustick's *Arabs in the Jewish State,* although events in late 1987 and early 1988 have overtaken its main theme, the explanation of Israeli Arab political quiescence. On the Druzes, see Gabriel Ben-Dor's *The Druzes in Israel: A Political Study.* On West Bank Arabs, the collection *Palestinian Society and Politics,* edited by Joel S. Migdal, is recommended, as is Meron Benvenisti's continuing *West Bank Data Project.* The *Journal of Palestine Studies* is an important resource as well, containing useful articles such as that by Elia Zureik.

The Israel Pocket Library, which contains material originally published in the *Encyclopedia Judaica,* has several books in the series that address aspects of Israeli society. These include *Society, Religious Life, Jewish Values,* and *Education and Science.* The material in these books is now dated but still valuable for the period before the October 1973 War. (For further information and complete citations, see Bibliography.)

Chapter 3. The Economy

A woman with a hat typical of headgear worn by kibbutz members

SINCE THE FOUNDING of Israel in 1948, the Israeli economy has experienced two distinct periods: one spanning the years 1948 through 1972, and another stretching from 1973 to 1988. The three prominent features of the Israeli economy during the first period were the ingathering of the exiles (resulting in a very high rate of population growth), considerable importing of capital, and rapid growth of total and per capita gross national product (GNP—see Glossary). During this period, the Israeli economy grew at a very rapid rate, averaging an annual GNP increase of 10.4 percent annually.

Between 1973 and 1986, by contrast, GNP growth declined to about 2 percent per annum, with no increase in per capita output. At the same time, the rate of inflation—which from 1948 through 1972 was in single digits—increased to a high of 445 percent in 1984. In 1975, 1983, and 1984, the Israeli economy came close to exhausting its potential sources of short-term financing to cover its balance of payments deficits.

In July 1985, the government instituted an emergency program to interrupt the hyperinflation that was threatening the survival of the economy. By the end of 1985, the rate of inflation had been reduced to 20 percent. Even more remarkable was the elimination of the government's budget deficit in fiscal year (FY—see Glossary) 1985. At the beginning of FY 1986, the budget deficit remained close to zero. The emergency program ended fourteen years of steadily worsening inflation and devaluations and reversed years of government overspending. The relative stability the program achieved was seen as the necessary precondition to an assault on the underlying structural shortcomings responsible for the slow growth of the economy since 1973.

Overview of the 1948–72 Period

The years immediately following the state's creation in 1948 were difficult for the Israeli economy. The new state possessed no natural or financial resources, no monetary reserves, little economic infrastructure, and few public services. A sizable portion of the existing Arab population fled the new state, while impoverished and afflicted Jewish refugees poured in from the European displaced persons camps and, later, from the Arab countries. In contrast to the 1930s, when Jewish immigrants to the Yishuv (or prestate Israel)

141

had arrived with ample financial and human capital, after 1948 most immigrants lacked the wealth and skills needed by the new state.

The new state had to supply food, clothing, shelter, and employment for its new citizens; set up civil and community services; and establish an independent foreign exchange, monetary, and fiscal system. Given the shortage of private capital, the burden of dealing with these problems naturally fell upon the public sector. The financial capital needed to deal with the influx of immigrants was drawn either from the high level of domestic savings, or from capital imports (such as foreign loans and grants), or foreign private sector investments (such as Israeli bonds). The government's solution to the capital shortage included an austerity program of stringent price controls and rationing. The government also decided to promote investment projects in agriculture and housing through the use of public funds rather than through private capital markets. The public sector thus gained control over a large part of Israel's investment resources and hence over the country's future economic activity.

The result of this long-term state intervention was the development of a quasi-socialist economy, which, in terms of ownership, was divided into three sectors: private, public, and Histadrut (see Glossary), the abbreviation of HaHistadrut HaKlalit Shel HaOvdim B'Eretz Yisrael (General Federation of Laborers in the Land of Israel). The Histadrut, the umbrella organization of trade unions, quickly became one of the most powerful institutions in Israel. Although Histadrut-owned enterprises generally behaved like privately owned firms, the collective nature of the labor organization precluded the timely demise of economically inefficient enterprises. Public sector firms were owned by local authorities and quasi-governmental bodies such as the Jewish Agency (see Glossary). As in the case of the Histadrut-run corporations, criteria other than profit maximization dominated the economic operation of these firms.

The Israeli service sector, therefore, became totally dominated by the government and the Histadrut. Histadrut-affiliated cooperatives achieved a near monopoly in such areas as public transport and the production and marketing of many agricultural products. The Jewish Agency acquired Israel's two major banks, which together made up 70 percent of the banking system; and the two largest insurance companies were (and in 1988 continued to be) owned by the Histadrut (see Financial Services, this ch.).

The importance of the government and the Histadrut was not limited to the service sector. They became increasingly involved in the industrial sector as well. Whereas the percentage of plants owned by the public and Histadrut sectors in 1972 was less than 2.5 percent, their share of total industrial employment was 27 percent. Similarly their share of total industrial output in 1972 was 34 percent. This situation continued until 1988, when discussions were initiated to decrease government control of business activity.

The major factor accounting for the increased role in industry of the public and Histadrut sectors was the development of Israel's defense industry. After the June 1967 War and the French arms embargo that followed, the Israeli government decided to build as many domestic weapons systems as it could. In the 1980s, companies such as Israel Aircraft Industries and Israel Military Industries continued to be state owned and among the largest firms in the country. The Histadrut-owned Tadiran Electronic Industries became a major defense contractor and the state's largest electronics firm. Similarly, the government-owned Israel Chemicals Limited and its subsidiaries held the sole rights to mine potash, bromine, and other raw materials in the Dead Sea area. The oil refineries, as well as the retail gas distributors, were also mostly government owned.

Economic Growth and Structural Change

Between 1948 and 1972, Israel's GNP rose by more than 10 percent per annum on average. Thereafter, Israel's growth rate slowed to an annual average of 2 percent. Not only was Israel's economic growth rate much lower after 1972, it was also far less stable. The reasons most often cited for this slowdown include a sharp increase in defense spending, the 1982–83 energy crisis, and increased expenditures on social welfare.

A breakdown of Israel's GNP into categories of consumption, investment, government expenditures, and net exports for the years 1960 through 1986, highlights some of the difficulties experienced by a small, open economy burdened with a massive defense expenditure. During this period, Israel experienced chronic current account deficits and increased government expenditures. The trade deficit, which accounted for an average of 20 percent of annual GNP from 1960 through 1964, reached a high of 35 percent in 1973. It declined to 16 percent in 1986, however, primarily because the real value of exports increased while the real value of imports remained unchanged.

Until the June 1967 War, defense spending ranged from 10 to 16 percent of GNP. Between 1970 and 1982, however, defense spending escalated to over 25 percent of GNP—a high ratio, even for the volatile Middle East. A significant share of defense spending

143

originated from military imports. In the aftermath of the October 1973 War, military imports equaled 17 percent of GNP. About one-quarter to one-third of this defense expenditure was paid for by United States aid. After 1984 the increase in United States aid reduced the defense burden in Israel virtually to pre-1967 levels. In 1986, the defense burden declined to 10 percent of GNP.

The sharp upturn in world oil prices in 1973 increased the cost of oil imports by more than 3 percent of GNP in that year. The oil price increases of 1979, which occurred at about the same time as the return to Egypt of the Sinai oil fields, are estimated to have had an even more devastating effect on the Israeli economy. The total direct losses to the Israeli economy caused by the increase in energy prices from 1973 to 1982 have been estimated at US$12 billion—the equivalent of one year's GNP.

In addition to these external shocks, the economy had to accommodate substantial increases in spending on domestic welfare programs in the early 1970s. In response to domestic social unrest, the government introduced large-scale social programs to improve education, housing, and welfare assistance for the urban poor. These programs were designed before 1973, but were implemented after the economy had begun to stagnate.

Slowdown of Economic Growth

The economy's behavior during the 1961–72 and 1973–88 periods was starkly different. The growth of capital stock declined modestly from an 8.9 percent annual increase during the first period to a 6 percent annual increase during the second period. A major decline occurred, however, in gross domestic product (GDP—see Glossary). From a 9.7 percent annual growth rate in the first period, GDP fell to a 3.4 percent annual growth rate in the second period. Furthermore, labor inputs (measured either as employed persons or total hours of work) declined from the first to the second period. The annual increase in employed persons from 1961 through 1972 averaged 3.6 percent; employed persons increased only 1.5 percent annually from 1973 through 1981. Similarly, total hours worked increased by an annual rate of 3.9 percent during the first period as compared to 1 percent during the second period. If the growth of the economy is measured as GDP per employed person, then Israeli performance declined from 6.1 percent to 1.9 percent over the two periods. If GDP per hour of work is used, Israel's performance declined from 5.8 percent to 2.4 percent. Finally, if GDP growth is measured per unit of capital, it declined from 0.8 percent a year between 1961 and 1972 to −2.6 percent a year from 1973 through 1981.

View of the National Water Carrier
that brings water from the north to foster agriculture in the Negev
Courtesy Embassy of Israel, Washington

Until 1973 the rise in labor and capital productivity was the major growth-generating ingredient in the Israeli economy, accounting for about 43 percent of total output growth and for 72 percent of the increase in output per worker hour. By contrast, beginning in 1973, increases in capital stock accounted for 64.7 percent of total growth. The contribution of labor and capital productivity to total output declined to 18 percent, and its contribution to the increase in output per worker hour declined to 25 percent. Between 1961 and 1981, the relative contributions of capital per unit of labor and of total labor and capital productivity to the increase in labor productivity were reversed. In large part, this reversal explains the slowdown in Israel's growth after 1972.

Three factors apparently led to a decline in the growth of business sector employment from 1973 through 1981. First, the growth rate of new people entering the labor force dropped, primarily because net immigration declined from an annual increase of 3.8 percent in the 1961–72 period to 2.5 percent in the 1973–81 period. Second, because of the increase in the income tax rate at higher levels of income, the average rate of labor force participation among men declined from 73.6 to 64.9 percent, while the rate for women increased from 29.2 to 33.4 percent. Fewer families found it worthwhile for the husbands to work at higher-taxed, high-paying jobs;

instead, the wives worked at lower-paying, lower-taxed jobs. Finally, the influx of Arab employees from the West Bank and the Gaza Strip declined in the 1973–81 period. In all, the share of business sector employment relative to the whole economy declined from 77.2 percent in the 1961–72 period to 73.6 percent in the 1973–81 period.

By 1988 the potential sources of large-scale net immigration had almost run dry. Since 1979 (as of 1988, 1979 was the last year during which the Soviet Union had permitted large numbers of Soviet Jews to leave) the rate of net immigration had been low; during several years, it had been surpassed by emigration. In 1987 immigration increased slightly, although this addition to the labor pool was insufficient to increase Israel's growth rate. The immigration of Oriental Jews had also decreased significantly by the 1980s. Given the low probability of sizable immigration from the United States or the Soviet Union, observers concluded that a return to the rapid economic growth of the 1950s and 1960s depended on Israel's ability to substitute alternative sources of sustained growth. Possibilities in this area were the new, science-based and high technology industries.

Changes in Investment Patterns

Gross investment reached an exceptionally high level of 30 percent of GNP in the period ending in the early 1970s, but subsequently dropped to 20 percent of GNP in 1986. While this figure is substantially lower than that achieved by earlier Israeli performance, it is internationally an acceptable standard of investment and private savings.

Nonetheless, concern existed in Israel about the extent of public-sector debt. Since 1973 the government has incurred a substantial domestic and foreign debt that has resulted in a significant reduction in the proportion of private savings available for investment. From 1970 through 1983, private savings averaged slightly above 10 percent of GNP. The success of the Economic Stabilization Program adopted in July 1985 in order to cut back on government spending led to an increase in private saving, however; by 1986, private savings stood at 21 percent of GNP.

Unlike the unstable trend in private savings recorded in the banking sector, investment in housing has taken a consistently high share of GNP, hitting a 40 percent peak in 1980. This high level of investment in housing, which many economists argue is not justified economically, further constrained the rise of gross business investment. For example, despite the rise of the share in GNP of gross investment in manufacturing during the 1970s, Israel's

1982–86 average share of 4 percent clearly is below international norms.

The lack of uniformity in government investment incentives and in the rate of return on capital within the manufacturing sector may be responsible for the mix of Israeli investments. Economists generally agree that inefficiencies have arisen as a result of excessive substitution of capital for labor, underused capacity, and inappropriate project selection. Government policy has been identified as the primary factor causing capital market inefficiencies by crowding out business investment, creating excessively high average investment subsidies, and introducing capital market controls based on inefficient discretionary policy.

The 1967 Law for the Encouragement of Capital Investment provided for the following incentives to "approved-type" enterprises: cash grants, unlinked long-term loans at 6.5 percent interest, and reduced taxes. The Treasury assumed full responsibility for any discrepancy between the linked rates paid to savers and the unlinked rates charged to investors. Because inflation in the mid-1970s reached levels close to 40 percent, the real interest rate paid on long-term loans was close to −30 percent per annum, with a total subsidy on long-term loans reaching a high of 35 percent in 1977. These extremely favorable interest rates and implied subsidies led to an excessive substitution of capital for labor.

The investment system has been characterized by the following factors: private firms generally are not allowed to issue bonds, the government establishes the real interest paid to savers and the nominal interest paid by investors, and the economy is plagued by high and unpredictable rates of inflation. These conditions have maintained an excess demand for investment. The result has been a continuous need to ration loans—and an implicit role for government discretion in project approval. Thus, since the late 1960s, as a result of capital market controls, the government has been making industrial policy.

Changes in Industrial Structure

The industrial structure of the economy can be seen in terms of the allocation of GDP, employment, and foreign capital among the tradable, nontradable, semitradable, and service sectors. The tradable sector includes agriculture, manufacturing, and transportation; nontradables include public services and construction; and semitradables include business and financial services, commerce, tourism, and personal services. Public services include the activities of government, national institutions, and local authorities;

147

education, research, and scientific organizations; health, religious, political, and trade-union groups; and defense.

Up to 1981, the economy allocated approximately 40 percent of its GDP to the tradable sector and about 33 to 35 percent to the nontradable sector. This distribution was mirrored in the allocation of civilian employment across the two sectors. The size of the public service sector in 1981 was 21 percent of GDP and 28 percent of civilian employment. Some economists argue that this latter figure is very high relative to the international norms for a developing country. It is not high, however, when compared to developed socialist countries in Europe. Some economists also argue that Israel's high level of nontradables can be explained by the high level of capital inflows from abroad, by a high demand for public services and construction as a result of immigration, and by defense needs.

From 1955 through 1972, the real output of tradables increased relative to that of nontradables. Most of this increase was attributable to the importance of physical capital in the form of machinery and increased productivity. After 1972 the importance of machinery declined, while that of labor increased. Educated workers were being absorbed into the public and financial services; simultaneously, manufacturing productivity was declining. Increased demand favored nontradables, and the share of tradables in both employment and output further declined. The overriding factor remained the rapid increase in the educated labor force.

Changes in Labor Force

In the 1950s and 1960s, through a state effort to absorb the large number of immigrant children into the public school system, the government assured itself of a future supply of educated workers. The demand for more educated workers was provided by the rapid expansion of public services, which are inherently human-capital intensive. Growth in public services resulted from the rapid and sustained economic growth that lasted until the early 1970s, and from the high rate of population growth.

In the 1970s, the education level of the labor force continued to rise markedly. Unlike the experience of other Western economies, the increased supply of educated workers in Israel did not, on average, depress the relative wage level of those with more schooling; nor did it markedly worsen the employment condition of more educated workers as compared with workers with a secondary education. The continued increase in demand for education-intensive services and for more sophisticated goods and services generally have so far precluded the negative effects experienced

A self-propelled irrigation machine in operation in the Negev Desert
Courtesy Embassy of Israel, Washington
Growing tomatoes under plastic
near the Sea of Galilee
Courtesy Embassy of Israel, Washington

in other countries. The widespread high level of human capital is
expected to continue into the twenty-first century as long as investment in education continues to be profitable.

The Public Sector

The two most important tools of economic policy in Israel have
been the budget and foreign exchange control. Through the budget,
the government can deal with all financial activities of the public
sector. Defined in its broadest terms, the public sector includes the
central government, local authorities, and national institutions
(where the central government clearly dominates). In 1986 government and private nonprofit institutions represented about 20
percent of GDP, which was about a 20 percent increase over
the public sector's importance in 1968. Similarly, the provision of
government-owned housing and rental services increased by 28 percent, rising from 8.4 percent of GDP in 1968 to 11 percent in 1986.
Overall, in 1986 the business sector represented 69 percent of GDP,
whereas the public sector, in all of its dimensions, represented 31
percent of GDP.

Government Budget

By 1988 the government had been operating under a deficit for
more than a decade. Between 1982 and 1984, the deficit equaled
between 12 and 15 percent of GNP. After the implementation of
the July 1985 Economic Stabilization Program, the government
succeeded in balancing its budget (see The Economic Stabilization Program of July 1985, this ch.). This balance was achieved
not only because the government raised taxes and reduced spending, but also because the reduced inflation increased the real value
of tax revenues. During FY 1986, the expansion of the economy
compensated for the reduction in direct and indirect taxes. The
government also initiated plans to reduce further its public debt
(see table 5; table 6, Appendix A).

Before the July 1985 reforms, the tax system was considered to
be very progressive on individual income but barely touched corporate income. After the reforms, which included a new corporate
tax law, large sums of taxes were collected from business sectors
that previously had been untaxed. Personal income tax ranged from
a base rate of 20 percent (payable on incomes equivalent to about
US$500 per month) to a top rate of 60 percent on a monthly income
of about US$2,100. Corporate income tax generally was 45 per-
cent. Few corporations, however, actually paid this rate once various government subsidies were included in the calculation.

Moshav Margalit in Galilee
Courtesy Embassy of Israel, Washington

Provision of Civilian Services

Civilian public services have employed a high proportion of the labor force and consequently have absorbed a high share of Israel's GNP. Spending on health, education, and welfare services rose from 17 percent of GNP in 1968 to 20 percent in the early 1970s. The level of spending on civilian public services remained constant at about 20 percent through 1986. The share of the total civilian labor force employed in civilian public services rose from 22 percent in 1968 to 30 percent in 1986.

The civilian services primarily responsible for these high outlays were education and health services, whose share increased from 50 percent of the total in 1969 to more than 60 percent in 1986. At the other end of the scale were economic and general services, whose expenditures declined from 33 percent of the total in 1969 to 23 percent in 1986. The share of other welfare services (including immigrant absorption services) remained constant. The decline of general and economic services reflected a transfer of some of these functions from the public sector to the business community and a decline in direct government intervention in the economy.

Unlike social welfare and economic services, which were directly funded by the government, until the early 1970s education and health services received substantial funding from foreign sources.

151

In 1968, for example, the government financed only 70.5 percent of Israel's education services. By 1978 the government's share had increased to 84.5 percent. Whereas in 1968 the Jewish Agency financed about 20 percent of the total national expenditure on education from foreign aid funds, by 1978 only 7.6 percent came from foreign aid, and this percentage has decreased further since. The result was an added burden on the taxpayer, equal to approximately 22 percent of the national expenditure on education. Direct private financing of education expenditures contracted from 9.5 percent of the total in FY 1968 to 1.7 percent in FY 1978. The key element explaining this latter drop was the institution of free, compulsory secondary education in the late 1970s.

Health services' funding followed a similar pattern. The government's share rose from 53 percent in 1968 to 62 percent in 1980. Here, however, the Jewish Agency's participation decreased even more sharply, from 20 percent of the total national expenditure on health in 1968 to nearly zero in 1980. The added burden of government financing from internal sources over the decade was almost 30 percent.

In both health and education, the trend illustrated a transition from foreign financing to internal resources and a switch from direct private financing (and independent fundraising by nonprofit institutions) to the imposition of a greater burden on the central fiscal system. In the past, when these services were expanded, the cost often was carried by aid from abroad. As this source began to dwindle, the cost increasingly shifted to the government, which for political reasons could not reduce these public civil expenditures.

Provision of Defense Services

Throughout its existence, Israel has been obliged to devote a considerable part of its resources to national defense. Since 1973, Israel's annual defense expenditure has equaled that of the Netherlands and exceeded that of Sweden. In per capita terms, Israel's expenditure has been two to three times as large as theirs. Defense expenditures in the Netherlands and Sweden each amounted to 3 to 4 percent of GNP in FY 1976; in Israel, they amounted to more than 25 percent of GNP. The persistence of a high defense expenditure over a very long period makes Israel's situation unique.

The simplest definition of the defense burden is the total budgeted resources diverted to defense and thus precluded from other uses by citizens. Other resource costs include the opportunity cost of labor working for the defense sector and therefore unavailable to other sectors, thus reducing civilian output. Finally, foreign currency spent on military imports is unavailable for civilian imports.

Although estimates of the defense burden suffer from inadequate data, the Central Bureau of Statistics publishes data on the noncivilian component of public consumption, which is used as a proxy for defense expenditures. Apart from the war years of 1967 and 1973, the annual fluctuations have been dominated by long-term changes in defense costs (commonly referred to as "ratchets" or step functions). By 1986 defense expenditure had declined to a range from 10 to 16 percent of GNP, depending on the measure used.

These official data do not include information on forfeited earnings of conscripted soldiers, forfeited earnings of persons on reserve duty, and costs of casualties, stockpiling, civil defense, land devoted for army training, and many other government and civilian expenditures ascribed to defense. Although it is impossible to assign a rough order of magnitude to the items mentioned, some economists have speculated that they are not insignificant components of the civilian public sector. This becomes clear when one considers that the length of time devoted to conscription, reserve duty, and regular army duty has been lengthened (see Conscription; Reserve Duty, ch. 5). Government defense functions involved in operations in the West Bank and the Gaza Strip add a further cost to the defense burden.

The cost of defense also includes direct defense imports and military aid from the United States. In FY 1986, Israel received United States military aid in the range of US$3 billion. A large share of these funds has regularly been spent in the United States (see table 7, Appendix A).

On the other side of the defense-burden equation are the beneficial by-products associated with military activity. The most important benefits are education, absorption of immigrants, agricultural settlement, and the development and manufacture of weapons and equipment. An example of these beneficial by-products was the development of the Kfir interceptor, which created jobs for technicians and laborers (see Defense Industries, ch. 5). In short, when estimating Israel's defense burden it is important to consider the cost reductions implicit from these beneficial by-products.

Taxation

From 1961 to 1983, government expenditures grew far more rapidly than Israel's GNP, primarily because of the sharp increase in defense outlays from the latter half of the 1960s through the 1970s. Taxation was insufficient to finance the increase in government spending. Although gross taxes increased, net taxes declined continuously during the period. To meet the deficit, the government resorted to domestic and foreign borrowing.

By the mid-1970s, the government increasingly relied on foreign sources to finance the domestic deficit. These growing debts were equivalent to almost 14 percent of each year's GNP, during a time when GNP was growing at less than 2 percent a year.

In the second half of the 1970s, the tax system collected approximately 47 percent of GNP, compared with 35 percent in the 1960s and 41 percent in the first half of the 1970s. This rise occurred mainly in direct taxes and taxation of domestically produced goods, while taxes on imports declined by a small margin. During FY 1981, direct taxes represented 25.7 percent of GNP; they were 14.3 percent of GNP in FY 1961. Taxes on domestic production represented 12 percent of GNP in FY 1981, a decline from the FY 1961 high of 13.9 percent. The introduction of the value-added tax on both domestic and foreign goods added a tax base of 8.7 percent of GNP in FY 1981.

In FY 1986, income taxes collected represented 33 percent of GNP. Value-added taxes represented 20 percent of GNP and customs duties represented 4 percent of GNP. In late 1987, the government announced plans to revamp the tax structure in the light of the 1985 Economic Stabilization Program (see The Economic Stabilization Program of July 1985, this ch.).

Industry

The Histadrut directly owns or controls a significant portion of Israeli industry. The separation of industries among the public, private, and Histadrut sectors of the economy, however, is not a simple one. Many important enterprises are partners with either or both the Histadrut and the government. Most big industrial concerns, such as the Nesher cement and Shemen vegetable oil plants, are owned either solely by Histadrut (through its industrial conglomerate, Koor Industries) or in partnership with private investors. About 10 percent of FY 1985 industrial output was produced by joint ventures of the private and Histadrut sectors.

In FY 1985, private-sector industrial ownership was as follows: electronics, 51 percent; textiles, 92 percent; clothing, 97 percent; machinery, 61 percent; food and tobacco, 60 percent; leather goods, 80 percent; wood products, 72 percent; paper products, 81 percent; and printing and publishing, 86 percent.

Manufacturing, particularly for export, has been a major component of GDP. In FY 1985, manufacturing contributed 23.4 percent of GDP. Industrial production grew at a rate of 3.6 percent in 1986, compared with 3 percent in 1984. Most of this growth has been in export products. For many years, export growth was led by the electronics and metallurgic industries, especially in the field of military equipment. In the 1980s, exports from the textile, clothing and fashion industries expanded, as did exports of food products of various sorts. Following a slump in the 1980s, diamond exports made a strong recovery after 1985 (see table 8, Appendix A).

Electronics

In the 1980s, high-technology industries received the greatest attention from the government. Israeli electronics companies competed worldwide and in some cases were leaders in their fields. Israel's Scitex was a leading image-processing firm, Laser Industries led in laser surgery, Elbit led in defense electronics, and Fibronics led in fiberoptic communication. In 1985 the electric and electronic equipment industry represented 4.5 percent of industrial establishments, 12 percent of industrial employment, and almost 13 percent of industrial revenues.

Despite the success of the electronics industry in the 1980s, experts predicted that in the 1990s this sector will face a shortage of engineers and technicians. A major reason for this shortage is the lower net pay for engineers in Israel relative to the United States. An identical 1985 gross salary of US$30,000 in Israel and in California would generate a net income of US$9,000 in Israel and US$20,000 in California. Although the Israeli would consume a higher amount of social services than his or her counterpart in California, a wide gap would remain between the two salaries. As long as this gap exists, Israel will have difficulty keeping skilled engineers.

Biotechnology

Israel's biotechnology industry is relatively new and an offspring of its American counterpart. Its creation in the late 1960s resulted from the establishment in Israel of subsidiaries of foreign pharmaceutical companies. The first of these was a subsidiary formed by Miles Laboratories with the Weizmann Institute of Technology, called Miles-Yeda. This was followed by the Hebrew University-Weizmann Institute subsidiary, Ames-Yissum. Over time, these firms became wholly Israeli-owned entities. Gradually, foreign venture capitalists began to initiate other independent biotechnology entities in Israel. As of the early 1980s, Israeli venture capitalists had begun creating their own science-based entities.

Many economists call biotechnology a "natural" Israeli industry. Its primary input has been data from research and university laboratories. The only other major ingredient has been American capital to support research and development activity. The main areas of research in the mid-1980s included genetic engineering,

155

human and animal diagnostics, agricultural biofertilization, and aquatic biotechnology.

Diamonds

Israel's diamond industry in the 1980s differed considerably from its 1950s' version. Until the early 1980s, a handful of large firms dominated the Israeli diamond industry. The nucleus consisted of European Jewish cutters who had immigrated during the Yishuv. In the 1970s, Israel surpassed Antwerp as the largest wholesale diamond center, accounting for more than 50 percent of all cut and polished gem diamonds. Diamonds were the only export in which Israel was more than a marginal supplier.

Unlike other industries, the diamond industry was affected entirely by external factors not under Israeli control. The diamond industry imported rough diamonds, cut and polished them, and then exported them. The slump in the industry from 1980 through 1982 surprised many Israeli firms that had speculative stockpiles. The result was a complete restructuring of the industry in FY 1984, and the creation of approximately 800 new and smaller manufacturing units. These small entities in mid-1986 concentrated exclusively on cutting, leaving the marketing to larger export firms. This latter task was supported by the 2,000-member Israel Diamond Exchange and the 300-member Israel Precious Stones and Diamonds Exchange, together with the quasi-governmental Israel Diamond Institute.

The success of this revitalization can be seen in the trade figures for the industry. In 1982 net diamond exports were US$905 million, equal to 18 percent of total exports; in 1986, however, diamond exports had grown to nearly US$1.7 billion, or approximately 24 percent of total exports.

Chemicals, Rubber, and Plastics

The chemical industry began in the early 1920s, when a small plant was started to extract potash and bromine from the Dead Sea. In the past, the chemical industry concentrated on the sale of raw materials, such as potash and phosphates, and their processed derivatives. In the early 1980s, the industry undertook a comprehensive research and development program, which has substantially transformed it. Helping Israel to become one of the world's largest chemical-producing nations was the industry's development of new treatment processes for ceramics, glass, textiles, plastics, and wood. In 1986 the chemicals, rubber, and plastics industries together provided 15.6 percent of total industrial sales and engaged 11 percent of the industrial labor force.

*Western pilgrims on the Via Dolorosa
in the Old City of Jerusalem pass a seller of bagels.
Courtesy Les Vogel*

In the 1980s, Israel Chemicals Limited (ICL)—a government-owned corporation—was the largest chemical complex and also dominated Israel's mineral resources industry. Its subsidiaries included the Dead Sea Works, Dead Sea Bromine, and Negev Phosphates. ICL also was parent to smaller research, desalination, telecommunications, shipping, and trucking firms. In addition, ICL owned Amsterdam Fertilizers in the Netherlands and Broomchemie, Guilin Chemie, and Stadiek Dunger in the Federal Republic of Germany (West Germany).

In the plastics field, Kibbutz Industries Association—a member of the Histadrut—accounted for more than 60 percent of Israel's plastics output and more than 75 percent of plastics exports. Virtually all the successful plastics establishments were kibbutz owned.

Clothing and Textiles

During the mid-1950s, Israel, like other developing countries, promoted the textile and apparel industry to be a ready source of employment. By 1985 the textile and clothing industry was represented by 1,523 establishments. These businesses employed about 46,000 workers (representing 15 percent of industrial workers) and earned revenues equal to approximately US$13 million, or 8.8 percent of total industrial earnings. In 1988 Israel continued

157

to promote this industry as a source of employment for unskilled and semiskilled immigrants and for local Israeli Arab labor.

The textile and apparel industries were characterized by many small firms and a few large, vertically integrated companies (including Polgat Enterprises, considered one of the most efficient producers in the world). Like other Israeli industries, the textile and apparel industry depended for its survival on its ability to export to Europe and the United States. Given the generally high tariff barriers in Europe and the United States on such products, the agreement Israel signed with the European Economic Community (EEC) in 1977, the Israel-EEC Preferential Agreement, as well as the United States-Israel Free Trade Area Agreement (as of 1987) have lowered and will lower further these tariffs, thus making Israeli textile and apparel products marginally competitive. Duty savings were not expected to play a major role in increasing Israel's trade competitiveness in these markets as long as Israeli wages in these industries were higher then comparable wages in Asia. Because they pay higher wages, Israeli textile and apparel producers have continued to concentrate on the more expensive segment of the market.

Construction

In 1987 the construction industry came to a turning point. Whereas in the preceding five years, the construction industry was characterized by a decline in output of about 2 percent per year, in 1987 the output grew at about 8 percent and returned to its 1984 level. The only subsectors where expanding business activity has led to increased demand for space have been electricity, transport, and communications.

The shrinking of the construction sector beginning in the late 1970s became much sharper in the 1980s. This contraction reflected not only an absolute decline in output but also a decline in productivity (over the preceding thirteen years, total productivity had been falling by an average of 2 percent per year). The share of the construction sector in the overall business sector declined from 19 percent in 1972 to 9 percent in 1987. In 1988 the construction period required for residential housing was twice as long as for most industrialized countries in Europe or for the United States.

Tourism

Tourism has always been an important source of foreign currency for Israel. In 1984 this industry earned US$1.08 billion. The Israeli airlines earned an additional US$210 million in tourist-related business. In 1986, 929,631 tourists arrived by air and 18,252 arrived by sea. Another 17,563 tourists arrived from Jordan by land via the Allenby Bridge. Sixty percent of total 1986 tourists originated in Europe; an additional 20 percent originated in the United States.

Although the 1986 figures are respectable, they represent a decline by 13 percent over the preceding three years. Moreover, the 1986 figure for American tourists is 41 percent lower than comparable figures for the years 1983 through 1985. This decline in tourism to Israel in 1986 reflected a general decline in American tourism to the Middle East, which was caused by security considerations and by a weakening of the United States dollar against European currencies.

Energy

Israel depends almost totally on imported fuel for its energy requirements; domestic production of crude petroleum and natural gas is negligible. After the June 1967 War, Israel acquired a large portion of its oil supply from captured Egyptian fields in the Sinai Peninsula. In 1979 these fields were returned to Egypt. Exploration within Israel was continuing in the mid-1980s, with interest centered on the Dead Sea and northern Negev areas, as well as in the Helez region along the coastal plain near Ashqelon (see fig. 8). Despite having spent about US$250 million between 1975 and 1985 searching for oil, Israel remained almost devoid of domestic energy sources. By 1986 domestic and foreign oil exploration in Israel ground to a near halt, although Occidental Petroleum (headed by Armand Hammer) continued its seismic studies in preparation for future drilling.

Because of the failure to find economically worthwhile deposits of fossil fuels, Israel has devoted large sums to developing other energy sources, particularly solar energy. In fact, Israel has long been an acknowledged leader in this field. Overall, the structure of Israel's energy economy has changed considerably since 1973. Between 1982 and 1984, about 50 percent of Israel's electricity came from coal. By 1985 oil-to-coal conversion programs made coal the source of 17 percent of Israel's primary energy. It appeared unlikely in 1988 that a major improvement in Israel's energy balance would occur.

The Arab oil embargo and the Iranian Islamic Revolution have forced Israel to diversify both its coal and oil imports. In 1986 Israel's major sources of coal were Australia, South Africa, and Britain. The bulk of Israel's oil came from Mexico and Egypt.

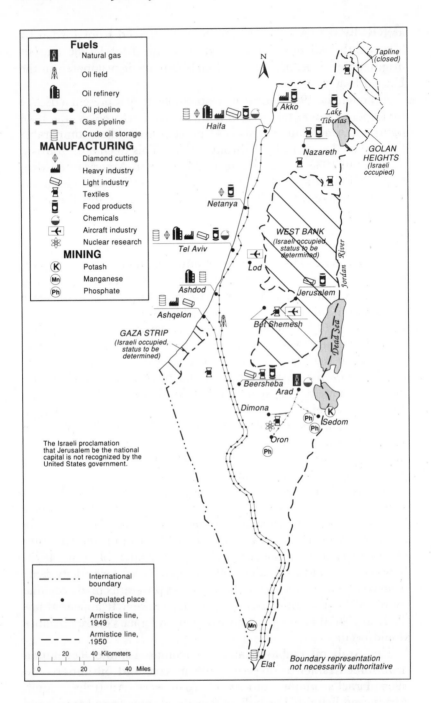

Figure 8. Economic Activity, 1988

Agriculture

Historically, agriculture has played a more important role in Israeli national life than its economic contribution would indicate. It has had a central place in Zionist ideology and has been a major factor in the settlement of the country and the absorption of new immigrants although its income-producing importance has been minimal. As the economy has developed, the importance of agriculture has declined even further. For example, by 1979 agricultural output accounted for just under 6 percent of GDP. In 1985 agricultural output accounted for 5.1 percent of GDP, whereas manufacturing accounted for 23.4 percent.

In 1981, the year of the last agricultural census (as of 1988), there were 43,000 farm units with an overall average size of 13.5 hectares. Of these, 19.8 percent were smaller than 1 hectare, 75.7 percent were between 1 and 9 hectares, 3.3 percent were between 10 and 49 hectares, 0.4 percent were between 50 and 190 hectares, and 0.8 percent were more than 200 hectares. Of the 380,000 hectares under cultivation in that year, 20.8 percent was under permanent cultivation and 79.2 percent under rotating cultivation. The farm units also included a total of 160,000 hectares of land used for purposes other than cultivation. In general, land was divided as follows: forest, 5.7 percent; pasture, 40.2 percent; cultivated, 21.5 percent, and desert and all other uses, 32.6 percent. Cultivation was based mainly in three zones: the northern coastal plains, the hills of the interior, and the upper Jordan Valley.

Agricultural activities generally were conducted in cooperative settlements, which fell into two principal types: kibbutzim and moshavim (see Glossary). Kibbutzim often served strategic or defensive purposes in addition to purely agricultural functions. In the 1980s, such settlements usually engaged in mixed farming and had some processing industry attached to them. A moshav provides its members with credit and other services, such as marketing and purchasing of seeds, fertilizer, pesticides, and the like. By centralizing some essential purchases, the moshavim were able to benefit from the advantages of size without having to adopt the kibbutz ideology (see Distinctive Social Institutions, ch. 2).

The agricultural sector declined in importance from 1952 to 1985. This decline reflected the rapid development of manufacturing and services rather than a decrease of agricultural productivity. In fact, from 1966 through 1984, agriculture was far more productive than industry.

Efficient use of the factors of production and the change in their relative composition explain a significant portion of the increased

161

productivity in the agricultural sector. From 1955 to 1983, the agricultural sector cut back on employed persons and increased the use of water, fertilizer, and pesticides, leading to a substantial increase in productivity. Other factors that contributed to increased productivity included research, training, improved crop varieties, and better organization. These changes in factor utilization led to a twelvefold increase in the value of agricultural production, calculated in constant prices, between 1950 and 1983.

In absolute terms, the amount of cultivated land increased from 250,000 hectares in FY 1950 to 440,000 hectares in FY 1984. Of this total, the percentage of irrigated land increased from 15 percent in FY 1950 (37,500 hectares) to around 54 percent in FY 1984 (237,000 hectares). The amount of water used for agricultural purposes increased from 332 million cubic meters in FY 1950 to 1.2 billion cubic meters in FY 1984.

The most dramatic change over this period was the reduction in the agricultural labor force. Whereas the number of workers employed in agriculture in the early 1950s reached about 100,000, or 17.4 percent of the civilian labor force, by 1986 it had dropped to 70,000, or 5.3 percent of the civilian labor force.

Agriculture has benefited from high capital inputs and careful development, making full use of available technology over a long period. Specialization in certain profitable export crops, in turn, has generated more funds for investment in agricultural production and processing, as has the development of sophisticated marketing mechanisms. In particular, Israel has had success in exporting citrus fruit, eggs, vegetables, poultry, and melons (see table 9, Appendix A).

Another factor important in Israel's agricultural development has been the sector's impressive performance in foreign trade. The rapid growth of agricultural exports was accompanied by a general increase in total exports. Between 1950 and 1983, a prominent development was the decline (by 65 percent) in the importance of citrus fruit exports in relation to total raw agricultural exports. This decrease was more than balanced by the increase in importance of processed agricultural products, whose exports increased by 4,000 percent over the same period.

Financial Services

In the late 1980s, Israel's financial system consisted of various financial intermediaries providing a range of services from short-term overdraft privileges to the financing of long-term investments in construction, industry, agriculture, and research and development. This financial system was concentrated among a limited number of large banking groups under the supervision and control of the Bank of Israel.

The government-owned Bank of Israel is Israel's central bank. Its legal powers and functions allow it to determine policies and regulate activities in all fiscal areas, including interest rates, money supply, foreign currency, and export financing and control. As part of its duties, the Bank of Israel seeks to create institutions specializing in defined sectors of business or customers. Consequently, banking corporations have been divided into two main groups: ordinary banking institutions, such as banks, foreign banks, and merchant banks—all of which are subject to liquidity regulations on both assets and liabilities—and specialized banking institutions, such as mortgage banks, investment finance banks, financial institutions, and joint services companies.

The financial system in 1988 consisted of five major bank groups: Bank HaPoalim, Bank Leumi Le Israel, Israel Discount Bank, United Mizrahi Bank, and the First International Bank of Israel. Given the high degree of concentration (the three largest bank groups accounted for more than 80 percent of total bank assets), banks operated in an oligopolistic environment, with little competition in determining lending and borrowing rates.

The financial system provided three types of credit instruments: short-term, nondirected credit financing; short-term, directed credit financing, and long-term and medium-term credit financing. The granting of directed credit was the responsibility of the Bank of Israel. This credit, however, actually was provided by joint funds of the Bank of Israel and the commercial banks, and it was primarily intended to meet the working capital requirements of export enterprises. Seventy-five percent of these funds were in foreign currency, with interest charges calculated on the basis of United States dollar credits.

Apart from directed credit, the other major form of short-term capital was nondirected credit, which was composed of overdraft facilities. This credit facility provided the customer with great flexibility at a nonindexed fee, which adjusted with inflation on a periodic basis. The other loans that were denominated in new Israeli shekels (NIS—see Glossary) were either indexed to the consumer price index or, if nonindexed, were fixed-term credits.

Medium-term and long-term loans (exceeding eighteen months) were primarily directed government loans. These credit flows were supervised by investment finance banks such as the Industrial Development Bank of Israel. The government generally determined how medium-term and long-term investment was encouraged and how it was financed. In an economy with a need for short-term capital, long-term financing was also used for financial activities other than investment.

Government intervention in investment financing has taken forms such as direct budget credits, development loans, and investment grants (under the Law for the Encouragement of Capital Investment). Since 1974 development loans—whose interest rates were not adjusted for changes in the rate of inflation—have contained a subsidy element that arises from the differential between the low interest rate paid by the borrower on the one hand and a reasonable market rate of interest plus the expected rate of inflation on the other. Beginning in 1979, the government linked development loans, thus reducing this subsidization. Despite this linkage, the persistent high rate of inflation had kept the effective real interest on these linked loans negative.

Although Israel had a well-developed banking system, it did not have a well-developed stock market in 1988. The Tel Aviv Stock Exchange (TASE), founded in 1953, had never developed properly because of the government's domination of activities relating to the raising and allocation of capital. TASE thus remained a shallow market, poorly regulated and dominated by the major banks, who assumed all stock market roles—brokers, underwriters, issuers, fund managers, counselors, and investors.

Between 1975 and 1983, private corporations increasingly raised more of their capital on the stock exchange. Most of the shares sold were highly overvalued and carried little or no voting rights. By the end of 1982, the total value of the shares registered on the TASE reached more than US$17 billion; in real terms, the value had more than doubled in a year and had multiplied fivefold since 1979. This development stood in sharp contrast to Israel's stagnant GNP growth and the worsening trade and debt position of the economy. In January 1983, however, the market sharply declined. In a matter of days, most speculators lost 50 to 70 percent of the value of their stocks. Mutual funds, which had been responsible for much of the market manipulation, became nearly valueless.

In October 1983, the shares of the banks (which up to that point had been unaffected by the market malaise) finally collapsed. Their crash precipitated a dramatic change in the development of Israel's banking system.

The banking industry had expanded spectacularly in the 1970s, both at home and abroad. This process had forced the banks to increase their capital base rapidly. The gradual advance of inflation in the economy, and its distorting effect on financial statements drawn up under historic accounting rules, only added to this thirst

Worker assembling electronic equipment
Courtesy Embassy of Israel, Washington

for capital. But in a capital market dominated by the government, which was able and willing to issue endless quantities of index-linked bonds, the banks found this capital difficult to raise.

The banks' solution was to transform their shares into index-linked paper by creating a system that ensured that the price of their shares would keep pushing upward, irrespective of the underlying market forces. Over the years, bank shares were perceived as a riskless investment. By 1983 the price of bank shares was steadily becoming more detached from their true value. When it became obvious in 1983 that the government would have to devalue its currency, many people began to liquidate their holdings of shekel-denominated assets in favor of foreign currency. The assets most widely held and most easily liquidated were bank shares. The selling wave began in the summer of 1983 and peaked in October, forcing the government to intervene. In 1988 the government undertook to secure the US$7 billion obligation (equal to the public's holding of bank shares) at the United States dollar value before the crash. The closing of the TASE, on October 6, 1983, became known as the "economic day of atonement" and represented the end of the speculators' paradise created and supported by leading Israeli banks.

Transportation and Communications

Beginning in 1948, the government invested large sums to develop a first-class transportation infrastructure. The main projects undertaken were the construction of the Qishon element of the harbor at Haifa and the Ashdod port, the building of railroads between Haifa and Tel Aviv and from Tel Aviv south to Beersheba, Dimona, and Zin, and the construction of several major roads in the center of the country as well as many new roads in peripheral regions (see fig. 9).

Rapid economic growth and the removal of the limitation on importing private cars and buses created a growing demand for transportation services in the early 1960s. This demand was met by increased public transportation services and by private transportation expenditures. In 1984 the subsidy on public transport equaled US$13 million. In 1985 Israel's 13,410 kilometers of roads were used by 776,000 vehicles, of which about 624,000 were private cars, about 115,000 were trucks and other commercial vehicles, and about 5,500 were buses. In 1988 there were two main public carriers—Egged, with about 4,000 buses operating throughout the country, and Dan, with approximately 1,500 buses. Both of these carriers were cooperatives that charged subsidized tariffs determined by agreement with the government.

Israel also had a government-run railroad system. In 1986 there were 528 kilometers of state-owned railroad linking Jerusalem, Tel Aviv, Haifa, and Beersheba. The government had a long-term plan to extend the Beersheba line along the Dead Sea and south to Elat and to develop a rapid rail line from Petah Tiqwa to Tel Aviv. Total railroad passenger traffic was 2,814,000 in 1985, and total freight carried (primarily phosphates, grains, coal, and potash) was 6,086,000 tons. Given the government status of the rail system, however, it could not compete with other transportation modes. Between 1965 and 1985, railroad use declined because of cutbacks in rail services. In 1986 travel by truck or car was faster than by rail on all lines except the Haifa-Tel Aviv line, where it was identical.

As a result of Israel's geopolitical situation, almost 99 percent of its trade was transported by ship. Thus, in the first twenty years of statehood, the government made a special effort to build a commercial fleet. In 1985 about 9,205 tons of freight were unloaded at Israeli ports: 55 percent at Haifa, 39.3 percent at Ashdod, and 5.7 percent at Elat. During the same year, 7,088 tons were loaded: 22 percent in Haifa, 68.7 percent at Ashdod, and 9.3 percent at Elat. In the 1970s, two additional, specialized ports were opened: an oil terminal at Ashqelon and a coal terminal at Hadera. These open-sea, offshore ports were operated by special port administrations independent of the Israel Ports Authority.

The merchant fleet was 3,050,000 deadweight tons in 1984. The main shipping companies were (in order of importance) Zim, El Yam, Dizengoff, and Maritime Fruit Carriers. During the late 1960s, two structural and technological changes took place in the shipping industry. First, improved cargo-handling technologies and containerization led to the use of more specialized ships. Second, ships increased in size, especially bulk carriers and tankers. Despite these changes—and the importance placed on sea transportation— Zim (owned by the government, the Histadrut, and the Israel Corporation) and El Yam continued to sell unprofitable old ships in the hope of becoming profitable.

In 1988 Israel had one international airport at Lod, but special charter flights also used smaller airports such as Qalandiyah, near Jerusalem, and Elat. El Al, the government-owned national carrier, flew a total of 36.3 million kilometers in 1984, carrying 1,450,000 passengers on 9,646 international flights. In 1985 approximately 455,000 passengers arrived in Israel on charter flights. Inland air services were provided by Arkia Israeli Airlines, which operated flights to major cities.

Israel: A Country Study

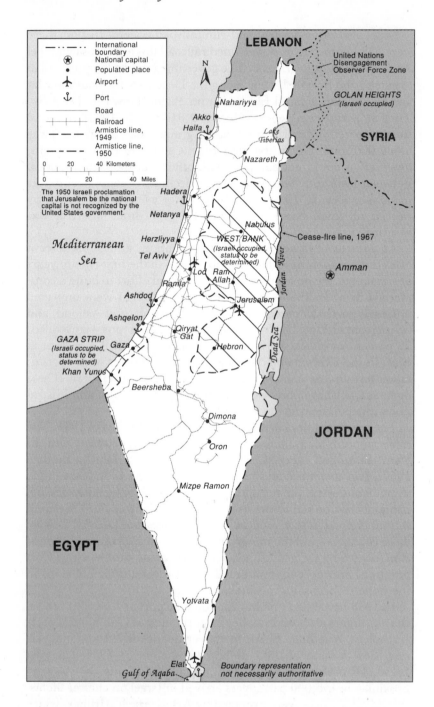

Figure 9. Transportation System, 1988

168

Like other developing countries, Israel has constantly battled the excess demand for telecommunications services. The telecommunications industry is characterized by its high capital intensity—it requires a full cable network system. In 1988 Israel was still lagging in the development of a telecommunications system adequate to meet the needs of its clients. While the industry was expanding, it continued to represent a major weakness of the economy.

Israel has long been plagued by delays in building new telephone exchanges and laying cables to meet the growing needs of the citizenry, businesses, and the new age of computer communication. Israel had about 1.9 million telephones in FY 1986. More than 250,000 citizens, however, remained on waiting lists to receive telephones that year. Some Israelis had been waiting seven or more years for telephones. Around 99 percent of the telephones in Israel were connected to the international direct dialing system.

Three ground satellite stations in 1988 facilitated satellite connections between Israel and the rest of the world. Overseas connections also were possible through underwater cables. In April 1988, Israel announced plans for a five-year telecommunications development program, costing approximately US$2 billion. The plan included an undersea cable from Israel to Europe and the installation of various satellite and cable television facilities. In addition, a multicapacity transatlantic cable was being planned in 1988 to provide 600 channels for communication with the North American continent. Furthermore, in May 1988 the cornerstone was laid for a US$170 million Voice of America transmission relay station in the Nahal HaArava north of Elat.

Foreign Trade

In 1988 Israel had a quasi-open economy. Its chronic trade imbalance reflected the country's military burden, its need to import capital and raw materials, and its excess civilian consumption. This trade deficit had long been covered by transfers and loans of various sorts. Despite drops in the prices of oil and other commodities (the effects of which were felt mainly in 1986) and improvement in Israel's terms of trade because of the fall in value of the United States dollar and the parallel strengthening of European currencies, the balance of trade worsened in 1986. The drop reflected a surge in inventory rebuilding after the 1984–85 recession.

Despite their high level, Israeli tariffs were not the major trade barrier. In addition to the standard specific and ad valorem tariffs, Israel also imposed a purchase tax, compulsory surcharges, unlinked deposits, excise duties, stamp duties, and a value-added tax on all imported products. These taxes were designed to regulate

169

domestic demand and to raise revenue. Lacking a mechanism by which to deal with dumping and other unfair trade practices, the government historically used the unilaterally imposed compulsory surcharge as a convenient measure by which to protect domestic products from foreign competition. Most of these charges, however, were rebatable to exporters as part of the export subsidy program. The brunt of these taxes, therefore, was borne by the nonexport sector.

One potentially discriminatory nontariff barrier arose from the administration of the purchasing tax. For purposes of the purchasing tax, the taxable value of an imported product must reflect its domestic wholesale price. The percentage difference between the imputed wholesale price and the tariff-included import price represents the markup, known by the Hebrew acronym TAMA. As long as the TAMA reflects the true wholesale markup, there is no increased protectionism. Only to the extent that the true markup is less than the TAMA, is there an implicit hidden tariff in Israel.

From 1970 to 1986, Israel's primary exports consisted of basic manufactures, machines, and transportation equipment, chemicals, and miscellaneous manufactures. Primary imports were basic manufactures, machines, and transportation equipment. The United States has been Israel's single largest trading partner, providing a market for approximately 25 percent of Israel's exports and supplying about 20 percent of its nonmilitary imports (see table 10, Appendix A).

Although as of 1988 the United States was Israel's largest individual trading partner, the majority of trade has been with the European Economic Community (EEC). Since 1975 Israel-EEC trade has been governed by the Israel-EEC Preferential Agreement. This agreement eliminated tariff barriers on trade in manufactured goods between the two entities. Under its terms, imports of Israeli manufactured products were granted duty-free entry to the EEC in July 1977, except for certain products (considered to be import-sensitive by the EEC) on which full duty elimination was delayed until December 1979. Because the EEC offered trade preferences to other developing countries and because Greece, Spain, and Portugal entered the EEC, Israel did not receive significant preferential benefits from the EEC. Israel eliminated duties on about 60 percent of its manufactured imports from the EEC in January 1980, and complete duty-free treatment was to be phased in by January 1989.

The Israel-EEC Preferential Agreement also attempted to provide for a substantial reduction in trade barriers for agricultural products. Although the EEC agreed to make tariff reductions on

*Israeli-invented Koffler
nuclear accelerator at the
Weizmann Institute of Science,
Rehovot
Courtesy Embassy
of Israel, Washington*

*Solar energy absorbers
used in producing electricity
Courtesy Embassy
of Israel, Washington*

Israel: A Country Study

about 80 percent of its agricultural imports from Israel, Israeli exporters still had to comply with the EEC's Common Agricultural Policy nontariff requirements and often were faced with quotas and voluntary export restraint agreements. As a result, reciprocal Israeli agricultural tariff concessions to the EEC have been very limited.

Israel-United States trade was far less distorted by tariff and nontariff barriers, at least from the United States' side. The overwhelming majority of Israeli exports entered the United States market duty free. By contrast, a large share of United States exports to Israel not only were subject to substantially higher tariffs, but also were subject to a variety of nontariff barriers, including a substantial "hidden tariff."

Total Israeli exports to the United States were about US$2.3 billion in 1986. Of this amount, only 2.4 percent (US$57.6 million) was subject to duty. Duties collected on these products were US$5.4 million, an average rate of 9.6 percent. Because the ad valorem equivalent tariff rate is calculated as the ratio of duties collected to dutiable value, this figure overstates the average tariff rate on Israeli exports to the United States.

The leading General System of Preferences (GSP) exports to the United States from 1978 through 1986 consisted of jewelry, X-ray equipment, gold necklaces, telephone equipment and parts, electromedical equipment and parts, office machines, and radiation equipment. Apart from jewelry, all the other major GSP exports were high-technology goods.

The product composition of dutiable exports helped explain the low overall duty paid. The primary reason for the low duties paid was that, between 1978 and 1980, the United States subjected diamond imports (Israel's principal export), to a 1 to 2 percent duty. As of 1981, these items entered at a zero most favored nation (MFN) rate. The other major export items that entered the United States at a zero MFN duty rate included potassium chloride, airplanes, emeralds, aircraft parts, potassium nitrate, and antiques. Major exports that remained dutiable in 1986 included agricultural products, footwear, textiles, and apparel.

Informed sources claimed that an elimination of United States duties under the United States-Israel Free Trade Area (FTA) Agreement on these products would lead to an estimated increase of approximately 1 percent of total Israeli exports to the United States. The major categories affected will be agricultural products such as cheeses, olives, and processed tomato products, and textile and apparel items such as swimsuits, knitwear, undergarments, and thread. Very few high-technology products will be affected by the FTA agreement.

Balance of Payments

Israel has had a balance of payments deficit throughout its existence, primarily because of its heavy defense burden and the costs associated with immigration. This deficit has been covered by capital transfers in the form of loans and, in recent years, grants. These grants historically have come from Diaspora Jewry. Since 1974 the United States government has become by far the most important source of financial support, at first in the form of loans, but since 1979 in the form of grants.

The balance of payments position fluctuated widely, following major shifts in economic policy. Between 1980 and 1983, the civilian portion of the import deficit rose rapidly, with a mounting increase in the foreign debt. In 1984 and 1985, these trends reversed themselves as increased United States grants halted the rise in foreign debt and capital exports.

At the end of 1986, Israel's net foreign debt totaled about US$19 billion. The size of this debt was less of a burden than it would appear, however, because US$10 billion of it was owed to the United States government and had a long repayment period. A further US$5.5 billion was owed primarily to Diaspora Jewry (see table 11, Appendix A).

In August 1986, the Israeli exchange rate was pegged to a five-country currency basket. The exchange rate remained fixed until January 1987. This policy, combined with a US$750 million United States emergency grant-in-aid and a reduction in oil prices, led to increased stabilization of Israel's inflation. In the first quarter of 1988, the dollar-NIS exchange rate stood at NIS1.60 = US$1.00.

The Economic Stabilization Program of July 1985

The Economic Stabilization Program adopted in July 1985 involved the simultaneous implementation of several measures. First, the exchange rate was devalued by 18.8 percent and was fixed at the level of NIS1.50 equaled US$1.00. This rate was allowed to fluctuate within a 2-percent band. Second, domestic prices were allowed to rise by 17 percent and thereafter were frozen with a stringent price control. Third, subsidies were reduced by US$750 million, as taxes were increased and a budget cut of US$750 million was implemented. Fourth, the regular anticipated cost-of-living adjustment was suspended. This resulted in a 20 to 30 percent erosion in real wages. Under Histadrut pressure, the government was forced to adjust wages to counter the effects of the devaluation. By March 1986, real wages had recovered their losses. Finally, monetary policy became extremely restrictive. Because the inflation rate was reduced to 20 percent by the end of the year, the return on unlinked shekel deposits became unprecedented. This situation induced a shift of capital from linked dollar deposits to unlinked shekel deposits. Although the government had conceived this program as a short-term, emergency program, it was extended several times because of its success. By the end of 1986, many of the price controls were removed with no visible "repressed inflation" appearing.

Many observers believe that this economic program was successful because its two anchors were the exchange rate and wage stability. The stability in these two prices, coupled with the new notion that inflation would erode the government's real revenues, forced the government to borrow more. The program's impact on the rate of inflation, which peaked at 445 percent in FY 1984, was little short of sensational. By the end of 1986, the inflation rate had stabilized at 20 percent—the lowest rate since 1972.

Outside factors also helped the success of this stabilization program. The program's introduction coincided with the acceleration of the fall of the United States dollar on international markets. Concurrently, the decline in oil prices lowered the cost of increased imports spurred by increased Israeli export and capital market earnings.

The success up to 1988 of the measures taken has encouraged the government to consider additional reforms. In the fall of 1987, discussion began regarding reforming the tax system, initiating a privatization program, and streamlining the tariff structure.

* * *

Information on the Israeli economy is extensive. Basic data are contained in the annual *Statistical Abstract of Israel* published by the Central Bureau of Statistics and the *Annual Report* published by the Bank of Israel. The Ministry of Finance's annual *Budget in Brief* provides considerable data and text on the budget. Additional data and text are included in the *Bank of Israel Economic Review* (published quarterly) and *Bank of Israel Recent Economic Developments* (published irregularly), and in the Central Bureau of Statistics' *Monthly Bulletin of Statistics.* An additional general source covering a range of economic subjects is the monthly *Israel Economist.*

The best up-to-date work on the Israeli economy and Israeli developments from 1968 to 1978 is *The Israeli Economy: Maturing Through Crises,* edited by Yoram Ben-Porath. The best coverage of the period from 1948 to 1968 can be found in Nadav Halevi and Ruth Klinov-Malul's *The Economic Development of Israel.* Other, more specialized, books include: *Israel: A Developing Society,* edited by A. Arian; Salomon J. Flink's *Israel, Chaos and Challenge: Politics vs. Economics;* Fanny Ginor's *Socio-Economic Disparities in Israel;* David Horowitz's *Enigma of Economic Growth: A Case Study of Israel;* Michael Michaely's *Foreign Trade Regimes and Economic Development: Israel;* Howard Pack's *Structural Change and Economic Policy in Israel;* Don Patinkin's *The Israeli Economy;* Ira Sharkansky's *What Makes Israel Tick: How Domestic Policy-Makers Cope with Constraints;* and Michael Wolffsohn's *Israel, Polity, Society, and Economy, 1882–1986.*

The best report on economic developments in the occupied territories is Raphael Meron's *Economic Development in Judea-Samaria and the Gaza District: Economic Growth and Structural Change, 1970–80.* (For further information and complete citations, see Bibliography.)

Chapter 4. Government and Politics

Sephardic chief rabbi, Orthodox woman with wrapped bandana, and Arab male with qafiyah

ISRAELI GOVERNMENTAL AND POLITICAL structures stem from certain premises and institutional arrangements generally associated with West European parliamentary democracies, East European and Central European institutions and traditions, and even some Middle Eastern sociopolitical patterns. These influences were transmitted though the unique history, political culture, and political institutions of Israel's formative prestate period and the Middle Eastern environment in which it is situated. The legitimacy of Israeli society and the identification by the majority Jewish population with the state and its institutions rest on several foundations: Zionist Jewish nationalism, the existence of an outside threat to Israeli security, Judaism, collectivism, and democracy. These bases are affected by the Arab/Palestinian-Israeli conflict (hereafter the Arab-Israeli conflict) and by the pluralist nature of Israeli society, in which a substantial Arab minority participates in the country's political system, but has an ambivalent role within the majority Jewish society (see Minority Groups, ch. 2).

The Israeli political system is characterized by certain West European democratic arrangements: elected government, multiparty competition, a high level of voter participation in local and national elections, an independent judiciary that is the country's foremost guardian of civil liberties, a vigorous and free press, and the supremacy of civilian rule. Other features, such as collectivism and a lack of expression of the liberal component in Israeli politics, are distinctly East European and Central European in origin. These features are expressed by the absence of a written constitution limiting the powers of government and imposing restraints on the majority to safeguard the rights of individuals, particularly in matters of civil rights and relations between state and religious interests. In the late 1980s, increasing disagreement over some fundamental questions, for instance, the state's territorial boundaries and the role of religion in the state, led to a breakdown in the pre-1967 national consensus over such issues. Such disagreement has resulted in intense ideological polarization as reflected in electoral and parliamentary stalemates between the two major political parties—Likud (Union) and the Israel Labor Party (generally referred to as the Labor Party or simply Labor)—and their allies.

In July 1984, the political system faced a challenge of unprecedented magnitude. For the first time in the country's thirty-six-year postindependence history, neither major party was able to form a coalition government without the other's equal participation. The result, the National Unity Government formed in September 1984, represented a milestone in the country's political development. That development had already undergone an unprecedented shock in May 1977, when the left-of-center Labor Party was voted out of office for the first time after nearly half a century of unbroken political dominance in pre- and post-state Israel. In 1977 a newly mandated regime was ushered in under Prime Minister Menachem Begin, who led the right-of-center Likud Bloc and who differed sharply with the Labor Party over political philosophy and both domestic and foreign policy. Likud was reconfirmed in power by the 1981 elections, but it suffered an almost irreparable blow with Begin's resignation in September 1983, which followed a series of failed policies concerning the 1982 invasion of Lebanon and the domestic economy. The less charismatic and more cautious Yitzhak Shamir succeeded Begin. Under the terms of the National Unity Government, established in September 1984, the leader of the Labor Party, Shimon Peres, was entrusted with the formation of a government with himself as prime minister, on the written understanding that he would relinquish the prime ministership in two years' time—halfway through the parliamentary term—to his designated "vice prime minister" (or vice premier) Shamir. The next elections to the Knesset (parliament—see Glossary) were held in November 1988; by reproducing the same inconclusive electoral results as in 1984, they led to the formation of a second Likud-and-Labor-led National Unity Government, except that this time Labor joined as a junior partner. Following a period of protracted coalition bargaining, Shamir was reinstated as prime minister, with Peres moving from the Ministry of Foreign Affairs to the Ministry of Finance. Moshe Arens, a former Likud minister of defense and a Shamir ally, was appointed minister of foreign affairs, and Labor's Yitzhak Rabin became minister of defense.

From 1984 to 1988, the National Unity Government acted as a joint executive committee of Labor and Likud. Under its direction, the Israel Defense Forces (IDF) withdrew to an Israeli-dominated security zone in southern Lebanon; Israel's runaway inflation, which had plagued the economy under previous Likud rule, was curbed; and divisive political debates on major national issues were, to some extent, subdued (see The Economic Stabilization Program of July 1985, ch. 3). Nevertheless, on major issues such as participation in United States-sponsored peace initiatives to resolve the Arab-Israeli conflict, the exchange of "land for peace," and the political future of the West Bank (see Glossary) and Gaza Strip territories, unity between Labor and Likud was lacking. The unity cabinet became deadlocked as each partner continuously strove to advance its own foreign policy agenda. In the latter half of the unity government's term, from 1986 to 1988, consensus on domestic issues disintegrated as the parties prepared for the 1988 Knesset elections. For the most part, this breakdown in consensus continued following the elections; although the United States began a dialogue with the Palestine Liberation Organization (PLO), the government continued to preserve the status quo on security issues.

The Constitutional Framework

The Declaration of the Establishment of the State of Israel, proclaimed by the Provisional Government and the Provisional Council of State on May 14, 1948, mentions a draft constitution to be prepared by a constitutional committee and to be adopted by an elected constituent assembly not later than October 1, 1948. After convening on February 14, 1949, the Constituent Assembly, however, instead of drafting a constitution, on February 16 converted itself into a legislative body (the first Knesset) and enacted the Transition Law, commonly referred to as the "small constitution." The Constituent Assembly could not agree on a comprehensive written constitution, primarily for fear that a constitution would unleash a divisive conflict between religious and state authorities, a fear that continued to exist in late 1988. The ensuing parliamentary debate, from February 1 through June 13, 1950, between those favoring a written constitution and those opposing it was a microcosm of the conflict between state and religious interests that would continue to agitate Israeli political life.

Proponents argued that under a bill of rights incorporated into a constitution Israel would benefit from the experience of other nations that had adopted written safeguards to ensure religious freedom, minority rights, equal rights, and civil liberties. A written constitution, they asserted, would also safeguard the principle of the separation of powers and, in a period of rapid immigration, referred to in Israel as the "ingathering of exiles," would be a unifying factor, unequivocally establishing the supremacy of civil law.

Opponents contended that the domestic and external circumstances of Israel in 1949 were not auspicious for the adoption of a constitution. They stressed that a written constitution would be politically divisive because the controversial issue of the boundaries between state and religion would inevitably be raised in formulating the principles, goals, and nature of the state as codified in a constitution (see The Role of Judaism, ch. 2). Prime Minister

David Ben-Gurion, the leading opponent of a written constitution, maintained that the Proclamation of Independence, however great an event, was merely the beginning of a long process in Israel's evolution as a democratic state and not "the redemption." Perhaps most significantly, Ben-Gurion and Mapai (Mifleget Poalei Eretz Yisrael, Israel Workers' Party—see Appendix B), the Labor Party's predecessor, had already formed an alliance with Orthodox religious parties by entering into a "historical partnership" with Mizrahi (Spiritual Center—see Appendix B) in 1933. As part of the Mapai-Mizrahi agreement of June 19, 1947, they obtained unity among the various groups in the Yishuv (the prestate Jewish community) by promising the leaders of the ultra-Orthodox Agudat Israel (Society of Israel—see Appendix B) that the status quo on issues involving state and religion would be maintained in the new state. Some observers felt that Ben-Gurion and other Labor leaders grossly underestimated the long-term consequences of delaying resolution of the role of religion in a modern Jewish state. In later years, the Orthodox-dominated Ministry of Religious Affairs, Ministry of Interior, rabbinate, rabbinic courts, and municipal religious councils gained a virtual monopoly in patronage and resources over Israel's organized Jewish religious institutions to the detriment of the more moderate Conservative and Reform movements of Judaism. As a consequence of the resurgence of right-wing fundamentalist religious movements, the influence of secular elements in Israeli society, especially of Labor and its allies, was ultimately diminished.

The Israeli solution to the lack of a constitution has been a "building-block" method. In June 1950, the Knesset passed a compromise resolution, known as the "Harari decision" (named after Knesset member Izhar Harari), approving a constitution in principle but postponing its enactment until a future date. The resolution stated that the constitution would be evolved "chapter by chapter in such a way that each chapter will by itself constitute a fundamental law." It stipulated: "The chapters will be submitted to the Knesset to the extent to which the Committee [for Constitution, Law, and Justice of the Knesset] completes its work, and the chapters will be incorporated in the constitution of the State." By 1988 nine Basic Laws had been enacted to deal with the Knesset (1958), Israeli Lands (1960), the Presidency (1964), the Government (1968), the State Economy (1975), the Army (1976), Jerusalem (1980), the Judiciary (1984), and Elections (1988). These Basic Laws, transcending regular legislation, may be amended or changed only by a special majority; in most cases the majority required is at least 80 members of the 120-member Knesset.

Moreover, to ensure the country's stability, the Basic Laws may not be amended, suspended, or repealed by emergency legislation.

Apart from the nine Basic Laws, as of the end of 1988 there were a number of ordinary laws that legitimized the structure, functions, and actions of state institutions. These ordinary statutes were intended eventually to take the form of Basic Laws, presumably with appropriate revisions to account for changing needs and circumstances. Among these laws were the Law of Return (1950), Nationality Law (1952), the Judges Law (1953), the State Education Law (1953), the Courts Law (1957), the State Comptroller Law (1958), and the Knesset Elections Law (1969). Legislation such as the Law of Return, the Nationality Law, and the State Education Law sought to resolve fundamental secular-religious disagreements. In the judgment of most Israeli observers, however, the enactment of such laws did not resolve fundamental controversies because Orthodox figures later sought to overturn them. For example, in 1988 the government was engaged in a legislative struggle involving renewed attempts by Orthodox religious parties to amend the 1950 Law of Return, the country's basic immigration law, by granting Orthodox religious authorities exclusive power to decide who is Jewish and to exclude people who had converted to Judaism through the Reform or Conservative movements. On June 14, 1988, the Knesset defeated two such bills by votes of sixty to fifty-three and sixty to fifty-one.

The question of human rights and civil liberties has been an important concern of all Israeli governments. It is reflected, for instance, in the Declaration of the Establishment of the State of Israel, sometimes considered analogous to the United States Declaration of Independence. The Israeli declaration reads in part: "The State of Israel will . . . foster the development of the country for the benefit of all its inhabitants; it will be based on freedom, justice, and peace as envisaged by the prophets of Israel; it will ensure complete equality of social and political rights to all its inhabitants irrespective of religion, race or sex; it will guarantee freedom of religion, conscience, language, education and culture." The declaration contains sections that were intended to grant constitutional authority for the establishment and operation of state organs during the immediate postindependence years. Apart from that legal significance, however, the declaration lacks the status of a formal constitution against which the legality of other enactments can be tested. This is especially true regarding the issue of fundamental civil rights.

In the absence of an expressed bill of rights, Israeli governments have relied on the court system to safeguard civil rights and liberties.

Israeli citizens have enjoyed a large measure of civil rights as a result of high standards of fairness in the administration of justice in Israel proper. Nonetheless, certain infringements have been caused by the dictates of internal security (see Israeli Arabs, Arab Land, and Arab Refugees, ch. 1). According to a United States Department of State report on human rights practices in Israel released in February 1988, "Israel is a parliamentary democracy which guarantees by law and respects in practice the civil, political, and religious rights of its citizens . . . As in the past, the most significant human rights problems for Israel in 1987 derived from the strained relations between the Israeli authorities and some Israelis on the one hand and the Arab inhabitants of the occupied territories on the other hand."

A number of attempts have been made to introduce proposals for a detailed constitution. The latest occurred in August 1987, when the Public Council for a Constitution for Israel, a group of Tel Aviv University professors led by Uriel Reichman, dean of its faculty of law, launched a campaign to enact a constitution. The group argued that the existing Basic Laws were not tantamount to a constitution because such topics as judicial review and a bill of rights were not covered and because most of the Basic Laws were regular laws that could be amended by a simple majority vote of the Knesset. A written constitution, in contrast, would spell out the relationship among the different branches of government and establish a type of secularized bill of rights between the individual and the state. The group advocated three necessary reform measures as essential for a democratic and constitutional state: the direct election of the prime minister; the safeguarding of all Basic Laws so that they could be rescinded only by a two-thirds or three-fifths Knesset majority; and the establishment of a well-defined system of judicial review. While the proposal had little chance of Knesset passage, it aroused renewed interest in the reform of the Israeli electoral, legislative, and judicial systems (see Prospects for Electoral Reform, this ch.).

Government

The President

The 1964 Basic Law provides that the president is the titular head of state (see fig. 10). The president is elected through secret balloting by an absolute majority of the Knesset on the first two ballots, but thereafter by a plurality, for a term of five years. Israeli presidents may not serve more than two consecutive terms, and any resident of Israel is eligible to be a presidential candidate. The office falls vacant upon resignation or upon the decision of three-quarters of the Knesset to depose the president on grounds of misconduct or incapacity. Presidential tenure is not keyed to that of the Knesset in order to assure continuity in government and the nonpartisan character of the office. There is no vice president in the Israeli governmental system. When the president is temporarily incapacitated or the office falls vacant, the speaker of the Knesset may exercise presidential functions.

Presidential powers are usually exercised based on the recommendation of appropriate government ministers. The president signs treaties ratified by the Knesset and laws enacted by the legislature except those relating to presidential powers. The president, who has no veto power over legislation, appoints diplomatic representatives, receives foreign envoys accredited to Israel, and appoints the state comptroller, judges for civil and religious courts, and the governor of the Bank of Israel.

Although the president's role is nonpolitical, Israeli heads of state perform important moral, ceremonial, and educational functions. They also play a part in the formation of a coalition cabinet, or "a government" as the Israelis call it. They are required to consult leaders of all political parties in the Knesset and to designate a member of the legislature to organize a cabinet. If the member so appointed fails, other political parties commanding a plurality in the Knesset may submit their own nominee. The figure called upon to form a cabinet is invariably the leader of the most influential political party or bloc in the Knesset.

As of 1988, all Israeli presidents have been members of, or associated with, the Labor Party and its predecessors, and all have been considered politically moderate. These tendencies were especially significant in the April 1978 election of Labor's Yitzhak Navon, following the inability of the governing Likud coalition to elect its candidate to the presidency. Israeli observers believed that, in counterbalance to Prime Minister Begin's polarizing leadership, Navon, the country's first president of Sephardi (see Glossary) origin, provided Israel with unifying symbolic leadership at a time of great political controversy and upheaval. In 1983 Navon decided to reenter Labor politics after five years of nonpartisan service as president, and Chaim Herzog (previously head of military intelligence and ambassador to the United Nations) succeeded him as Israel's sixth president.

The Cabinet

The separation of powers between the executive and legislative branches in the Israeli political system generally follows the British

Israel: A Country Study

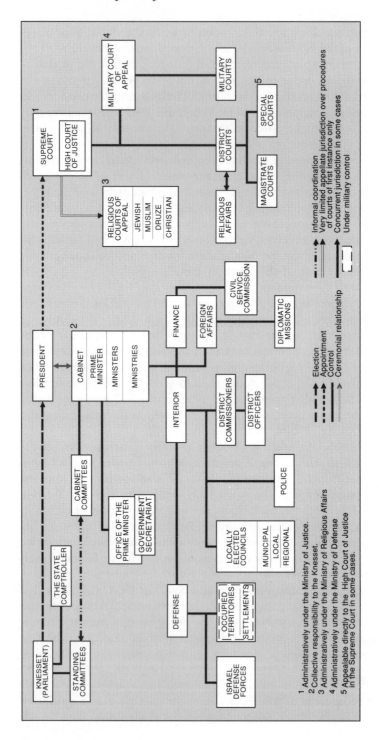

1 Administratively under the Ministry of Justice.
2 Collective responsibility to the Knesset.
3 Administratively under the Ministry of Religious Affairs.
4 Administratively under the Ministry of Defense.
5 Appealable directly to the High Court of Justice in the Supreme Court in some cases.

Figure 10. Government System, 1988

186

pattern. The cabinet is the top executive policy-making body and the center of political power in the nation. It consists of the prime minister and an unspecified number of ministers. The head of government must be a Knesset member, but this is not a requirement for ministers. In practice, most ministers have been Knesset members; when non-Knesset members are considered for cabinet posts, their selection is subject to Knesset approval. A deputy prime minister and deputy ministers may be appointed from among the membership of the Knesset, usually as a result of coalition bargaining, but in this instance only the deputy prime minister is considered a regular cabinet member. As stated above, in September 1984, the National Unity Government established the position of vice prime minister, or vice premier. The vice prime minister, who was the leader of one of the two major parties in the unity coalition, was considered the second leading cabinet minister.

The cabinet takes office upon confirmation by the Knesset, to which it is collectively responsible for all its acts. To obtain this consent, the prime minister-designate must submit a list of cabinet members along with a detailed statement of basic principles and policies of his or her government. The cabinet can be dissolved if it resigns en masse, if the Knesset passes a motion of censure against it, or if the prime minister resigns or dies. The prime minister's resignation invalidates the cabinet, but resignations of individual ministers do not have this effect. Since independence all cabinets have been coalitions of parties, each coalition having been formed to achieve the required total of sixty-one or more Knesset seats. Although often based on political expediency, coalition formation is also concerned with ideological and issue compatibility among the participating groups. Cabinet posts are divided among coalition partners through behind-the-scenes bargaining and in proportion to the parliamentary strength of the parties involved, usually at the ratio of one cabinet portfolio for every three or four Knesset seats. This formula may be dispensed with, however, in times of national emergency or electoral and political stalemate. The first precedent in this direction occurred after the June 1967 War when a "national unity government" was formed by co-opting three opposition party leaders as cabinet ministers. This move, which was achieved without the standard cabinet formation procedure, was designed to demonstrate internal solidarity in the face of an external threat.

The members of coalition governments are obligated to fulfill their commitments to the coalition at the time of seeking a vote of confidence from the Knesset. A cabinet member may be dismissed for failing to support the government on any matter that is included in the original coalition pact except where the minister's dissenting vote in the Knesset for reasons of "conscience" is specifically approved in advance by the minister's party. This obligation also applies in the formation and maintenance of a national unity government, with the exception of times of emergency when opposition elements co-opted into the cabinet may disagree with the mainstream of the coalition on any matters other than those they have pledged to support. At a minimum, coalition members must vote with the government on issues of national defense, foreign policy, the budget, and motions of censure. Failure to do so constitutes grounds for their expulsion; ministers may simply withdraw from the government in protest if they cannot reconcile themselves to the mainstream.

As a rule, the cabinet meets at least once a week on Sunday morning or whenever extraordinary reasons warrant. Cabinet deliberations are confidential; this is especially true when the body meets as a session of the ministerial Committee for Security Affairs.

The cabinet conducts much of its work through four standing committees dealing with economic affairs, legislation, foreign affairs and security, and home affairs and services. The committees meet once a week and may set up special ad hoc committees of inquiry to scrutinize issues affecting coalition unity or other urgent questions. A cabinet member may be assigned to one or more committees. Committee decisions are final unless challenged in plenary cabinet sessions.

As compensation for serving in the cabinet, Knesset members' salaries and accompanying benefits are supplemented by the government. Ministers are given a car and a driver and offices in Tel Aviv and Jerusalem. The government provides them with an official residence in Jerusalem and covers personal expenses such as travel, hotels, and food on official business. They also receive comprehensive medical insurance and other allowances.

Until November 1988, the unity cabinet included, in addition to Prime Minister Shamir, nineteen ministers with portfolio, including the vice-prime minister and two deputy prime ministers. The jurisdictions of their portfolios were agriculture, communications, defense, economics and planning, education and culture, energy and infrastructure, finance, foreign affairs, health, housing and construction, immigration and absorption, industry and trade, interior, justice and tourism (both ministries were headed by one minister), labor and social affairs, police, religious affairs, science and development, and transportation. In addition, there were six ministers without portfolio. Upon approval of the second unity government by the Knesset in December 1988, the new cabinet consisted of twenty-eight ministers, the largest in the country's history. Its size was expanded to accommodate political demands by the coalition partners.

Interministerial coordination is the responsibility of the four standing cabinet committees and the Office of the Prime Minister, especially the Government Secretariat, which is located in that office. Headed by the secretary to the government (the position is also known as government secretary or cabinet secretary), the secretariat prepares the agenda for meetings of the cabinet and cabinet committees, maintains their records, coordinates the work of ministries, and informs the public of government decisions and policies.

Also in the Office of the Prime Minister are the Prime Minister's Bureau, which deals with confidential matters concerning the chief executive, and a staff of advisers on political and legal issues, national security, terrorism and counterterrorism, the media, petitions and complaints, Arab affairs, and welfare affairs. The most influential advisory personnel carry the title of "director general and political adviser" to the prime minister. Other constituent units of the office include the State Archives and Library, Government Names Committee, Government Press Office, National Council for Research and Development, Technological and Scientific Information Center, Atomic Energy Commission, Institute for Biological Research, National Parks Authority, and Central Bureau of Statistics.

The Civil Service

As of late 1988, government employees were recruited through a merit system, with appointment, promotion, transfer, termination, training, discipline, and conditions of employment regulated by law. They were prohibited, especially in the senior grades, from engaging in partisan politics by the Civil Service (Restriction of Party Activities and Fund-Raising) Law of 1959. As of 1988, there were approximately 100,000 government employees, excluding the Israel Police, teachers (who were technically municipal employees), civilian workers in the defense establishment, and employees of the State Employment Service and the autonomous Israel Broadcasting Authority.

The civil service was headed by a commissioner appointed by the cabinet and directly responsible to the minister of finance. The commissioner, who like other senior government officials carried the rank of director general, had broad responsibility for the examination, recruitment, appointment, training, and discipline of civil service personnel. In practice, however, except in the senior grades, these matters were left to the discretion of the various ministries. The commissioner was also chairman of the Civil Service Board, consisting of three directors general representing government ministries and three members representing the public. The purpose of the board was to administer the civil service pension system. In addition, the office of the commissioner directed the operation of the Central School of Administration in Jerusalem and furnished administrative services to the Civil Service Disciplinary Court. Civil servants were automatically members of the Civil Servants' Union—a practice that has been in effect since 1949 when the union became part of the General Federation of Laborers in the Land of Israel (HaHistadrut HaKlalit shel HaOvdim B'Eretz Yisrael, known as Histadrut—literally, organization). Any basic changes in the conditions of government employment must have the concurrence of the union. The mandatory retirement age for civil service workers was sixty-five, and pensions ranged from 20 to 70 percent of terminal salary, depending on length of service.

The Knesset

The Knesset is a unicameral parliament and the supreme authority of the state. Its 120 members are elected by universal suffrage for a four-year term under a system of proportional representation. Basic Law: the Knesset provides for "general countryside, direct, equal, secret, and proportional" elections. This provision means that if, for example, in a national election a given party list received approximately 36,000 votes, it would be entitled to two seats in the Knesset. As a result, the top two names on the party's list would obtain Knesset seats. The legislative authority of the Knesset is unlimited, and legislative enactments cannot be vetoed by either the president or the prime minister nor can such enactments be nullified by the Supreme Court. The regular four-year term of the Knesset can be terminated only by the Knesset, which can then call for a new general election before its term expires.

The Knesset also has broad power of direction and supervision over government operations. It approves budgets, monitors government performance by questioning cabinet ministers, provides a public forum for debate of important issues, conducts wide-ranging legislative inquiries, and can topple the cabinet through a vote of no confidence that takes precedence over all other parliamentary business. The Knesset works through eleven permanent legislative committees, including the House Committee, which handles parliamentary rules and procedures, and the Law and Justice Committee, usually referred to as "Law." The jurisdictions of the remaining committees are the constitution, finance, foreign affairs

The Knesset, or Parliament, of Israel, Jerusalem
Courtesy Embassy of Israel, Washington

and security, immigration and absorption, economics, education and culture, internal affairs and environment, labor and welfare, and state control. Committee assignments are made by the Arrangements Committee, a committee consisting of representatives of the various parties established at the beginning of each Knesset session, enabling each party to determine for itself where it wants its stronger delegates placed. Committee assignments are for the duration of the Knesset's tenure. Committee chairmen are formally elected at the first meeting of each respective committee upon the nomination of the House Committee. As a rule, however, the chairmanship of important committees is reserved for members of the ruling coalition. If a member resigns from his or her party, the place on the committee reverts to the party, even if the member remains in the Knesset.

Among the first tasks of a new Knesset is to assign members to the various standing committees and to elect a speaker, his or her deputies, and the chairmen of committees. The speaker is assisted by a presidium of several deputies chosen by the Knesset from the major parties. At a minimum, the Knesset is required to hold two sessions a year and to sit not fewer than eight months during the two sessions. The Knesset meets weekly to consider items on its agenda, but not on Fridays, Saturdays, and Sundays in deference to its Muslim, Jewish, and Christian members. Agendas are set

191

by the speaker to permit the questioning of ministers and the consideration of proposals from the government or motions from members. Time allocations to individual members and parties are made in advance by the speaker so as to preclude filibusters or cloture. Other than national emergencies, budgetary issues have usually been the most important items dealt with by the Knesset at any of its session.

Following the British pattern, legislation is generally introduced by the cabinet; to a lesser extent it is initiated by various Knesset committees; and in limited cases, private bills are initiated by individual Knesset members. Bills are drafted by the ministries concerned in consultation with the Ministry of Justice. By majority vote of the cabinet, draft bills are sent to the speaker of the Knesset for legislative action. Proposed bills are considered by appropriate committees and go through three readings before being voted on by the Knesset after the third reading. Any number of Knesset members present constitutes a quorum, and a simple majority of those present is required for passage. Exceptions to this rule apply in the election or removal of the president of the state, removal of the state comptroller, changes to the system of proportional elections, and changes to or repeal of Basic Laws; in these instances, required majorities are specified by law.

Apart from the Knesset, which is the principal source of legislation, such public institutions as ministries, local authorities, and independent bodies can frame rules and regulations or subsidiary legislation on a wide range of matters. Subsidiary legislation has the effect of law, but it can be declared invalid by the courts when it contravenes any enactment of the Knesset.

Knesset members are granted extensive legal immunity and privileges. Their special legal status, which many observers regard as excessive, ranges from parliamentary immunity to protection from criminal proceedings for the entire period of Knesset membership. Immunity extends to acts committed before becoming a Knesset member, although such immunity can be removed by the Knesset upon the recommendation of the House Committee. Knesset members are also exempt from compulsory military service. The official language of the Knesset is Hebrew, but Arab members may address the legislature in Arabic, with simultaneous translation provided.

The State Comptroller

The power of the Knesset to supervise and review government policies and operations is exercised mainly through the state comptroller, also known as the ombudsman or ombudswoman. The state comptroller is appointed by the president upon the recommendation of the House Committee of the Knesset for a renewable term of five years. The incumbent is completely independent of the government and is responsible to the Knesset alone (the state controller's budget is submitted directly to the Knesset's Finance Committee and is exempt from prior consideration by the Ministry of Finance). The state comptroller can be relieved only by the Knesset or by resignation or demise. During the incumbent's term of office, he or she may not be a member of the Knesset or otherwise engage in politics and is prohibited from any public or private activity that could create a conflict of interest with the independent performance of the duties of the office. The state comptroller, although lacking in authority to enforce compliance, has broad investigative powers and employs hundreds of staff members, including accountants, lawyers, and other relevant professionals. Since 1949, when the state comptrollership was created, three individuals have held the office, with each having served for an extended period.

The principal function of the state comptroller is to check on the legality, regularity, efficiency, economy, and ethical conduct of public institutions. The checks are performed by continuous and spot inspections of the financial accounts and activities of all ministries, the armed forces and security services, local government bodies, and any corporations, enterprises, or organizations subsidized or managed by the state in any form.

The state comptroller acts in conjunction with the Finance Committee of the Knesset and reports to it whenever necessary. The state comptroller may recommend that the Finance Committee appoint a special commission of inquiry, but having no statutory authority of its own it relies on the Knesset to impose sanctions on errant bodies. The state comptroller's office is divided into five major inspection units. The first four are concerned with ministries, defense services, local authorities, and corporations; the fifth deals with public complaints concerning government bodies.

The Judicial System

The Judiciary Law of 1984 formalized the judicial structure consisting of three main types of courts: civil, religious, and military. There also are special courts for labor, insurance, traffic, municipal, juvenile, and other disputes. Each type of court is administratively responsible to a different ministry. Civilian courts come under the Ministry of Justice; religious courts fall under the Ministry of Religious Affairs, and military courts come under the Ministry of Defense (see The Role of Judaism, ch. 2; Discipline and Military

Justice, ch. 5). In the administration of justice, however, all courts are independent and Israelis generally concede their fairness.

Legal codes and judicial procedures derive from various sources. Laws applicable to Israeli Jews in matters of personal status are generally based on the Torah (see Glossary) and the halakah (see Glossary). Influences traceable to the British Mandate period include parts of Ottoman legal codes, influenced by the Quran, Arab tribal customary laws, and the Napoleonic Code. In general, British law has provided the main base on which Israel has built its court procedure, criminal law, and civil code, whereas American legal practice has strongly influenced Israeli law regarding civil rights.

The status of the judiciary and the definition and authority of the court structure are spelled out in the Judges Law of 1953, the Courts Laws of 1957, the Rabbinical Courts Jurisdiction (Marriage and Divorce) Law of 1953, the Dayanim Law of 1955 (sing., *dayan,* rabbinical court judge), the Qadis Law of 1961 (sing., *qadi,* Muslim religious judge), the Druze Religious Courts Law of 1962 (*qadi madhab,* Druze religious judge), the Jurisdiction in Matters of Dissolution of Marriages (Special Cases) Law of 1969, and the Judiciary Law of 1984. The principal representative of the state in the enforcement of both criminal and civil law is the attorney general, who is responsible to the minister of justice. As was the case during the British Mandate, courts do not use the jury system; all questions of fact and law are determined by the judge or judges of the court concerned, and the system upholds the principle of innocence until proven guilty.

The president, on the recommendation of a nominating committee chaired by the minister of justice, appoints civil courts judges. The nominating committee consists of the president of the Supreme Court, two other justices of the highest court, two members of the Knesset, one cabinet member in addition to the minister of justice, and two practicing lawyers who are members of the Israel Bar Association, a body established in 1961 charged with certifying lawyers for legal practice. The independence of committee members is safeguarded in part by a procedure whereby, except for the minister of justice and the president of the Supreme Court, they are elected through secret ballot by the members of their respective institutions. Whereas the composition of the committee is meant to depoliticize the nominations process, political considerations require the inclusion of at least one religious justice on the Supreme Court, as well as the representation on the nominating committee of Sephardim and women.

The president of the state, on the recommendation of nominating committees, also appoints judges of religious courts, except Christian courts. Nominating committees, chaired by the minister of religious affairs, are organized to ensure the independence of their members and to take account of the unique features of each religious community. Religious courts of the ten recognized Christian communities are administered by judges appointed by individual communities (see Minority Groups, ch. 2).

Civil and religious judges hold office from the day of appointment; tenure ends only upon death, resignation, mandatory retirement at age seventy, or removal from office by disciplinary judgment as specified by law. Transfers of judges from one locality to another require the consent of the president of the Supreme Court. The salaries of all judges are determined by the Knesset. Judges may not be members of the Knesset or engage in partisan political activity.

Before assuming office, all judges, regardless of religious affiliation, must declare allegiance to the State of Israel and swear to dispense justice fairly. Judges other than *dayanim* must also pledge loyalty to the laws of the state; *dayanim* are subject only to religious law. The implication is that Jewish religious law suspersedes the man-made laws of the Knesset; where the two conflict, a *dayan* will follow religious law in matters of personal status. Israeli civil libertarians view this as a blemish on the judiciary system because, as Israeli political scientist Asher Arian points out, religious laws "restrict certain liberties taken for granted in other liberal systems."

At the top of the court hierarchy is the Supreme Court, located in Jerusalem and composed of a number of justices determined by the Knesset. In late 1988, there were eleven justices: a president or chief justice, a vice president, and nine justices. The court has both appellate and original jurisdiction. A minimum of three justices is needed for a court session.

The Supreme Court hears appeals from lower courts in civil and criminal cases. As a court of first instance, it may direct a lower district court to hold a retrial in a criminal case if the original verdict is based on questionable evidence, subject to the stipulation that penalties imposed at retrial should not exceed the severity of those originally imposed. In addition, the Supreme Court has original jurisdiction over petitions seeking relief from administrative decisions that fall outside the jurisdiction of any court. In this role, the Supreme Court sits as the High Court of Justice and may restrain government agencies or other public institutions by such writs as habeas corpus and mandamus, customary under English common law. In its capacity as the High Court of Justice, it may also order a religious court to deal with a case concerned with its competence as a religious body, but only on petitions raised before a verdict is handed down. In this regard, the Supreme Court is limited to the procedural question and may not impinge on the merits of the case.

The Supreme Court serves as the principal guardian of fundamental rights, protecting the individual from any arbitrary action by public officials or agencies. It does not have the power of judicial review and cannot invalidate Knesset legislation. It is empowered, however, to nullify administrative rules and regulations or government and local ordinances on the ground of their illegality or conflict with Knesset enactments. As the highest court of the land, the Supreme Court may also rule on the applicability of laws in a disputed case and on jurisdictional disputes between lower civil courts and religious courts. There is no appeal from its decisions.

The second tier of the civil court structure consists of six district courts located in Jerusalem, Tel Aviv, Ramla, Haifa, Beersheba, and Nazareth (see fig. 1). As courts of first instance, district courts hear civil and criminal cases outside the jurisdiction of lower courts. Their jurisdiction includes certain matters of personal status involving foreigners. If the foreigners concerned consent to the authority of religious courts, however, there is concurrent jurisdiction over the issue. The district court at Haifa has additional competence as a court of admiralty for the country as a whole.

District courts also hear appeals from magistrate courts, municipal courts, and various administrative tribunals. Israel's twenty-eight magistrate courts constitute the most basic level of the civil court system. They are located in major towns and have criminal as well as civil jurisdiction. There are a small number of municipal courts that have criminal jurisdiction over any offenses committed within municipal areas against municipal regulations, local ordinances, by-laws, and town-planning orders.

The civil court structure includes bodies of special jurisdiction, most notably traffic courts; juvenile courts; administrative tribunals concerned with profiteering, tenancy, and water; and tribal courts specific to the Southern District having jurisdiction in any civil or criminal cases assigned to them by the president of the district court or the district commissioner. Disputes involving management-employee relations and insurance claims go to regional labor courts. The courts, established in 1969, are located in Jerusalem, Tel Aviv, Haifa, and Beersheba. Appeals from the decisions of these courts are made directly to the National Labor Court, located in Jerusalem. Finally, distinct from court-martial proceedings is the military

Yitzhak Shamir,
Prime Minister of
Israel and head of
the Likud Party
Courtesy Embassy
of Israel, Washington

Shimon Peres,
leader of the Labor Party
Courtesy Embassy
of Israel, Washington

197

court system, empowered to prosecute civilians for offenses against defense emergency regulations.

Local Government

As of late 1988, there were two levels of local government: the central government operated the upper or district level; citizens elected the lower and relatively autonomous municipal level officials. The system of district administration and local government was for the most part based on statutes first promulgated during the Ottoman era and perpetuated under the British Mandate for Palestine and under Yishuv policies. Since independence it has been modified to deal with changing needs and to foster local self-rule. As of late 1988, local government institutions had limited powers, experienced financial difficulties, and depended to a great extent on national ministries; they were, nevertheless, important in the political framework.

Israel consisted of six administrative districts and fourteen subdistricts under, respectively, district commissioners and district officers. The minister of interior appointed these officials, who were responsible to him for implementing legislative and administrative matters. District officials drafted local government legislation, approved and controlled local tax rates and budgets, reviewed and approved by-laws and ordinances passed by locally elected councils, approved local public works projects, and decided on grants and loans to local governments. In their activities, local officials were also accountable to the Office of the State Comptroller. Staff of other ministries might be placed by the minister of interior under the general supervision of district commissioners.

Israel's local self-government derived its authority from the by-laws and ordinances enacted by elected municipal, local, and regional councils and approved by the minister of interior. Up to and including the municipal elections of 1973, mayors and members of the municipal councils were elected by universal, secret, direct, and proportional balloting for party lists in the same manner as Knesset members. Council members in turn chose mayors and municipal council chairpersons. After 1978 mayoral candidates were elected directly by voters in a specific municipality, while members of municipal and local councils continued to be elected according to the performance of party lists and on the basis of proportional representation (see The Knesset, this ch.).

Population determined the size of municipal and local councils. Large urban areas were classified as municipalities and had municipal councils. Local councils were designated class "A" (larger) or class "B" (smaller), depending on the number of inhabitants in villages or settlements. Regional councils consisted of elected delegates from settlements according to their size. Such councils dealt mainly with the needs of cooperative settlements, including kibbutzim and moshavim (see Glossary). The extensive local government powers of the minister of interior included authority to dissolve municipal councils; district commissioners had the same power with regard to local councils.

Local authorities had responsibility for providing public services in areas such as education, health care and sanitation, water management, road maintenance, parks and recreation, and fire brigades. They also levied and collected local taxes, especially property taxes, and other fees. Given the paucity of locally raised tax revenues, most local authorities depended heavily on grants and loans from the national Treasury. The Ministry of Education and Culture, however, made most of the important decisions regarding education, such as budgets, curriculum, and the hiring, training, and licensing of teachers. Nationwide, in 1986 local authorities contributed approximately 50 percent to financing local budgets. In 1979 the figure was about 29 percent. Over the years, municipalities have relied on two other methods for raising funds: cities such as Jerusalem, Tel Aviv, and Haifa used special municipal endowment funds, particularly for cultural purposes; and Project Renewal, a collaboration among local authorities, government ministries, and the Jewish Agency (see Glossary) provided funds to rehabilitate deteriorated neighborhoods.

Local government employees came under the Local Authorities Order (Employment Service) of 1962. The statutes pertaining to the national Civil Service Commission did not cover them.

The Local Government Center, a voluntary association of major cities and local councils, was originally established in 1936, and reorganized in 1956. It represented the interests of local governing bodies vis-à-vis the central authorities, government ministries, and Knesset committees. It also represented local authorities in wage negotiations and signed relevant agreements together with the Histadrut and the government. The center organized conferences and advisory commissions to study professional, budgetary, and managerial issues, and it participated in various national commissions.

Civilian Administration in the West Bank and the Gaza Strip

A civilian administration has been set up in the West Bank and the Gaza Strip as an interim measure pending final resolution of the political future of these two areas, which are not part of Israel proper. While Labor was in power, Israeli-sponsored municipal

elections were held in the West Bank in 1976. The civilian administration of the area until late 1987 employed approximately 13,000
to 14,000 Palestinian civil servants. The Palestinian uprising
(*intifadah*) in the West Bank and the Gaza Strip that began in December 1987, however, had a profound impact on the relationship
between the civilian administration and the Palestinian inhabitants
of the occupied territories (see Introduction; Palestinian Uprising,
December 1987–, ch. 5).

National Institutions

As of late 1988, Israel had a number of so-called "nongovern-
ment public sector" organizations, also known as "national institutions." For all practical purposes, they constituted an integral
part of the government system, performing functions that were vital
to the fulfillment of Zionist aspirations and to the maintenance of
Israeli society. Political parties competed for leadership and
patronage within them. During the Mandate period, these organizations served as the British administration's officially recognized
governing bodies for the Jewish community in Palestine. The Jewish
Agency Executive, for instance, was recognized by the governments
of Britain, the United States, and other states and international
organizations, including the United Nations (UN). In the process
of their work, the organizations acquired considerable experience
in self-rule, not to mention jealously guarded bureaucratic
prerogatives.

These bodies engaged in fund-raising in the Diaspora (see Glossary), operated social welfare services, and were involved in education and cultural work. They operated enterprises, including
housing companies; organized immigration; and promoted Zionist
work. After Israel achieved independence, many of these services
were taken over by the state, but others remained under the control of these well-entrenched organizations. They came to function side by side with the government, and their activities often
overlapped, especially in the field of social welfare services. Until
the early 1970s, these organizations were almost completely dominated by Israeli governments; later, the organized representatives
of Diaspora Jewry began to function more independently.

World Zionist Organization and the Jewish Agency

Principal among these bodies were the World Zionist Organization (WZO—see Glossary) and the Jewish Agency. The Jewish
Agency for Palestine was established in 1929 under the terms of
the League of Nations Mandate for Palestine as the operative arm
of the WZO in building a Jewish national homeland. In 1952 the

Knesset enacted the World Zionist Organization-The Jewish Agency (Status) Law, defining the WZO as "also the Jewish Agency." The 1952 law expressly designated the WZO as "the authorized agency which will continue to operate in the State of Israel for the development and settlement of the country, the absorption of immigrants from the Diaspora and the coordination of activities in Israel of Jewish institutions and organizations active in those fields." The same statute granted tax-exempt status to the Jewish Agency and the authority to represent the WZO as its action arm for fund raising and, in close cooperation with the government, for the promotion of Jewish immigration. The specifics of cooperation were spelled out in a covenant entered into with the government in 1954. The 1954 pact also recognized the WZO and the Jewish Agency as official representatives of world Jewry.

These two bodies played a significant role in consolidating the new State of Israel, absorbing and resettling immigrants, and enlisting support from, and fostering the unity of, the Diaspora. Their activities included organizing immigration, resettling immigrants, assisting their employment in agriculture and industry, education, raising funds abroad, and purchasing land in Israel for settlers through the Jewish National Fund (Keren Kayemet). In principle, the WZO was responsible mainly for political and organizational matters important to Zionists—Jewish education in the Diaspora and supervision of the Jewish National Fund—whereas the Jewish Agency's main concern was for financial and economic activities. In practice, the division of functions was more often obscured, resulting in a duplication of efforts and a bureaucratic morass.

In 1971 the relationship between the WZO and the Jewish Agency was reconstituted as part of a continuing effort to improve the operations of these bodies and to harmonize and strengthen ties between the state and the Diaspora. The need for this step was thought to be particularly acute after the June 1967 War, when contributions to Israel from previously uncommitted sections of the Diaspora reached unprecedented proportions. Impressed by the show of support, the congress of the WZO, which is usually convened every four years, directed the Jewish Agency to initiate discussions with all fund-raising institutions working for Israel. The purpose of these negotiations was to establish a central framework for cooperation and coordination between the Jewish Agency and other fund-raising groups. These discussions led to an agreement in 1971 whereby the governing bodies of the Jewish Agency were enlarged not only to provide equal representation for Israeli and Diaspora Jews but also to ensure a balance in geographical representation. The reconstitution helped to address the long-standing grievance of non-Zionist and non-Israeli supporters of Israel that the Jewish Agency was dominated by Israel-based Zionists.

Under the 1971 rearrangement, the WZO was separated in terms of its functions, but not its leadership, from the Jewish Agency. This was necessary because of the restrictive provision of the United States tax code pertaining to contributions and gifts. Those of its activities that were ''political'' or otherwise questionable from a tax-exemption standpoint had to be grouped separately and placed under the WZO. The organization was directed to ''continue as the organ of the Zionist movement for the fulfillment of Zionist programs and ideals,'' but its operations were to be confined mainly to the Diaspora. Among the main functions of the WZO after 1971 were Jewish education, Zionist organizational work, information and cultural programs, youth work, external relations, rural development, and the activities of the Jewish National Fund. For the most part, these functions were financed by funds funneled through the Jewish Agency, which continued to serve as the main financial arm of the WZO. However, because of United States tax law stipulations, funds allocated for the WZO by the Jewish Agency were required to come from those collected by Keren HaYesod (Israel Foundation Fund—see Glossary), the agency's financial arm in countries other than the United States.

The Jewish Agency's task was not only to coordinate various fund-raising institutions but also to finance such programs as immigration and land settlement and to assist immigrants in matters of housing, social welfare, education, and youth care. The United Jewish Appeal (UJA, sometimes designated the United Israel Appeal) raised the agency's funds in the United States. In the 1980s, contributions and gifts from the United States usually accounted for more than two-thirds of the total revenue of the Jewish Agency. In 1988 American Jews donated US$357 million to Israel through the UJA.

The Jewish National Fund was the land-purchasing arm of the WZO. It dealt mainly with land development issues such as reclamation, afforestation, and road construction in frontier regions. Keren HaYesod provided partial funding for programs, which were implemented in close cooperation with the Jewish Agency and various government ministries.

Histadrut

As of the late 1980s, the Histadrut (HaHistadrut HaKlalit shel HaOvdim B'Eretz Yisrael, General Federation of Laborers in the

Land of Israel) continued to be a major factor in Israeli life as the largest voluntary organization in the country. It also wielded an enormous influence on the government's wage policy and labor legislation, and was influential in political, social, and cultural realms (see Distinctive Social Institutions, ch. 2). The largest trade union organization, and largest employer in Israel after the government, the Histadrut has opened its membership to almost all occupations. Its membership in 1983 was 1,600,000 (including dependents), accounting for more than one-third of the total population of Israel and about 85 percent of all wage earners. About 170,000 Histadrut members were Arabs. Founded in 1920 by Labor Zionist parties, traditionally it has been controlled by the Labor Party, but not to the exclusion of other parties (see Multiparty System, this ch.). Almost all political parties or their affiliated socioeconomic institutions were represented in the organization.

The Histadrut performed functions that were unique to Israeli society, a legacy of its nation-building role in a wide range of economic, trade union, military, social, and cultural activities. Through its economic arm, Hevrat HaOvdim (Society of Workers), the Histadrut operated numerous economic enterprises and owned and managed the country's largest industrial conglomerates. It owned the country's second largest bank (Bank HaPoalim) and provided the largest and most comprehensive system of health insurance and also operated medical and hospital services. In addition, it coordinated the activities of domestic labor cooperative movements, and through its International Department, as well as organizations such as the Afro-Asian Institute, it maintained connections with labor movements in other countries.

Israeli political parties have regularly contested elections to the Histadrut Conference (Veida), held every four years. They also have contested elections to the National Labor Council and to the country's seventy-two local labor councils. Voting results in these elections have often paralleled or preceded trends in parliamentary and municipal elections.

The Histadrut Conference elects a General Council and an Executive Committee. The committee in turn elects a forty-three member Executive Bureau, which administers day-to-day policy. The Histadrut's secretary general, its most powerful official, is elected by the Executive Committee. As in the past, in late 1988 the Histadrut's secretary general, Israel Kaissar, was a Labor Party leader and a member of its Knesset delegation.

Political Framework: Elite, Values, and Orientations

When Israel became independent, its founding political elite, associated mainly with Mapai, had almost three decades of experience in operating self-governing institutions under the British Mandate. The top Mapai/Labor Party leaders continued to dominate Israeli politics for another three decades. Their paramount influence for over half a century as founders, architects, and prime movers of a Jewish national homeland has had an enduring effect on their successor generation and the political scene in Israel. The elite, political culture, social structure, and social makeup of any nation entwine in complex ways and in the process shape the character and direction of a given political system. This process holds true especially in Israel, where ideological imperatives and their institutionalization have constituted an important part of the country's evolution.

The first generation of Israeli leaders came to Palestine (which they called Eretz Yisrael, or Land of Israel) mainly during the Second Aliyah (see Glossary) between 1900 and 1914 (see Labor Zionism, ch. 1). The Ashkenazim (Jews of European origin), who constituted the majority among the Yishuv's mostly Labor Zionist political and socioeconomic elites, were impelled by Zionist ideals. The majority held to Labor Zionism, while others adhered to moderate General Zionism (sometimes called Political Zionism) or right-wing Revisionist Zionism. To the early immigrants, the themes promoted by the different Zionist movements provided powerful impulses for sociopolitical action. These pioneers were essentially Labor Zionists with an abiding faith in the rectitude of values that stressed, among other things, the establishment of a modern Jewish nation promoting mutual assistance under the principle of ''from each according to his ability, to each according to his needs,'' abolition of private ownership of the means of production, and the idea that human consciousness and character were conditioned by the social environment. They also held that Jewish land should be developed in a collectivist agricultural framework, that well-to-do Jews in the Diaspora should materially aid the cause of the Jewish homeland, and that the Jews of the Diaspora should seek the fullest measure of redemption by immigrating to the new Yishuv. In addition, collectivist values of East European and Central European origin, in which the founding generation had been socialized, affected the political orientation of Israel both before and after independence.

The value system of the first generation came to be exemplified first and foremost in the communal and egalitarian kibbutz and to a lesser extent in the moshav. Together these institutions accounted for less than 3 percent of the Jewish population at any given time, but they have held a special place in Israeli society as the citadel of pioneer ideology. They also gave Israel a distinctive self-image as a robust, dedicated, egalitarian, "farmer- or citizen-soldier" society. The kibbutzim also produced numbers of national leaders out of proportion to their small population; they also provided the country with some of its best soldiers and officers.

The founding generation of Israeli leaders, including David Ben-Gurion, Yitzhak Ben-Zvi, Berl Katznelson, Moshe Sharett, and later, Levi Eshkol and Golda Meir, in effect shaped the country's socioeconomic structures and political patterns. These people were instrumental in establishing the original Labor Zionist parties beginning in 1905, in merging them to establish Mapai in 1930, and in organizing the Histadrut and Jewish self-defense institutions, such as the Haganah (see Glossary), which later became the Israel Defense Forces (IDF) in 1948. These formative, nation-building organizations, along with the quasi-governmental Elected Assembly (Asefat Hanivharim—see Glossary), the National Council (Vaad Leumi), the WZO, and the Jewish Agency, served as the Yishuv's national institutions, shaping the character of postindependence Israel.

From its earliest days, Mapai, which had an interlocking leadership with the Histadrut, dominated Israeli public life, including the top echelons of the IDF, the WZO, and the Jewish Agency. Its legitimacy as a ruling party was seldom questioned because it was identified with the mystique of the Zionist struggle for independence, patriotism, and the successful consolidation of statehood. The essentially secular political values espoused by Mapai leaders were endorsed by most of the Jewish population. The absence of effective alternative governing elites or countervalues within the country's multiparty coalition-type government system made it difficult to challenge the Mapai-controlled political mainstream. Moreover, political patterns from the 1920s until the June 1967 War generally discouraged the rise of radical right-wing or left-wing destabilizing tendencies. This trend was rooted in the overall political dominance of Israel's Labor Party and its predecessors and the strength of the mutual restraints inherent in Israel's political subcultures.

Mainstream Israeli society is composed of persons who represent pluralistic cultural and political backgrounds. Politically, some Israeli Jews have liberal West European orientations; others were reared in more collectivist Central European and East European environments, or in authoritarian Middle Eastern political cultures. Some are religiously more traditional than others, but even among Orthodox Jews, shades of conviction vary substantially over the role of Jewish customary laws and the relationship between the state and religion. Thus, the founding generation had to develop a political system that reconciled and accommodated the varied needs of a wide range of groups.

The political system within Israel proper, excluding the West Bank and the Gaza Strip, is geared to the broadest possible level of public participation. Political activities are relatively free, although authoritarian and antidemocratic tendencies were evident among some of the leaders and supporters of right-wing ultranationalist parties and factions. In the late 1980s, the impetus to "agree to disagree" within the democratic framework of conciliation began to show some weakening as a result of intense polarizing controversies over the future of the occupied territories and various disputes over issues concerning the state and religion.

By the early 1970s, Jews of Sephardic origin (popularly referred to in Israel as Oriental Jews) outnumbered their Ashkenazic counterparts as a demographic group. The older Sephardim were, in general, from politically authoritarian and religiously traditional North African and Middle Eastern societies that regarded the Central European and West European secular and social democratic political value spectrum as too modern and far-reaching as compared to their own. They were accustomed to strong authoritarian leaders rather than ideals emphasizing social democratic collectivism and popular sovereignty. Nonetheless, a sizable proportion of Sephardim joined Labor's ranks both as leaders and rank-and-file party members.

Oriental Jews came to be referred to in the 1960s as "the Second Israel"—the numerically larger but socially, culturally, economically, and politically disadvantaged half of the nation (see Jewish Ethnic Groups, ch. 2). Not all Orientals were economically deprived, but nearly all of those who were relatively poor belonged to Sephardic communities. The communal gap and attendant tensions between Ashkenazic and Sephardic Jews have naturally engaged the remedial efforts of successive governments, but results have fallen far short of Oriental expectations. The problem was partly rooted in the country's political institutions and processes. Ashkenazic dominance of sociopolitical and economic life had been firmly institutionalized before independence. Over the years, however, Sephardic representation substantially increased in the country's major political parties, and as of the 1980s, Sephardic Jews occupied leadership positions in many municipalities.

Not surprisingly, beginning in the 1950s, most Sephardim tended to vote against Mapai and its successor, Labor. Both were perceived as representing the Ashkenazic establishment, even though Sephardim were always represented among the ranks of party leaders. In the 1950s and early 1960s, while many Sephardim were impressed with Ben-Gurion's charismatic and authoritative leadership, they nevertheless tended to support Herut, the major opposition party led by Menachem Begin, whose right-wing populism and ultranationalist, anti-Arab national security posture appealed to them. Paradoxically, the socialist-inspired social welfare system, a system built by Mapai and sustained by Labor and the Labor-dominated Histadrut, benefited the Sephardim particularly. In general, the Sephardim tended to support the right-wing Gahal/Likud blocs that for years had advocated a substantial modification of the welfare system so as to decrease its socialist emphasis. In terms of long-range electoral trends, the Sephardic position did not augur well for the Labor Zionist elite of the Labor Party.

Pressure for greater political representation and power has come from the younger, Israeli-born generation of both Ashkenazic and Sephardic origins. As a group, they were less obsessed with the past than their elders. The youth have been moving toward a strong, industrialized, capitalist, Western-style, middle-class society as the national norm. Although some younger right-wing ultranationalists and right-wing religious advocates continued to be imbued with the extremist nationalism and religious messianism of their elders—as shown, for example, by their support of parties favoring annexation of the occupied territories—most of the younger generation were more secular, pragmatic, and moderate on such issues.

The concerns of secular young people went beyond the question of "Who is a Jew"—which they continuously had to confront because of right-wing religious pressures—to such critical issues as the quality of education, social status, economic conditions, and the comforts of modern life. Their primary interests have been how to make Israel more secure from external threat and how to improve the quality of life for all. Nevertheless, for many Israelis, the founding ideologies remained a ritualized part of national politics.

Urbanization and industrialization were equally potent forces of change; their adulterating effect on Israel's founding ideology has been particularly significant. They have led to new demands, new opportunities, and new stresses in social and economic life affecting all social and political strata. The older commitment to agriculture, pioneering, and collectivism has crumbled before the relentless pressure of industrialization and the bridging of the gap between urban and rural life. Collective and communal settlements have become increasingly industrialized; factories and high-technology industries have been set up; the mass media have faciliated an influx of new information and ideas; and additional layers of bureaucratic and institutional arrangements have emerged.

Kibbutz idealism, the pride of Israel, has declined, especially among increasingly individualistic and consumer-oriented young people. To stem this tide and to retain young members, kibbutz federations and individual kibbutzim have established many educational and vocational programs and activities.

As the 1970s began, the social base of Israeli politics had become highly complex, and political fluidity resulted. A major catalyst in creating a new mood was the October 1973 War, known in Israel as the Yom Kippur War, which dealt a crushing blow to popular belief in Israel's strength and preparedness in the face of its Arab adversaries (see The October 1973 War, ch. 5). The result was a loss of confidence in the political and national security elite, headed at the time by Prime Minister Golda Meir, Minister of Defense Moshe Dayan, and Minister-Without-Portfolio Israel Galilee. After the war, in which Egyptian and Syrian forces scored military gains, many charges and countercharges concerned inadequate military preparedness. Nevertheless, Meir's government returned to power in the country's parliamentary elections held on December 31, 1973. Apparently, despite widespread misgivings, many Israelis believed that continuity was preferable to change and uncertainty under Begin's newly formed and untried center-right Likud Bloc (see The Likud Bloc, this ch.).

Meir's resignation from the prime ministership in April 1974 resulted in a succession crisis and the departure of the last of Labor's old guard party leaders, mostly in their late sixties and seventies, such as Meir, Pinchas Sapir, and Israel Galilee. Meir's departure triggered political infighting among the Labor elite, specifically between the former Mapai and Rafi (Israel Labor List—see Appendix B) factions; a new generation centered around the triumvirate of Yitzhak Rabin, Shimon Peres, and Yigal Allon, succeeded Meir.

The second most striking political development in the 1970s was the ascendance of a new right-wing counterelite in May 1977. An upset victory in the ninth parliamentary elections, called an "earthquake" by some, brought Begin's center-right Likud to power, ending Labor's half a century of political dominance. The new political elite won primarily because of the defection of former Labor leaders and previous Labor voters to the Democratic Movement for Change (DMC), which had been founded in 1976 by Yigal Yadin and several other groups. Despite the subsequent collapse of the DMC and the defection of moderates from the Likud-led cabinet—for example, former Minister of Defense Ezer Weizman formed his own list Yahad (Together—see Appendix B) in 1981 and Minister of Foreign Affairs Moshe Dayan created Telem—Likud's success in the tenth parliamentary elections of 1981 resulted from its continued ability to present itself as a viable governing group and a party dedicated to ultranationalism and territorial expansionism.

The top echelons of the Israeli political elite as of the late 1980s were still predominantly of European background; many of them had either immigrated to Palestine during the 1930s and the 1940s or had been born in the Yishuv to parents of East European or Central European origin. A growing number of Oriental politicians, however, were making their mark in the top ranks of all the major parties and at the ministerial and subministerial levels. A majority of the elite had a secular university education, while a minority had a more traditional religious education. The political elite was overwhelmingly urban—most resided in Tel Aviv, Jerusalem, or Haifa. A minority, particularly the Sephardim, came from the newer development towns. Among the elite who resided in rural areas most, especially members of Labor and its satellites, represented communal kibbutzim and, to a lesser extent, moshavim.

By occupational category, professional party politicians constituted by far the largest single group, followed, in numerical order, by lawyers, kibbutz officials, educators, Histadrut or private sector corporate managers, journalists, ex-military officers, and, to a lesser degree, functionaries of religious institutions. Many of the elite were in the forty-to-mid-sixty age bracket. In 1988 the political elite numbered more than 200 individuals, excluding the broader social elite encompassing business, military, religious, educational, cultural, and agricultural figures. The number would be greater if senior officials in such key offices as the Office of the Prime Minister and the ministries of defense, foreign affairs, finance, and commerce, as well as the Histadrut and its industrial and financial enterprises and trade unions, were included.

The power of individual members of the elite varied depending on their personal reputation and their offices. The most influential were found in the cabinet. Members of the Knesset came next. Elected mayors of large municipalities such as Tel Aviv, Jerusalem, and Haifa had considerable importance because of the influence of local politics on national-level politics. In addition, the president, Supreme Court justices, and the head of the Office of the State Comptroller had the prestige of cabinet members although they lacked decision-making responsibility.

During the late 1980s, the criteria for entrance into the top elite were more open and competitive than previously. Political parties, and, to some extent, the civil service, continued to be the principal vehicles for upward mobility. Under the country's electoral system of proportional representation, participation in party politics

plexceptpalfor positions cases

remained essential for gaining top positions, except in limited cases of co-optation from nonparty circles, principally the military. In earlier periods, party nominating committees primarily determined a politician's entry into a parliamentary delegation; in the 1980s, internal party elections increasingly governed this decision. This system placed a high premium on partisan loyalty, membership in a party faction, and individual competence.

The political establishment, whether in office or in opposition, secularist or Orthodox, left-wing or right-wing, has remained basically loyal to the state. Establishment interpretations of classical Zionist ideologies have varied according to the adherents' diverse backgrounds and political and religious orientations, but internal political cleavages have not undermined the essential unity of Israeli society and political institutions. Except for certain segments among a minority of extremist right-wing religious or secular ultranationalists, most Israeli citizens have sought to maintain democratic values and procedures; their differences have centered mainly on tactics rather than on the goal of realizing a modern, democratic, prosperous social welfare state.

Multiparty System

Political power in Israel has been contested within the framework of multiparty competition. Parliamentary elections are held every four years, and, unlike many parliamentary systems, the electorate votes as a single national constituency. Power has revolved around the system of government by coalition led by one of the two major parties, or in partnership among them. From the establishment of Mapai in 1930 until the 1977 Knesset elections, Labor (and its predecessor, Mapai) was the dominant party. Labor's defeat in the 1977 Knesset election, however, transformed the dominant party system into a multiparty system dominated by two major parties, Labor and Likud, in which neither was capable of governing except in alliance with smaller parties or, as in 1984 and 1988, in alliance with each other.

Since 1920, when the first Elected Assembly was held, no party has been able to command a simple majority in any parliamentary election. Israel has always had a pluralistic political culture featuring at least three major polarizing social and political tendencies: secular left-of-center, secular right-of-center, and religious right-of-center. No single tendency was dominant in the 1980s. Political fragmentation, as marked by the proliferation of parties, is a long-standing feature of Israeli society. For example, in the prestate period, between 1920 and 1944, from twelve to twenty-six party lists were represented in the Elected Assembly. In the first Knesset election in 1949, twenty-four political parties and groups competed. Since then the number has fluctuated as a result of occasional splits, realignments, and mergers. However, dominance by two major parties and a multiplicity of smaller parties remained deeply embedded in Israeli political culture (for details of individual political parties, see Appendix B).

In addition to political operations, party functions during the prestate period included "democratic integration," that is, the provision of social, economic, military, and cultural services for party members and supporters. During the postindependence period, party politics, in particular regarding competition between Labor and Likud and their respective allies, continued to be vigorous. Many analysts saw signs of a political crisis looming with the emergence of extremist minor parties and extraparliamentary protest movements (e.g., Kach and Gush Emunim). These groups challenged the traditional parties on such issues as the roles of the state and religion and the future territorial boundaries of the Jewish state.

Israel's major parties originated from the East European and Central European branches of the WZO, founded by Theodor Herzl in 1897, and from political and religious groups in the Mandate period. For example, a faction called the Democratic Zionists, including among its members Chaim Weizmann, Israel's first president, was active in 1900; Mizrahi (Spiritual Center), an Orthodox religious movement, was founded in 1902; and the non-Marxist Labor Zionist HaPoel HaTzair (The Young Worker), was established in 1905. Aaron David Gordon, the latter group's spiritual leader, was instrumental in founding the first kibbutz and moshav soon after the party's establishment (see Political Zionism, ch. 1). Moreover, in 1906 the Marxist Poalei Tziyyon (Workers of Zion—see Appendix B) was created to initiate a socialist-inspired class struggle in Palestine. Ber Borochov was its ideological mentor, and Ben-Gurion and Ben-Zvi were among its founding leaders. Vladimir Jabotinsky founded the right-wing Revisionist Party in 1925 to oppose what he considered the WZO executive's conciliatory policy toward the British mandatory government and toward the pace of overall Zionist settlement activity in Palestine.

These early, formative experiences in political activity produced three major alignments. All were Zionist, but they had varying shades of secularism and religious orthodoxy. Two of the alignments were secular but ideologically opposed. The first consisted of leftist or socialist labor parties of which Mapai, founded in 1930, was the dominant party. The second consisted of centrist-rightist parties; Herut (Freedom Movement—see Appendix B), founded in 1949, the Revisionist Party's successor and the present Likud's mainstay, dominated that alignment. Herut, which had become part of Likud, eventually won a mandate to govern in 1977 under Begin. The third major political alignment consisted of Orthodox religious Zionists. A fourth category of minor Zionist parties also emerged, traditionally allied with one of the two major alignments; non-Zionist communist Arab or nationalist Arab parties constituted the fifth grouping.

In the late 1980s, the stated values of Israeli political parties, including religious, communist, Arab nationalist, and mainstream parties, could not properly be placed on the left-right or liberal-conservative spectrum except, perhaps, on the issue of the future of the occupied territories. The positions advocated by Labor, Likud, Orthodox religious parties, and the constellation of smaller parties allied to them have varied greatly. On the extreme left, the most anti-Western element in Israeli politics was Rakah (New Communist List—see Appendix B), a Moscow-oriented group with a contingent of former Sephardic Black Panther activists that appealed to Palestinian Arab nationalist sentiment. Of the long-established minor parties, the moderate left-of-center Mapam (formally Mifleget Poalim Meuchedet, United Workers' Party—see Appendix B), which from 1969 to 1984 constituted a faction in the electoral alignment with Labor, the Citizens' Rights Movement (see Appendix B), and Shinui (Change—see Appendix B), were Labor's traditional satellites. Labor, in alignment with Mapam from 1969 until 1984, favored a negotiated settlement concerning the occupied territories involving the exchange of land for peace.

On the center-right of the political spectrum were Likud and its satellite parties, Tehiya, Tsomet, and Moledet. On the fringe right was Kach, which the Knesset outlawed in 1988 because of its racist platform that wished to expel all Arabs from the occupied territories. Likud, especially its Herut component, favored retaining much of the occupied territories to regain what it considered to be the ancient boundaries of Eretz Yisrael. The positions of the religious parties—the National Religious Party (NRP—see Appendix B), Agudat Israel, Shas (Sephardic Torah Guardians—see Appendix B), and Degel HaTorah (Torah Flag—see Appendix B)—generally coincided with the right-of-center parties, although the NRP trade-union component has continued its alliance with Labor in the Histadrut.

Israeli parties have engaged in many activities even in nonelection years. Indoctrination of young people has been important, although in the case of the Labor Party it had markedly lessened in the 1980s in comparison to the prestate period. Political parties retained much of their early character as mutual aid societies.

Consequently, voters have tended to support the country's political parties as a civic duty. Membership in a registered party has not been a requirement for voting, but formal party membership was high and party members have accounted for 25 to 50 percent of the vote.

Except for small Arab and communist groups, Israeli political parties have been basically Zionist in their orientation. Given the shades of interpretation inherent in Zionism, parties drew their support from adherents who might be secular, religious, or antireligious, adherents of social welfare policies or free enterprise (the distinction was not always clear because Mapai/Labor in fact created Israel's capitalist economy), advocates of territorial compromise or territorial expansion. In general, attempts to organize parties on the basis of ethnic origin—for example, in the cases of Yemeni, Iraqi, or Moroccan Jews—had been unsuccessful until the early 1980s, when the Sephardi-based Tami (Traditional Movement of Israel—see Appendix B) and Shas were formed.

With the exception of religious parties, Israeli parties possessed national constituencies but also engaged in politics based on territorial subdivisions and local interests. Increasingly during the late 1980s, local party branches enjoyed greater independence in selecting local personalities in internal party nominations for mayoral, municipal council, Histadrut, and Knesset elections, as well as their own party's central committees and conventions. This independence resulted in part from the growing tendency to vote on the basis of individual merit—mayoral elections, for example, reflected an emerging pattern of split-ticket voting—rather than traditional party loyalty. This trend, if sustained, was likely to lead to the decentralization of party control, if only to ensure that voters will support the same party in national as well as local elections.

Alignment Parties

Labor Party

Until 1977 Mapai and the Labor Party dominated the political scene. Labor became Israel's dominant party as a result of its predecessors' effective and modernizing leadership during the formative prestate period (1917–48). The Labor Party (see Appendix B) resulted in 1968 from the merger of Mapai, Ahdut HaAvoda (Unity of Labor—see Appendix B), and Rafi (see fig. 11). In addition, shortly before the 1969 elections an electoral Alignment (Maarakh) occurred between Labor and the smaller Mapam Party. Although the two parties retained their organizational

Israel: A Country Study

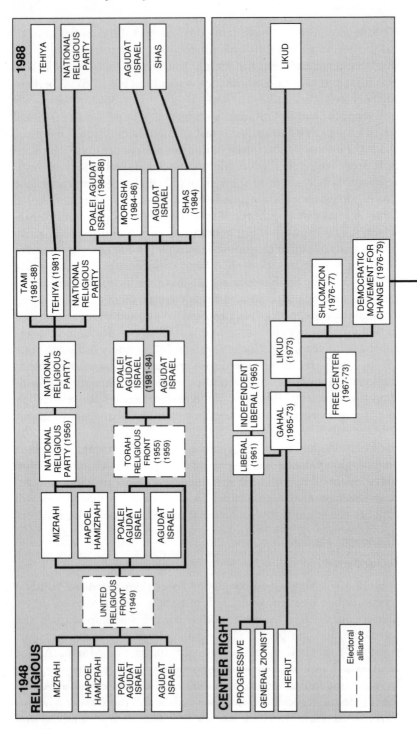

214

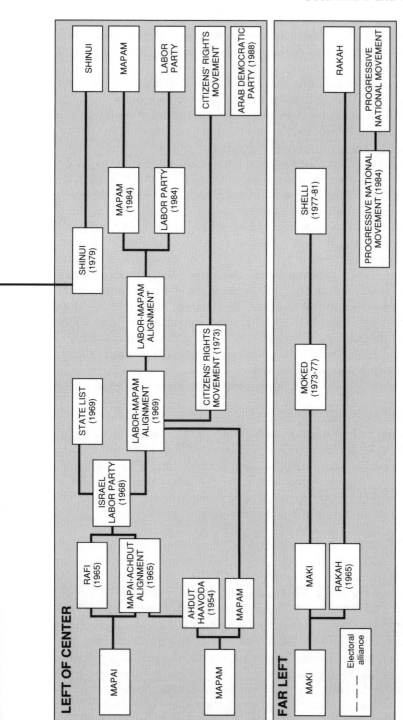

Figure 11. Evolution of Political Parties, 1948–88 (Simplified)

215

independence, they shared a common slate in elections to the Knesset, the Histadrut, and local government offices. The Alignment lasted until 1984.

Labor's political dominance broke down, particularly following the June 1967 War, when the party split over its leaders' inability to reach a consensus concerning the future of the West Bank, the Gaza Strip, and the Sinai Peninsula; there was agreement only on the need to retain the Golan Heights to ensure strategic depth against Syria. Later, the October 1973 War dealt a blow to public confidence in Labor from which its leadership was unable to recover. The war also exacerbated a number of crises confronting the party such as those concerning leadership succession. Although the party survived the Knesset elections of December 31, 1973, with a slightly reduced plurality, the war led to the resignation of Prime Minister Meir's government on April 10, 1974. The new leadership team of Yitzhak Rabin, Shimon Peres, and Yigal Allon, which assumed power in June 1974, proved unable to govern effectively or to resolve major issues such as the future of the occupied territories. Following its electoral defeat in the 1977 Knesset elections, the Labor Party provided the principal opposition to Likud in the elections of 1981, 1984, and 1988. In the 1988 Knesset elections, the Labor Party, despite its efforts to present a revived platform advocating territorial compromise, gained only thirty-nine seats, down from forty-four in 1984.

In 1988 the dominant personalities in Labor, in addition to Peres and Rabin, included former president Yitzhak Navon, former IDF Chief of Staff Moredechai Gur, and former Likud Defense Minister Ezer Weizman, who joined Labor in preparation for the 1984 elections. Labor's biggest problem in the 1980s has been the gradual decline in its electoral support among growing segments in the electorate, notably Orientals and the young.

Mapam

A moderate, left-of-center Labor Zionist party, Mapam has had representatives in the Knesset since the inception of the state; it won three seats in the November 1988 Knesset elections. Opposition to the formation of the unity government in September 1984 led Mapam to withdraw from its fifteen-year-long electoral alignment with Labor. The 1988 Knesset elections represented the first time in twenty years that Mapam had contested an election independently. Mapam's top leaders included the party's secretary general, Elazar Granot, and Knesset member Yair Tzaban.

Mapam has advocated a strong national security and defense posture, with many of its members playing leading roles in the IDF.

At the same time, it has urged continuing peace initiatives and territorial compromise, and has opposed the permanent annexation of the territories occupied in the June 1967 War beyond minimal border changes designed to provide Israel with secure and defensible boundaries. Mapam has long believed in Jewish-Arab coexistence and friendship as a means of hastening peace between Israel, the Palestinians, and the Arab states.

Citizens' Rights Movement (CRM)

Founded in 1973 by Shulamit Aloni, a former Labor Party Knesset member, the CRM has played an active role in calling for strengthening civil rights in Israel, particularly regarding issues involving the boundaries between the state and religion, and in advocating a peace settlement with the Palestinians and the Arab states based on territorial compromise. In the 1988 Knesset elections, the party increased its representation to five seats, compared with three in 1984. The party has traditionally allied itself with Labor, although it has refused to join Labor in unity governments with Likud. The CRM received considerable support from the country's liberal community, and prominent among its leaders were Knesset members Yossi Sarid (formerly of the Labor Party); Ran Cohen, a high-ranking reservist in the IDF; and Mordechai Bar-On and Dudy Zucker, leaders of the Peace Now (see Appendix B) movement.

Shinui (Change)

Founded in 1977 by Amnon Rubenstein, a law professor at Tel Aviv University and a columnist for *Ha'aretz*, Shinui represented a large faction in the Democratic Movement for Change (DMC). The DMC won fifteen seats and played a major role in toppling the Labor Party in the 1977 Knesset elections. Within less than three years, however, the DMC broke up over the issue of continued participation in the Likud government. During the next decade Shinui served as an ally of Labor and was a leading advocate for constitutional and electoral reform and greater flexibility on the Palestinian problem. In the November 1988 elections, Shinui's Knesset representation declined from three to two seats.

The Likud Bloc

In the ninth Knesset elections in May 1977, the center-right Likud alliance emerged victorious and replaced the previously dominant Labor alignment for the first time in the history of independent Israel. The Likud Bloc, founded in 1973, consisted of the Free Center, Herut (Tnuat HaHerut or Freedom Movement—

see Appendix B), Laam (For the Nation—see Appendix B), and Gahal (Freedom-Liberal Bloc—see Appendix B). In large part, Likud was the direct ideological descendant of the Revisionist Party, established by Vladimir Jabotinsky in 1925 (see Revisionist Zionism, ch. 1).

The Revisionist Party, so named to underscore the urgency of revision in the policies of the WZO's executive, advocated militancy and ultranationalism as the primary political imperatives of the Zionist struggle for Jewish statehood. The Revisionist Party demanded that the entire mandated territory of historical Palestine on both sides of the Jordan River, including Transjordan, immediately become a Jewish state with a Jewish majority. Revisionist objectives clashed with the policies of the British authorities, Labor Zionists, and Palestinian Arabs. The Revisionist Party, in which Menachem Begin played a major role, contended that the British must permit unlimited Jewish immigration into Palestine and demanded that the Jewish Legion be reestablished and that Jewish youths be trained for defense.

The Revisionist Party also attacked the Histadrut, whose Labor Zionist leadership under Ben-Gurion was synonymous with the leadership of the politically dominant Mapai. Ben-Gurion accused the revisionists of being ''fascists''; the latter countercharged that the policies being pursued by Ben-Gurion and his Labor Zionist allies, including Chaim Weizmann, were so conciliatory toward the British authorities and Palestinian Arabs and so gradual in terms of state-building as to be self-defeating.

In 1933 the Revisionist Party seceded from the WZO and formed the rival New Zionist Organization. After 1936 the revisionists rejected British and official Zionist policies of restraint in the face of Arab attacks, and they formed two anti-British and anti-Arab guerrilla groups. One, the Irgun Zvai Leumi (National Military Organization, Irgun for short) was formed in 1937; an offshoot of the Irgun, the Stern Gang also known as Lehi (from Lohamei Herut Israel, Fighters for Israel's Freedom), was formed in 1940 (see Historical Background, ch. 5). These revisionist paramilitary groups operated independently of, and at times in conflict with, the official Zionist defense organization, the Haganah; they engaged in systematic terror and sabotage against the British authorities and the Arabs.

After independence Prime Minister Ben-Gurion dissolved the Irgun and other paramilitary organizations such as Lehi and the Palmach (see Glossary). In 1948 remnants of the dissolved Irgun created Herut.

"WOULD YOU TRUST HIM (SHAMIR) AS A SHIP CAPTAIN?!"

*November 1988 election flyer of the Young Guard
faction of the Labor Party. The flag reads "Annexed!"*

In the mid-1960s, Herut took steps to broaden its political base and attain greater legitimacy. In 1963 it established the Blue-White (Tehelet-Lavan) faction to contest the previously boycotted Histadrut elections. In 1965 Herut and the Liberal Party (see Appendix B) formed Gahal (Gush Herut-Liberalim), a parliamentary and electoral bloc, to contest both Knesset and Histadrut elections. The final step in gaining greater political legitimacy occurred just before the outbreak of the June 1967 War, when Begin and his Gahal associates agreed to join the government to demonstrate internal Israeli unity in response to an external threat.

Gahal continued as part of the Meir cabinet formed after the 1969 elections. Gahal ministers withdrew from the cabinet in 1970 to protest what they believed to be Prime Minister Meir's conciliatory policy on territorial issues (see Foreign Relations, this ch.). In the summer of 1973, Gahal organized the Likud alignment in which Herut continued to be preeminent.

In the November 1988 elections, Likud lost one Knesset seat. Nevertheless, observers believed that demographic indicators favored continued support for Likud and its right-wing allies among young people and Orientals.

The most prominent leaders of Likud in 1988, as in previous years, were members of its Herut faction. They included Prime Minister Shamir; Minister of Foreign Affairs Moshe Arens, a likely

219

successor to Shamir as leader of Herut; Deputy Prime Minister and Minister of Housing David Levi, the chief Sephardic political figure; Minister of Commerce and Industry Ariel Sharon; and Deputy Minister of Foreign Affairs Benjamin Netanyahu.

Religious Parties

Israel's religious parties were originally organized not to seize the reins of power, but rather to engage in what American scholar Norman L. Zucker has called ''theopolitics''—to gain theological ends by means of political activity. From the Orthodox viewpoint, Israel remained an imperfect state as long as secular rather than religiously observant Jews constituted a majority. As of 1988, policy issues concerning religious parties included the question of ''Who is a Jew,'' maintaining Orthodox rabbinical control over marriage and divorce, increasing sabbath observance, observing kosher dietary regulations, maintaining and expanding the state religious education systems, ensuring the exemption of religious women and ultra-Orthodox men from military service, and such social issues as abortion.

Despite the minority position of adherents of Orthodox Judaism, several factors have enabled this religious bloc to maintain a central role in the state. Such factors have included the links between Judaism and Israeli nationalism; the political and organizational power of the religious parties—particularly the NRP and later Agudat Israel and Shas—in assuming a pivotal role in the formation and maintenance of coalition governments; and the inability of the Reform and Conservative Jewish religious movements, although powerful in the Jewish Diaspora, to penetrate effectively Israel's religious administrative apparatus. This apparatus consisted particularly of the Ministry of Religious Affairs, the Chief Rabbinate, the Chief Rabbinical Council, and local religious councils. The Reform and Conservative movements played a minor role in Zionism during the prestate period and thus allowed the Orthodox to dominate religious activities in the new state. Among the Orthodox there were varying forms of religious observance in accordance with halakah. The main division was between the ultra-Orthodox, who rejected Zionism and were associated with Agudat Israel and Shas, and the modern Orthodox, who attempted to reconcile Zionism and religious orthodoxy and were associated with the NRP.

Taken together, Israel's religious parties have over the years generally commanded from fifteen to eighteen seats in the Knesset, or about 12 to 15 percent of the Knesset. On occasion they have formed religious coalitions of their own, such as the United

Religious Front (see Appendix B) and the Torah Religious Front
(see Appendix B). The voter strength of the religious parties, particularly the NRP, made them ideal coalition partners for the two
major blocs. Because neither bloc has ever been able to achieve
a majority in the Knesset, the potentially pivotal position of the
religious parties has given them disproportionate political power.
One of the greatest shocks of the 1988 Knesset elections was the
surprising increase in strength of the Orthodox and ultra-Orthodox
parties, which went from thirteen to eighteen Knesset seats.

National Religious Party

The National Religious Party, Israel's largest religious party,
resulted in 1956 from the merger of its two historical antecedents,
Mizrahi (Spiritual Center—see Appendix B) and HaPoel HaMiz-
rahi (Spiritual Center Worker—see Appendix B). The NRP (as
Mizrahi prior to 1956) has participated in every coalition govern-
ment since independence. Invariably the Ministry of Religious
Affairs, as well as the Ministry of Interior, have been headed by
Knesset members nominated by this party.

Although the NRP increased from four to five Knesset seats in
the 1988 elections, it had not fully recovered from major political
and electoral setbacks suffered in the 1981 and 1984 elections. In
those elections, much of its previous electoral support shifted to
right-wing religio-nationalist parties. As a sign of its attempted
recovery, in July 1986 the NRP held its first party convention since
1973. The long interval separating the two conventions was caused
by factional struggles between the younger and the veteran leadership groups. In the 1986 convention, the NRP's second generation of leaders, members of the Youth Faction, officially took over
the party's institutions and executive bodies. The new NRP leader
was Knesset member Zevulun Hammer, former minister of education and culture in the Likud cabinet (1977–84) and secretary general of the party (1984–86). In 1986 Hammer succeeded
long-time member Yosef Burg as minister of religious affairs in
the National Unity Government. Hammer and Yehuda Ben-
Meir, coleader of the Youth Faction until 1984, were among the
founders of Gush Emunim in 1974 (see Extraparliamentary Religio-
Nationalist Movements, this ch.). Both leaders somewhat moder-
ated their views on national security, territorial, and settlement
issues following Israel's 1982 invasion of Lebanon, but the NRP's
declining political and electoral position and the increasing radicalization of its religiously based constituency led to a reversal in Hammer's views. As a result, in the 1986 party convention the Youth
Faction helped incorporate into the NRP the religio-nationalist

221

Morasha (Heritage), which was led by Rabbi Chaim Druckman and held two seats in the Knesset. In return, Rabbi Yitzhak Levi, the third candidate on the Morasha Knesset list, became the NRP's new secretary general. Moroccan-born Levi has been a fervent supporter of Gush Emunim and an advocate of incorporating the West Bank and the Gaza Strip into a greater Israel.

Until the 1986 party convention, the dominant faction in the NRP was LaMifneh (To the Turning Point). The center-most faction, LaMifneh advocated greater pragmatism and ideological pluralism. Burg, a Knesset member since 1949, who had held a variety of cabinet portfolios including interior (1974–84) and religious affairs (1982–86), led LaMifneh. Burg and Rafael Ben-Natan, former party organization strongman, were responsible for maintaining the "historical partnership" with the Labor Party that officially ended in 1977, but continued in some municipal councils and in the Histadrut.

In the 1988 internal party elections, the NRP took a number of steps to regain the support of segments of the Oriental Orthodox electorate that were lost to Tami in 1981 and, to a lesser extent, to Shas in 1988. The party also sought to regain the support of right-wing religious ultranationalists. In the internal party elections, the NRP nominated Moroccan-born Avner Sciaki for the top spot on its Knesset list, Zevulun Hammer for the second position, and Hanan Porat, a leader of Gush Emunim and formerly of Tehiya, in the third spot. As a result of these steps, the NRP attained greater ideological homogeneity and competed with Tehiya and Kach for the electoral support of the right-wing ultranationalist religious community.

Agudat Israel

During the prestate period, Agudat Israel, founded in 1912, opposed both the ideology of Zionism and its political expression, the World Zionist Organization. It rejected any cooperation with non-Orthodox Jewish groups and considered Zionism profane in that it forced the hand of the Almighty in bringing about the redemption of the Jewish people. A theocratic and clericalist party, Agudat Israel has exhibited intense factionalism and religious extremism. From 1955 to 1961 Agudat Israel formed a part of the Torah Religious Front (see Appendix B). Traditionally, the party's Knesset delegation has consisted only of Ashkenazi factions, although ultra-Orthodox Orientals also provided it considerable electoral support.

In preparation for the 1984 Knesset elections, grievances over a lack of representation in party institutions caused Orientals to defect and establish Shas. As a result, Agudat Israel's Knesset representation declined from four to two seats. In the 1988 Knesset elections, as part of an ultra-Orthodox electoral upswing, the Shas Knesset delegation increased from two to six seats.

The Council of Torah Sages, a panel of rabbis to which both religious and secular decisions had to be referred, contained representatives of each faction in Agudat Israel. The main factions represented two Hasidic (ultra-Orthodox) courts: the court of the Rabbi of Gur, which dominated the party and the Council of Torah Sages; and the court of Rabbi Eliezer Shakh.

Agudat Israel engaged in ultra-Orthodox educational and social welfare activities, as well as in immigrant absorption. It usually took the lead in initiating legislation on religious issues. The party has obtained exemptions from military service for its adherents.

Shas

Shas resulted in 1984 from allegations of Agudat Israel's inadequate representation of ultra-Orthodox Sephardim in the Council of Torah Sages, the party organization, and educational and social welfare institutions. The leader of Shas was Rabbi Yitzhak Peretz, who served as minister of interior in the National Unity Government until his protest resignation in 1987. As a theocratic party, Shas depended heavily for policy direction on its patrons, former Sephardic Chief Rabbi Ovadia Yoseph, and Rabbi Eliezer Shakh, former Ashkenazi head of the Agudat Israel-dominated Council of Torah Sages. Rabbi Shakh sanctioned the formation of Shas and its division into separate Sephardi and Ashkenazi factions. In the negotiations to form the National Unity Government in 1984, Shas outmaneuvered the NRP and gained the Ministry of Interior portfolio. As minister of interior, Rabbi Peretz became a source of controversy as a result of his promoting religious fundamentalism in general and the narrow partisan interests of Shas in particular.

Unlike Agudat Israel, Shas saw no contradiction between its religious beliefs and Zionism. It was far more anti-Arab than Agudat Israel and sought increased representation for its adherents in all government bodies, in Zionist institutions, and in the Jewish Agency. Despite its ethnic homogeneity, Shas was not immune from bitter infighting over the spoils of office, as shown by the rivalry between factions led by Rabbi Peretz and Rabbi Arieh Dari, leader of the party's apparatus, who remained director general of the Ministry of Interior until the National Unity Government's term ended in 1988. Shas gained four Knesset seats in the 1984 elections and increased the size of its delegation to six in 1988. In late

1988, it actually held eight Knesset seats when combined with the two seats gained by Degel HaTorah, a Shas Ashkenazi faction formed in 1988.

Central Religious Camp

In 1988 Rabbi Yehuda Amital of Jerusalem formed a new moderate religious party, the Central Religious Camp, in an attempt to counteract the growing popularity of right-wing ultranationalist religious parties. Rabbi Tovah Lichtenstein had the second position on the party's Knesset list. The party failed, however, to gain the minimum 1 percent of votes required for Knesset representation.

Right-Wing Ultranationalist Parties

Tehiya (Renaissance—see Appendix B), an ultranationalist party, arose in 1979 in reaction to NRP and Likud support for the 1978 Camp David Accords and the 1979 Treaty of Peace Between Egypt and Israel. The party consisted of religious and secular leaders and activists of Gush Emunim and the Land of Israel Movement. The leaders and parliamentary representatives of Tehiya were Yuval Neeman, party chairman and former minister of science and technology in the Likud-led cabinet (1981–84); Geula Cohen, formerly of Herut; Rabbi Eliezer Waldman, head of the Kiryat Arba Yeshiva; Gershon Shafet; and Kiryat Arba's ultranationalist attorney Eliakim Haetzni. Former IDF Chief of Staff Rafael Eitan ranked among the party's leaders until 1984, when he left to form his own list, Tsomet. Tehiya's platform advocated the eventual imposition of Israeli sovereignty over the West Bank and the Gaza Strip and the transfer of the Palestinian inhabitants of these territories to Arab countries. In the 1984 elections, Tehiya gained five Knesset seats, an increase of two from 1981. In 1988, however, Tehiya lost two seats to the newly formed Tsomet and Moledet parties.

Tsomet (Crossroads) was an extreme right-wing ultranationalist party founded in 1984 by Eitan. It gained two seats in the 1988 Knesset elections.

Moledet (Homeland) ran in 1988 on an extremist platform advocating the forcible "transfer" of Palestinian Arabs from the West Bank to Arab states. Led by retired IDF General Rehavam (Ghandi) Zeevi, the party won two seats in the 1988 Knesset elections.

Kach (Thus), another ultranationalist party, came into being around Rabbi Meir Kahane, an American-born right-wing Orthodox extremist. Characterized as an internal dictatorship under Kahane, Kach has advocated the forcible expulsion of Arabs from

Israel and the occupied territories, followed by the imposition of Israeli sovereignty there. A number of second-echelon party leaders have been implicated in Kach-supported terrorist activities. A terrorist attack on a bus carrying Arab passengers on Mount Hebron, near the town of Hebron, caused the imprisonment of Yehuda Richter, in second place on the Kach Knesset list. Avner Ozen, number four on Kach's 1984 list, was also imprisoned on terrorist charges. To counteract Kach's inflammatory political activities, in 1988 Likud and the Citizens' Rights Movement succeeded in passing a Basic Law empowering the Central Elections Board to prohibit a party advocating racism from contesting parliamentary elections in Israel and Kach was outlawed from participating in the November 1988 elections. Kach, largely funded by American supporters, had gained one seat in the 1984 elections after several earlier unsuccessful attempts to enter the Knesset.

Extraparliamentary Religio-Nationalist Movements

Gush Emunim (Bloc of the Faithful), a right-wing ultranationalist, religio-political revitalization movement, was formed in March 1974 in the aftermath of the October 1973 War. The younger generation of NRP leaders who constituted the party's new religious elite created Gush Emunim. Official links between Gush Emunim and the Youth Faction of the National Religious Party were severed following the NRP's participation in the June 1974 Labor-led coalition government, but close unofficial links between the two groups continued. Gush Emunim also maintained links to Tehiya and factions in the Herut wing of Likud.

The major activity of Gush Emunim has been to initiate Jewish settlements in the West Bank and in the Gaza Strip. From 1977 to 1984, Likud permitted the launching of a number of Jewish settlements beyond the borders of the Green Line (see Glossary). The Likud regime gave Gush Emunim the active support of government departments, the army, and the WZO, which recognized it as an official settlement movement and allocated it considerable funds for settlement activities.

A thirteen-member secretariat has governed Gush Emunim. A special conference elected nine of the group's secretaries and co-opted the other four from the leadership ranks of its affiliated organizations. Four persons have managed the movement's day-to-day affairs: Rabbi Moshe Levinger, a founder of Gush Emunim and the leader of the Jewish town of Kiryat Arba, near Hebron, on the West Bank; Hanan Porat, a founder of the organization and a former Tehiya Knesset member who later rejoined the NRP; Uri Elitzur, secretary general of Amana, Gush Emunim's

225

settlement movement; and Yitzhak Armoni, secretary general of Gush Emunim since September 1988. From 1984 to August 1988, American-born Daniella Weiss served as Gush Emunim's secretary general.

Amana was Gush Emunim's settlement arm. The Council of Settlements in Judea and Samaria (Yesha), chaired by Israel Harel, was the political organization representing the majority of Jewish settlements in the West Bank and the Gaza Strip. There were more than eighty such settlements, including those affiliated with nonreligious parties. Yesha dealt primarily with practical matters, such as the utilization of land and water, relations with Israeli military authorities and, if necessary, mobilizing political pressure on the government. Yesha has created affiliations between Gush Emunim settlements and Labor, the NRP, and Herut's Betar youth movement. Two factors shape Yesha, a democratically elected political organization: the right-wing and ultranationalist views of its members and its political dependency on external bodies such as government agencies. The group had five councils in Israel proper and six regional councils in the occupied territories.

Arab Parties

Israel's approximately 781,350 Arabs, constituting about 17.8 percent of the population, articulated their views through elected officials on the municipal and national levels and through the Arab departments within governmental ministries and nongovernmental institutions such as the Histadrut. In the past, most elected Arab officials traditionally affiliated with the Labor Party and its predecessors, which expected—erroneously as time has proved—that Israeli Arabs would serve as a "bridge" in creating peace among Israeli Jews, the Palestinians, and the Arab world. Beginning in the mid-1970s and throughout the 1980s, increasing numbers of Arab voters, especially younger ones, asserted themselves through organizations calling for greater protection of minority rights and the resolution of the Arab-Israeli conflict. Generally, Israeli Arabs remained attached to their religious, cultural, and political values, but their ethnic homogeneity has not necessarily resulted in political cohesion. Internal fissures among Christians, Sunni Muslims, and Druzes, Negev beduins and Galilee Arabs, and communist and noncommunist factions have made it difficult for them to act as a single pressure group in dealing with Israel's Jewish majority.

In 1988, despite their natural sympathy for the year-long uprising by their fellow Palestinians in the West Bank and the Gaza Strip, Israeli Arabs continued to be active participants in the Israeli electoral system. They increased their share in the total 1988 Knesset vote to more than 10 percent of the electorate, and the voting percentage among those eligible to participate was approximately 74 percent, as compared to 80 percent for Jewish voters. Israeli Arabs increased their voting support for Arab lists from 50 percent in 1984 to 60 percent in 1988.

As of 1988, Rakah (New Communist List), a predominantly Arab communist party, continued to adhere to the official Soviet line, yet explicitly recognized Israel's right to exist within its pre-1967 borders. Rakah succeeded Poalei Tziyyon, part of which split off in 1921 and became the Communist Party of Palestine. In 1948 it became the Communist Party of Israel, Miflaga Komunistit Yisraelit, known as Maki (see Appendix B), and in 1965 it split into two factions: Rakah with mainly Arab membership, and Maki, with mainly Jewish membership. In 1977 Maki and several other groups created Shelli (acronym for Peace for Israel and Equality for Israel), which disbanded before the 1984 elections. In the November 1988 elections, Rakah maintained its relatively constant share of 40 percent of the total Arab vote and four Knesset seats. In 1988 the party's secretary general was Meir Vilner, a veteran Israeli communist.

Within the Israeli Arab community, Rakah's strongest challenges came from two more radical parties, the Palestinian nationalist Sons of the Village, which had no Knesset seats, and the Progressive National Movement. The Progressive National Movement, also known as the Progressive List for Peace, came into being in 1984. Its platform advocated recognition of the PLO and the establishment of a Palestinian state in the West Bank and the Gaza Strip. In the November 1988 elections, the party, led by Muhammad Muari, received about 15 percent of the Arab vote; its Knesset delegation declined to one from the 1984 level of two.

The Arab Democratic Party, founded in early 1988 by Abdul Wahab Daroushe, a former Labor Party Knesset member, gained about 12 percent of the total Arab vote and one seat in the November 1988 Knesset elections. In a March 1988 interview, Daroushe acknowledged that his resignation from the Labor Party resulted from the Palestinian uprising in the West Bank and the Gaza Strip and the "diminishing choices" open to Israeli Arab politicians affiliated with the government and yet tied to the Arab community by a sense of shared ethnic identity. Echoing the sentiments of other Israeli Arabs, Daroushe has stated that "The PLO is the sole legitimate representative of the Palestinians" living outside Israel's pre-1967 borders.

Interest Groups

Major interest groups in Israel influencing the formulation of public policy have included the politically powerful Histadrut, the kibbutzim, and the moshavim, all of which were affiliated with or represented in most of the political parties. Reportedly, one of the main reasons for Labor to join the National Unity Government in 1988 was the opportunity for Peres, as minister of finance and chairman of the Knesset's Finance Committee, to bail out the Histadrut, the kibbutzim, and the moshavim, which were billions of dollars in debt.

As of the late 1980s, other economically oriented interest groups included employer organizations and artisan and retail merchant associations. In addition, there were major groups concerned with promoting civil rights, such as the Association for Civil Rights in Israel and the Association for Beduin Rights in Israel. Numbered among groups concerned with political issues such as the West Bank and the Gaza Strip, were movements such as Peace Now and Gush Emunim.

Furthermore, Diaspora Jewry might be considered, in the words of Canadian scholar Michael Brecher, an externally based foreign policy interest group. In the late 1980s, Diaspora Jewry, and especially American Jewry, had become increasingly critical of Israeli government policy, particularly over the handling of the West Bank and the Gaza Strip, and issues concerning religion and the state.

Prospects for Electoral Reform

The structural crisis facing the Israeli political system has been attributed to a number of factors. Such factors include the absence of a written constitution that provides for the separation of state and religion and safeguards the rights of the individual. Another factor often cited is the country's inability to form effective coalition governments and cabinets—a phenomenon caused by a breakdown of the dominant party system and the resulting inability of any one major party to garner a parliamentary majority. As a consequence, in forming coalitions each major party has had to depend heavily on smaller parties bent on promoting their own narrow interests.

Various reforms have been proposed to blunt the disruptive role of minor parties. One suggestion is to change the electoral system of pure proportional representation by raising the minimum percentage threshold required to obtain a Knesset seat. One of the most comprehensive studies of this problem, *The Political System in Israel: Proposals for Change,* edited by Baruch Zisar, argues that the negative features of the Israeli electoral system have so far outweighed its positive attributes. The study concludes that individual district constituencies may offer Israel the best form of electoral representation.

Following the stalemated results of the November 1988 Knesset elections, a committee composed of representatives of the two major parties was set up to study changes in the proportional representation system. In a newspaper interview, Shimon Peres admitted that "The democratic system in Israel has reached a point in which it has begun to be ineffective and a change is demanded in the electoral system."

Civil-Military Relations

The supremacy of civilian authorities over the military has rarely been challenged in Israel's history. The Lavon affair of 1954 remains the major exception (see The Emergence of the IDF, ch. 1). Factors weighing against military interference have included the prohibition on active officers engaging in politics and the population's broad support for the nonpartisan behavior of the armed forces. Given the ever-present external threat to Israeli security, however, the military looms large in everyday life. This has led some foreign observers to call Israel a "garrison democracy." The military has also served as a channel into politics, with political activity providing a "second career" for retired or reservist officers after they complete their military careers, usually between the ages of forty and fifty. This phenomenon has left its mark on Israeli politics as high-ranking retired or reservist IDF figures have often "parachuted" into the leadership ranks of political parties and public institutions.

The most frequent instances of this tendency have occurred during the demobilization of officers in postwar periods, for example, following the 1948, 1967, and 1973 wars. Until the June 1967 War, the great majority of reservist or retired officers joined Labor's ranks. In the 1950s, the first generation of such officers included Moshe Dayan, Yigal Allon, Yigal Yadin, Israel Galilee, and Chaim Herzog. After 1967, the number of such officers co-opted into the political elite rose sharply, with many for the first time joining center-right parties. Among those joining the Labor Party were Yitzhak Rabin, Haim Bar-Lev (*bar,* son of—see Glossary), Aharon Yariv, and Meir Amit. Ezer Weizman, Ariel (Arik) Sharon, Mordechai Zipori, and Shlomo Lahat joined Likud. Despite their widespread participation in politics, these ex-military officers have not formed a distinct pressure group. The armed forces have generally remained shielded from partisan politics. The only possible exception was the IDF's military action in Lebanon in June 1982, which disregarded the cabinet's decision on the limits of the advance. The invasion occurred while Ariel Sharon was minister of defense (1981–83) and Rafael Eitan was chief of staff (1979–83);

both individuals had stressed the independent policy role of the IDF (see The Military in Political Life, ch. 5).

Foreign Relations

The cabinet, and particularly the inner cabinet, consisting of the prime minister, minister of foreign affairs, minister of defense, and other selected ministers, are responsible for formulating Israel's major foreign policy decisions. Within the inner cabinet, the prime minister customarily plays the major role in foreign policy decision making, with policies implemented by the minister of foreign affairs. Other officials at the Ministry of Foreign Affairs include, in order of their rank, the director general, assistant directors general, legal and political advisers, heads of departments, and heads of missions or ambassadors. While the director general may initiate and decide an issue, commit the ministry by making public statements, and respond directly to queries from ambassadors, assistant directors general supervise the implementation of policy. Legal and political advisers have consultative, not operational, roles. Heads of departments serve as aides to assistant directors general, administer the ministry's departments, and maintain routine contact with envoys. The influence of ambassadors depends on their status within the diplomatic service and the importance to the ministry's policy makers of the nation to which they are accredited.

In the Knesset, the Foreign Affairs and Security Committee, with twenty-six members, although prestigious, is not as independent as the foreign affairs committees of the United States Congress. Its role, according to Samuel Sager, an Israeli Knesset official, is not to initiate new policies, but to "legitimize Government policy choices on controversial issues." Members of the committee frequently complain that they do not receive detailed information during briefings by government officials; government spokesmen reply that committee members tend to leak briefing reports to the media.

Israeli foreign policy is chiefly influenced by Israel's strategic situation, the Arab-Israeli conflict, and the rejection of Israel by most of the Arab states. The goals of Israeli policy are therefore to overcome diplomatic isolation and to achieve recognition and friendly relations with as many nations as possible, both in the Middle East and beyond. Like many other states, throughout its history Israel has simultaneously practiced open and secret diplomacy to further its main national goals. For example, it has engaged in military procurement, the export of arms and military assistance, intelligence cooperation with its allies, commercial trade, the importation of strategic raw materials, and prisoner-of-war exchanges and other arrangements for hostage releases. It has also sought to

Government and Politics

foster increased Jewish immigration to Israel and to protect vulnerable Jewish communities in the Diaspora.

Relations with Middle Eastern States

Despite the Arab-Israeli conflict, Israel has established formal diplomatic relations with Egypt and maintained a de facto peaceful relationship with Jordan. Israeli leaders have traveled to Morocco to discuss Israeli-Arab issues, and Morocco has often served as an intermediary between Israel and the other Arab states. In 1983 Israel signed a peace treaty with Lebanon, although it was quickly abrogated by the Lebanese as a result of Syrian pressure. Some secret diplomatic contacts may also have occurred between Israel and Tunisia.

Egypt

In late 1988, about ten years after the signing of the Camp David Accords and the Treaty of Peace Between Egypt and Israel (see The Peace Process, ch. 1), a "cool" peace characterized Egyptian-Israeli relations. These relations had originally been envisioned as leading to a reconciliation between Israel and the Arab states, but this development has not occurred. Egyptian-Israeli relations have been strained by a number of developments, including the June 1981 Israeli bombing of an Iraqi nuclear reactor, the Israeli invasion of Lebanon directed against Palestinian forces a year later, the establishment of an increasing number of Jewish settlements in the West Bank and the Gaza Strip, and the "watering down" of proposals for the autonomy of the Palestinian inhabitants of these territories as envisaged by the Camp David Accords and the Egyptian-Israeli peace treaty.

Relations between the two countries warmed somewhat during Peres's tenure as prime minister and minister of foreign affairs in the National Unity Government. They again cooled, however, following the establishment of the Likud-led cabinet in December 1988, and prime minister Shamir's rejection of Israeli participation in an international peace conference with the PLO. Nevertheless, the two countries continued to maintain full diplomatic relations, and in 1985 about 60,000 Israeli tourists visited Egypt, although Egyptian tourism to Israel was much smaller. Cooperation occurred in the academic and scientific areas as well as in a number of joint projects in agriculture, marine science, and disease control.

Another issue that had impeded normal relations between Egypt and Israel concerned the disposition of Taba, an approximately 100-hectare border enclave and tourist area on the Gulf of Aqaba in the Sinai Peninsula claimed by the two countries, but occupied by Israel. Following a September 1988 ruling in Egypt's favor by an international arbitration panel, official delegations from Israel and Egypt met to implement the arbitral award.

Jordan

Secret or "discreet" contacts between the leaders of the Yishuv and later of Israel and the Hashemite Kingdom of Transjordan or Jordan began in the early days of the British Mandate and continued into the late 1980s. These covert contacts were initiated with King Abdullah, the grandfather of King Hussein, Jordan's present ruler. Some observers have speculated that, together with Jordan's annexation of the West Bank in 1950, these contacts may have been responsible for Abdullah's assassination by a Palestinian gunman in East Jerusalem in July 1951. According to Israeli journalists Yossi Melman and Dan Raviv, Hussein renewed Jordan's ties with Israel in 1963. Following Jordan's ill-fated participation in the June 1967 War, secret meetings took place between Hussein and Israeli leaders in 1968, and they lasted until Begin's accession to power in 1977. This "secret" relationship was revived in 1984, following Labor's participation in the National Unity Government, and intensified in 1986–87. The participants reached agreements on Israeli-Jordanian cooperation on such issues as the role of pro-Jordanian Palestinian moderates in the peace process, setting up branches of Jordan's Cairo-Amman Bank in the West Bank, and generally increasing Amman's influence and involvement in the West Bank's financial, agricultural, education, and health affairs, thus blocking the PLO. The last reported meeting between Minister of Foreign Affairs Peres and King Hussein took place in London in November 1987, when the two leaders signed a "memorandum of understanding" on a peace plan. Upon his return to Israel, however, Peres was unable to win support for the agreement in the Israeli cabinet.

Morocco

Morocco has been noted for its generally good relations with its own Jewish community, which in 1988 numbered approximately 18,000; in 1948 there had been about 250,000 Jews in Morocco. Over the years discreet meetings have occurred between Moroccan and Israeli leaders. Beginning in 1976, King Hassan II began to mediate between Arab and Israeli leaders. Then Prime Minister Yitzhak Rabin reportedly made a secret visit to Morocco in 1976, leading to a September 1977 secret meeting between King Hassan and Foreign Minister Moshe Dayan. King Hassan also played a

Allenby Bridge across the Jordan River, a crossing point into Jordan, with Israeli and Jordanian soldiers talking
Courtesy Les Vogel

role in the Egyptian-Israeli contacts that led to the 1978 Camp David Accords. In July 1978, and again in March 1981, Peres, as opposition leader, made secret trips to Morocco. In May 1984, thirty-five prominent Israelis of Moroccan origin attended a conference in Rabat. This meeting was followed by an official visit in May 1985 by Avraham Katz-Oz, Israel's deputy minister of agriculture, to discuss possible agricultural cooperation between the two countries. In August 1986, Moroccan agricultural specialists and journalists reportedly visited Israel, and Chaim Corfu, Israel's minister of transport, attended a transportation conference in Morocco. On July 22 and 23, 1986, Prime Minister Peres met King Hassan at the king's palace in Ifrane. This was the first instance of a public meeting between an Arab leader and an Israeli prime minister since the Egyptian-Israeli meetings of the late 1970s. Hassan and Peres, however, were unable to agree on ways to resolve the Palestinian dimension of the Arab-Israeli conflict.

Iran

Until the overthrow of the shah's regime in 1979, Israel and Iran had established government missions in both countries although this relationship was never formalized by an exchange of ambassadors. Under the shah, from 1953 to 1979, Iran was one of Israel's primary suppliers of oil and a major commercial partner. In addition, the intelligence services of the two countries cooperated closely, and Israel exported military hardware and provided training and other assistance to Iranian military forces. These close, but discreet, relations were abruptly terminated in 1979, upon the coming to power of the regime of Ayatollah Sayyid Ruhollah Musavi Khomeini and Iran's joining of the anti-Israel camp. Shortly thereafter, Iran called for the "eradication" of the State of Israel through armed struggle and its replacement by a Palestinian state. As a symbolic gesture, the PLO was given the building of the former Israeli mission in Tehran.

In the 1980s, however, Israeli concern about the fate of the approximately 30,000 Jews remaining in Iran, interest in assisting Iran in its war with Iraq, and cooperation with the United States in its efforts to free American hostages held by Iranian-backed Shia (see Glossary) extremists in Lebanon, led to a renewal of contacts between Israeli and Iranian leaders and shipments of Israeli arms to Tehran. Israel reportedly sent arms to Iran in exchange for Iran's allowing thousands of Jews to leave the country.

Relations with the United States

For strategic security and diplomatic support, Israel has depended almost totally upon the United States. Since the establishment of the state in 1948, the United States has expressed its commitment to Israel's security and well-being and has devoted a considerable share of its world-wide economic and security assistance to Israel. Large-scale American military and economic assistance began during the October 1973 War, with a massive American airlift of vital military matériel to Israel at the height of the war. From 1948 through 1985, the United States provided Israel with US$10 billion in economic assistance and US$21 billion in military assistance, 60 percent of which was in the form of grants. From 1986 through 1988, total United States economic and military assistance to Israel averaged more than US$3 billion a year, making Israel the largest recipient of United States aid. Of the annual total, about US$1.8 billion was in Foreign Military Sales credits, and about US$1.2 billion was in economic assistance.

During the administration of President Ronald Reagan, the United States-Israeli relationship was significantly upgraded, with Israel becoming a strategic partner and de facto ally. A number of bilateral arrangements solidified this special relationship. In November 1983, the United States and Israel established a Joint Political-Military Group to coordinate military exercises and security planning between the two countries, as well as to position United States military equipment in Israel for use by American forces in the event of a crisis. In 1984 Israel and the United States concluded the United States-Israel Free Trade Area Agreement to provide tariff-free access to American and Israeli goods. In 1985 the two countries established a Joint Economic Development Group to help Israel solve its economic problems; in 1986 they created a Joint Security Assistance Group to discuss aid issues. Also in 1986, Israel began participating in research and development programs relating to the United States Strategic Defense Initiative. In January 1987, the United States designated Israel a major non-NATO ally, with status similar to that of Australia and Japan. Two months later, Israel agreed to the construction of a Voice of America relay transmitter on its soil to broadcast programs to the Soviet Union. In December 1987, Israel signed a memorandum of understanding allowing it to bid on United States defense contracts on the same basis as NATO countries. Finally, the two countries signed a memorandum of agreement in April 1988 formalizing existing arrangements for mutually beneficial United States-Israel technology transfers.

Israel has also cooperated with the United States on a number of clandestine operations. It acted as a secret channel for United States arms sales to Iran in 1985 and 1986, and during the same period it cooperated with the United States in Central America.

The United States-Israeli relationship, however, has not been free of friction. The United States expressed indignation with Israel over an espionage operation involving Jonathan Jay Pollard, a United States Navy employee who was sentenced to life imprisonment for selling hundreds of vital intelligence documents to Israel. During the affair, Israeli government and diplomatic personnel in Washington served as Pollard's control officers. Nevertheless, United States government agencies continued to maintain a close relationship with Israel in sensitive areas such as military cooperation, intelligence sharing, and joint weapons research.

The main area of friction between the United States and Israel has concerned Washington's efforts to balance its special ties to Jerusalem with its overall Middle Eastern interests and the need to negotiate an end to the Arab-Israeli conflict, in which the United States has played a major mediating role. In 1948 the United States hoped that peace could be achieved between Israel and the Arab states, but this expectation was quickly dashed when Arab nations refused to recognize Israel's independence. American hopes were dashed again when in 1951 Jordan's King Abdullah, with whom some form of settlement seemed possible, was assassinated and in 1953 when the Johnston Plan, a proposal for neighboring states to share the water of the Jordan River, was rejected.

The June 1967 War provided a major opportunity for the United States to serve as a mediator in the conflict; working with Israel and the Arab states the United States persuaded the United Nations (UN) Security Council to pass Resolution 242 of November 22, 1967. The resolution was designed to serve as the basis for a peace settlement involving an Israeli withdrawal from territories occupied in the June 1967 War in exchange for peace and Arab recognition of Israel's right to exist. Many disputes over the correct interpretation of a clause concerning an Israeli withdrawal followed the passage of the UN resolution, which was accepted by Israel. The resolution lacked any explicit provision for direct negotiations between the parties. Although the Arab states and the Palestinians did not accept the resolution, it has remained the basis of United States policy regarding the Arab-Israeli conflict.

In December 1969, the Rogers Plan, named after United States Secretary of State William P. Rogers, although unsuccessful in producing peace negotiations, succeeded in ending the War of Attrition between Israel and Egypt that followed the June 1967 War and established a cease-fire along the Suez Canal. In 1971 United States assistant secretary of state Joseph P. Sisco proposed an ''interim Suez Canal agreement'' to bring about a limited Israeli withdrawal from the canal, hoping that such an action would lead to a peace settlement. The proposal failed when neither Israel nor Egypt would agree to the other's conditions.

In October 1973, at the height of the Arab-Israeli war, United States-Soviet negotiations paved the way for UN Security Council Resolution 338. In addition to calling for an immediate cease-fire and opening negotiations aimed at implementing Resolution 242, this resolution inserted a requirement that future talk be conducted ''between the parties concerned,'' that is, between the Arabs and the Israelis themselves.

In September 1975, United States secretary of state Henry Kissinger's ''shuttle diplomacy'' achieved the Second Sinai Disengagement Agreement between Israel and Egypt, laying the groundwork for later negotiations between the two nations. The United States also pledged, as part of a memorandum of understanding with Israel, not to negotiate with the PLO until it was prepared to recognize Israel's right to exist and to renounce terrorism.

Another major United States initiative came in 1977 when President Jimmy Carter stressed the need to solve the Arab-Israeli conflict by convening an international peace conference in Geneva, cochaired by the United States and the Soviet Union. Although Egyptian President Anwar as Sadat conducted his initiative in opening direct Egyptian-Israeli peace talks without United States assistance, the United States played an indispensable role in the complex and difficult negotiation process. Negotiations ultimately led to the signing, under United States auspices, of the September 17, 1978, Camp David Accords, as well as the March 1979 Treaty of Peace Between Egypt and Israel. The accords included provisions that called for granting autonomy to Palestinians in the West Bank and the Gaza Strip through a freely elected self-governing authority during a five-year transitional period; at the end of the period the final status of the occupied territories was to be decided. Carter had hoped that this process would enable the Palestinians to fulfill their legitimate national aspirations while at the same time safeguarding Israeli security concerns. While criticizing the Begin government's settlement policy in the occupied territories, the Carter administration could not prevent the intensified pace of construction of new settlements.

Following Israel's invasion of Lebanon in early June 1982, on September 1, 1982, President Reagan outlined what came to be called the Reagan Plan. This plan upheld the goals of the Camp David Accords regarding autonomy for the Palestinians of the West Bank and the Gaza Strip and disapproved of Israel's establishment of any new settlements in these areas. It further proposed that at the end of a transitional period, the best form of government for the West Bank and the Gaza Strip would be self-government by the resident Palestinian population in association with Jordan. Under the plan, Israel would be obliged to withdraw from the occupied territories in exchange for peace, and the city of Jerusalem would remain undivided; its final status would be decided through negotiations. The plan rejected the creation of an independent Palestinian state. Although Labor leader Peres expressed support for the plan, Prime Minister Menachem Begin and the Likud opposed it, as did the PLO and the Arab states. The plan was subsequently shelved.

The United States nevertheless continued its efforts to facilitate Arab-Israeli peace. In March 1987, the United States undertook intensive diplomatic negotiations with Jordan and Israel to achieve agreement on holding an international peace conference, but differences over Palestinian representation created obstacles. In Israel, Likud prime minister Shamir and Labor minister of foreign affairs Peres were at odds, with Shamir rejecting an international conference and Peres accepting it. Peres and Labor Party minister of defense Rabin reportedly held talks with Jordan's King Hussein, who wanted the conference to include the five permanent members of the UN Security Council, as well as Israel, the Arab states, and the PLO. The Reagan administration, on the other hand, was reluctant to invite the Soviet Union to participate in the diplomatic process. The administration insisted that any prospective conference adjourn speedily and then take the form of direct talks between Israel and Jordan. The administration also insisted that the conference have no power to veto any agreement between Israel and Jordan.

A major difficulty involved the nature of Palestinian representation at a conference. A Soviet-Syrian communiqué repeated the demand for PLO participation, which Israel flatly rejected. The United States asserted that, as the basis for any PLO participation, the PLO must accept UN Resolutions 242 and 338 with their implied recognition of Israel's right to exist. Both the PLO mainstream and its radical wings were unwilling to agree to this demand. The Palestinian uprising (*intifadah*) in the West Bank and the Gaza Strip began in December 1987. In February 1988, Secretary of State George Shultz visited Israel, Egypt, Jordan, and Syria; in a statement issued in Jerusalem he called for Palestinian participation, as part of a Jordanian/Palestinian delegation, in an international peace conference. The PLO rejected this initiative. The United States proposal called for a comprehensive peace providing for the security of all states in the region and for fulfillment of the legitimate rights of the Palestinian people. The proposal consisted of an "integrated whole" and included the following negotiating framework: "early negotiations between Israel and each of its neighbors willing to do so," with the door "specifically open for Syrian participation"; "bilateral negotiations . . . based on United Nations Security Council Resolutions 242 and 338 in all their parts"; "the parties to each bilateral negotiation" to determine "the procedure and agenda of the negotiation"; "negotiations between an Israeli and a Jordanian/Palestinian delegation on arrangements for a transitional period for the West Bank and Gaza," with the objective of completing "these talks within six months"; and "final status negotiations" beginning "on a date certain seven months after the start of transitional talks," with the objective of completing the talks "within a year."

On March 26, 1988, Shultz met with two members of the Palestine National Council (PNC), which represents Palestinians outside Israel, various political and guerrilla groups within the PLO, and associated youth, student, women's, and professional bodies. According to a PLO spokesman, the PNC members, Professors Ibrahim Abu Lughod and Edward Said, both Arab Americans, were authorized by Yasir Arafat to speak to Shultz, and they later reported directly to the PLO leader about their talks. Little resulted from this meeting, however, and Shultz found no authoritative party willing to come to the conference table.

The United States once again involved itself in the peace process to break the stalemate among the Arab states, the Palestinians, and Israel following King Hussein's declaration on July 31, 1988, that he was severing most of Jordan's administrative and legal ties with the West Bank, thus throwing the future of the West Bank onto the PLO's shoulders. PLO chairman Yasir Arafat thereby gained new international status, but Shultz barred him from entering the United States to address the UN General Assembly in early December because of Arafat's and the PLO's involvement in terrorist activities. When Arafat, following his December 14 address to a special session of the UN General Assembly in Geneva, met American conditions by recognizing Israel's right to exist in "peace and security," accepted UN Resolutions 242 and 338, and renounced "all forms of terrorism, including individual, group and state terrorism," the United States reversed its thirteen-year policy of not officially speaking to the PLO.

The Israeli National Unity Government, installed in late December, denounced the PLO as an unsuitable negotiating partner. It did not accept the PLO's recognition of Israel and renunciation of terrorism as genuine.

Whether the United States-PLO talks would yield concrete results in terms of Arab-Israeli peace making remained to be seen as of the end of 1988. Notwithstanding the possibility of future progress, the new willingness of the United States to talk to the PLO demonstrated that, despite the special relationship between the United States and Israel and the many areas of mutual agreement and shared geopolitical strategic interests, substantial differences continued to exist between the United States and certain segments of the Israeli government. This was especially true with regard to the Likud and its right-wing allies.

Relations with the Soviet Union

In August 1986, the Soviet Union renewed contacts with Israel for the first time since severing diplomatic relations immediately following the June 1967 War. The Soviet Union had been an early supporter of the 1947 UN Partition of Palestine Resolution, and in 1948 it had recognized the newly established State of Israel. Relations between Israel and the countries of Eastern Europe, however, markedly worsened in the 1950s. The Soviet Union turned to Egypt and Syria as its primary partners in the Middle East, and in the early 1960s it began to support the Palestinian cause and supply the PLO and other Palestinian armed groups with military

Israel: A Country Study

hardware. But in the mid-1980s, the Soviet Union turned its attention to improving relations with Israel as part of its "new diplomacy" and a change in its Middle Eastern strategy.

Soviet and Israeli representatives held talks in Helsinki, Finland, on August 17, 1986. Although the talks did not lead to renewed diplomatic relations between the two countries, they indicated Soviet interest in improving ties with Israel. Israel viewed the Soviet initiative as an attempt to obtain Israel's agreement to participate in an international peace conference to resolve the Arab-Israeli conflict and to increase Soviet involvement in the Middle East as a counterweight to the United States. The Soviets raised three issues: the activity of the Soviet section based in the Finnish legation in Tel Aviv; consular matters connected with the travels of Soviet citizens to Israel; and Soviet property, mainly that belonging to the Russian Orthodox Church, in Israel. In talks with the Soviets, the Israelis demanded that greater numbers of Jews be permitted to emigrate to Israel, that a radical change take place in official Soviet attitudes toward its Jewish community, and that Moscow cease publishing virulent anti-Zionist tracts. Soviet and Israeli officials held a number of additional meetings in 1987.

A major group influencing improved relations between the two countries was the active Israeli lobby, the Soviet Jewry Education and Information Center. This lobby represented about 170,000 Soviet Jews living in Israel, who pressured the government not to restore diplomatic relations with Moscow until the Soviet Union permitted free Jewish emigration.

Despite its renewed contacts with Israel, the Soviet Union continued to support the PLO and the Palestinian cause through military training and arms shipments. Moscow also used various front organizations, such as the World Peace Council, to wage propaganda campaigns against the Israeli state in international forums.

Relations with Eastern Europe

Improved Israeli-Soviet relations led to increased ties with East European states as well. Israel and Poland reestablished diplomatic relations in September 1986. Trade and tourism between Israel and Hungary also improved in 1986. On August 6, 1986, a senior Romanian envoy visited Jerusalem and met with Prime Minister Peres to discuss relations with the Soviet Union. At the time, there was speculation that the Romanian president, Nicolae Ceauçescu, had helped arrange behind-the-scenes contacts between the Soviet Union and Israel. On August 30, 1986, talks followed between Yehuda Horam, head of the East European Division of the Israeli Ministry of Foreign Affairs, and Romanian officials. Also in

August, Mrs. Shulamit Shamir, the wife of then-Minister of Foreign Affairs Yitzhak Shamir, received an invitation to visit Bulgaria, the first such official Bulgarian gesture toward Israel. In January 1987, an Israeli delegation held negotiations with Polish, Bulgarian, and Hungarian representatives concerning agricultural cooperation.

Relations with Western Europe

Israeli relations with the states of Western Europe have been conditioned by European desires to further their own commercial interests and ties with the Arab world and their heavy dependence on Middle Eastern oil. Europeans have provided political support for Arab states and the Palestinian cause, even though Europe has served as the battleground for Arab and Palestinian terrorist groups. For example, beginning in the early 1970s, the ministers of foreign affairs of the European Community called for Israel to withdraw from territories occupied during the June 1967 War, expressed "reservations" over the 1978 Camp David Accords, and accepted the "association" of the PLO in solving the Palestinian problem.

Despite such official declarations, West European states have been important trading partners for Israel; about 40 percent of Israel's foreign trade occurred with European countries. Furthermore, there has been strong European-Israeli cooperation—except with Greece—in the area of counterterrorism. Britain was Israel's most important European trading partner although relations between the two countries were never free of tensions. In 1979, for example, Britain disallowed Israel's purchase of British crude oil after Israel lost oil deliveries from Iran and Sinai. Moreover, Britain imposed an arms embargo on Israel following its June 1982 invasion of Lebanon.

In the early 1950s, France and Israel maintained close political and military relations, and France was Israel's main weapons supplier until the June 1967 War. At that time, during Charles de Gaulle's presidency, France became highly critical of Israeli policies and imposed an arms embargo on Israel. In the early 1980s, French-Israeli relations markedly improved under the presidency of François Mitterrand, who pursued a more even-handed approach than his predecessors on Arab-Israeli issues. Mitterand was the first French president to visit Israel while in office.

Relations between Israel and the Federal Republic of Germany (West Germany) were "second in importance only to [Israel's] partnership with the United States," according to Michael Wolffsohn, a leading authority on the subject. In Wolffsohn's view, the dominant issues in West German-Israeli relations were: the question

241

of reparations (up to 1953); the establishment of diplomatic relations (up to 1965); the solidification of normal relations (through 1969); the erosion in the West German-Israeli relationship as Chancellor Willi Brandt—the first West German chancellor to visit Israel—began to stress Israel's need to withdraw from all territories occupied in the June 1967 War and to recognize the right of the Palestinian people to self-determination; and, finally, during the 1980s, under the Christian Democrats, West Germany's closer adherence to United States policies on Arab-Israeli issues.

In January 1986, Spain established full diplomatic relations with Israel despite pressures from Arab states and policy differences between Madrid and Jerusalem over the Palestinian question. This step concluded intensive behind-the-scenes Israeli efforts—begun upon the death of President Francisco Franco in 1975—to achieve normal relations with Spain. Prior to establishing diplomatic relations, the two countries discreetly collaborated in antiterrorism efforts, and there were close ties between Labor and Spain's Socialist Party.

Although in 1947 Turkey voted against the UN resolution to establish the Jewish state, in 1948 it became the first Muslim country to establish full diplomatic relations with Israel. The two countries subsequently maintained normal relations.

Relations with African States

Until the early 1970s, Israel sent hundreds of agricultural experts and technicians to aid in developing newly independent sub-Saharan African states, seeking diplomatic relations in return. The Arab countries, however, exerted pressure on such states to break ties with Israel. Most African states eventually complied with this pressure because of their need for Arab oil at concessionary prices and because of Arab promises of financial aid. Furthermore, Israel received heavy criticism from African nations because of its relations with South Africa. Moreover, Israeli support for the Biafran secessionist movement in Nigeria alarmed the members of the Organization of African Unity, many of whom faced threatening national liberation movements in their own countries. The June 1967 Israeli occupation of the West Bank, the Gaza Strip, and the Sinai Peninsula stirred a sense of unease among the African states; after the October 1973 War twenty-nine African states severed diplomatic relations with Israel. Malawi, Lesotho, and Swaziland were the only sub-Saharan countries to maintain diplomatic relations with Israel.

The African "embargo" of Israel began to collapse after the 1978 Camp David Accords and the establishment of diplomatic relations between Egypt and Israel. Following Zaire's lead in 1982, Liberia (1983), the Côte d'Ivoire (1986), Cameroon (1986), and Togo (1987) renewed diplomatic ties with Israel. Kenya, Gabon, Senegal, and Equatorial Guinea have also shown interest in renewing diplomatic relations. Several other African countries, although maintaining their diplomatic distance, nevertheless had unofficial ties with Israel, as expressed by the presence of Israeli advisers and technicians. Ghana had an Israeli "interests office," and Nigeria, Sierra Leone, and the Central African Republic all maintained unofficial ties with Israel.

Israeli military expertise and technical skills, particularly in desert reclamation, have often facilitated ties with the sub-Saharan nations. In Cameroon, Israel built a training center to assist in halting the advance of the Sahara Desert, and in Côte d'Ivoire, Israeli contractors undertook several major building projects. Israel also trained the elite armed units protecting the presidents of Cameroon, Liberia, Togo, and Zaire.

Israel has long had a special interest in Ethiopia, a partially Christian country, because of the presence of Falashas (Ethiopian Jews) in that country. Ethiopian-Israeli relations had been close until the overthrow of Emperor Haile Selassie and the imposition of a Marxist, pro-Soviet military regime in 1974. In 1978 Ethiopia received military aid from Israel as well as from the Soviet Union, Cuba, and Libya in its border war with Somalia. In 1984 and 1985, it was reported that, in exchange for Israeli military aid to Ethiopia in its battle against Muslim Eritrean secessionists supported by Arab states, Israel organized an airlift of more than 10,000 Falashas from Ethiopia to Israel. In 1988 it was estimated that between 10,000 and 15,000 Falashas still remained in Ethiopia.

Israel has also had a longstanding interest in South Africa because of its approximately 110,000 Jews and 15,000 Israelis. Israeli leaders justified trade with South Africa on the ground that it offered protection for the South African Jewish community and developed export markets for Israel's defense and commercial industries. Excluding the arms trade, in 1986 Israel imported approximately US$181.1 million worth of South African goods, consisting primarily of coal; it exported products worth about US$58.8 million.

Israel has traditionally opposed international trade embargoes as a result of its own vulnerability at the hands of the UN and Third World-dominated bodies. In 1987, however, Israel took steps to reduce its military ties with South Africa so as to bring its policies in line with those of the United States and Western Europe, which had imposed limited trade, diplomatic, and travel sanctions on South Africa. In a speech to the Knesset on March 19, then Minister

243

of Foreign Affairs Peres formally presented the Israeli cabinet's four-point plan to ban military sales contracts with South Africa (Israel's arms trade with South Africa was reportedly between US$400 and US$800 million a year); to condemn apartheid, which Peres characterized as ''a policy totally rejected by all human beings;'' to reduce cultural and tourist ties to a minimum; and to appoint an official committee to draft a detailed list of economic sanctions in line with those of the United States and other Western nations. The cabinet also announced its decision to establish an educational foundation for South African blacks and people of mixed race in Israel.

Relations with Asian States

Many Asian nations have not established full diplomatic relations with Israel because of their large Muslim populations and the close ties they have maintained, as part of the Non-Aligned Movement, with the Arab states and the PLO. Nevertheless, there were back-channel contacts between Israel and India, and Israel has maintained a consul in Bombay since 1948. In August 1977, Minister of Foreign Affairs Dayan covertly visited India to meet with Prime Minister Morarji Desai, but the meeting proved inconclusive. In addition, there has been a tacit relationship between Israel and the People's Republic of China in such fields as commerce, technical and agricultural programs, and arms sales. Israel has maintained friendly relations with Australia, New Zealand, Singapore, Sri Lanka, Taiwan, and Thailand. It also has diplomatic relations with Japan, although Japan's trade relations with the Arab states and Iran take precedence over those with Israel.

Relations with Latin America

The traditional pro-Western stance of most Latin American states has proven to be politically and economically advantageous to Israel, as they have tended to be more sympathetic to Israel in the UN than African or Asian countries. They have also been more willing to maintain economic and military relations with Israel. Although Latin American states are primarily Roman Catholic and follow the Vatican's position favoring the internationalization of Jerusalem, Israel has obtained crude oil from Mexico, it maintains a lucrative arms trade with Argentina and other countries, and it has assisted Latin American regimes in their counterinsurgency efforts against Cuban and Nicaraguan-supported guerrillas.

Communications Media

Western observers have considered the Israeli press for the most part to be highly independent and a reliable source of information.

The press has reflected accurately the range of political opinions in the country and played a leading role in investigating and uncovering many scandals involving official corruption and mismanagement. It has also covered developments in the West Bank and the Gaza Strip. In addition to providing news and information, Israel's press, television and radio, in effect constituted an "extra-parliamentary opposition," according to William Frankel, a British Jewish journalist who is an authority on Israel. The influence of the press is considerable; 1988 estimates were that on a daily basis more than 75 percent of all adult Israelis read one daily newspaper and that about 11 percent read two or more.

As of 1988, most daily newspapers were published in Hebrew; because Israel is a nation of immigrants, others appeared in Arabic, English, Yiddish, Russian, Polish, Hungarian, French, and German, with weeklies adding more languages to the list. Many of the country's daily newspapers, particularly the English-language *Jerusalem Post* and those printed in Hebrew, were founded by Zionist political parties during the prestate period, and they have continued to be politically affiliated with such parties. Since independence, however, the "party newspaper" has declined as political alignments have changed. For example, the consolidation of Israel's socialist parties led to the demise of some papers affiliated with the former parties. In addition, the management and editorial direction of some papers, such as the *Jerusalem Post* (circulation of 30,000 on weekdays, 47,000 on weekends), has become increasingly independent, production costs have risen, and party supporters have turned to rapidly growing independent dailies. Such papers have included *Ma'ariv* (Afternoon—circulation of 147,000 on weekdays, 245,000 on weekends), *Yediot Aharonot* (Latest News—circulation of 180,000 on weekdays, 280,000 on weekends), *Hadashot* (News), which was founded in 1984, and the influential *Ha'aretz* (The Land—circulation of 55,000 on weekdays, 75,000 on weekends), an independent morning daily. Israel's two leading and politically liberal dailies have been *Davar* (News—circulation of 39,000), the official organ of the Histadrut, and *Al HaMishmar* (On Guard—circulation of 25,000), published by Mapam.

In 1953 the Editors' Committee, whose prestate name was the Redaction Committee, was officially registered as an independent association serving as a channel between the government and the press, and as a "voluntary partner" in carrying out the military censorship code—an arrangement that involved the exchange of confidential information with the general staff of the IDF. This arrangement functioned relatively smoothly as long as there was consensus over national security issues; relations between the press and the IDF became more strained, however, following the 1982 invasion of Lebanon. Another organization concerned with media oversight, the Israel Press Council, came into being in 1963. The press council is a professional association responsible, among other matters, for administering the code of ethics binding journalists.

The Israel Broadcasting Authority (IBA), established in 1965 and modeled after the British Broadcasting Corporation, controlled the country's radio and television networks. It was subject to the general supervision of the Ministry of Education and Culture. The IBA, however, operated autonomously under a self-governing board of directors whose discretion over content and presentation, with the exception of a stormy period during Begin's prime minister-ship, was rarely limited. The two leading radio stations were the IBA and Galei Tzahal (Voice of the IDF), the highly popular IDF broadcasting station. In 1968 Israeli television began broadcast-ing in both Hebrew and Arabic.

According to two polls conducted in 1988 by Public Opinion Research of Israel, a plurality of Jewish Israelis (42 percent) con-sidered television news programs as their ''best source'' of inter-national news, followed by newspapers (27 percent) and radio (25 percent). Only 3 percent of Israelis relied on magazines to keep them informed. These figures revealed a dramatic shift from 1986 figures that indicated reliance on newspapers as the best source for news coverage (46 percent), followed by magazines (26 per-cent), and television (19 percent). The poll attributed the sharp increase in reliance on the broadcast media to the strong visual impact of the Palestinian uprising on Israeli society.

As of 1988, Israeli Arabic language daily newspapers were led by the Jerusalem-based *Al Anba* (The News), with a circulation of about 10,000. Rakah also published an Arabic paper, *Al Ittihad* (Unity). An increasing number of Israeli Arabs also read Hebrew dailies. *Al Quds* (Jerusalem), founded in 1968 for Arabs in Jerusa-lem and the West Bank, resulted from the merger of two veteran Palestinian dailies founded on the West Bank following Jordan's annexation of the territory in 1950. By 1988 the paper had largely transferred its operations to Amman. In the early 1970s, additional Palestinian papers appeared, including *Al Fajr al Jadid* (The New Dawn), with a circulation of about 3,000 to 5,000, and *Ash Shaab* (The People), with 2,000 to 3,000 readers. Weekly and monthly magazines and periodicals published in Arabic include the liter-ary monthly *Al Jadid* (The New); *At Taawun* (Cooperation), pub-lished by the Histadrut Arab Workers' Department; and the Mapam party's Arab organ *Al Mirsad* (The Lookout). Israeli Arab and Palestinian newspapers have relied on Israeli and international sources for their reports on Israeli government decisions and actions concerning Israel's Arab community and Palestinian communities on the West Bank and the Gaza Strip.

The Israeli Arab press has faced the same censorship constraints as have Jewish newspapers, namely, the Press Ordinance of 1933. This regulation was first enacted by the British mandatory authority. In 1948 it was adopted by Israel and administered by the Ministry of Interior to license, supervise, and regulate the press. The IDF had responsibility for administering censorship regulations, and, under an agreement with the Editors' Committee, most Hebrew-language newspapers could exercise self-censorship, with the censor receiving only articles dealing with national security matters. This arrangement, however, did not cover Palestinian publications in the West Bank and the Gaza Strip, whose editors were required to submit items for publication to the military administration on a nightly basis. Failure to abide by these regulations has resulted in warnings and newspaper shutdowns. As a result of these regulations, many West Bank newspapers have preferred to publish in Jerusalem, which has less rigid civilian legislation and courts. In late 1988, Israeli authorities, suspecting Palestinian journalists of involvement in the *intifadah,* censored and shut down many Palestinian newspapers and magazines in the West Bank and the Gaza Strip and arrested Arab journalists, including several members of the board of the Arab Journalists' Association.

* * *

The literature on the Israeli political system is extensive. Useful bibliographies and bibliographical essays on Israel include Gregory S. Mahler's *Bibliography of Israeli Politics;* Joshua Sinai's "A Bibliographic Review of the Modern History of Israel"; and *Books on Israel: Vol. I,* edited by Ian S. Lustick.

Comprehensive studies on Israeli government and politics include Yonathan Shapiro's *HaDemokratia Be Yisrael;* Asher Arian's *Politics in Israel: The Second Generation;* Michael Wolffsohn's *Israel, Polity, Society, and Economy, 1882–1986;* Bernard Reich's, *Israel: Land of Tradition and Conflict;* Howard M. Sachar's two-volume *A History of Israel;* William Frankel's *Israel Observed: An Anatomy of the State;* Bernard Avishai's *The Tragedy of Zionism: Revolution and Democracy in the Land of Israel;* and Mitchell Cohen's *Zion and State: Nation, Class, and the Shaping of Modern Israel.*

Aspects of Israeli government and politics are covered in a series of volumes on the Knesset elections of 1969, 1973, 1977, and 1981, edited by Asher Arian; *Israel at the Polls, 1981: A Study of the*

Knesset Elections, edited by Howard Penniman and Daniel J. Elazar; *The Roots of Begin's Success: The 1981 Israeli Elections,* edited by Dan Caspi, et al; *Israel in the Begin Era,* edited by Robert O. Freedman; Nathan Yanai's *Party Leadership in Israel: Maintenance and Change;* Samuel Sager's *The Parliamentary System of Israel; Local Government in Israel,* edited by Daniel Elazar and Chaim Kalchheim; and Yoram Peri's *Between Battles and Ballots: Israeli Military in Politics.* Two leading books on the Labor Party are Peter Y. Medding's *Mapai in Israel: Political Organisation and Government in a New Society* and Myron J. Aronoff's *Power and Ritual in the Israel Labor Party.* The religious parties are covered in S. Zalman Abramov's *Perpetual Dilemma: Jewish Religion in the Jewish State;* Norman L. Zucker's *The Coming Crisis in Israel: Private Faith and Public Policy;* Gary S. Schiff's *Tradition and Politics: The Religious Parties of Israel;* and Ian S. Lustick's *For the Land and the Lord: Jewish Fundamentalism in Israel.*

Foreign relations are discussed in Michael Brecher's *The Foreign Policy System of Israel, Decisions in Israel's Foreign Policy,* and *Decisions in Crisis: Israel, 1967 and 1973;* Bernard Reich's *Quest for Peace: United States-Israel Relations and the Arab-Israeli Conflict* and *The United States and Israel: The Dynamics of Influence;* Shlomo Aronson's *Conflict and Bargaining in the Middle East: An Israeli Perspective;* Gideon Rafael's *Destination Peace: Three Decades of Israeli Foreign Policy; Dynamics of Dependence: U.S.-Israeli Relations,* edited by Gabriel Sheffer; and Aaron S. Klieman's *Statecraft in the Dark: Israel's Practice of Quiet Diplomacy.* The Arab-Israeli peace process is discussed in William B. Quandt's *Camp David: Peacemaking and Politics* and Harold H. Saunders's *The Other Walls: The Politics of the Arab-Israeli Peace Process.* Finally, materials on various peace proposals include the Brookings Institution's report *Toward Arab-Israeli Peace.* (For further information and complete citations, see Bibliography.)

Chapter 5. National Security

Man in a military beret and woman in service cap

IN FEW COUNTRIES of the world have matters of national security played as pervasive a role in society as in Israel. The Israel Defense Forces (IDF—commonly known in Israel as Zahal, the Hebrew acronym for Zvah Haganah Le Yisrael) was organized to be the ultimate guarantor of national security. Israeli policy makers, however, have believed that strong armed forces alone were not enough to protect the state. All of the state's resources were to be marshalled and applied to national security. In 1960 David Ben-Gurion stated that Israeli security also depended on the integration of immigrants, the settlement and peopling of "empty areas," the dispersal of the population and establishment of industries throughout the country, the development of agriculture, the "conquest of the sea and air," economic independence, and the fostering of research and scientific skill at the highest level of technology in all branches of science. Israel's quest for national security has been a prime motivating factor behind the state's rapid development.

The quest for national security also has imposed great costs on the state and its citizens. Defense expenditures on a per capita basis, and as a percentage of gross national product (GNP—see Glossary), have been consistently higher in Israel than in almost any other country in the world. Moreover, the IDF has diverted scarce manpower from the civilian economy, and Israeli industry has been compelled to manufacture military matériel instead of the consumer items that would raise the standard of living. Defense spending has also fueled double digit inflation for protracted periods and created a large national debt.

The prominence given national security by Israeli society stems from the perceived massive security threat posed by Israel's Arab neighbors. Having founded the State of Israel in the wake of the Holocaust, in which Diaspora (see Glossary) Jews were defenseless against an enemy bent on their destruction, Israeli Jews were determined to devote considerable resources to defend their young nation. In 1988 most outside observers agreed that the IDF was stronger than ever and clearly superior to the armies of its Arab enemies. Unlike the years after the June 1967 War, however, Israelis in the late 1980s did not display overconfidence in their defense capability. The surprise Arab offensive in October 1973 had renewed Israel's fears of defeat at the hands of its Arab enemies. Israel's 1982 invasion of Lebanon restored confidence in the tactical superiority of the IDF, but it also engendered controversy. The invasion was opposed from its inception by many Israeli politicians and IDF officers, who referred to it as Israel's first imperial war. Moreover, the IDF's victory on the battlefield was not matched by strategic accomplishments. In 1988 the IDF confronted a new problem—sustained protest by Palestinians in the occupied territories.

Many observers in the late 1980s described Israel as a democratic garrison state and a praetorian society. Indeed, in many respects Israel resembled an armed camp, and a wide range of government policies, particularly in foreign affairs, was dictated by security considerations as advised by IDF commanders. Unlike many garrison states, however, in Israel the armed forces played an indirect role in politics, and the IDF was unlikely to abandon its tradition of strict subordination to civilian authority.

Nevertheless, national defense policy was a major component of civilian politics during 1988. The Palestinian uprising in the occupied territories, known as the *intifadah,* created a new threat to Israel's security. Although the army seemed able to contain the violence militarily, its resources were strained by the dual role of policing the territories while maintaining strong border defenses. A nationwide debate centered on the question of whether Israeli concessions were strategically preferable to further Jewish settlement in the occupied territories. With the growing sophistication and deadliness of modern armaments in the Middle East, the alternative to peace with Israel's neighbors was the specter of increasingly costly wars. Since Israel's birth forty years earlier, such conflicts already had cost nearly 12,000 Israeli lives.

Security: A Persistent National Concern
Historical Background

Ancient Jewish military tradition is deeply rooted in biblical history and begins with Abraham, who led an ad hoc military force. Joshua, who conquered Canaan, is an early hero, and David, who captured Jerusalem, is regarded by Israeli Jews as their greatest king and warrior. Solomon organized and maintained the first standing Jewish army (see Ancient Israel, ch. 1).

Little in the way of military tradition arose out of the nearly 2,000 years of the Diaspora. In fact, the lack of military prowess in the Jewish communities of the Diaspora was commonly viewed as a cause of their hardships and became a major motivation for building a strong defense establishment within Israel. As a result of the Russian pogroms of the 1880s, a small number of Jews began settling in the area of Palestine and, determined to end the centuries of persecution, created self-defense units called Shomrim, or Guardsmen, to protect the early settlements. In 1909 the Shomrim were formally organized throughout the area of Jewish settlement in Palestine and renamed HaShomer, or the Watchmen. Although HaShomer numbered fewer than 100 men at the organization's peak, these armed militias became extremely important to Israeli military tradition. Many members of HaShomer joined the Jewish Legion, which fought with the British against imperial Germany during World War I. They also established a precedent of armed self-defense of the Zionist movement, which during the War of Independence in 1948 would flower into the IDF.

Increasing tensions between the Arab communities and the growing Jewish communities of Palestine brought the need to expand the capacity of the Yishuv (see Glossary) for self-defense (see Events in Palestine: 1908–48, ch. 1). In 1920, after serious Arab disturbances in Jerusalem and in northern Palestine, HaShomer militias were disbanded and replaced by the Haganah (abbreviation for Irgun HaHaganah, Defense Organization), which was intended to be a larger and more wide-ranging organization for the defense of all Palestinian Jewry. By 1948, when it was disbanded so that the IDF would be the sole Israeli military organization, the Haganah was a force of about 30,000.

The Haganah, financed originally through the Zionist General Federation of Laborers in the Land of Israel (HaHistadrut HaKlalit shel HaOvdim B'Eretz Yisrael, known as Histadrut) and later through the Jewish Agency (see Glossary), operated clandestinely under the British Mandate, which declared the bearing of unauthorized arms by Palestinian Jews to be illegal. Arms and ammunition were smuggled into the country, and training was conducted in secret. In addition to guarding settlements, the Haganah manufactured arms, built a series of roads and stockades throughout Palestine to facilitate defense, and organized and defended groups of Jewish immigrants during periods under the Mandate when immigration was illegal or restricted.

Arab attacks on Jewish communities in 1921 and 1929 found the Haganah ill-equipped and ineffective: more than 100 Jews were killed in 1929 alone. When renewed Arab rioting broke out in Jaffa (Yafo) in 1936 and soon spread throughout Palestine, the Mandate authorities—realizing that they could not defend every Jewish settlement—authorized the creation of the Jewish Settlement Police, also known as Notrim, who were trained, armed, and paid by the British. In 1938 a British intelligence officer, Captain Orde Charles Wingate, organized three counterguerrilla units, called special night squads, manned by British and Jewish personnel. As both of these organizations contained a large number of Haganah members, their formation greatly increased the assets of the Haganah while providing a legal basis for much of their activities. Although these nearly continuous disturbances from 1936 to 1939 cost the lives of nearly 600 Jews and more than 5,000 Arabs, Israeli observers have pointed out that Jewish casualties would have been far greater were it not for the increasing effectiveness of these paramilitary units (see The Palestinian Revolt, 1936–39, ch. 1).

During these disturbances, the Haganah's policy of *havlaga,* or self-restraint, under which retaliation against the Arab community at large was strictly forbidden, was not aggressive enough for some. Under Vladimir (Zeev) Jabotinsky and later Menachem Begin, these dissidents in 1937 established the National Military Organization (Irgun Zvai Leumi, known both as the Irgun and by the acronym Etzel). Initially the Irgun waged a campaign of terror, sabotage, and reprisal against the Arabs. After the British government issued a white paper in May 1939 extending the Mandate for ten years and placing limits on Jewish immigration, however, the Irgun turned its terrorist activities against the British troops in Palestine in an all-out struggle against the Mandate authority.

With the outbreak of World War II, Irgun leaders settled on a policy of cooperation with the British in the war effort; but a hard core within the organization opposed the policy and accordingly split off from the larger body. This group, led by Avraham Stern, formed the Fighters for Israel's Freedom (Lohamei Herut Israel—Lehi), known as the Stern Gang. The Stern Gang, which included Begin and later Yitzhak Shamir, specialized in the assassination of British and other officials. At their peaks, the Irgun contained about 4,000 men; the Stern Gang, 200 to 300. Defeat of Nazi Germany in 1945 precipitated a resumption of anti-British activities by both Haganah and Irgun in pursuance of their common ultimate goal, the establishment of a national home and the creation of a sovereign Jewish state.

During World War II, about 32,000 Palestinian Jews, both men and women, volunteered for the British army. In 1944 about 5,000 of these were formed into the Jewish Brigade, which fought successfully in Italy in 1945. With so many of its members serving abroad, the ranks of the Haganah were depleted, and in 1941 its leaders decided to raise a mobile force—the Palmach (abbreviation of Pelugot Mahatz—Shock Forces—see Glossary)—of approximately 3,000 full-time soldiers, whose mission was to defend the Yishuv. Trained with the aid of the British, the Palmach was the first full-time standing Jewish army in more than 2,000 years and is considered the direct forerunner to the IDF. For many years, the vast majority of IDF officers were veterans of either the Palmach or the Jewish Brigade.

War of Independence

When Israel achieved its independence on May 14, 1948, the Haganah became the de facto Israeli army. On that day, the country was invaded by the regular forces of Egypt, Lebanon, Iraq, and Syria. Eleven days later, Israel's provisional government issued an order that provided the legal framework for the country's armed forces. The order established the official name Zvah Haganah Le Yisrael and outlawed the existence of any other military force within Israel.

The dissident Irgun and Stern Gang were reluctant to disband. Fighting between Irgun and regular military forces broke out on June 21 when the supply ship *Altalena* arrived at Tel Aviv with 900 men and a load of arms and ammunition for the Irgun. The army sank the ship, destroying the arms, and many members of the Irgun were arrested; both organizations disbanded shortly thereafter. A more delicate problem was how to disband the Palmach, which had become an elite military unit within the Haganah and had strong political ties to the socialist-oriented kibbutzim. Nonetheless, David Ben-Gurion, Israel's first prime minister and minister of defense, was determined to see the IDF develop into a single, professional, and nonpolitical national armed force. It was only through his skill and determination that the Palmach was peacefully abolished and integrated into the IDF in January 1949.

The ranks of the IDF swelled rapidly to about 100,000 at the height of the War of Independence. Nearly all able-bodied men, plus many women, were recruited; thousands of foreign volunteers, mostly veterans of World War II, also came to the aid of Israel. The newly independent state rapidly mobilized to meet the Arab invaders; by July 1948, the Israelis had set up an air force, a navy, and a tank battalion. Weapons and ammunition were procured abroad, primarily from Czechoslovakia. Three B-17 bombers were bought in the United States through black market channels, and shortly after one of them bombed Cairo in July 1948, the Israelis were able to establish air supremacy. Subsequent victories came in rapid succession on all three fronts. The Arab states negotiated separate armistice agreements. Egypt was the first to sign (February 1949), followed by Lebanon (March), Transjordan (April), and finally Syria (July). Iraq simply withdrew its forces without signing an agreement. As a result of the war, Israel considerably expanded its territory beyond the United Nations (UN) partition plan for Palestine at the expense of its Arab neighbors. Victory cost more than 6,000 Israeli lives, however, which represented approximately 1 percent of the population. After the armistice, wartime recruits were rapidly demobilized, and the hastily raised IDF, still lacking a permanent institutional basis, experienced mass resignations from its war-weary officer corps. This process underscored the basic manpower problem of a small population faced with the need to mobilize a sizable army during a wartime emergency. In 1949, after study of the Swiss reservist system, Israel introduced a three-tiered system based on a small standing officer corps, universal conscription, and a large pool of well-trained reservists that could be rapidly mobilized.

In early 1955, Egypt began sponsoring raids launched by fedayeen (Arab commandos or guerrillas) from the Sinai Peninsula, the Gaza Strip, and Jordan, into Israel (see fig. 1). As the number and seriousness of these raids increased, Israel began launching reprisal raids against Arab villages in Gaza and the West Bank (see Glossary) of the Jordan. These retaliatory measures, which cost the lives of Arab civilians and did little to discourage the fedayeen, became increasingly controversial both within Israel and abroad. Shortly thereafter Israeli reprisal raids were directed against military targets, frontier strongholds, police fortresses, and army camps.

In addition to these incidents, which at times became confrontations between regular Israeli and Arab military forces, other developments contributed to the generally escalating tensions between Egypt and Israel and convinced Israeli military officials that Egypt was preparing for a new war. Under an arms agreement of 1955, Czechoslovakia supplied Egypt with a vast amount of arms, including fighter aircraft, tanks and other armored vehicles, destroyers, and submarines. The number of Egyptian troops deployed in Sinai along the Israeli border also increased dramatically in 1956. In July Egypt nationalized the Suez Canal; shortly thereafter Egypt closed the Strait of Tiran, at the southern tip of Sinai, and blockaded Israeli shipping.

1956 War

Fearing these actions to be signs of an imminent Egyptian invasion, Israel rapidly mobilized its reserves. On October 29, under Major General Moshe Dayan, the IDF launched a preemptive attack into Sinai. Israeli advances on the ground were rapid, and, supported by air cover, by November 2 they had routed the Egyptian forces and effectively controlled the entire peninsula. With Israeli troops on the east bank of the Suez Canal, British and French

United Nations checkpoint
in the occupied territories, on the road to Damascus
Courtesy Jean E. Tucker
A view of a Palestinian refugee camp in Gaza
Courtesy International Committee for the Red Cross (Jean-Luc Ray)

troops landed at Port Said and demanded withdrawal of both sides from the Canal. The UN met in an emergency session and demanded that the British and French leave Suez, which they did in December 1956 in response to both United States and UN pressure, and that Israel withdraw to the Armistice line of 1949, which it did somewhat reluctantly in March 1957 after the United Nations Emergency Force (UNEF) had been stationed in the Gaza Strip and at Sharm ash Shaykh on the Strait of Tiran.

Israel's victory in the 1956 War (known in Israel as the Sinai Campaign) thus afforded it a modicum of increased security by virtue of the UN presence. Far more important, however, was that it enhanced Israel's standing as a military power and as a viable nation. Although many Israelis felt that the military victory was nullified by the UN demand to withdraw from Sinai, Israel had achieved significant psychological gains at a cost of fewer than 170 lives.

The decade after the 1956 War was the most tranquil period in the nation's history. The Egyptian armistice line remained quiet, and there were few incidents along the Jordanian line until 1965, when Egyptian-sponsored guerrilla raids by Al Fatah first occurred. Beginning in 1960, there were repeated guerrilla activities and shellings of Israeli settlements from the Golan Heights of Syria, but these incidents remained localized until 1964.

Underlying tensions, however, did not abate. By the early 1960s, both sides considered a third round of war inevitable. An ominous arms race developed. Egypt and Syria were supplied with Soviet aid and military hardware, and Israel suddenly found European powers—the Federal Republic of Germany (West Germany), Britain, and especially France—to be willing suppliers of modern armaments. Jordan continued to receive arms from Britain and the United States.

Tensions mounted in 1964, when, after Israel had nearly completed a massive irrigation project that involved diverting water from the Jordan River into the Negev Desert, Syria began a similar project near the river's headwaters that would have virtually dried the river bed at the Israeli location. Israel launched air and artillery attacks at the Syrian site, and Syria abandoned the project. Guerrilla incursions from Syria and Jordan steadily mounted, as did the intensity of Israeli reprisal raids.

In April 1967, increased Syrian aircraft-shelling of Israeli border villages encountered an Israeli fighter attack during which six Syrian MiGs were shot down. Syria feared that an all-out attack from Israel was imminent, and Egypt, with whom Syria had recently signed a mutual defense treaty, began an extensive military buildup in early May. On May 18, Egypt's president, Gamal Abdul Nasser, demanded the withdrawal of UN forces from Gaza and Sinai; Secretary General U Thant promptly acceded and removed the UNEF. Four days later, Nasser announced a blockade of Israeli shipping at the Strait of Tiran, an action that Israel since the 1956 War had stressed would be tantamount to a declaration of war. Jordan and Iraq rapidly joined Syria in its military alliance with Egypt.

June 1967 War

On May 30, mounting public opinion led to the appointment of Dayan as minister of defense. Levi Eshkol, who had been both prime minister and minister of defense since Ben-Gurion's resignation in 1963, retained the prime minister's position. Dayan immediately made a series of public declarations that war could be avoided, while secretly planning a massive preemptive strike against the Arab enemy. On the morning of June 5, Israel launched a devastating attack on Arab air power, destroying about 300 Egyptian, 50 Syrian, and 20 Jordanian aircraft, mostly on the ground. This action, which virtually eliminated the Arab air forces, was immediately followed by ground invasions into Sinai and the Gaza Strip, Jordan, and finally Syria. Arab ground forces, lacking air support, were routed on all three fronts; by the time the UN-imposed cease-fire took effect in the evening of June 11, the IDF had seized the entire Sinai Peninsula to the east bank of the Suez Canal; the West Bank of Jordan, including East Jerusalem; and the Golan Heights of Syria. Unlike the aftermath of the 1956 War, however, the IDF did not withdraw from the areas it occupied in 1967.

Israel was ecstatic about its swift and stunning victory, which had been achieved at the relatively low cost of about 700 lives. The IDF had proven itself superior to the far larger forces of the combined Arab armies. More important, it now occupied the territory that had harbored immediate security threats to Israel since 1948. For the first time since independence, the Israeli heartland along the Mediterranean Sea was out of enemy artillery range. The exploits of what was known in Israel as the Six-Day War soon became legend, and the commanders who led it became national heros.

Although control of the occupied territories greatly improved Israel's security from a geographical standpoint, it also created new problems. The roughly 1 million Arabs within the territories provided potential cover and support for infiltration and sabotage by Arab guerrillas. From shortly after the June 1967 War until 1970, a steady stream of men and weapons were sent into the West Bank by a number of guerrilla groups, in particular Al Fatah (see Palestinian Terrorist Groups, this ch.). Incidents of sabotage and clashes with Israeli security forces were commonplace. In the spring of 1970, the guerrilla strategy reverted to shelling Israeli towns from across the Jordanian and Lebanese borders. International terrorism, aimed at focusing world attention on the grievances of Palestinian Arabs against Israel, also appeared after the June 1967 War.

Hostilities on the Egyptian front were far more serious. The decimated Egyptian army was rapidly resupplied with advanced Soviet weapons, and the Soviet presence at the Suez Canal increased dramatically. In October 1967, the Israeli destroyer and flagship *Elat* was sunk by a missile fired from an Egyptian ship docked in Port Said; Israel retaliated with the destruction of Egyptian oil refineries at Suez. A year later, shelling began along the canal, and a new round of fighting, commonly known as the War of Attrition, commenced. For nearly two years, until a new cease-fire was imposed on August 7, 1970, Egypt (with growing and direct support from the Soviet Union) threw an increasingly heavy barrage of artillery and missiles at fortified Israeli positions along the east bank of the canal, while Israel stood its ground and launched a series of fighter-bomber raids deep into the Egyptian heartland. This deadly but inconclusive conflict culminated on July 30, 1970, when Israeli and Soviet-piloted fighters clashed in a dogfight near the Suez Canal. Israeli pilots reportedly shot down four MiGs and lost none of their own, but this direct confrontation with a nuclear superpower was a frightening development and helped bring about the cease-fire.

Although activity aimed against Israel by Palestinian guerrillas continued throughout the early 1970s, Israel felt relatively secure vis-à-vis its Arab neighbors after the War of Attrition. Israel's military intelligence was convinced that Syria would launch a war only in concert with Egypt and that Egypt would go to war only if it were convinced that its air power was superior to Israel's. This theory, which became so institutionalized in Israeli military thinking as to be dubbed "the concept," contributed to the country's general sense of security. Defense expenditures declined markedly from 1970 levels, the annual reserve call-up was reduced from sixty to thirty days, and in 1973 the length of conscription was reduced from thirty-six to thirty-three months.

October 1973 War

The October 1973 War (known in Israel as the Yom Kippur War and in the Arab world as the Ramadan War) developed

*Israeli liaison officers visit beduins
in the southern Sinai Peninsula, November 1975
Courtesy United Nations (Zuhair Saade)*

rapidly, and the coordinated Egyptian-Syrian offensive caught Israel by surprise. On September 28, Palestinian guerrillas detained an Austrian train carrying Soviet Jews en route to Israel. Subsequent Egyptian and Syrian military deployments were interpreted by Israel as defensive actions in anticipation of Israeli reprisals. For one week, Israel postponed mobilizing its troops. Not until the morning of Yom Kippur (October 6), about six hours before the Arab offensive, were Israeli officials convinced that war was imminent; a mobilization of the reserves was then ordered. In the early days of the war, the IDF suffered heavy losses as Egyptian forces crossed the Suez Canal and overran Israeli strongholds, while Syrians marched deep into the Golan Heights. Israel launched its counteroffensive first against the Syrian front, and only when it had pushed the Syrians back well east of the 1967 cease-fire line (by October 15) did Israel turn its attention to the Egyptian front. In ten days of fighting, Israel pushed the Egyptian army back across the canal, and the IDF made deep incursions into Egypt. On October 24, with Israeli soldiers about one kilometer from the main Cairo-Ismailia highway and the Soviet Union threatening direct military intervention, the UN imposed a cease-fire.

After several months of negotiations, during which sporadic fighting continued, Israel reached a disengagement agreement in

January 1974, whereby the IDF withdrew across the canal and
Israeli and Egyptian troops were separated in Sinai by a UNEF-
manned buffer zone. Israel signed a similar agreement with Syria
on May 31, 1974, whereby Israel withdrew to the 1967 cease-fire
line in the Golan Heights and a United Nations Disengagement
Observer Force (UNDOF) occupied a buffer zone between Israeli
and Syrian forces. On September 4, 1975, after further negotiations, the Second Sinai Disengagement Agreement was signed between Egypt and Israel that widened the buffer zone and secured
a further Israeli withdrawal to the east of the strategic Gidi and
Mitla passes.

Israel's military victory in 1973 came at a heavy price of more
than 2,400 lives and an estimated US$5 billion in equipment, of
which more than US$1 billion was airlifted by the United States
during the war when it became apparent that Israel's ammunition
stores were dangerously low. This action, and the threatened Soviet
intervention, raised more clearly than ever the specter of the Arab-
Israeli conflict escalating rapidly into a confrontation between the
superpowers. The October 1973 War also cost Israel its self-
confidence in its military superiority over its Arab enemy. The
government appointed a special commission, headed by Chief
Justice Shimon Agranat, president of the Israeli Supreme Court,
to investigate why Israel had been caught by surprise and why so
much had gone wrong during the war itself. The commission's
report, completed in January 1975, was highly critical of the performance of the IDF on several levels, including intelligence gathering, discipline within the ranks, and the mobilization of reserves.
The euphoria of the post-1967 era faded.

1982 Invasion of Lebanon

Since 1970, Israeli settlements near the southern border of
Lebanon had been exposed to harassing attacks from forces of the
Palestine Liberation Organization (PLO), which had been driven
out of Jordan. On three occasions, in 1970, 1972, and 1978, Israel
had retaliated by ground operations carried out up to Lebanon's
Litani River. The inhabitants of southern Lebanon deeply resented
the conversion of their region to a battlefield by the PLO. Supported by Israeli arms and training since 1973, they formed a militia
under Saad Haddad, a major in the Lebanese Army. Israeli support was gradually extended to other Christian militias, including
the Phalangist movement of Pierre Jumayyil (also seen as Gemayel),
as the Christian Maronites increasingly found themselves pressured
by the involvement of the PLO in the 1975 Lebanese Civil War.
A complicating element was the presence of the Syrian army in

Lebanon, tolerated by Israel on the understanding that Israel's security interests in southern Lebanon would not be threatened.

The Israeli government rejected appeals by Maronite Christians for direct Israeli military intervention to evict the PLO and Syrians from Lebanon. Pierre Jumayyil's son Bashir, however, determined to embroil Israel against Syria, staged an incident in 1981 in the city of Zahlah using approximately 100 Phalangist militiamen who had been infiltrated to attack Syrian positions. Jumayyil persuaded Israel to honor an earlier pledge for air strikes, which resulted in the downing of two Syrian helicopter transports. Syrian President Hafiz al Assad responded by stationing SA-6 surface-to-air missiles (SAMs) in the vicinity of Zahlah. Other SAMs and surface-to-surface missiles were deployed on the Syrian side of the border. Although the Phalangists abandoned Zahlah, the net effect was that Syrian air defense missiles were deployed in Lebanon, a situation that Israel regarded as an unacceptable shift in the balance of power in the area.

Meanwhile Israel had conducted preemptive shelling and air strikes to deter PLO terrorist attacks on settlements in Galilee in northern Israel. The PLO fought back by shelling Israeli towns in Upper Galilee and coastal areas, especially after a devastating Israeli air raid against a heavily populated Palestinian neighborhood in West Beirut that killed more than 100 people and wounded more than 600. In July 1981, United States Middle East Special Ambassador Philip Habib negotiated a truce in the artillery duel. During this cease-fire, PLO leader Yasir Arafat reinforced his position by purchases of artillery rockets and obsolete tanks of Soviet manufacture. The forces under his control, the Palestine Liberation Army (PLA), were transformed from a decentralized assemblage of terrorist and guerrilla bands to a standing army.

When, in early June 1982, terrorists of the Abu Nidal organization, a PLO splinter group, badly wounded the Israeli ambassador in London during an assassination attempt, Israel seized the pretext for launching its long-planned offensive. The Israeli cabinet's authorization for the invasion, named Operation Peace for Galilee, set strict limits on the incursion. The IDF was to advance no farther than forty kilometers, the operation was to last only twenty-four hours, there would be no attack on Syrian forces and no approach to Beirut. Because of these limits, the IDF did not openly acknowledge its actual objectives. As a result, the IDF advance unfolded in an ad hoc and disorganized fashion, greatly increasing the difficulty of the operation.

When IDF ground forces crossed into Lebanon on June 6, five divisions and two reinforced brigade-size units conducted the three-pronged attack. On the western axis, two divisions converged on Tyre and proceeded north along the coastal highway toward Sidon, where they were to link up with an amphibious command unit that had secured a beachhead north of the city. In the central sector, a third division veered diagonally across southern Lebanon, conquered the Palestinian-held Beaufort Castle, and headed west toward Sidon, where it linked up with the coastal force in a pincer movement. The PLO was the only group to resist the IDF advance. Although many PLO officers fled, abandoning their men, the Palestinian resistance proved tenacious. In house-to-house and hand-to-hand combat in the sprawling refugee camps near Tyre and Sidon, the Palestinians inflicted high casualties on the IDF. In the eastern sector, two Israeli divisions thrust directly north into Syrian-held territory to sever the strategic Beirut-Damascus highway. A brigade of Syrian commandos, however, ambushed the Israeli column in mountainous terrain, approximately five kilometers short of the highway. Syria's strong air defense system prevented the Israeli air force from attacking the entrenched Syrian positions. Nevertheless, in a surprise attack on Syrian SAM sites in the Biqa Valley, the Israelis destroyed seventeen of nineteen batteries. The Syrian air force was decimated in a desperate air battle to protect the air defense system.

With total air superiority, the IDF mauled the Syrian First Armored Division, although in the grueling frontal attacks the Israelis also suffered heavy casualties. Still stalled short of the Beirut-Damascus highway, the IDF was on the verge of a breakthrough when, on June 11, Israel bowed to political pressure and agreed to a truce under United States auspices (see fig. 12).

The Siege of Beirut and Its Aftermath

The cease-fire signaled the start of a new stage in the war, as Israel focused on PLO forces trapped in Beirut. Although Israel had long adhered to the axiom that conquering and occupying an Arab capital would be a political and military disaster, key Israeli leaders were determined to drive the PLO out of Beirut. Israel maintained the siege of Beirut for seventy days, unleashing a relentless air, naval, and artillery bombardment. The Israeli air force conducted what was called a ''manhunt by air'' for Arafat and his lieutenants and on several occasions bombed premises only minutes after the PLO leadership had vacated them. If the PLO was hurt physically by the bombardments, the appalling civilian casualties earned Israel world opprobrium. Morale plummeted among IDF officers and enlisted men, many of whom personally opposed the war. Lebanese leaders petitioned Arafat, who had threatened to fight the IDF until the last man, to abandon Beirut to spare further civilian suffering. Arafat's condition for withdrawal was that a multinational peacekeeping force be deployed to protect the Palestinian families left behind. Syria and Tunisia agreed to host departing PLO fighters. An advance unit of the Multinational Force, 350 French troops, arrived in Beirut on August 11, followed within one week by a contingent of 800 United States marines. By September 1, approximately 8,000 Palestinian guerrillas, 2,600 PLA regulars, and 3,600 Syrian troops had evacuated West Beirut.

Taking stock of the war's toll, Israel announced the death of 344 of its soldiers and the wounding of more than 2,000. Israel calculated that hundreds of Syrian soldiers had been killed and more than 1,000 wounded, and that 1,000 Palestinian guerrillas had been killed and 7,000 captured. By Lebanese estimates, 17,825 Lebanese had died and more than 30,000 had been wounded.

On the evening of September 12, 1982, the IDF, having surrounded the Palestinian refugee camps of Sabra and Shatila, dispatched 300 to 400 Christian militiamen into the camps to rout what was believed to be the remnant of the PLO forces. The militiamen were mostly Phalangists but also included members of the Israeli-sponsored South Lebanon Army (SLA). The IDF ordered its soldiers to refrain from entering the camps, but IDF officers supervised the operation from the roof of a six-story building overlooking part of the area. According to the report of the Kahan Commission created later by the Israeli government to investigate the events, the IDF monitored the Phalangist radio network and fired flares from mortars and aircraft to illuminate the area. Over a period of two days, the Christian militiamen massacred 700 to 800 Palestinian men, women, and children.

Minister of Defense Ariel Sharon, the architect of Israel's war in Lebanon, was forced to resign his portfolio in the wake of the Sabra and Shatila investigation, although he remained in the cabinet. He was replaced by former ambassador to the United States Moshe Arens, who wanted Israel to withdraw promptly from Lebanon, if only to avoid further antagonizing Washington.

Israel withdrew its forces to the outskirts of the capital but it no longer had a clear tactical mission in Lebanon. Israel intended its continued presence to be a bargaining chip to negotiate a Syrian withdrawal. While awaiting a political agreement, the IDF had to fight a different kind of war. Turned into a static and defensive garrison force, it was now caught in a crossfire between warring factions. Its allies in Lebanon, the Christian Maronite militias, proved to be incapable of providing day-to-day security and holding territory taken from the PLO. The hostility engendered among

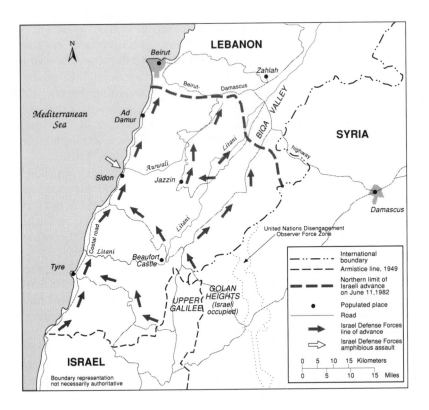

Figure 12. Israel's 1982 Invasion of Lebanon

the predominant Shia population of southern Lebanon over the prolonged Israeli occupation was in some ways potentially more dangerous than the threat posed by Palestinian guerrillas. In November 1983, the blowing up of the Israeli command post in Tyre signaled the beginning of full-scale guerrilla warfare by Shia groups, some of which were linked militarily and ideologically to Iran. During 1984, more than 900 attacks—hit-and-run ambushes, grenade assaults, and antipersonnel mine detonations—took place upon Israeli troops. Realizing that to attempt to hold a hostile region like southern Lebanon indefinitely contravened its basic strategic doctrine, the IDF pulled back its forces between January and June 1985, leaving only a token force to patrol a narrow security zone with its proxy, the SLA.

Israeli Concepts of National Security

The need for a strong military posture in the face of the perceived

Arab threats to Israel's survival has been endorsed with near unanimity by Israeli policy makers and citizens. Nevertheless, the question of which strategies best ensure national defense has often caused
acrimonious national, as well as international, controversy. Events
subsequent to Ben-Gurion's initial concepts of national security
laid down when Israel was founded in 1948, particularly Israel's
occupation of Arab territories since the June 1967 War, have modified the foundations for Israel's concepts of national security.

Dormant War

Israelis traditionally viewed the Arab-Israeli conflict as a struggle for survival, convinced that even one military defeat would mean
the end of their country. National defense became the first priority, with proportionately more human and material resources devoted to defense than in any other nation in the world. Israelis
regarded major conflicts, such as occurred in 1967 and 1973, as
"rounds" or battles in a continuous war. Even when it was not
engaged in outright combat with its Arab enemies, Israel remained
in what General Yitzhak Rabin, who became minister of defense
in 1984, called a "dormant war" that, "like a volcano," could
erupt with little warning into a major conflagration.

Extensive Threat

Another premise was that every Arab country was at least a
potential member of a unified pan-Arab coalition that could attack Israel—a concept sometimes referred to by Israeli strategic
planners as the "extensive threat." To confront this extensive
threat, the IDF aimed to have the capability to defend Israel not
only against an attack by a single Arab adversary or an alliance
of several Arab states, but also against the combined forces of all
Arab countries. Israeli strategists felt that planning for such a worst-
case scenario was prudent because Arab states had often rhetori-
cally threatened such a combined attack. The concept of extensive
threat also justified requests for greater military aid from the United
States and protests against United States military support of moderate Arab states that, from the American perspective, posed no credi-
ble threat to Israel's security. Some Israeli military leaders insisted
that, despite the 1978 Camp David Accords, Egypt remained a
major potential enemy in any future Arab-Israeli war. Moreover,
some Israeli strategists worried about threats from outside the Arab
world. In a 1981 speech, then Minister of Defense Sharon stated
that "Israel's sphere of strategic and security interests must be
broadened in the 1980s" to confront new adversaries in Africa and

Asia, and cited Pakistan as one potential threat. Some strategists even envisioned Israeli clashes with Iran and India.

At the other end of the spectrum were those who felt that the concept of extensive threat exaggerated the danger to Israel. Some Israeli strategists argued in the late 1980s that the Arab-Israeli conflict was evolving into a bilateral contest between Israel and Syria to which other Arab actors were becoming peripheral. They considered that the IDF for pragmatic reasons should deploy its limited resources to counter the threat of a cross-border attack by Syria. Speaking in 1987, Minister of Defense Rabin stated that Egypt had placed itself "outside the circle of nations at war with Israel" and that the Treaty of Peace Between Egypt and Israel had "significantly altered the Middle East balance of power in Israel's favor."

Demographic and geographic pressures arising from Israel's small size and concentrated population meant that a war fought within Israel would be extremely costly in terms of civilian casualties and damage to the economic infrastructure. Morale and, hence, future immigration would also suffer. It was therefore an ironclad rule of Israeli strategists to transfer military action to enemy territory, and no regular Arab troops have hit on Israeli soil since 1948. Because Israel could never defeat its Arab enemy permanently, no matter how many victories or "rounds" it won on the battlefield, and because in each full-scale war it incurred the risk, however minimal, of combat being conducted on its territory or even a defeat that would destroy the state, Israel's official policy was to avoid all-out war unless attacked. Deterrence therefore became the main pillar of Israel's national security doctrine.

Strategic Depth

Israel considered an offensive rather than a defensive strategy the best deterrent to Arab attack. Because of the absence until 1967 of the depth of terrain essential for strategic defense, Israel could ensure that military action was conducted on Arab territory only by attacking first. Moreover, Israel feared that a passive defensive strategy would permit the Arabs, secure in the knowledge that Israel would not fight unless attacked, to wage a protracted low-level war of attrition, engage in brinkmanship through incremental escalation, or mobilize for war with impunity. Paradoxically, then, the policy of deterrence dictated that Israel always had to strike first. The Israeli surprise attack could be a "preemptive" attack in the face of an imminent Arab attack, an unprovoked "preventive" attack to deal the Arab armies a setback that would stave off future attack, or a massive retaliation for a minor Arab infraction.

Israel justified such attacks by the concept that it was locked in permanent conflict with the Arabs.

The occupation of conquered territories in 1967 greatly increased Israel's strategic depth, and Israeli strategic thinking changed accordingly. Many strategists argued that the IDF could now adopt a defensive posture, absorb a first strike, and then retaliate with a counteroffensive. The October 1973 War illustrated that this thinking was at least partially correct. With the added security buffer of the occupied territories, Israel could absorb a first strike and retaliate successfully.

But when Sharon was appointed minister of defense in 1981, he advocated that Israel revert to the more aggressive pre-1967 strategy. Sharon argued that the increased mechanization and mobility of Arab armies, combined with the increased range of Arab surface-to-surface missile systems (SSMs), nullified the strategic insulation and advanced warning that the occupied territories afforded Israel. Israel, therefore, faced the same threat that it had before 1967 and, incapable of absorbing a first strike, should be willing to launch preventive and preemptive strikes against potential Arab threats. After the 1982 invasion of Lebanon, for which Sharon was substantially responsible, the aggressive national security posture that he advocated waned in popularity. By 1988, however, Iraq's use of SSMs against Iran and Saudi Arabia's acquisition of long-range SSMs from China suggested to some Israeli strategists that the concepts of extensive threat and preemption should again be given more weight.

Potential Causes of War

Israel made clear to the Arabs that certain actions, even if not overtly hostile or aimed at Israel, would trigger an Israeli preemptive attack. Israel announced various potential causes of war. Some causes, such as interference with Israeli freedom of navigation in the Strait of Tiran, were officially designated as such. In 1982 Sharon listed four actions that would lead to an attack: the attempt by an Arab country to acquire or manufacture an atomic bomb, the militarization of the Sinai Peninsula, the entry of the Iraqi army into Jordan, and the supply of sophisticated United States arms to Jordan. In 1988 the government of Israel continued to communicate potential causes to its Arab adversaries. Their tacit acquiescence in these unilateral Israeli demands constituted a system of unwritten but mutually understood agreements protecting the short-term status quo.

Since the establishment of Israel, the IDF has been obliged to deal with terrorist actions, cross-border raids, and artillery and missile barrages of the various Palestinian organizations under the loose leadership of the PLO. The IDF's approach in contending with PLO activity has combined extreme vigilance with prompt and damaging retaliatory measures, including punishment of Arab nations giving sanctuary to terrorists and guerrillas. The presence of innocent noncombatants was not accepted as a reason for withholding counterstrikes. Although striving to limit harm to uninvolved persons, the Israelis gave priority to the need to demonstrate that acts of terrorism would meet with quick retribution in painful and unpredictable forms.

Israeli strategists believed the periodic outbreak of war to be virtually inevitable and that once war broke out it was essential that it be brief and lead to decisive victory. The requirement of a rapid war followed from at least two factors. During full mobilization, virtually the entire Israeli population was engaged in the defense effort and the peacetime economy ground to a halt. Sustaining full mobilization for more than several weeks would prove disastrous to the economy, and stockpiling sufficient supplies for a long war would be difficult and very costly. Experience from past wars also showed Israel that prolonged hostilities invited superpower intervention. As a result, Israeli strategists stressed the need to create a clear margin of victory before a cease-fire was imposed from the outside. This concept was extended in the 1980s, when Israeli military leaders formulated the strategy of engaging in a "war of annihilation" in the event of a new round of all-out warfare. Israel's goal would be to destroy the Arab armies so completely as to preclude a military threat for ten years. Such a scenario might prove elusive, however, because destroyed equipment could be quickly replaced, and the Arab countries had sufficient manpower to rebuild shattered forces.

Nuclear and Conventional Deterrents

The concept of deterrence assumed a new dimension with the introduction of nuclear weapons into the equation. In December 1974, President Ephraim Katzir announced that "it has always been our intention to develop a nuclear potential. We now have that potential." Ambiguously, Israeli officials maintained that Israel would not be the first nation to introduce nuclear weapons into the Middle East. Experts assumed that Israel had a rudimentary nuclear capability. In September 1986, the testimony and photographs provided by Mordechai Vanunu, a technician who had worked at Israel's Dimona nuclear facility in the Negev Desert, led experts to conclude that Israel had a nuclear capability far greater than previously thought (see Nuclear Weapons Potential, this ch.).

Although viewed as its ultimate guarantor of security, the nuclear option did not lead Israel to complacency about national security. On the contrary, it impelled Israel to seek unquestioned superiority in conventional capability over the Arab armies to forestall use of nuclear weapons as a last resort. The IDF sought to leverage its conventional power to the maximum extent. IDF doctrine and tactics stressed quality of weapons versus quantity; integration of the combined firepower of the three branches of the armed forces; effective battlefield command, communications, and real-time intelligence; use of precision-guided munitions and stand-off firepower; and high mobility.

The debate over secure borders rested at the heart of the controversy over Israel's national security. Some strategists contended that only a negotiated settlement with the Arabs would bring peace and ensure Israel's ultimate security. Such a settlement would entail territorial concessions in the occupied territories. Proponents of exchanging land for peace tended to be skeptical that any border was militarily defensible in the age of modern warfare. In their eyes, the occupied territories were a liability in that they gave Israel a false sense of security and gave the Arabs reason to go to war.

Others believed Israel's conflict with the Arab states was fundamentally irreconcilable and that Israeli and Arab territorial imperatives were mutually exclusive. They held that ceding control of the occupied territories would bring at best a temporary peace and feared that the Arabs would use the territories as a springboard to attack Israel proper. Israeli military positions along the Golan Heights and the Jordan Rift Valley were said to be ideal geographically defensible borders. Others viewed the occupied territories as an integral part of Israel and Israeli withdrawal as too high a price to pay for peace. Extending beyond national security, the controversy was enmeshed with political, social, and religious issues—particularly the concept of exchanging "land for peace" that formed the basis of UN Security Council resolutions 242 and 338.

Autonomy

Autonomy was another cornerstone of Israeli strategic doctrine, but autonomy did not mean independence. The Israeli military acknowledged a heavy dependence on the United States as a supplier of military matériel and as a deterrent to possible Soviet intervention on the side of the Arabs during times of war. Precisely because of this dependence, however, Israel felt it necessary to take autonomous action—often in defiance of strong United States objections. In numerous actions, such as the 1973 encirclement of the Egyptian Third Army and the 1982 siege of West Beirut, Israel

271

signaled to Washington that its national interests were not always congruent with those of the United States. More important, Israel proved to its Arab adversaries that despite any political pressure they exerted on Washington, the United States could not extract concessions from Israel. Another dimension of autonomy was that Israel would not make a settlement with the Arabs by placing itself in an indefensible position in return for security guarantees from the United States. In general, foreign policy was subservient to defense policy, and Israeli policy makers felt that Israel should never sacrifice its strategic strength for improved foreign relations with the United States, the Arab states, or other countries, even if such improved relations made war less likely. As Dayan said, "Israel has no foreign policy—only a defense policy."

International and Domestic Security Concerns
The Arab Military Threat

As of 1988, experts considered the IDF superior to any combination of Arab forces that was likely to be massed against it in a future conflict. The total manpower and firepower that could be directed against Israel far outweighed the battlefield resources that Israel could muster, yet Israel's dynamic military leadership, troop proficiency, and sophisticated weaponry still promised to be decisive, as they had been in previous wars. The Arab nations remained deeply divided over a host of issues in mid-1988, including their postures toward Israel. Although the Camp David peace process between Egypt and Israel failed to achieve normalization of relations, Israel no longer considered Egypt part of the circle of hostile states. Nevertheless, Israeli planners did not rule out an upheaval in Egyptian politics that would renew the risk of military confrontation. With the Sinai region effectively demilitarized, the element of surprise that had initially worked in Egypt's favor in the October 1973 War would not be available. In any future conflict, Egyptian forces would have to cross 130 kilometers of desert exposed to Israeli air power. Jordan's military weakness vis-à-vis Israel and its exposure to Israeli retaliation seemed to rule out military action except as a reluctant ally in a larger Arab coalition. The modernization of Jordan's army and air force was continuing, however, with the help of the United States and France. Many important Israeli targets were within the range of Jordanian artillery and rockets.

Syria posed the paramount threat. The Syrian armed forces had pursued a massive build-up of offensive and defensive manpower and equipment in an effort to maintain parity with Israel. Although the inflexibility of their military strategy had resulted in crushing defeats in engagements with the IDF, the Syrians had proved to be skillful and stubborn fighters during the Lebanon conflict. The concentrations of Syrian troops facing the Golan Heights probably could make initial gains in a thrust against the IDF, but would absorb heavy punishment once the Israelis mobilized for a counterattack.

Like other Arab states, Saudi Arabia had upgraded its naval and air arms, improving its capability to defend its air space and control activities in the Red Sea area. Saudi Arabia's outlook and strategic doctrine were primarily defensive, and its primary objective was stability in the Middle East to minimize the danger to its oil facilities and other vital installations. Nevertheless, from Israel's perspective, that country had the potential to undertake offensive air operations in conjunction with other Arab air forces. In the eyes of Israeli strategists, Saudi Arabia's 1988 purchase of long-range missiles from China and its acquisition of Tornado fighter-bombers from Britain enhanced its role in a future conflict.

The Iraqi army had not played a decisive role in previous wars. During the October 1973 fighting, two Iraqi brigades were quickly overcome in the IDF drive toward Damascus. If Iraq again attempted to advance its forces to support Syria and Jordan, they would, like those of Egypt, be vulnerable to Israeli air strikes. Nevertheless, as of late 1988, Israeli officers were less confident of their ability to neutralize Iraq's armed potential. During the war with Iran, the Iraqi army had expanded to more than twenty divisions and had acquired combat experience and skill in the use of sophisticated weaponry. Iraq also had demonstrated the capacity and willingness to resort to chemical weapons. On the other hand, Iraq was economically drained and presumably tired of fighting after the eight-year struggle with Iran. Israeli military analysts felt, moreover, that tensions would persist in the Persian Gulf and that Iraq's armed forces would be unlikely to welcome military involvement elsewhere.

The buildup of the Arab armies between the October 1973 War and the mid-1980s was both qualitative and quantitative. Egypt, Syria, and Jordan had expanded the total of their divisions from twenty to twenty-five during this period. Of these, the number of armored and mechanized divisions rose from ten to twenty-two. Israeli planners estimated that Iraq could contribute another ten divisions, increasing the Arab disparity over Israel even more (see fig. 13).

The lifting of restrictions on arms sales by the Western powers, combined with the increased resources at the disposal of oil-exporting countries, enabled the Arab powers vastly to expand their

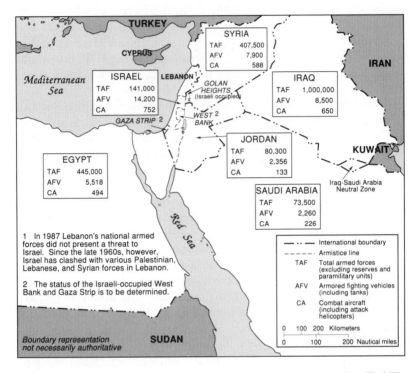

Source: Based on information from International Institute for Strategic Studies, *The Military Balance, 1987–1988,* London, 1987, 96–114.

Figure 13. Comparison of Military Forces of Israel and Neighboring Countries, 1987

sophisticated weaponry between 1973 and 1988. The tank inventories of Egypt, Jordan, and Syria rose by 60 percent, while their stocks of aircraft, helicopters, and armored personnel carriers roughly doubled. Both Syria and Iraq had acquired high performance aircraft of Soviet design. To the Arab countries' primary land weapons had been added more self-propelled artillery, guided antitank missiles, new munitions—including cluster and homing shells—improved fire-control systems, and laser rangefinders. Previously vulnerable air defenses now could be shielded using advanced mobile missile systems acquired from both East and West. Most of the strategic sites in Israel were exposed to Syrian striking power in the form of Soviet-supplied SS-21 SSMs, with a range of 120 kilometers and far greater accuracy than the earlier generation FROG-7 (70 kilometers) and Scud-B (300 kilometers).

Israel could draw only tentative conclusions regarding the improvement in Arab military leadership and manpower resources. Arab field commanders had not yet demonstrated the successful adaptation of modern command and control systems to battlefield situations. Arab forces had in the past shown greater effectiveness in static defense than in mobile offensive operations. The paucity of qualified technical personnel in the Arab armies, attributed to deficiencies in education and training, continued to detract from the ability of the Arab armed forces to employ modern weaponry with full efficiency. The superior skills of Israeli pilots had been decisive in the 1982 invasion of Lebanon and in earlier engagements. Although the rising level of weapons technology presented more of a problem to the Arab nations than to Israel, the Arabs' Soviet systems were simpler to use and maintain than their more sophisticated United States counterparts. The improved performance of the Iraqi air force against Iran after 1985 offered some evidence that the disparity in pilot skills and experience might be narrowing.

Palestinian Terrorist Groups

The PLO was formed in 1964 as an umbrella body for a number of elements of the Palestinian resistance movement. Its main constituent force was Al Fatah (Movement for the Liberation of Palestine), whose head, Yasir Arafat, assumed control of the PLO in 1968. At the outbreak of the invasion of Lebanon in 1982, Al Fatah numbered 6,500 armed men organized into regular units. Another PLO faction was the Popular Front for the Liberation of Palestine (PFLP), ideologically close to the Soviet Union and led by a Christian, George Habash. The PFLP was bitterly opposed to compromise with Israel. Numbering about 1,500 adherents in 1982, it was responsible for some of the most deadly international terrorist actions against Israel and its supporters. Other leftist groups had splintered from the PFLP, including the Democratic Front for the Liberation of Palestine (DFLP), the Popular Front for the Liberation of Palestine-General Command (with ties to Syria and Libya), and the Palestine Liberation Front (Iraq-supported). The Palestine Liberation Army (PLA), numbering nearly 4,000 men in 1982, was established in 1964 as the military arm of the PLO. In practice, however, the Syrian general staff controlled the PLA's contingents of Palestinian troops and the Jordanian army controlled one brigade in Jordan. The Abu Nidal organization, an anti-Arafat group supported by Libya and Syria, was responsible for many terrorist actions in Western Europe and against pro-Arafat Palestinians.

Initially linked to Syria, Al Fatah came into its own after the June 1967 War, when the West Bank and the Gaza Strip fell under Israeli control. Palestinian refugees poured into Jordan, where the PLO established virtually autonomous enclaves, and from which it launched guerrilla raids. Israel's retaliation inflicted heavy damage within Jordan. The PLO refused demands from King Hussein that it cease operations and, in a sharp conflict with Jordanian forces in 1970 and 1971, was driven out of Jordan. Shifting its headquarters to Lebanon, the PLO adopted a more formal military structure, benefiting from an abundant flow of arms from other Arab nations. In spite of the danger of Israeli reprisals, the Lebanese government was forced to accept the independent political and military presence of the PLO in Lebanon.

Airliner hijackings had been an element in the PLO's strategy since 1967. In retaliation against an attack on an El Al airliner in Athens in 1968, Israel mounted a helicopter raid against the Beirut International Airport, destroying thirteen Arab-owned aircraft. A number of deadly terrorist incidents and guerrilla attacks against Israeli West Bank settlements occurred during the 1970s. In an attempt at hostage-taking, the Black September group, an extremist faction of Al Fatah, killed eleven Israeli athletes at the Munich Olympics in 1972. A climax in the terrorist campaign occurred in March 1978, when Al Fatah raiders landed on the Israeli coast south of Haifa, attacking a bus and cars on the Tel Aviv-Haifa highway. Thirty-five Israelis were killed and at least seventy-four were wounded. In reaction to the highway attack, the IDF launched Operation Litani in April 1978, a three-month expedition to clear the PLO guerrillas from Lebanese border areas. Within one week, the strong IDF force had driven back the PLO and established complete control in southern Lebanon up to the Litani River.

Nevertheless, the PLO had not been dealt a decisive blow. With Soviet help, it began to accumulate substantial numbers of heavy weapons, including long-range artillery, rocket launchers, antiaircraft weapons, and missiles. Between 1978 and 1981, numerous IDF raids against PLO installations in southern Lebanon were answered within hours by random artillery and rocket attacks on Israeli border settlements. By mid-1981, the reciprocal attacks were approaching the intensity of full-scale hostilities. Punishing bombing raids by the Israeli air force included an attack aimed at PLO headquarters in Beirut that caused many civilian casualties. Although a truce was arranged with the help of United States ambassador Philip Habib on July 24, 1981, acts of PLO terror did not abate inside Israel, in the West Bank, and in foreign countries. Israel considered the continued presence of long-range

Israeli forces withdrawing from
occupied area of southern Lebanon, June 1978
Courtesy United Nations (Y. Nagata)

weapons threatening its northern population centers an unacceptable threat. In June 1982, Israel justified its invasion of Lebanon
as the response to an assassination attempt against its ambassador
in London by the Abu Nidal group. At the outset of the war, the
PLO had approximately 15,000 organized forces and about 18,000
militia recruited among Palestinian refugees. In spite of the large
quantity of weapons and armor it had acquired, it never reached
the level of military competence needed to meet the IDF in regular combat. When three division-size IDF armored columns bore
down on the 6,000 PLO fighters defending the coastal plain below
Beirut, the Palestinians fought tenaciously even though they were
poorly led and even abandoned by many senior officers. Effective
resistance ended within a week when the IDF closed in on the Beirut
suburbs (see 1982 Invasion of Lebanon, this ch.).

To avoid the domestic and international repercussions of the
bloody street fighting that an attack on the PLO headquarters in
West Beirut would have entailed, an agreement was negotiated
whereby the PLO troops and command would evacuate Lebanon
and withdraw to other Arab states willing to receive them. By
September 1982, more than 14,000 PLO combatants had withdrawn. About 6,500 Al Fatah fighters sailed from Beirut. Most
of the others crossed into Syria, and smaller contingents went to

other Arab countries. As of 1987, it was believed that between 2,000 and 3,700 guerrillas were still in Syria, 2,000 were in Jordan, and smaller groups were quartered in Algeria, the Yemen Arab Republic (North Yemen), the People's Democratic Republic of Yemen (South Yemen), Iraq, Sudan, and Tunisia. By 1988, however, many PLO fighters had filtered back into Lebanon. About 3,000 armed men aligned with Al Fatah were located in two camps near Sidon, forty kilometers south of Beirut, and an additional 7,000 fighters aligned with Syria reportedly were deployed in bases and refugee camps in eastern and northern Lebanon.

Much of the Arab terrorism directed against Israel during the mid-to-late 1980s was conducted by Syrian-sponsored Palestinian groups that rejected Arafat. To a lesser extent, terrorist threats resulted from Libyan involvement or from Al Fatah and its Force 17. Terrorists made a number of attempts to infiltrate the Israeli coast by sea and the anti-Arafat Abu Musa faction mounted several terrorist attacks in Jerusalem. The Damascus-based PFLP waged a relentless campaign to inhibit the development of moderate Palestinian leadership in the occupied territories. The shadowy Abu Nidal was believed responsible for a number of actions in which Israel was not necessarily the primary target. These included the hijacking of an Egyptian airliner with the loss of many lives in late 1985, and shooting and grenade attacks at the El Al counters of the Rome and Vienna airports a few months later.

The Shia population of southern Lebanon had initially welcomed the IDF as adversaries of the PLO. By 1984, however, they had turned against the Israelis because of the dislocation caused by the Israeli occupation. Protests turned to violence in the form of hundreds of hit-and-run attacks by Shia gunmen against Israeli troops. The situation eased with the end of the Israeli occupation in mid-1985.

Southern Lebanon continued to be a potentially dangerous base for guerrilla attacks in 1988, following the partial reorganization of PLO elements in Lebanon and the introduction of hundreds of Shia radicals of the Hizballah (Party of God) movement supported by Iran. Numerous attempts had been made by terrorist squads to penetrate Israel's border defenses. A zone inside Lebanese territory eighty kilometers long and averaging ten kilometers in depth was patrolled by 1,000 IDF troops backed by 2,000 SLA militiamen recruited among Christian Maronites. The IDF conducted periodic sweeps of this zone to discourage cross-border infiltration and shelling by the PLO. The frontier itself was protected by antipersonnel mines, an electronic fence, acoustic, radar and night-vision systems, fortified positions, and mobile patrols.

The Palestinian uprising (*intifadah*) that broke out in December 1987 in the West Bank and Gaza Strip apparently was launched spontaneously and was not directly controlled by the PLO. Burying their longstanding rivalries, local members of Al Fatah, PFLP, DFLP, the Palestinian Communist Party, and fundamentalists of the Islamic Holy War faction provided leadership through "popular committees" in camps and villages. A loose coordinating body, the Unified National Command of the Uprising, distributed leaflets with guidance on the general lines of resistance. By August 1988, a separate Islamic fundamentalist organization had emerged. Known as Hamas, the Arabic acronym for a name that translates as the Islamic Resistance Movement, it rejected any political settlement with Israel, insisting that a solution would come only through a holy war (see Palestinian Uprising, December 1987– , this ch.).

Jewish Terrorist Organizations

Several small Jewish groups had been linked with terrorist attacks against Arabs in the West Bank and East Jerusalem. None of these presented a significant security problem to the IDF as of 1988. The best known of these organizations, the Gush Emunim Underground (sometimes called the Jewish Terror Organization), was formed in 1979 by prominent members of Gush Emunim, a group of religious zealots who had used squatter tactics to carry on a campaign to settle the West Bank after the October 1973 War. The underground perceived the 1978 Camp David Accords and the 1979 Treaty of Peace Between Egypt and Israel as betraying the Begin government's policy of retaining the territories conquered by Israel.

The principal terrorist actions of the Gush Emunim Underground were carried out between 1980 and 1984. In 1980 car bombings of five West Bank Arab mayors resulted in crippling two of the mayors. In 1983, the Hebron Islamic College was the target of a machinegun and grenade attack that killed three Arab students and wounded thirty-three others. In 1984 an attempt was made to place explosive charges on five Arab buses in East Jerusalem. This plot was foiled by agents of Israel's internal security force, Shin Bet, leading to arrest and prison sentences for eighteen members of the underground. The security services also uncovered a well-developed plan to blow up the Dome of the Rock, one of Islam's most sacred shrines, on Jerusalem's Temple Mount.

Another anti-Arab terrorist group, Terror Against Terror (known as TNT) was established by Kach, the right-wing extremist political movement of Rabbi Meir Kahane. TNT was responsible for numerous beatings and bombings and several murders of Arabs, beginning in 1975. Defending Shield (Egrof Magen), a Jewish vigilante group of West Bank settlers formed in 1983, was responsible for a number of attacks and vandalization of Arab property on the West Bank. During the *intifadah,* beginning in late 1987, there were many reports of Jewish vigilantism, including shootings, punitive raids on refugee camps, and assaults on Arab motorists in retaliation for rock-throwing attacks by Arab youths. Most of these appeared to be spontaneous actions by settlers of individual communities.

The Israel Defense Forces

Command Structure

The IDF had no commander in chief designated as such. The Basic Law: The Army, 1976, vested command in the government. In fact, the minister of defense acted as the highest authority over the IDF and was its link to civilian political authorities. The minister of defense was a civilian (although usually a retired military officer). The cabinet was required to give prior approval to major military policies and operations. Under normal circumstances, the standing Foreign Affairs and Security Committee of the cabinet exercised this responsibility. The invasion of Lebanon in 1982 demonstrated, however, that a domineering minister of defense could, by misleading the cabinet or withholding information, act contrary to the government's wishes. Periodic reports on the status of the military were provided to the Israeli parliament, the Knesset, through its Foreign Affairs and National Security Committee and on budgetary matters through the Finance Committee.

The highest ranking IDF officer, the only officer to hold the rank of lieutenant general, was the chief of staff, who was chairman of the general staff and was responsible to the minister of defense. The general staff was in charge of "professional" matters, such as organization, training, and the planning and execution of military operations. The chief of staff in late 1988, Lieutenant General Dan Shomron, had held the position since April 1987. He was appointed by the minister of defense for a term that was nominally three years but that could be shortened or extended. Within the Ministry of Defense, the senior civilian officer beneath the minister was the director general, who supervised defense production, infrastructure, the budget, and other administrative and technical matters. As the supreme commander of the IDF, however, the minister of defense could intervene in all IDF matters (see fig. 14).

The general staff had as its members the chief of general staff branch (operations), the chiefs of manpower, logistics, and intelligence; the three area commanders; and the commanding officers of the air force, navy, and ground corps. The ground corps commander was responsible for training, doctrine, and development of equipment for the four combat corps of paratroop/infantry, armor, artillery, and engineers. Operational control of the ground forces went through a separate chain of command from the chief of staff directly to the three area commanders—Northern (forces facing Syria and Lebanon); Central (forces facing Jordan); and Southern (forces facing Egypt)—who in turn exercised command over divisions and brigades.

The navy and air force were not, nor had ever been, designated as separate services. Officially known as the Sea Corps (Hel Yam) and the Air Corps (Hel Avir), the navy and air force, however, enjoyed more autonomy within the IDF structure than their official designations would suggest. Their commanders had the status of senior advisers to the chief of staff. Along with the ground force area commanders, the commanders of the air force and navy held two-star rank.

Ground Forces

The Israeli government did not disclose information on the overall size of the IDF, or the identity, location, and strength of units. In 1988 the International Institute for Strategic Studies in London estimated the strength of the ground forces at 104,000 troops, including 16,000 career soldiers and 88,000 conscripts. An additional 494,000 men and women were regularly trained reserves who could be mobilized within seventy-two hours. The staffs of each of the ground forces' three area commanders were divided into branches responsible for manpower, operations, training, and supply. The authority of the area commanders extended to the combat units and ground force bases and installations located within their districts, as well as area defense, including the protection of villages, especially those near the frontier. During combat, area commanders also coordinated activities of naval and air force units operating on fronts within their areas.

The army was organized into three armored divisions, each composed of two armored and one artillery brigade, plus one armored and one mechanized infantry brigade upon mobilization. An additional five independent mechanized infantry brigades were available. The reserves consisted of nine armored divisions, one

Israel: A Country Study

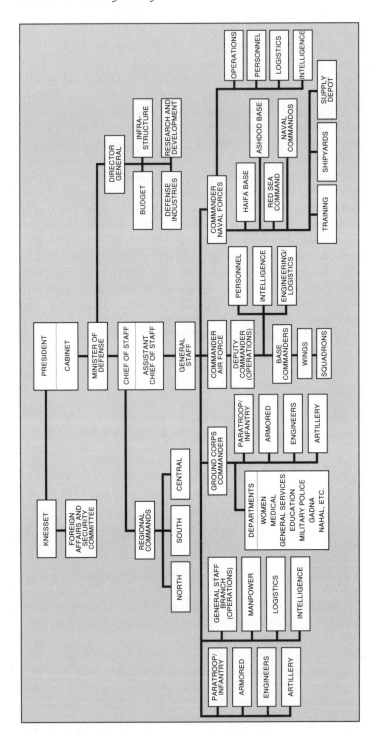

Figure 14. Organization of National Defense, 1988

282

airmobile mechanized division, and ten regional infantry brigades for border defense. In practice, unit composition was extremely fluid and it was common for subunits to be transferred, especially when a particular battalion or brigade was needed in a combat zone far from its regular divisional station.

The IDF did not organize permanent divisions until after the June 1967 War. As of 1988, their composition remained flexible, leading military analysts to regard the brigade as the basic combat unit of the IDF. Brigade commanders exercised considerable autonomy, particularly during battle, following the IDF axiom that the command echelon must serve the assault echelon.

Between 1977 and 1987, the IDF reconfigured its units as its tank inventory grew, reducing the number of infantry brigades while increasing the number of armored brigades from twenty to thirty-three upon mobilization. Although maintained with a full complement of equipment, most of the armored brigades were only at cadre strength.

The Israeli ground forces were highly mechanized. Their equipment inventory included nearly 4,000 tanks and nearly 11,000 other armored vehicles (see table 12, Appendix A). Their armored personnel vehicles almost equaled in number those of the combined armies of Egypt, Jordan, and Syria. The offensive profile of the army was bolstered significantly by the artillery forces (principally self-propelled and equipped with advanced fire control systems and high-performance munitions). Antitank capabilities had been upgraded with modern rocket launchers and guided missile systems.

As of 1988, most Israeli ground forces were positioned on the northern and eastern border areas facing Jordan, Syria, and Lebanon. After the Syrian army shifted most of its troops out of Lebanon following the IDF withdrawal in June 1985, more than six Syrian divisions were concentrated in the Golan-Damascus area. The IDF responded by constructing several defensive lines of mines and antitank obstacles in the Golan Heights, and by reinforcing its troop strength there, mainly with regular armored and infantry units. Reserve units training in the vicinity also could be mobilized in case of need. Other ground forces were deployed in defending the Lebanese border against infiltration.

Navy

By far the smallest arm of the IDF, the navy in 1987 consisted of about 1,000 officers and 8,000 enlisted personnel, including 3,200 conscripts. An additional 1,000 reserve personnel would be available on mobilization. Long neglected, the navy won acclaim for its successful engagements with the Syrian and Egyptian navies during the October 1973 War, when it sank eight Arab missile boats without the loss of a single Israeli vessel. The Soviet Union replaced Syria's wartime losses and provided an additional nine missile boats. The Egyptian fleet also introduced new and more advanced equipment after the 1973 conflict. With more than 140 units as of 1988, the Egyptian fleet was larger than that of Israel. Nevertheless, foreign observers believed that the balance of naval power still rested with Israel because of its technological and tactical superiority.

During the 1980s, sea infiltration by PLO terrorists presented the most immediate naval threat. With few exceptions the navy succeeded in thwarting such attacks, using missile boats to detect mother ships on the high seas, fast patrol craft for inshore patrolling, and offshore patrol aircraft for visual or radar detection of hostile activity. Nevertheless, Israeli defense planners accorded the navy the lowest priority among the IDF's three arms and, although it had been expanded, some Israeli defense experts warned that modernization was lagging behind that of the navies of the Arab states.

Although reduced in scope from earlier plans, a modernization program for the navy approved in 1988 included the acquisition of three Saar 5-class corvettes to be built in the United States and three Dolphin-class diesel submarines to be built in West Germany, and the upgrading of existing patrol boats. The 1,000-ton Saar 5s, which would be the most potent surface vessels in the fleet, would each be equipped with Harpoon and Gabriel missiles, as well as a helicopter. They would considerably enhance the navy's range and offensive capability.

In 1988 the fleet contained approximately seventy combat vessels, including three submarines, three missile-armed hydrofoils, twenty-two fast attack craft equipped with Israeli-built Gabriel missiles, and thirty-two coastal patrol boats (see table 13, Appendix A). In assembling its fleet, the navy had shunned large vessels, preferring small ships with high firepower, speed, and maneuverability. The Reshef-class fast attack craft, the heart of the Israeli fleet, had a range of about 2,400 kilometers. The fleet operated in two unconnected bodies of water—on the Mediterranean Sea, where major naval ports were located at Haifa and Ashdod, and on the Gulf of Aqaba, with a naval facility at Elat. The first Reshefs were stationed in the Red Sea but were redeployed to the Mediterranean, via the Cape of Good Hope, after the return of the Sinai Peninsula to Egypt. As of 1988, the naval units protecting shipping on the Gulf of Aqaba were primarily Dabur-class coastal patrol boats.

The navy had not established a marine corps, although it had created an elite unit of about 300 underwater commandos who had proved to be highly successful in amphibious assault and sabotage operations. Its naval air arm was limited to maritime reconnaissance conducted with Israeli-produced Seascan aircraft and rescue and surveillance missions performed with Bell helicopters. With a moderate number of landing craft, Israel could deliver small forces of troops and armored equipment for beach landings in the eastern Mediterranean. This capability was demonstrated in June 1982, when these amphibious units successfully landed an assault force of tanks, armored personnel carriers, engineering equipment, and paratroops behind PLO positions near Sidon on the Lebanese coast.

Air Force

By a tremendous effort, Israel assembled a motley group of combat aircraft when Arab air forces attacked it after the declaration of independence in 1948. The first airplanes came from Czechoslovakia, which furnished propeller-driven Messerschmitts and reconditioned Spitfires from World War II. Czechoslovakia also trained the first Israeli pilots, although these few were quickly supplemented by hundreds of experienced volunteers from a number of countries. The prestige of the air force was enhanced after its spectacular success during the June 1967 War, and the subsequent decade saw an unprecedented increase in its manpower and equipment resources. Since 1971 the air force has also assumed full responsibility for air defense.

In 1988 the air force consisted of about 28,000 men, of whom approximately 9,000 were career professionals, and 19,000 were conscripts assigned primarily to air defense units. An additional 50,000 reserve members were available for mobilization.

The air force commander, who was directly responsible to the chief of staff, supervised a small staff consisting of operations, training, intelligence, quartermaster, and manpower branches, at air force headquarters in Tel Aviv. Orders went directly from the air force commander to base commanders, each of whom controlled a wing of several squadrons. As of 1988, Israel had nineteen combat squadrons, including twelve fighter-interceptor squadrons, six fighter squadrons, and one reconnaissance squadron.

The mainstays of the combat element of 524 aircraft were of four types: the F-16 multirole tactical fighter, the first of which became operational in Israel in 1980; the larger and heavier F-15 fighter designed to maintain air superiority, first delivered in 1976; the F-4 Phantom, a two-seater fighter and attack aircraft, delivered to Israel between 1969 and 1977; and the Kfir, an Israeli-manufactured fighter plane first delivered to the air force in 1975, and based on the French-designed Mirage III. The air force also kept in service as a reserve older A-4 Skyhawks first acqu. 1966. All of these models were expected to be retained in th, ventory into the next century, although the Skyhawks would used primarily for training and as auxiliary aircraft.

Israel's project to design and build a second-generation indigenous jet fighter, the Lavi (lion cub), was cancelled in 1987 because of expense. Instead, Israel was to take delivery of seventy-five advanced F-16C and F-16D fighters produced in the United States. The air force inventory also included a large number of electronic countermeasure and airborne early warning aircraft, cargo transports and utility aircraft, trainers, and helicopters. Boeing 707s had been converted for in-flight refueling of F-15s and F-16s (see table 14, Appendix A).

Israeli air force commanders pointed out that the ratio of combat aircraft available to Israel and the total of all Arab air forces, including Egypt and Libya, was on the order of 1:4 in 1987. Nevertheless, Israel's superior maintenance standards and higher pilot-to-aircraft ratio meant that it could fly more sorties per aircraft per day. Israel also enjoyed an advantage in precision weapons delivery systems and in its ability to suppress Arab air defense missile systems.

With little expansion of the air force contemplated, emphasis was placed on motivating and training pilots and relying on versatile, high performance aircraft. The Israeli air force repeatedly demonstrated its superior combat performance. During the June 1967 War, waves of successive bombings of Egyptian and Syrian airfields caused tremendous damage. The Arab air forces lost 469 aircraft, nearly 400 of them on the ground. Only forty-six Israeli planes were destroyed. The October 1973 War was marked by a large number of dogfights in which the Israelis prevailed, claiming the destruction of 227 enemy airplanes at a cost of 15 Israeli aircraft. On the other hand, sixty Israeli airplanes were lost in missions in support of ground forces. In the Lebanon fighting in 1982, Israeli airplanes destroyed most of the Syrian missile sites in the Biqa Valley. The Israeli air force also dominated the air battle, bringing down ninety Syrian aircraft without a loss.

The air force had demonstrated its ability to bring Israel's military power to bear at distant points and in unconventional operations. In 1976 its transport aircraft ferried troops to the Entebbe airport in Uganda to rescue passengers on a commercial airplane hijacked by Arab terrorists. In June 1981, F-16 fighter-bombers destroyed the Osiraq (Osiris-Iraq) nuclear research reactor near Baghdad, Iraq, flying at low levels over Saudi Arabian and Iraqi territory to evade radar detection. In 1985 Israeli F-15s refueled in flight and bombed the headquarters of the PLO near Tunis, Tunisia, at a distance of more than 2,000 kilometers from their bases.

Nahal

The Pioneer Fighting Youth (Noar Halutzi Lohem—Nahal) was an organization that combined military service with agricultural training in a tradition that recalled the vision of the original Zionist pioneers. The primary activity of Nahal, one of the "functional commands" within the IDF organizational structure, was the establishment and maintenance of military and agricultural outposts or settlements. Nahal's military missions were to provide advance warning, to serve as a first line of defense against ground attack along the borders, to prevent infiltration, and to assist and support Israeli occupation authorities in the territories. Its nonmilitary missions were to develop previously unused land for agriculture, to assist in the socialization of immigrant and delinquent youth, and, since 1967, to assert Israeli rule in the immediate area surrounding new settlements. Many military commanders, however, felt that the program siphoned off some of the best quality recruits for lower priority duty. Under pressure from the army, the system was altered so that only about one-third of a conscript's service was in agricultural training and on a kibbutz, the remaining time being devoted to regular military activities.

In 1988 Nahal had an estimated total strength of 5,000 men and women who had volunteered upon call-up. The basic unit was the platoon, which ranged from about twenty to eighty young people depending on assignment. A small headquarters served as a command element for a number of platoons located in the same general area. Platoons were assigned either to reinforce existing frontier settlements or to establish new ones in areas unsuitable for development by the civilian population. Strategic considerations were fundamental in selecting locations for Nahal units. Some sites were later abandoned as no longer useful; others became permanent civilian settlements.

Gadna

The Youth Corps (Gdudei Noar—Gadna), another IDF "functional command," consisted in 1988 of more than 30,000 young men and women aged fourteen to seventeen, who were formed into battalions, each under the command of an IDF captain. One of numerous youth groups, Gadna was administered by the Ministry of Education and Culture, with IDF officers serving as advisers to the ministry. Obligatory for most secondary-school students,

Gadna introduced them to the common Israeli experience of army life and indoctrinated them as to Israel's special security situation. Time spent in training increased from fifteen days yearly plus one hour per week during the ninth year of school to roughly forty days a year in the twelfth year of school. Over the years, its emphasis had shifted from weapons familiarity and drilling to sports, physical fitness, and camping. Gadna also participated in the socialization of recent immigrants and the rehabilitation of juvenile delinquents to qualify them for military service. It had not been mobilized for military tasks since the War of Independence in 1948, although Gadna members had performed support services during later emergencies.

Conscription

Military service in Israel was mandatory, beginning at age eighteen, for male and female citizens and resident aliens. The length of compulsory military service has varied according to IDF personnel needs. In 1988 male conscripts served three years and females twenty months. New immigrants, if younger than eighteen years of age upon arrival, were subject to the same terms of conscription when they reached eighteen. Male immigrants aged nineteen to twenty-three served for progressively reduced periods, and those twenty-four or older were conscripted for only 120 days. Female immigrants over the age of nineteen were exempted from compulsory service. Immigrants who had served in the armed forces of their countries of origin had the length of their compulsory service in Israel reduced.

Exemptions for Jewish males were rare, and about 90 percent of the approximately 30,000 men who reached age eighteen each year were drafted. Several hundred ultra-Orthodox students studying at religious schools, yeshivot (sing., yeshiva—see Glossary) followed a special four-year program combining studies and military duty. The Ministry of Defense estimated, however, that in 1988 about 20,000 of the most rigidly Orthodox yeshiva students, who felt little allegiance to Zionism and the Israeli state, were escaping the draft through an endless series of deferments. From a strictly military point of view, their value to the IDF would be limited because of restrictions on the jobs they would be able or willing to perform. Although the military served kosher food and adhered to laws of the Jewish sabbath and holidays, secular soldiers were lax in their observance.

An academic reserve enabled students to earn a bachelor's degree before service, usually in a specialized capacity, following basic training; such students reported for reserve duty during summer vacations. Conscientious objectors were not excused from service, although an effort was made to find a noncombatant role for them. The minimum physical and educational standards for induction were very low to insure that a maximum number of Jewish males performed some form of service in the IDF. Conscripts were screened on the basis of careful medical and psychological tests. Those with better education and physical condition were more likely to be assigned to combat units. Sons and brothers of soldiers who had died in service were not accepted for service in combat units unless a parental waiver was obtained.

Several elite units were composed exclusively of volunteers. They included air force pilots, paratroops, the submarine service, naval commandos, and certain army reconnaissance units. Because of the large number of candidates, these units were able to impose their own demanding selection procedures. The air force enjoyed first priority, enabling it to select for its pilot candidates the prime volunteers of each conscript class. Conscripts also could express preferences for service in one of the regular combat units. The Golani Infantry Brigade, which had acquired an image as a gallant frontline force in the 1973 and 1982 conflicts, and the armored corps were among the preferred regular units.

Women in the IDF

Standards for admission to the IDF were considerably higher for women, and exemptions were given much more freely. Only about 50 percent of the approximately 30,000 females eligible annually were inducted. Nearly 20 percent of eligible women were exempted for "religious reasons"; nearly 10 percent because they were married; and most of the remaining 20 percent were rejected as not meeting minimum educational standards (eighth grade during the 1980s). A law passed in 1978 made exemptions for women on religious grounds automatic upon the signing of a simple declaration attesting to the observance of orthodox religious practices. This legislation raised considerable controversy, and IDF officials feared that the exemption could be abused by any nonreligious woman who did not wish to serve and thus further exacerbate the already strained personnel resources of the IDF. Women exempted on religious grounds were legally obliged to fulfill a period of alternative service doing social or educational work assigned to them. In practice, however, women performed such service only on a voluntary basis.

Female conscripts served in the Women's Army Corps, commonly known by its Hebrew acronym, Chen. After a five-week period of basic training, women served as clerks, drivers, welfare workers, nurses, radio operators, flight controllers, ordnance personnel, and course instructors. Women had not engaged in direct combat since the War of Independence.

Reserve Duty

The Defense Service Law required that each male conscript, upon completion of his active-duty service, had an obligation to perform reserve duty (*miluim*) and continue to train on a regular basis until age fifty-four. Very few women were required to do reserve duty but were subject to call-up until the age of thirty-four if they had no children. The duration of annual reserve duty depended on security and budgetary factors, as well as specialty and rank. After 1967 reserve duty generally lengthened as the IDF experienced a growing manpower need. The average length of reserve duty was temporarily increased from thirty to sixty days in early 1988 to help deal with the Palestinian uprising. After about age thirty-nine, reservists no longer served in combat units.

This comprehensive reserve system, the most demanding of any in the world, was vital to Israel's defense posture. It allowed the country to limit the full-time manpower within the IDF, thus freeing vitally needed people for civilian tasks during most of the year. Because of the reserve system, the IDF could triple in size within forty-eight to seventy-two hours of the announcement of a full mobilization. The system was burdensome for most Israeli citizens but provided a source of escape from everyday routine for some. Most Israelis regarded reserve duty as a positive social phenomenon, making an important contribution to democracy by reducing class distinctions. Nevertheless, it was undeniably a source of discontent to many, especially those assigned to dangerous and disagreeable patrol and policing duties in southern Lebanon and in the occupied territories. In the past, evasion of reserve duty had been regarded as a violation of the individual's duty to the nation, verging on treasonous behavior. In September 1988, however, the media revealed the existence of a bribery ring of doctors and senior IDF personnel officers that sold medical exemptions for sums ranging from US$300 to US$500. The lengthy military obligation was also believed to be a major cause of emigration, although the number who had left Israel for this reason could not be accurately estimated. The IDF required Israeli citizens of military age to obtain the permission of their reserve unit before traveling abroad.

Training

Upon induction at the age of eighteen, conscripts were assigned to one of three types of basic training: generalized, for women and

Israel Defense Forces members training in amphibious operations
Courtesy Embassy of Israel, Washington
Soldier operating antiaircraft gun
Courtesy Israel Defense Forces

for men with some physical limitation; corps, for conscripts assigned to noninfantry units, such as armor or artillery; and brigade, for all infantry recruits. Generalized basic training, which was an orientation program including the use of basic military weapons, lasted one month. Corps training lasted from three to four months, encompassing infantry-type training and indoctrination into the recruits' assigned corps. It was followed by advanced training of a more specialized nature, after which trainees were assigned to their permanent corps units. Brigade basic training, the most arduous, lasted from four to five months. It was conducted at training bases of the individual infantry and airborne brigades and, upon completion, the company created at the beginning of basic training remained together as a company in the brigade.

Basic training was an extremely strenuous indoctrination into the IDF, involving forced marches, bivouacs, night exercises, and obstacle courses, focused on operations at the squad and platoon level. It also stressed strengthening the recruits' knowledge of the country's origins and traditions, and identification with national ideals and goals. Visits were made to kibbutzim, moshavim (sing., moshav—see Glossary), and places venerated in Jewish or IDF history. Basic training also served as a melting pot, bringing together different ethnic groups and individuals from a variety of socioeconomic backgrounds. The IDF played an especially important role in the education and assimilation of new immigrants.

After about five months of service with their field units, all soldiers were evaluated for their leadership potential. About half qualified for further training as squad leaders, tank commanders, and other types of noncommissioned officers (NCOs). Those selected were assigned to a junior command course of three to four months. Considered exceptionally demanding, the course was conducted mostly in the field, where the students acted in rotating command roles in daytime and nighttime exercises. Those successfully completing the course either returned to their original units as junior NCOs for a further six to ten months or were assigned as basic training instructors. During this phase, they were further evaluated for their potential as officers. This evaluation included ratings by their fellow soldiers, recommendations by commanders, and screenings by military psychologists. Those who were not selected or who rejected officer training (often because they were reluctant to serve the necessary additional year), remained as NCOs until they had completed their three-year tour of active service.

All officer candidates were selected from among conscripts who had distinguished themselves in their initial period of service; Israel had no military academy as a source of officers. Three secondary schools stressed military training, however, and assigned students to military camps during summer vacations. Graduates of these high schools were given the rank of corporal on enlistment and most went on to become officers. After junior officers completed their obligatory service, they either shifted to reserve officer status or signed contracts (renewable every three to five years) as career soldiers within the standing ranks of the IDF. A wide variety of Jewish social and economic backgrounds were represented in the officer corps, although sabras (see Glossary), Ashkenazim (see Glossary), and members of kibbutzim and moshavim were represented well beyond their respective percentages in the society as a whole.

The IDF course for officer candidates was conducted at a single base but was divided into three types: the six-month infantry course for infantry and paratroop units; the two-month combat arms course for officers in armor, artillery, engineering, and air defense; and the two-month basic officer course for all candidates for the support services. The latter two courses were each followed by specialized three-month courses given by the corps to which the officer was assigned. Those who completed the course (the failure rate was as high as 50 percent) returned to their units commissioned as second lieutenants to be assigned as platoon commanders. Such officers generally served for two further years of active duty, followed by many years of reserve officer status.

About 10 percent of junior officers joined the permanent service corps after their national service, signing up for an initial period of two to three years. They usually were assigned as company commanders, sometimes after filling a staff or training position. Some of the young officers attended the company commanders' course run by their corps, although the bulk of those officers in the course tended to be reservists. Those men opting for longer careers in the military were later assigned to the Command and Staff School, a year-long course designed primarily for majors as a prerequisite to promotion to lieutenant colonel. A small number of brigadier generals and promotable colonels, along with senior civilian officials, attended a one-year course at the National Defense College dealing with military, strategic, and management subjects. A few senior IDF officers attended staff colleges abroad, mainly in Britain, France, and the United States.

Promotions for regular officers were rapid. Company commanders were generally about twenty-five years of age, battalion commanders thirty, and brigade commanders thirty-five to forty. Retirement was obligatory at age fifty-five, although most officers left the service between forty and forty-five years of age, in accordance with a "two career" policy that encouraged and assisted officers to move into responsible civilian jobs.

Minorities in the IDF

Christian and Muslim Arabs were exempted from obligatory service and, although they could volunteer, were often screened out by security checks. Beginning in 1987, however, the IDF made efforts to boost recruitment of Christian Arabs and beduins. It was believed that this policy portended the ultimate introduction of compulsory service in these two communities, although there was certain to be resistance by both the IDF and the minority communities. As of 1988, Israel's Druze and Muslim Circassian minorities were subject to conscription (see Minority Groups, ch. 2).

In 1956 Druze leaders, feeling that being exempted from military service denied them full rights of citizenship, requested that their constituency be drafted. During the 1980s, however, resentment grew within the Druze community because they were drafted while other Arabs were exempt. In 1987 the IDF appointed its first Druze general.

Minorities tended to serve in one of several special units: the Minorities Unit, also known as Unit 300; the Druze Reconnaissance Unit; and the Trackers Unit, which comprised mostly beduins. In 1982 the IDF general staff decided to integrate the armed forces by opening up other units to minorities, while placing some Jewish conscripts in the Minorities Unit. In 1988 the intelligence corps and the air force remained closed to minorities.

Pay and Benefits

Traditionally, conditions of service in the IDF were Spartan; Israeli soldiers served out of a patriotic desire to defend the homeland rather than for material benefits. During the 1980s, however, as manpower needs of the IDF grew substantially—particularly the requirement to attract skilled technicians from the civilian sector—material considerations became more important. The nearly continual cycle of increases in pay and benefits were meant to attract additional manpower and to compensate for the ever-rising cost of living.

Salaries for career soldiers were linked to salaries in the civilian sector; thus, compensation for education, skills, and responsibilities in the IDF was at least commensurate with that in the civilian sector, where wages were largely standardized. In spite of the relatively high pay and allowances, conditions of service were often onerous and comforts were few. Accommodations within units were austere. Extended separations from family and frequent relocations were common. Career soldiers received supplements and benefits unavailable to civilians, but it was difficult, if not impossible, for a career soldier to moonlight, a practice prevalent among civilians.

Basic pay was low and, because it changed more slowly than other salary components, had become progressively less significant in the soldier's total pay. Supplements were added for cost of living and families, based on size. Costs of higher education and free medical care were provided for all family members, and exchange and commissary facilities offered substantial discounts on purchases. The IDF subsidized housing in three ways: the IDF could provide base quarters at minimal rents, long-term, low-interest loans for purchase of homes, or assisted rentals in the civilian market. A generous retirement program covered those who had completed ten years of service and reached the age of forty. Every officer with the rank of lieutenant colonel or above had a car for both official and private use; lower-ranking officers had the use of cars on a shared basis. During annual leave, an officer could go to one of several seaside family resorts operated by the IDF.

Conscript soldiers received pay and benefits far below those of the career soldier. Pay was minimal, amounting to about US$25 a month for a private in 1986. Married soldiers received a monthly family allowance based on family income, as well as a rent and utility allowance. A demobilization grant was paid upon discharge, and unemployment compensation and a partial income tax exemption were available for up to one year. Discharged soldiers theoretically received preference in hiring. Former conscripts choosing to settle in development areas could obtain loans to purchase apartments.

Pay and benefits for the reservist while on active duty also were less than for the career soldier. Reservist pay was supplemented by pay from civilian employment. Employers regularly contributed a small percentage of the employee's salary to the National Security Fund, from which the employer then drew to pay the reservist while he or she was on active duty. Self-employed reservists could put money into the fund to receive a salary while on duty; if they chose not to contribute they received only subsistence pay while on active duty. Reservists could use the post exchange only while on active duty.

Retired officers received from 2 to 4 percent of their final pay for each year of service, depending on their job. Retired pilots, for example, received 4 percent and were said to live quite comfortably in retirement. In addition, retired officers and NCOs continued to receive a reduced portion of their in-service benefits. Disabled veterans received extra allowances and benefits. Retiring officers usually sought a second career; the IDF helped the transition into civilian life by offering occupational training (a course in business management, for example) and by paying the retired officer's full salary for up to one year depending on rank and seniority, while the officer searched for satisfactory civilian employment.

Rank, Insignia, and Uniforms

Three basic commissioned officer ranks existed in the IDF: commander of tens (*segen*); commander of hundreds (*seren*); and commander of thousands (*aluf*). All other ranks were variations of these, with prefixes and suffixes to indicate relative seniority. Thus, a lieutenant general was *rav aluf*, a major general was *aluf*, a brigadier general was *tat aluf*, and a colonel was *aluf mishne*. A captain was *seren* and a major was *rav seren*. Rank titles were the same for the ground forces, the navy, and the air force. The rank of lieutenant general was held by only one officer serving on active duty, the chief of staff. Major generals included each of the three area commanders, the commander of the ground corps, the chiefs of the five branches of the general staff, and the commanders of the navy and air force.

United States equivalents for enlisted ranks were less exact than for officers. The three senior NCO grades were often equated to warrant officer rank; status and function were much alike. The lowest career NCO rank was sergeant (*samal*).

For ground forces' officers, rank insignia were brass on a red background; for the air force, silver on a blue background; and for the navy, the standard gold worn on the sleeve. Officer insignia were worn on epaulets on top of both shoulders. Insignia distinctive to each service were worn on the cap (see fig. 15).

Enlisted grades wore rank insignia on the sleeve, halfway between the shoulder and the elbow. For the army and air force, the insignia were white with blue interwoven threads backed with the appropriate corps color. Navy personnel wore gold-colored rank insignia sewn on navy blue material.

The service uniform for all ground forces personnel was olive green; navy and air force uniforms were beige. The uniforms consisted of shirt, trousers, sweater, jacket or blouse, and shoes. The navy had an all white dress uniform. Green fatigues were the same for winter and summer. Heavy winter gear was issued as needed. Women's dress paralleled that of men but consisted of a skirt, a blouse, and a garrison cap. Headgear included a service cap for dress and semi-dress and a field cap worn with fatigues. Army and air force personnel also had berets, usually worn in lieu of the service cap. The color of the air force beret was blue-gray; for armored corps, mechanized infantry, and artillery personnel, it was black; for infantry, olive drab; for paratroopers, red; for combat engineers, gray; and for the Golani Infantry Brigade, purple. For all other army personnel, except combat units, the beret for men was green and for women, black. Women in the navy wore a black beret with gold insignia.

Awards and Decorations

Awards and decorations carried considerable prestige in the IDF simply because so few were given. Scarcely 1,000 had been awarded from the War of Independence through the Lebanon invasion of 1982. Under a revised system of military decorations instituted in 1973, all soldiers decorated since 1948 received one of three medals that would be used subsequently to honor those who acquitted themselves in an outstanding manner while serving in the IDF. Each medal was accompanied by a ribbon worn above the left breast pocket. The least prestigious, Etour HaMofet, awarded for exemplary conduct, was accompanied by a blue ribbon. Etour HaOz, awarded for bravery, was accompanied by a red ribbon. The highest medal, Etour HaGevora, awarded for heroism, had been presented to fewer than thirty IDF soldiers as of 1988. Its color was yellow in commemoration of those Jews who had committed acts of heroism while forced to wear the yellow Star of David during the Nazi era and during the Middle Ages.

Campaign ribbons were awarded for service in the War of Independence (1948–49), the 1956 Sinai Campaign, the wars of 1967 and 1973, and the 1982 invasion of Lebanon. Badges could be worn by those who served in the Palmach and in the Jewish Brigade before the formation of the IDF. In addition, soldiers were awarded a special emblem representing six months of service in a front-line combat unit. Each independence day, the president of Israel awarded certificates to 100 outstanding soldiers, both conscripts and careerists, for exceptional soldierly attributes.

Discipline and Military Justice

Military discipline was characterized by informality in relations between officers and enlisted men and apparent lack of concern for such exterior symbols as smartness on the parade ground and military appearance and bearing. Little attention was devoted to military drills and ceremonies, and uniform regulations were not always strictly enforced. Although the IDF historically viewed such visible manifestations of traditional military discipline as unimportant as long as the level of performance in combat remained high, shortcomings revealed during the October 1973 War resulted in

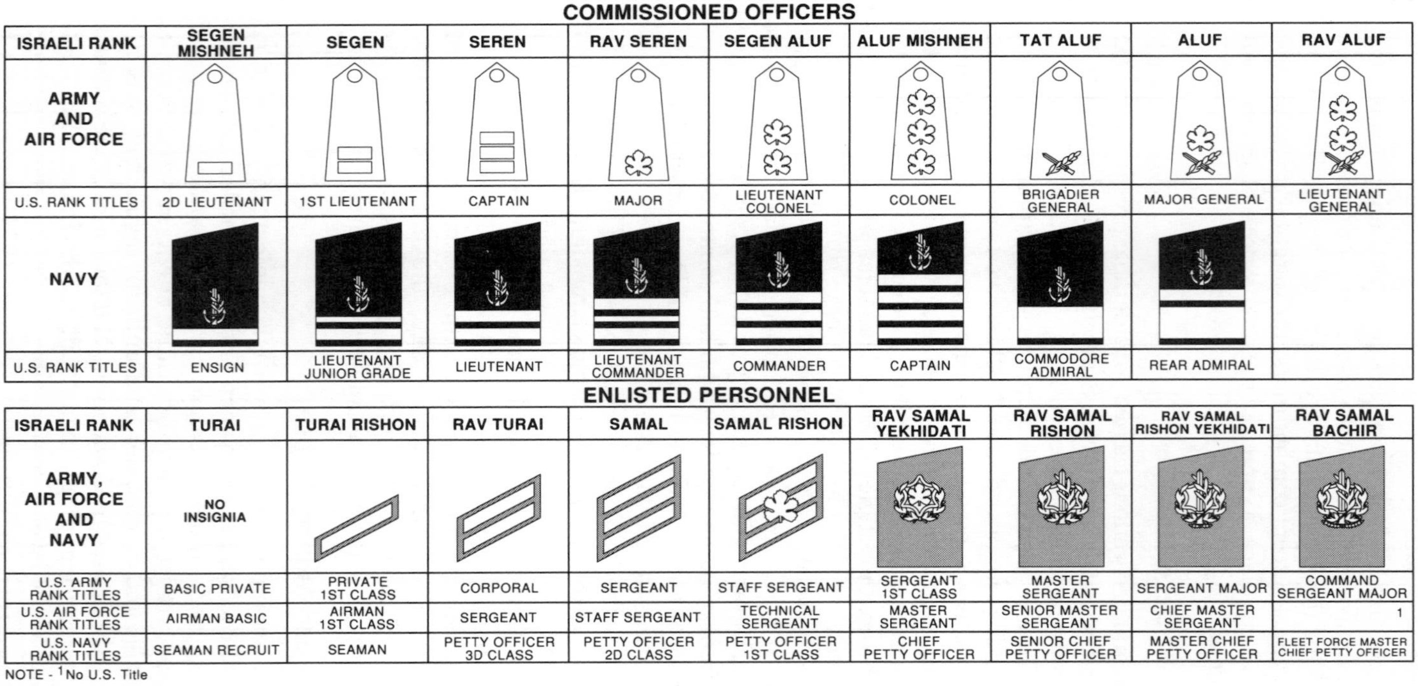

COMMISSIONED OFFICERS

ISRAELI RANK	SEGEN MISHNEH	SEGEN	SEREN	RAV SEREN	SEGEN ALUF	ALUF MISHNEH	TAT ALUF	ALUF	RAV ALUF
ARMY AND AIR FORCE									
U.S. RANK TITLES	2D LIEUTENANT	1ST LIEUTENANT	CAPTAIN	MAJOR	LIEUTENANT COLONEL	COLONEL	BRIGADIER GENERAL	MAJOR GENERAL	LIEUTENANT GENERAL
NAVY									
U.S. RANK TITLES	ENSIGN	LIEUTENANT JUNIOR GRADE	LIEUTENANT	LIEUTENANT COMMANDER	COMMANDER	CAPTAIN	COMMODORE ADMIRAL	REAR ADMIRAL	

ENLISTED PERSONNEL

ISRAELI RANK	TURAI	TURAI RISHON	RAV TURAI	SAMAL	SAMAL RISHON	RAV SAMAL YEKHIDATI	RAV SAMAL RISHON	RAV SAMAL RISHON YEKHIDATI	RAV SAMAL BACHIR
ARMY, AIR FORCE AND NAVY	NO INSIGNIA								
U.S. ARMY RANK TITLES	BASIC PRIVATE	PRIVATE 1ST CLASS	CORPORAL	SERGEANT	STAFF SERGEANT	SERGEANT 1ST CLASS	MASTER SERGEANT	SERGEANT MAJOR	COMMAND SERGEANT MAJOR
U.S. AIR FORCE RANK TITLES	AIRMAN BASIC	AIRMAN 1ST CLASS	SERGEANT	STAFF SERGEANT	TECHNICAL SERGEANT	MASTER SERGEANT	SENIOR MASTER SERGEANT	CHIEF MASTER SERGEANT	1
U.S. NAVY RANK TITLES	SEAMAN RECRUIT	SEAMAN	PETTY OFFICER 3D CLASS	PETTY OFFICER 2D CLASS	PETTY OFFICER 1ST CLASS	CHIEF PETTY OFFICER	SENIOR CHIEF PETTY OFFICER	MASTER CHIEF PETTY OFFICER	FLEET FORCE MASTER CHIEF PETTY OFFICER

NOTE - 1 No U.S. Title

Figure 15. Ranks and Insignia of the Israeli Defense Forces, 1988

a renewed concern with discipline. The Agranat Commission, which studied the failures of the October 1973 War, criticized the casualness of relations between ranks and suggested that lax discipline had led to deficiencies in such vital areas as the maintenance of weapons. After 1973 there was some tightening up, but the general feeling was that stringent spit-and-polish style disciplinary measures were unnecessary and would run counter to the egalitarian traditions of Zionism. Veteran commanders feared that too much emphasis on formal discipline risked weakening the reliance on personal commitment, bravery, and unit pride that had repeatedly brought victory to the IDF.

The predominance of reserves in the IDF also made it difficult to enforce rigid military discipline. Relations between enlisted reservists and their officers were informal. Because of intermixing, this attitude tended to be transferred to regular troops as well. In some of the most elite units, saluting was scorned and officers and enlisted men addressed each other by first names. To argue with an officer as an equal was not uncommon.

During the 1970s, certain kinds of unlawful activities— particularly drug abuse, but also thefts and violent behavior— increased markedly within the IDF. Most commentators attributed the problem to the post-1973 policy of conscripting former criminal offenders. The increase in drug abuse, particularly hashish, also was attributed to increased availability of illegal drugs in society as a whole. Career soldiers convicted of possession of illegal drugs risked dismissal. Most of those who did not adjust well to military life were assigned to service support units where they would not affect the overall motivation and readiness of the IDF.

The IDF took pride in promoting a humanistic spirit among its members and in seeking to avoid unnecessary bloodshed and civilian casualties whenever possible, a concept known as "purity of arms." But with the 1982 invasion of Lebanon, a degree of indifference and brutalization set in. The difficulty of fighting hidden guerrillas in a complex but generally hostile environment, plus the absence of well-defined political and military goals, eroded standards of conduct and morale. Troops often acted with contempt for civilian life and property. Whereas previously it had been unheard of, especially among elite units, for reservists to try to evade duty, commanders now struggled against reservist efforts to avoid service based on medical or other pretexts.

As the uprising in the occupied territories intensified during 1988, Israeli psychologists noted further evidence of these tendencies. The policy of placing esprit de corps above tight discipline militated against effective policing operations to contain violence. Excesses resulted when immature soldiers were ordered to administer beatings, break bones, or damage Arab property. Junior officers found it difficult to interpret orders flexibly or to contain emotionally charged troops who regarded Arab protesters as inferior beings (see Palestinian Uprising, December 1987–, this ch.).

The Military Justice Law of 1955, which embraced the entire range of legal matters affecting the military establishment, governed the conduct of IDF personnel. Under its provisions, a separate and independent system of military courts was established; military offenses were defined and maximum authorized punishments were specified in each case; and pretrial, trial, and appeal procedures and rules of evidence were described in detail. Military law applied to all military personnel, including reservists on active duty, civilian employees of the IDF, and certain other civilians engaged in defense-related activities. Punishments included confinement to camp, loss of pay, reprimand, fine, reduction in rank, imprisonment up to life, and death (although as of 1988 neither life imprisonment nor the death penalty had ever been imposed on IDF personnel).

Courts-martial of the first instance included district courts, naval courts, field courts, and special courts with jurisdiction over officers above the rank of lieutenant colonel. All courts except the special court were composed of three members, at least one of whom had to be a legally qualified military judge. The special court could have three or five members. No member could be of lower rank than the accused. The district court was the basic court-martial of first instance. The minister of defense could authorize the establishment of field courts in times of fighting.

The accused could act as his or her own defense counsel or elect to be represented by another military person or by a civilian lawyer authorized to practice before courts-martial. A three-member court-martial empaneled from members of the Military Court of Appeal decided appeals.

The IDF in the Occupied Territories

In the course of the June 1967 War, Israel occupied the West Bank, East Jerusalem, the Golan Heights, the Gaza Strip, and the Sinai Peninsula. As a result of the 1979 Treaty of Peace Between Egypt and Israel, the Sinai Peninsula was restored to Egypt. Israel unilaterally annexed East Jerusalem soon after the June 1967 War, reasserting this fact in July 1980, and in 1981 it annexed the Golan Heights (see fig. 16). As of 1988, the West Bank and the Gaza Strip, with a combined population of at least 1,400,000 Arabs, remained under the jurisdiction of the Ministry of Defense. The 57,000 Jews residing in settlements in the two territories in 1988 came under the central government of Israel proper (see figs. 17 and 18).

The primary mission of the military government was to maintain internal security in the West Bank and the Gaza Strip. The Border Police, the Shin Bet, the Israel Police, and the IDF all shared in the task of maintaining order. Immediately upon occupation of the territories in June 1967, Israel launched an intense pacification program. Harsh measures were used to suppress local noncooperation campaigns, strikes, and especially terrorist activities. Local residents whom Israeli officials deemed subversive were deported, Arab homes believed to house anti-Israeli activists and their supporters were destroyed, and dissenters could be placed in administrative detention for up to six months. These and other repressive measures derived from the emergency regulations of the British Mandate period.

Military Government

The minister of defense held responsibility for administration and security of the Arab population of the occupied territories. Until 1981, actual command passed from the minister of defense to the Department of Military Government, a functional command within the general staff, and from this department to the regional commanders of the Gaza Strip and the West Bank in their roles as military governors. The military governors exercised primarily a coordinating function because day-to-day operations in the territories were carried out not by military officers, but by civilian representatives of the various ministries.

In 1981 Israel established a separate civilian administration in the territories to exercise the civil powers of the military government. This administration lacked authority to enact legislation. The civilian officials who carried out these executive functions nominally drew their authority from the military government; in fact, they were part of the permanent staff of Israeli ministries and received directives from their ministerial superiors. This relinquishment of responsibility by the Ministry of Defense and its assumption by Israeli civil authorities gathered momentum under governments controlled by the right-wing Likud Bloc, whose policies sought to achieve de facto annexation by subordinating all civilian matters in the occupied territories to ministries of the government in Jerusalem.

A civilian "coordinator of activities" in the Ministry of Defense acted in the name of the minister of defense to advise, guide, coordinate, and supervise all government ministries, state institutions, and public authorities in the occupied territories. In 1988 the

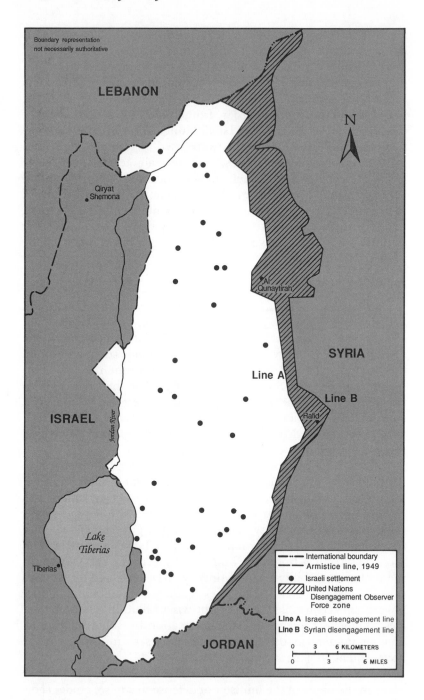

Figure 16. Israeli Settlements in the Golan Heights, 1985

coordinator was Shmuel Goren. Neither the minister of defense nor the coordinator of activities, however, had veto powers over officials answerable to civilian ministries in Jerusalem.

Local government in areas of the West Bank occupied by Palestinians consisted of twenty-five towns having municipal status and eighty-two village councils operating under the Jordanian Village Management Law. After 1981, when the Israeli civil administration deposed nine West Bank mayors, Israeli officials ran most municipalities. Under them, Arabs held the vast majority of government administrative and staff positions. Until the latter part of 1988, when King Hussein cut off all funds to the West Bank, Jordan paid the salaries of about 5,000 of these civil servants. The remaining 16,000, who were mostly teachers, had their Israeli salaries supplemented by a Jordanian bonus averaging US$100 monthly.

Jewish settlements in the West Bank were incorporated into fourteen local authorities. These authorities functioned under special military government legislation identical to the local authorities legislation that applied in Israel. The Ministry of Interior supervised their budgets and in general the West Bank settlements functioned as though they were in Israel proper.

Palestinian Uprising, December 1987–

During the first twenty years of Israeli occupation, security in the territories fluctuated between periods of calm and periods of unrest. Discontent was chronic, however, especially among the younger Palestinians in refugee camps. Nearly half the Arab population of the occupied territories lived in twenty camps in the West Bank and eight camps in the Gaza Strip, in overcrowded and unsanitary conditions. The camps had existed since the flight of Arabs displaced after the partition of Palestine in 1948. Communal conflict was liable to break out at any time between Palestinians and Israeli settlers. Friction also arose from security measures taken by Israeli authorities to counter perceived threats to order.

An upsurge of instability and violence in 1987 resulted partly from deliberate provocations by PLO factions and PLO dissident groups, but much of it generated spontaneously. Violence by Israeli settlers increased, including the initiation of unauthorized armed patrols and physical harassment of Palestinians. Although some settlers were arrested, the Palestinians asserted that the authorities were lenient with Israelis who violated security regulations.

The escalating level of Palestinian unrest precipitated a series of protests and violent demonstrations that began on December 9, 1987, in the West Bank and the Gaza Strip, and later spread to Arab communities in Jerusalem and Israel itself. Thousands of

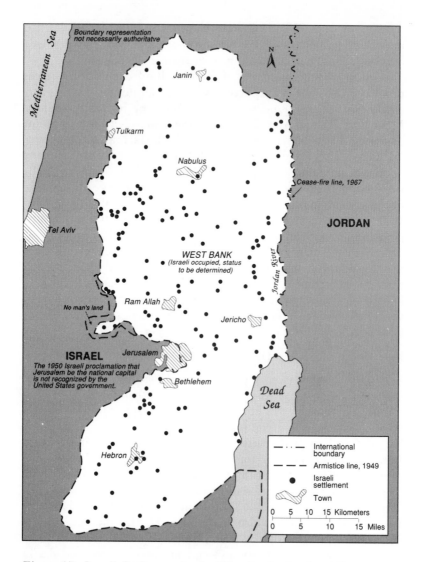

Figure 17. Israeli Settlements in the West Bank, October 1986

mostly teen-aged Palestinians banded together, setting up barri-
cades in refugee camps, confronting soldiers and Border Police,
and attacking road traffic with rocks. Unlike previous demonstrations, the violence did not appear to be directed or coordinated
by the PLO and continued almost unabated for many months.
By October 1988, more than 250 Palestinians had been killed
and 5 Israeli deaths had occurred. Although mass violence had

diminished, many individual incidents of rock-throwing and the tossing of gasoline bombs by small roving bands continued to occur. The army's retaliation was tougher and more rapid, with aggressive use of clubs and plastic bullets, demolition of houses, orchards, wells, and gardens, and economic sanctions against recalcitrant villages.

The young IDF conscripts called upon to impose order at first responded erratically, in some cases with restraint and in other cases with brutality. Lacking proper equipment and training in riot control, the soldiers often fired indiscriminately at Arab protesters, causing many casualties. Later, after troops were ordered to use batons and rifle butts, demonstrators were often badly beaten both before and after arrest, suffering fractured bones. There were reports of soldiers entering Arab houses to administer collective punishment and beating and harassing doctors and nurses in hospitals where wounded Arabs were being treated. Under mounting international criticism for the harsh and undisciplined behavior of the IDF, the military authorities acquired additional riot control equipment, including rubber and plastic bullets, tear gas, and specially-equipped command cars. New tactics were introduced, notably the deployment of large forces to snuff out riots as soon as they began. The IDF instituted a code of conduct and a special one-week training program in internal security.

The uprising forced the IDF to cancel normal troop training and exercises. About 15,000 soldiers—several times the normal number—were assigned to maintain security in the West Bank and the Gaza Strip. The military authorities later replaced most of the conscripts with reservists who had demonstrated greater restraint when confronted by rock-throwing demonstrators. Nonetheless, several hundred reservists, disagreeing with Israeli policy, refused to serve in the occupied territories.

As of mid-1988, fifteen soldiers had been court-martialed for some of the most serious offenses, including a widely publicized case in which four Arab demonstrators had been severely beaten and then buried under a load of sand. Other soldiers had faced lower-level disciplinary proceedings. There was growing evidence that the morale of the IDF was eroding as a result of the stress of daily confrontations with hostile demonstrators. Senior officers contended that the riot control mission had induced a crisis of confidence that would affect the army's performance in orthodox conflict. The IDF's reputation as a humane, superbly trained, and motivated force had clearly been tarnished.

IDF commanders said that they had reduced the number of soldiers assigned to riot control duty by nearly one-third since the mass demonstrations had tapered off but feared that the cost of

Figure 18. Israeli Settlements in the Gaza Strip, January 1988

controlling the uprising (estimated at US$300 million) would necessitate curtailing IDF equipment purchases. Although they foresaw that the violence might continue indefinitely, they did not regard it as a serious threat in strategic terms.

Armed Forces and Society

Economic Impact

The burden of maintaining a large, modern national security

establishment has always weighed heavily on the vulnerable Israeli economy. The total defense budget for Israeli fiscal year (FY—see Glossary) 1988, including United States assistance of US$1.8 billion, amounted to US$5.59 billion. Its principal components were local spending on equipment, supplies, and construction worth US$2.05 billion, personnel costs equivalent to US$1.25 billion, and purchases abroad of US$1.87 billion.

The defense budgets for FY 1987 and FY 1986 totaled US$5.6 billion and US$4.98 billion, respectively. The budget submission to the Knesset indicated that the objective was to maintain overall local costs—i.e., those items not supported by United States assistance—at the same level in both FY 1987 and FY 1988. Several factors made it difficult to compare the defense effort on a year-to-year basis. For example, defense budgets were affected by the immediate costs and later savings associated with cancellation of the Lavi fighter aircraft project. The additional wages needed for the extended call-up of reservists in 1988 to help contain the uprising in the occupied territories also depleted resources available for normal defense requirements.

As the largest single item in the government budget, defense spending absorbed a major share of the budgetary cuts within the Economic Stabilization Program of July 1985. The cumulative reductions in domestic defense spending from FY 1983 through FY1986 were estimated at US$2.5 billion, representing a 20 percent decrease in total domestically financed military expenditures. The defense burden as a ratio of GNP had averaged about 9 percent until 1966. Real defense expenditures increased dramatically as a result of the June 1967 War and the October 1973 War. They subsequently remained steady at about 10 to 15 percent of GNP, excluding foreign military purchases, and accounted for 20 to 25 percent of GNP when foreign military purchases (almost entirely funded by the United States) were included.

The Israeli government estimated the defense-related foreign exchange burden at US$2.1 billion in FY 1985 and predicted that it would remain at about that level during the foreseeable future. This included self-financed military imports, indirect imports (such as fuel and materials for the defense industry), and debt servicing of defense-related loans. The Ministry of Finance estimated that these expenditures contributed 53 percent of Israel's total deficit in the balance of payments in 1985. According to the ministry, the share of defense expenditures in the national budget, exclusive of debt servicing, was 43 percent in FY 1984, falling to 39 percent in FY 1985 and FY 1986 (see Provision of Defense Services, ch. 3).

According to an analysis by the United States Arms Control and Disarmament Agency, Israel ranked among the five or six highest countries in the world in terms of military expenditures as a ratio of GNP. It ranked eighth in terms of military expenditures per capita (US$875 in 1985) and second after Iraq in relative size of the armed forces (47.9 uniformed personnel per 1,000 population). Israel ranked about twenty-fifth in the world, below a number of Arab and communist countries, in terms of military expenditures as a ratio of total central government expenditures, based on 1985 defense budgets.

The economic burden of national security was perhaps most apparent in terms of manpower, a vital resource in an industrialized nation of only about 4.4 million people. The proportion of soldiers to civilians at any given time was eight times higher than the world average and historically had been far higher than in any other country. This impact was magnified during mobilization of the reserves, which has been increasingly frequent since 1973, when the failure to mobilize promptly proved to be a costly mistake. A full mobilization of the nation's nearly 500,000 reserves acted as a sudden brake on virtually all economic activity. Even partial mobilizations, which regularly occurred several times annually, had a profound impact on national production, as did the yearly periods of active duty served by each reservist. Such economic disruption was a principal reason why Israeli strategists emphasized that wars must be of brief duration (see Israeli Concepts of National Security, this ch.).

The IDF as a Socializing Factor

The tradition of the IDF as a social service institution dates from 1949, when it played a major role in tackling sudden and widespread epidemics in transit camps for the flood of immigrants to the new nation. In the same year, Ben-Gurion envisioned a vital educational mission for the military. The IDF has fulfilled this mission both indirectly and directly. The common experience of conscription for about 90 percent of Jewish males and 50 percent of Jewish females has itself fostered the homogenization of disparate elements of Israeli society. The IDF made a concerted effort to integrate within its various units persons from different social backgrounds. Sephardim and Ashkenazim, men and women from kibbutzim and cities, and sabra and immigrant Jewish youth often mixed for the first time in their lives in the IDF.

More specifically, the IDF administered an educational program that helped immigrant Sephardic youth, many of whom had been deprived of basic education as children, to integrate into the Ashkenazi-dominated society of Israel. Perhaps the most important educational function of the IDF was the teaching of the national

A street demonstration in the occupied territories;
Palestinians are carrying the Palestinian flag, which is forbidden.
Courtesy Palestine Perspectives

language, Hebrew. Young immigrants could defer their entry until they had an adequate grasp of the language and if needed could be assigned to a three-month intensive course in Hebrew at the beginning of their service.

Conscripts who had failed to complete grade school attended a special school prior to discharge in order to bring them to junior high school level. In 1981, 60 percent of conscripts had the equivalent of a high school education. It was estimated that by 1990 this percentage would increase to 80 percent, while those insufficiently educated for military service would diminish to almost none. A variety of other educational opportunities, including secondary and vocational school courses, was available to soldiers. The IDF educational system also extended to civilians. Gadna and Nahal members were deployed in rural settlements of recent immigrants, where they taught material similar to that taught immigrant soldiers and informed the new arrivals of state services available to them (see Nahal; Gadna, this ch.).

Some Israeli sociologists, however, have criticized the IDF's treatment of immigrant Sephardim. A 1984 study found that new Oriental Jewish immigrants held lower ranks than did sabra Ashkenazim of similar qualifications. Oriental immigrants also tended to be assigned to the least prestigious IDF corps. A disproportionate number of new immigrants served in peripheral support corps, such as the Civil Defense Corps, the Guard Corps, and the General Service Corps. Oriental immigrants were underrepresented in the air force and in glamorous elite units, and those who served in combat instead of support corps were overrepresented in the Artillery Corps and the Combat Engineering Corps, where they were relegated to the most dangerous and physically laborious positions. These newer immigrants also were more liable to serve in units posted far from their homes and to be taught skills that could not be transferred to the civilian job market. The study concluded, however, that this situation was caused not by prejudice in the IDF but, on the contrary, by regulations permitting a shorter period of service for those who were beyond the regular recruitment age of eighteen or who were married and had children. The majority of newer immigrants served less than one-third the time that nonimmigrants did, and most remained at the rank of private. The brief service experience limited their absorption into military life and mobility within the defense organization. Their immigrant status and their adjustment to Israeli society were thus prolonged and the likelihood of improving their status later as civilians was reduced.

A newer aspect of the social impact of the IDF was its role in the socialization of delinquent and formerly delinquent youth. In the early 1970s, the IDF reversed its previous policy and began conscripting all but the most serious offenders among delinquent youth in an attempt both to increase its manpower pool and to provide remedial socialization in the context of military discipline. By 1978 it was clear that the policy was only partially successful. Approximately half the youths (generally the less serious offenders) released from detention to join the IDF had adjusted successfully; the other half had been less successful. Many returned to criminal activity and contributed to growing disciplinary problems within the IDF that included rising drug use among soldiers and thefts and violent crimes within IDF units. Others could not adjust to army life and simply left or were expelled from the IDF. Despite the problems associated with the new policy, IDF officials were proud of their role in youth rehabilitation and felt that the opportunity afforded delinquent youth to be reintegrated into society outweighed the associated disciplinary problems.

The Military in Political Life

The Jewish military organizations of Palestine before Israeli independence were fiercely political. The Haganah and Palmach were closely associated with socialist-labor Mapai (see Appendix B) and the kibbutz programs, whereas the Irgun was intimately connected with the right-wing Revisionist Zionism of Vladimir Jabotinsky and his disciple, Begin (see Revisionist Zionism, ch. 1). As the chief architect of the IDF, Ben-Gurion was determined to eliminate all political overtones from Israel's unified, national army and to establish clear civilian supremacy over the military. He was extraordinarily successful in his efforts in that during the first forty years of its history the IDF never overtly challenged the authority of the civilian government. This did not mean, however, that the IDF was a nonpolitical institution. On the contrary, in the late 1980s the political impact of the armed forces remained pervasive and profound. IDF officers influenced government foreign affairs and national security policy through official and unofficial channels. Under Ben-Gurion's successor, Levi Eshkol, the political system was opened to permit greater interaction between the civilian leadership and the military high command. The shift permitted the chief of staff to advance the views of the IDF directly to the cabinet and Knesset committees. The growing number of former officers in political life also helped to legitimate the involvement of the military in strategic policy debates.

Under Israeli law, the cabinet, which could be convened as the Ministerial Committee for Security Affairs in order to enforce the secrecy of its proceedings, set policy relating to national security. The Foreign Affairs and Security Committee of the Knesset approved national security policy. The minister of defense often was the principal policy formulator (although this depended on his personality and the personalities of the prime minister and the chief of staff) and could make decisions without consulting fellow cabinet members if an urgent need arose. During the first twenty years of Israel's existence, membership in the ruling Labor Party often was a prerequisite for appointment to a high level staff position. Political qualifications for top assignments gradually declined in importance during the 1970s, although the chief of staff's perceptions of Israel's security were necessarily consonant with the aims of the government.

When Prime Minister Begin served as his own minister of defense from 1980 to 1981, his chief of staff, Lieutenant General Rafael Eitan, could assert the IDF position not only on defense matters but also on foreign policy and economic questions. When Sharon—a retired major general highly respected within the officer corps—became defense minister in 1981, the focus of decision making in both defense and foreign policy shifted to him. The minister of defense after 1984, Rabin, also was a retired officer. Under him, the balance of authority continued to rest with the Ministry of Defense as opposed to the military establishment; however, Rabin did not exercise the monopoly of control that had existed under Sharon.

Although considered primarily the implementer of policy, the IDF influenced many sectors of society. It had a major voice in strategic planning, in such social matters as education and the integration of immigrants, and in the government's role in the occupied territories. Moreover, the enormous impact of the defense establishment on the economy made its claims on the nation's resources of major political significance.

The high command had ample opportunity to convey its views to the civilian leadership. The chief of staff and the chief of military intelligence met regularly with the Committee on Foreign Affairs and Security and the Finance Committee of the Knesset. The chief of staff participated regularly in cabinet meetings and gave opinions on government security policy. The setbacks at the outset of the October 1973 War gave rise to an exceptional period when senior officers influenced political decisions through their contacts with members of the cabinet and the Knesset. The situation was complicated by the involvement of former senior officers who had entered political life and who served as reserve officers in the war. A committee created to investigate the errors committed during the first days of the war led to the enactment in 1976 of the new Basic Law: the Army governing the IDF. The government expended much effort to redefine the roles of the prime minister, minister of defense, and chief of staff. The new legal requirements, however, proved less important than the personalities of the individuals holding those positions at any given time.

Private consultations with the high command were viewed as essential in light of the cabinet's need to be informed on security issues. Public statements of opinion concerning Israel's defense policy (such as when and where to go to war, or when, how, or with whom to make peace) were generally considered to be in the realm of politics and improper for active-duty personnel. It became clear that many senior officers had moral and political reservations over the scope and tactics employed in the 1982 invasion of Lebanon, but their dissent did not escalate into open protest. One exception was the highly controversial case of Colonel Eli Geva, who asked to be relieved of his command when his brigade was given the mission of leading the army's entry into Beirut, an act that was bound to cause many civilian casualties. Many officers regarded Geva's conduct as outright insubordination. Others agreed that it was proper for him to decline the performance of his military obligations when they conflicted with his conscience. In spite of his

outstanding record as a combat leader, Geva was released from
further service.

Members of the IDF could vote and engage in normal political
activity, albeit with certain restraints. They could join political parties or politically oriented groups and attend meetings, but they
were barred from taking an active role as spokespersons either for
the IDF or for a political group. Analysts found little difference
between the political orientation of military personnel and of
civilians. Retired officers entering politics were not concentrated
in a particular part of the political spectrum. Few officers were associated with the small minority of groups upholding autocratic
political values. Most appeared to accept unreservedly the prevailing
democratic political culture. Compared with most countries, Israel
had far less separatism, distinction between life styles, or social distance between civilians and the officer corps.

The vast majority of the citizenry did not regard the practice
of retired officers "parachuting into politics" as threatening to
civilian control of the military. No ex-IDF officer had assumed a
cabinet position until 1955, and not until after the June 1967 War
did it become a common practice. Israeli law prohibited retired
officers from running for the Knesset until 100 days after their retirement, but no such law existed regarding cabinet positions.

Retired officers pursuing political careers were likely to be called
back to active duty because retired officers remained reserve officers
until age fifty-five. The problems that eventually could arise became apparent in 1973, when Major General Sharon retired in
July to join the opposition Likud Party only to be recalled to active duty during the October 1973 War. Sharon was highly critical of the conduct of the war, becoming the most vocal participant
in the so-called War of the Generals, in which a number of active,
retired, and reserve general officers engaged in a public debate over
the management of the war for several months during and after
the hostilities. Sharon was elected to the Knesset in the December
1973 elections. Once there, he continued to criticize government
policy while he remained a senior reserve officer. As a result of
this situation, the government barred Knesset members from holding senior reserve appointments.

Despite the prominence and visibility of former military officers
at the highest level of government, former officers have not formed
a cohesive and ideologically united group. Although two of the most
prominent military figures of the period, Sharon and Eitan (chief
of staff from 1978 to 83) were regarded as right wing on Arab-
Israeli issues, many more senior officers were moderates, less

persuaded than the Likud government or the public that military force was the answer.

There has been little evidence of an identifiable military or officer caste dedicated to protecting the army's own interests. Militarism was deeply antithetical to the democratic, civilian-oriented concept of Israeli society held by the vast majority of Israelis. Society has, however, held prominent military personalities in high esteem and treated them as national heroes. This was particularly true after the stunning victory of the June 1967 War. After the near disaster in 1973 and the controversies surrounding operations in Lebanon in 1982, however, the prestige of the professional military suffered. The Lebanon experience raised in its most acute form the question of how effectively the civilian government could control the military establishment. IDF operations ordered by Sharon and Eitan often had been contrary to the government's decisions and the cabinet had been kept ignorant of the military situation. The cabinet's inability to oppose effectively Sharon and Eitan was made possible by the passive attitude of Prime Minister Begin, the relative lack of operational military experience among other cabinet ministers, and the deliberate manipulation of reports on the fighting. For a time, the checks and balances that had previously prevented the defense establishment from dominating the civilian decision-making authority seemed in jeopardy. Political protest arose in the government, among the public, in the news media, and even in sectors of the army that forced a reassessment of the actions of the military leadership. Although no structural changes were introduced, Sharon was removed from the Ministry of Defense and a more normal pattern of military-civilian relations was restored. In 1988, Chief of Staff Shomron, Deputy Chief of Staff Major General Ehud Barak, and West Bank Commander Major General Amran Mitzna, all were perceived to be political liberals. They were, however, careful not to draw attention in public to possible differences with the government over its handling of the uprising in the occupied territories.

Defense Production and Sales

The manufacture of small weapons and explosives for the forerunners of the IDF had begun in secret arms factories during the 1930s. The War of Independence was fought with Sten guns, grenades, light mortars, antitank guns, flamethrowers, and light ammunition, much of it produced in Israel with surplus United States machinery acquired as scrap after World War II. After independence and the departure of the British, massive imports of wartime surplus aircraft, tanks, and artillery were possible. The

Israeli arms industry made a specialty of upgrading and overhauling such equipment. The Israeli-designed Uzi submachine gun, adopted by the security forces of many nations, was a major export success, providing needed revenue for the arms industry. The Czechoslovak arms agreement with Egypt in 1955 and the 1956 War gave further impetus to weapons production. The decision to become a major producer of armaments was inspired by the arms embargo imposed by France—then Israel's main supplier of arms—just before the outbreak of the June 1967 War. By the mid- to late 1970s, indigenous suppliers were delivering an increasing share of the IDF's major weapons systems. These systems included the Reshef missile boat, the Kfir fighter plane, the Gabriel missile, and the Merkava tank. The Kfir, based on plans of the French Mirage III acquired clandestinely through a Swiss source, was powered with a United States General Electric J79 engine, but embodied Israeli-designed and Israeli-produced components for the flight control and weapons delivery systems.

Domestic production reduced foreign exchange costs for imports, provided a degree of self-sufficiency against the risk of arms embargoes, and facilitated the adaptation of foreign equipment designs to meet Israeli requirements. A high concentration of well-qualified scientists, engineers, and technicians, a growing industrial base, and a flow of government resources toward military research and development facilitated the rapid expansion of locally produced military equipment. Officials asserted that spinoffs from the arms industry, especially in electronics, had stimulated the civilian high technology sector, thus contributing indirectly to export earnings. This claim has been disputed by Israeli economists who concluded that the US$700 million spent annually on military research and development would have produced five times the value in export earnings had it been spent directly on civilian research and development. Even among government leaders, there was growing realization that the defense industry had become too large and that the government should not be obliged to come to the rescue of large defense firms in financial difficulty.

Defense Industries

Israel's more than 150 defense and defense-related firms (thousands of other firms were engaged in subcontracting) fell into one of three ownership categories: state-owned enterprises, privately owned firms, and firms with mixed state and private ownership. One firm, Armament Development Authority, commonly known as Rafael, was the main military research and development agency responsible for translating the ordnance requirements of IDF field units into development projects. Rafael had a unique status under the direct supervision of the Ministry of Defense.

Total employment in the defense sector reached a peak of 65,000 persons in the mid-1980s, more than 20 percent of the industrial work force. By 1988, however, retrenchment of the defense budget and shrinkage of the world arms market had exposed the defense industry to severe financial losses and layoffs that reduced the work force to about 50,000 employees.

The largest of the defense firms was the government-owned conglomerate, Israel Aircraft Industries (IAI) that manufactured the Kfir and Arava aircraft, the Ramta light armored car, Gabriel anti-ship missiles, and high-speed patrol boats. IAI began in 1933 as a small machine shop, later catering to the maintenance and upgrading of the motley collection of aircraft acquired during the War of Independence. It continued to specialize in the overhaul and retrofitting of the whole range of aircraft in the air force inventory. Until the cancellation of the Lavi project in 1987, IAI had been entrusted with the development of the advanced fighter aircraft.

The factories of Israel Military Industries (IMI), another government-owned conglomerate, produced the Uzi submachine-gun, the Galil rifle, explosives, propellants, artillery shells, and light ammunition. IMI also specialized in the upgrading and conversion of tanks and other armored vehicles. Tadiran Electronic Industries was the largest private firm engaged in defense production, notably communications, electronic warfare, and command and control systems, as well as the pilotless reconnaissance aircraft of which Israel had become a leading manufacturer. Soltam, another private firm, specialized in mortars and artillery munitions.

Growth of the defense industry was achieved by a mixture of imported technology and Israeli innovation. Israeli firms purchased production rights and entered into joint ventures with foreign companies to manufacture both end products and components. Nearly every electronics firm had links of some sort with United States producers. Purchase agreements for foreign military equipment frequently specified that production data and design information, together with coproduction rights, be accorded to Israel. Nevertheless, American firms often were reluctant to supply advanced technology because of fears that Israel would adapt the technology for use in items to be exported to third countries on an unrestricted basis. Some American firms also feared that collaboration would encourage Israeli competition in already saturated world markets.

Nuclear Weapons Potential

Israel had been involved in nuclear research since the country's inception. With French assistance that began about 1957, Israel constructed a natural uranium research reactor that went into operation at Dimona, in the Negev Desert in 1964. Dimona's operations were conducted in secret, and it was not brought under international inspection. According to a 1982 UN study, Israel could have produced enough weapons-grade plutonium at Dimona for a number of explosive devices. Under an agreement with the United States in 1955, a research reactor also was established at Nahal Soreq, west of Beersheba. This reactor was placed under United States and subsequently International Atomic Energy Agency (IAEA) inspection. The Nahal Soreq facility was not suspected of involvement in a weapons program.

American and other Western specialists considered it possible that Israel had developed a nuclear weapons capability incorporating enriched uranium as an alternative to plutonium. The United States suspected that up to 100 kilograms of enriched uranium missing from a facility at Apollo, Pennsylvania, had been taken in a conspiracy between the plant's managers and the Israeli government. In 1968, 200 tons of ore that disappeared from a ship in the Mediterranean probably were also diverted to Israel. Foreign experts found indications that Israel was pursuing research in a laser enrichment process although no firm evidence had been adduced that Israel had achieved a capability to enrich uranium. In a 1974 analysis, the United States Central Intelligence Agency (CIA) expressed the belief that Israel had already produced nuclear weapons. Among the factors leading to this conclusion were the two incidents of disappearance of enriched uranium and Israel's costly investment in the Jericho missile system.

Officially, Israel neither acknowledged nor denied that nuclear weapons were being produced. The government held to the unvarying formulation that ''Israel will not be the first to introduce nuclear weapons into the Middle East.'' As of 1988, Israel had not acceded to the Treaty on the Non-Proliferation of Nuclear Weapons (1968). It was, however, a party to the Treaty Banning Nuclear Weapons Tests in the Atmosphere, in Outer Space, and Under Water (1963). There was no evidence that Israel had ever carried out a nuclear test, although some observers speculated that a suspected nuclear explosion in the southern Indian Ocean in 1979 was a joint South African-Israeli test.

In 1986 descriptions and photographs were published in the London *Sunday Times* of a purported underground bomb factory.

The photographs were taken by a dismissed Israeli nuclear technician, Mordechai Vanunu. His information led experts to conclude that Israel had a stockpile of 100 to 200 nuclear devices, a far greater nuclear capability than had been previously estimated.

A nuclear attack directed against targets almost anywhere in the Middle East would be well within Israel's capacities. Fighter-bombers of the Israeli air force could be adapted to carry nuclear bombs with little difficulty. The Jericho missile, developed in the late 1960s, was believed to have achieved a range of 450 kilometers. An advanced version, the Jericho II, with a range of nearly 1,500 kilometers, was reported to have been test-flown in 1987.

Foreign Military Sales and Assistance

By the late 1980s, Israel had become one of the world's leading suppliers of arms and security services, producing foreign exchange earnings estimated at US$1.5 billion annually, which represented one-third of the country's industrial exports. Because the defense industry was not subsidized by the government, it was indispensable for major arms manufacturers to develop export markets, which accounted in some cases for as much as 65 percent of total output. Foreign military sales at first consisted primarily of the transfer of surplus and rehabilitated equipment stocks and the administration of training and advisory missions. Particularly after the October 1973 War, however, foreign sales of surplus IDF stocks and weapons systems from newly developed production lines increased dramatically. Rehabilitated tanks and other Soviet equipment captured from Egypt and Syria were among the products marketed abroad. In addition to its economic and trade value, the expansion of the arms industry assured Israel of the availability of a higher production capacity to supply the IDF at wartime levels. It also provided Israel with opportunities to develop common interests with countries with which it did not maintain diplomatic relations and to cultivate politically useful contacts with foreign military leaders.

Initially, most of Israel's arms sales were to Third World countries, but, owing to financial difficulties faced by these clients and to competition from new Third World arms producers such as Brazil and Taiwan, different sales strategies had to be adopted. In part through joint ventures and coproduction, Israel succeeded in breaking into the more lucrative American and West European markets. By the early 1980s, more than fifty countries on five continents had become customers for Israeli military equipment. Among Israel's clients were communist states (China and Romania), Muslim states (Morocco, Turkey, Indonesia, and Malaysia), and so-called pariah states (South Africa and Iran). To some degree, Israel was restricted in its marketing by United States controls over arms transactions involving the transfer of components or technology of United States origin. In one well-publicized case, the United States vetoed the sale of twelve Kfir fighters to Uruguay in 1978. Intimidation of potential buyers by Arab states also presented a problem. Observers believed that Arab pressure played a part in decisions by Austria and Taiwan not to purchase the Kfir and in Brazil's decision not to choose the Gabriel missile for its navy.

The broader issues of Israel's foreign military sales program were decided by a cabinet committee on weapons transfers. Routine applications to sell arms to countries approved by this committee were reviewed by the Defense Sales Office of the Ministry of Defense. The primary concerns were that arms supplied by Israel not fall into the hands of its enemies and that secret design innovations not be compromised. After 1982, however, security restrictions were relaxed to permit export of high technology weapons and electronics.

South Africa was believed to be one of Israel's principal trade partners in spite of the mandatory UN resolution of 1977 against arms shipments to the Pretoria government. South Africa was known to have acquired 6 Reshef missile boats, more than 100 Gabriel missiles, and radar and communications systems, and to have obtained Israel's assistance in upgrading its British-built Centurion tanks. The South African-manufactured Cheetah fighter airplane unveiled in 1986 was a copy of the Kfir C-2 produced in collaboration with IAI. Subsequent to the passage of the Comprehensive Anti-Apartheid Act of 1986 in the United States, which mandated a cut-off of military aid to countries selling arms to South Africa, Israel announced that it would not enter into any new arms contracts with Pretoria. Existing contracts, however, which would not be canceled, were reported to be valued at between US$400 and US$800 million.

Military cooperation between Israel and Iran had been extensive since the 1960s, under the shah's regime. After a brief rupture of relations when Ayatollah Sayyid Ruhollah Musavi Khomeini came to power in 1979, cooperation resumed. The Israeli minister of defense in 1982 acknowledged the negotiation of an arrangement worth US$28 million, including spare parts for United States-manufactured airplanes and tanks in the early 1980s. The Israeli motivating factor was the belief that it was to Israel's strategic advantage to help Iran in its war against Iraq, an Arab state bitterly hostile to Israel. Although Israel announced an embargo of arms transactions after disclosure of its involvement in the plan to trade arms for the release of United States hostages in Lebanon, a stricter directive had to be issued in November 1987, following reports that weapons of Israeli origin continued to reach the Iranians.

Prior to the mass severance of diplomatic relations with Israel after the October 1973 War, Israel had actively promoted military collaboration with a number of African countries. Training or advisory missions had been established in at least ten African states. During the 1980s, Israel quietly resumed these activities in several places, most notably Zaire. Israel dispatched teams there to train elite units and to help reorganize and rearm a division deployed in Shaba Region. Israel also equipped and trained Cameroon's presidential guard unit. Limited pilot training programs were extended to Liberia and to Ciskei, a South African homeland (see Relations with African States, ch. 4).

Military Cooperation with the United States

The military partnership between the United States and Israel was by 1988 a flourishing relationship that encompassed not only military assistance but also intelligence sharing, joint weapons research, and purchases of Israeli equipment by the United States armed forces. During the early years of Israeli independence, the United States had been reluctant to become a major source of arms, a position dictated by the view that the United States could best contribute to resolving the Arab-Israeli dispute by avoiding identification with either party to the conflict. The United States continued to deal with Israeli arms requests on a case-by-case basis until the October 1973 War, when it became virtually the sole outside source of sophisticated weaponry. The high level of United States aid was intended to insure that Israel maintained the capability to defend itself against any potential combination of aggressors and to give Israel the confidence to enter into negotiations with its Arab neighbors.

Israel had great difficulty in obtaining the modern arms it needed until the mid-1950s, when France became its main supplier. Even after the announcement of a major arms agreement between Egypt and Czechoslovakia in 1955, the United States was unmoved by the argument that this development justified deliveries to Israel to maintain a balance of forces in the Middle East. It did, however, relax its stance by authorizing the transfer to Israel of Mystère IV fighter planes manufactured in France with United States assistance and F-86 Sabre jets manufactured in Canada under United States license. In 1958 the United States consented to a modest sale of 100 recoilless rifles to help Israel defend itself from neighbors receiving shipments of both Soviet- and Western-made tanks.

Sales of Hawk antiaircraft missiles in 1962 and M-48 Patton tanks in 1966 represented a shift in policy, but were justified as "occasional, selective sales" to balance the large shipments of sophisticated Soviet arms to Egypt, Syria, and Iraq. A more decisive turn in United States policy occurred in 1968 when, following the failure of efforts to reach an understanding with the Soviet Union on limiting the supply of arms to the Middle East and the imposition of a complete embargo by France on arms sales to Israel, Washington approved the sale of fifty F-4 Phantom jets.

By the early 1970s, the flow of United States military supplies to Israel had acquired considerable momentum, although it was not always considered sufficient by Israeli leaders concerned with Egypt's aggressive actions along the Suez Canal. In 1972 and 1973, the Israeli air force was bolstered by additional deliveries of F-4 aircraft as well as A-4 Skyhawks. After the outbreak of the October 1973 War, President Richard M. Nixon ordered the airlift of urgently needed military supplies to Israel. President Nixon followed this action by seeking from Congress US$2.2 billion in emergency security assistance including, for the first time, direct aid grants. By 1975 a steady flow of aircraft, Hawk missiles, self-propelled artillery, M-48 and M-60 tanks, armored personnel carriers, helicopters, and antitank missiles enabled Israel to recover from the heavy equipment losses suffered during the war. For the first time, the United States government approved the sale to Israel of more advanced F-15 and F-16 interceptor aircraft.

In conjunction with the IDF redeployment following the Egyptian-Israeli peace treaty of 1979, the United States provided US$3.2 billion in special aid. More than one-third of this amount was used to finance the construction of two airbases in the Negev, replacing three bases evacuated in the Sinai. Egypt also benefited from a vastly increased level of aid; but Israel sharply disputed Washington's later package proposal to sell US$4.8 billion worth of aircraft to Israel, Egypt, and Saudi Arabia. Israel's objections to the delivery of sophisticated fighter aircraft to Saudi Arabia grew stronger when the United States decided in 1981 to allow Saudi Arabia to purchase airborne warning and control system (AWACS) aircraft.

In 1983 the United States and Israel established the Joint Political-Military Group (JPMG) to address the threat to American and Israeli military interests in the Middle East posed by the Soviet Union. The JPMG contemplated joint military planning, combined exercises, and the prepositioning of United States military equipment in Israel. In the same year, the United States agreed to assist Israel in constructing its own Lavi fighter aircraft by furnishing technology, engines, flight controls, and other components. Although the United States was committed to contribute US$1.75 billion to the Lavi, the project was cancelled in 1987 under United States pressure (with considerable support from senior Israeli officers) because of cost overruns that were causing unacceptable strains to the entire Israeli defense program.

As part of the growing military partnership, aircraft from United States Navy aircraft carriers in the Mediterranean used Israeli bombing ranges in the Negev; Israel loaned the United States older Kfir fighters with characteristics similar to the Soviet MiG-21 to use for combat training; antiterrorist teams from the two countries trained together; and joint submarine exercises were held. Israel also participated in advanced weapons research programs. In 1986 the United States granted Israel the right, along with Britain and West Germany, to compete for subcontracts for the Strategic Defense Initiative. In 1988 the United States announced that it would provide Israel US$120 million to continue research on the Hetz antiballistic missile system. Purchases of Israeli products by the United States Department of Defense (including bridge-laying equipment, mine-laying and mine-clearing systems, and electronic and communications items) amounted to more than US$200 million in 1986.

Israel benefited more than any other country from United States military assistance, at a level of approximately US$1.8 billion annually in the mid- and late 1980s. Only Egypt (US$1.3 billion in 1988) approached this sum. Military aid to Israel, which had been in the form of both grant aid and military sales on concessional credit terms, changed to an all-grant form beginning in United States fiscal year (FY) 1985 (see table 15, Appendix A). The US$1.2 billion provided each year in economic aid enabled Israel to service the foreign debt incurred by past purchases of military matériel. United States assistance accounted for more than one-third of all Israeli defense spending during this period. Nevertheless, in terms of purchasing power, the level of direct military aid was less than the US$1 billion received in 1977.

In spite of the intimate degree of cooperation in the military sphere, discord occasionally arose over the purposes to which United States equipment had been applied. Under the terms of military assistance agreements, Israel could use the equipment only for purposes of internal security, for legitimate self-defense, or to participate in regional defense, or in UN collective security measures. Israel also agreed not to undertake aggression against any other state. The United States condemned the Israeli air strike against Iraq's Osiraq (acronym for Osiris-Iraq) nuclear research installation

near Baghdad in 1981 using F-16 aircraft escorted by F-15s. A
pending shipment of F-16s was suspended for a time and the sus-
pension was extended when the Israeli air force bombed PLO targets in West Beirut, resulting in significant civilian casualties. The
United States lifted the ban after a few months without a formal
finding as to whether Israel had violated its commitments by using
United States-supplied aircraft on the two raids.

The United States objected to Israel's use of cluster bombs during Operation Litani, its incursion into Lebanon in 1978. A commitment was obtained from Israel that it would restrict the use of
cluster bombs that cast lethal projectiles over a wide area to "hard"
targets. In 1982, however, the United States held up further deliveries of the bombs when it learned that they were being used in
the invasion of Lebanon. In 1986, with the embargo still in force,
the United States launched an investigation into the unapproved
sale of equipment by private American firms enabling Israel to
manufacture the bombs.

In addition to cooperation on matériel, cooperation between the
two countries on intelligence matters had begun in the early 1960s,
when Israel furnished the United States with captured Soviet missiles, antitank weapons, and artillery shells for evaluation and testing. The United States shared reconnaissance satellite data with
Israel, although after Israel apparently used satellite photographs
to aid in targeting the Osiraq reactor, the data reportedly were limited to information useful only for defensive purposes relating to
Arab military deployments on or near Israel's borders. In September 1988, however, Israel announced that it had launched its own
scientific satellite which was to be followed by other satellites in
orbits characteristic of observation satellites.

The Israel Police

Law enforcement was entrusted to a single national police force,
called simply the Israel Police, which had a personnel strength of
20,874 men and women in 1986. The Israel Police had responsibility for preventing and detecting crime; apprehending suspects,
charging them, and bringing them to trial; keeping law and order;
and traffic control. Since 1974 the police had also controlled internal security, especially the prevention of border infiltration and
terrorism. With the abolition of the Ministry of Police in 1977,
the Israel Police came under the jurisdiction of the Ministry of Interior. The minister of interior appointed the police commanding
officer, the inspector general. Since 1967 Israeli police have functioned in the occupied territories under the authority of the military governors. In March 1988, after the murder of one Arab

policeman, at least half of the 1,000 Palestinian police in the occupied territories heeded leaflets and radio broadcasts calling upon
them to resign.

The country was divided into four police districts and a number of subdistricts. The heavily populated metropolitan area of Tel
Aviv constituted one district that was divided into three subdistricts. The Southern District, with six subdistricts, comprised central
and southern Israel down to the Negev Desert. The Northern District, with five subdistricts, included Haifa, Galilee, and the coastal
area north of Tel Aviv. A fourth district was formed in the Negev
following the return to Egypt of the Sinai Peninsula as part of the
Camp David Accords in 1979. The occupied territories were divided
between the northern and southern districts.

The subdistricts exercised authority over individual police stations. Most operations, including the investigation of crimes, were
carried out at the police station level, subject to guidance from the
appropriate functional bureau of the national headquarters in
Jerusalem. The principal bureaus of national headquarters were
Operations (patrolling, traffic, and internal security); Investigation (criminal investigation, intelligence, criminal identification,
fraud); and Administration (personnel, training, communications,
finance). These bureaus had counterparts at the district level.

Subordinate Forces

The Border Police, a paramilitary force of about 5,000 men, was
part of the Israel Police and reported directly to the inspector general. Its primary mission was to patrol the northern border and
the occupied territories to guard against infiltration and guerrilla
attacks. It also provided security to ports and airports. Border Police
units were available to assist regular police in controlling demonstrations and strikes. With a reputation for rigorous enforcement
of the law, the Border Police often behaved in a manner that caused
resentment among the Arab population. The Border Police recruited among Druze and Arab Christian minorities for operations
in Arab areas. The Special Operational Unit of the Border Police
was intensively trained and equipped to deal with major terrorist
attacks but was reportedly underused because the army continued
to handle this mission in spite of the formal transfer of the internal
security function to the police.

Civil defense units of the army reserve also formed an auxiliary
force that through daytime foot patrols assisted the police in crime
prevention, surveillance against sabotage, and public order. The
Civil Guard, founded after the October 1973 War, was a force of
more than 100,000 volunteers, including women and high school

students. Its primary activities were nighttime patrolling of residential areas, keeping watch on the coastline, manning roadblocks, and assisting the police during public events. Civil Guard patrols were armed with rifles.

Recruitment and training criteria for police resembled those for military service. The minimal education requirement for constables was ten years of schooling, although, with the rising level of education and increasingly sophisticated nature of police work, most recruits met more than the minimum standards. Low police wages in relation to other employment opportunities and the poor public image of the police contributed to the force's chronic inability to fill its ranks. Since new immigrants tended to be available as potential recruits, fluency in Hebrew was not a condition for employment, although a special course helped such recruits achieve a working knowledge of the language. Somewhat more than 15 percent of the Israel Police were women, most of whom were assigned to clerical work, juvenile and family matters, and traffic control. Women were not assigned to patrol work.

It was possible to enter the police force at any one of four levels— senior officer, officer, noncommissioned officer, or constable— depending on education and experience. Except for certain specialized professionals, such as lawyers and accountants who dealt with white collar offenses, most police entering as officers had relevant military experience and had held equivalent military ranks.

Advancement was based principally on success in training courses, and to a lesser degree on seniority and the recommendation of the immediate superior officer. Assignment to the officers' training course was preceded by a rigorous selection board interview.

The National Police School at Shefaraam, southwest of Nazareth, offered courses on three levels: basic training, command training, and technical training. The six-month basic training course covered language and cultural studies, the laws of the country, investigation, traffic control, and other aspects of police work. Command training for sergeants (six months) and officers (ten months) included seminar-type work and on-the-job experience in investigation, traffic, patrolling, and administration. The Senior Officers' College offered an eight-month program in national policy, staff operations, criminology, sociology, and internal security. Technical courses of varying duration covered such specialized areas as investigations, intelligence, narcotics, and traffic.

The Israel Police traditionally has placed less emphasis on physical fitness, self-defense, and marksmanship than police organizations in other countries. A special school for physical fitness, however, was introduced in the 1980s. Another innovation during this period was the postponement of the six-month basic course until after a recruit completed a six-month internship with several experienced partners. The only preparation for the initial field experience was a ten-day introductory course on police jurisdiction. The internship phase weeded out recruits who could not adapt to police work. Moreover, the recruit then had the option of choosing one of the two areas of concentration into which the basic course was divided—patrol, traffic, and internal security, or investigation and intelligence.

Police Reform

In an attempt to analyze the growth of organized crime and the degree of effectiveness of the police, in 1977 the government appointed a Commission to Examine the Topic of Crime in Israel, known as the Shimron Commission. The group's report cited many shortcomings in the Israel Police, including the neglect of training, especially of investigators, high turnover, weak enforcement of traffic laws, a need for improved community relations, lack of communications and transportation equipment, poor supervision of precinct operations, and duplication of activities between national and district headquarters. Many of the administrative reorganizations recommended by the Shimron Commission were adopted, but implementation of major reforms lagged. In early 1980, the unusual step was taken of introducing an outsider, General Herzl Shafir, a recently retired IDF officer, as inspector general. Following an intensive six-month study of police problems, Shafir developed a five-year strategy to reorganize the police. Known as Tirosh (new wine), the strategy included plans for the expanded use of computers to determine the most efficient employment of manpower and resources; innovative approaches to community relations; the routine rotation of personnel to counter staleness and petty corruption; major redeployment of police resources, including 2,000 new policemen to patrol 800 new local beats; the establishment of forty-five new police stations, many of them in Arab communities of Israel; and a 40 percent cutback in administrative personnel.

After one year in office, Shafir was dismissed on the ground of inability to accept civilian control. He had demonstrated political insensitivity by ordering a police raid on the files of the Ministry of Religious Affairs to investigate suspicions of fraud and bribery involving the minister. Despite the institution of many aspects of the Tirosh program, the lack of strong leadership after Shafir's departure thwarted the comprehensive reforms that he had advocated. In particular, Shafir's vision of transplanting the high esprit de corps of the IDF to the Israel Police failed; morale, which had surged as a result of his efforts, reportedly sank back to its previous low state.

Intelligence Services

Many observers regarded Israel's intelligence community as among the most professional and effective in the world and as a leading factor in Israel's success in the conflict with the Arab states. Its missions encompassed not only the main task of ascertaining plans and strengths of the Arab military forces opposing Israel but also the work of combating Arab terrorism abroad, collecting sensitive technical data, and conducting political liaison and propaganda operations.

The intelligence community had four separate components, each with distinct objectives. The Central Institute for Intelligence and Special Missions (Mossad Merkazi Le Modiin Uletafkidim Meyuhadim—commonly known as Mossad) had a mission analogous to that of the United States Central Intelligence Agency, being responsible for intelligence gathering and operations in foreign countries. The General Security Service (Sherut Bitahon Kelali—commonly known as Shin Bet or Shabak) controlled internal security and, after 1967, intelligence within the occupied territories. The prime minister supervised Mossad and Shin Bet. Military intelligence, the Intelligence Branch of the general staff (Agaf Modiin—known as Aman), had responsibility for collection of military, geographic, and economic intelligence, particularly within the Arab world and along Israel's borders. Military intelligence was under the jurisdiction of the minister of defense, acting through the chief of staff. The Center for Research and Strategic Planning, formerly the Research Division of the Ministry of Foreign Affairs, prepared analyses for government policy makers based on raw intelligence as well as longer analytical papers.

Mossad

Mossad, with a staff of 1,500 to 2,000 personnel, had responsibility for human intelligence collection, covert action, and counterterrorism. Its focus was on Arab nations and organizations throughout the world. Mossad also was responsible for the clandestine movement of Jewish refugees out of Syria, Iran, and Ethiopia. Mossad agents were active in the communist countries, in the West, and at the UN. Mossad had eight departments, the largest of which, the Collections Department, had responsibility for espionage operations, with offices abroad under both diplomatic and unofficial cover. The Political Action and Liaison Department conducted political activities and relations with friendly foreign intelligence services and with nations with which Israel did not have normal diplomatic relations. In larger stations, such as Paris, Mossad customarily had under embassy cover two regional controllers: one to serve the Collections Department and the other the Political Action and Liaison Department. A Special Operations Division, believed to be subordinate to the latter department, conducted highly sensitive sabotage, paramilitary, and psychological warfare projects.

Israel's most celebrated spy, Eli Cohen, was recruited by Mossad during the 1960s to infiltrate the top echelons of the Syrian government. Cohen radioed information to Israel for two years before he was discovered and publicly hanged in Damascus Square. Another Mossad agent, Wolfgang Lotz, established himself in Cairo, became acquainted with high-ranking Egyptian military and police officers, and obtained information on missile sites and on German scientists working on the Egyptian rocket program. In 1962 and 1963, in a successful effort to intimidate the Germans, several key scientists in that program were targets of assassination attempts. Mossad also succeeded in seizing eight missile boats under construction for Israel in France, but which had been embargoed by French president Charles de Gaulle in December 1968. In 1960, Mossad carried out one of its most celebrated operations, the kidnapping of Nazi war criminal Adolph Eichmann from Argentina. Another kidnapping, in 1986, brought to Israel for prosecution the nuclear technician, Mordechai Vanunu, who had revealed details of the Israeli nuclear weapons program to a London newspaper. During the 1970s, Mossad assassinated several Arabs connected with the Black September terrorist group. Mossad inflicted a severe blow on the PLO in April 1988, when an assassination team invaded a well-guarded residence in Tunis to murder Arafat's deputy, Abu Jihad, considered to be the principal PLO planner of military and terrorist operations against Israel.

Aman

Military intelligence, or Aman, with an estimated staff of 7,000 personnel, produced comprehensive national intelligence estimates for the prime minister and cabinet, daily intelligence reports, risk of war estimates, target studies on nearby Arab countries, and communications intercepts. Aman also conducted across-border agent operations. Aman's Foreign Relations Department was responsible for liaison with foreign intelligence services and the activities of Israeli military attachés abroad. Aman was held responsible for the failure to obtain adequate warning of the Egyptian-Syrian attack that launched the October 1973 War. Many indications of the attack were received but faulty assessments at higher levels permitted major Arab gains before the IDF could mobilize and stabilize the situation.

During preparations for the invasion of Lebanon in 1982, Aman correctly assessed the weaknesses of the Christian militia on which Israel was depending and correctly predicted that a clash with the Syrian garrison in Lebanon was inevitable. The chief of intelligence, Major General Yehoshua Saguy, made these points to the general staff and privately to the prime minister. But, although he was present at cabinet meetings, he failed to make his doubts known to avoid differing openly with Begin and Sharon. Saguy was forced to retire after the Kahan Commission found that he had been delinquent in his duties regarding the massacres at the Sabra and Shatila Palestinian refugee camps (see The Siege of Beirut and its Aftermath, this ch.).

Small air force and naval intelligence units operated as semi-autonomous branches of Aman. Air force intelligence primarily used aerial reconnaissance and radio intercepts to collect information on strength levels of Arab air forces and for target compilation. In addition to reconnaissance aircraft, pilotless drones were used extensively to observe enemy installations. Naval intelligence collected data on Arab and Soviet naval activities in the Mediterranean and prepared coastal studies for naval gunfire missions and beach assaults.

Shin Bet

Shin Bet, the counterespionage and internal security service, was believed to have three operational departments and five support departments. The Arab Affairs Department had responsibility for antiterrorist operations, political subversion, and maintenance of an index on Arab terrorists. The Non-Arab Affairs Department, divided into communist and noncommunist sections, concerned itself with all other countries, including penetrating foreign intelligence services and diplomatic missions in Israel and interrogating immigrants from the Soviet Union and Eastern Europe. The Protective Security Department had responsibility for protecting Israeli government buildings and embassies, defense industries, scientific installations, industrial plants, and El Al.

Shin Bet monitored the activities of and personalities in domestic right-wing fringe groups and subversive leftist movements. It was believed to have infiltrated agents into the ranks of the parties of the far left and had uncovered a number of foreign technicians spying for neighboring Arab countries or the Soviet Union. All foreigners, regardless of religion or nationality, were liable to come under surveillance through an extensive network of informants who regularly came into contact with visitors to Israel. Shin Bet's network of agents and informers in the occupied territories destroyed the PLO's effectiveness there after 1967, forcing the PLO to withdraw to bases in Jordan.

Shin Bet's reputation as a highly proficient internal security agency was tarnished severely by two public scandals in the mid-1980s. In April 1984, Israeli troops stormed a bus hijacked by four Palestinians in the Gaza Strip. Although two of the hijackers survived, they were later beaten to death by Shin Bet agents. It appeared that the agents were acting under orders of Avraham Shalom, the head of Shin Bet. Shalom falsified evidence and instructed Shin Bet witnesses to lie to investigators to cover up Shin Bet's role. In the ensuing controversy, the attorney general was removed from his post for refusing to abandon his investigation. The president granted pardons to Shalom, his deputies who had joined in the cover-up, and the agents implicated in the killings.

In 1987 Izat Nafsu, a former IDF army lieutenant and member of the Circassian minority, was released after his 1980 conviction for treason (espionage on behalf of Syria) was overturned by the Supreme Court. The court ruled that Shin Bet had used unethical interrogation methods to obtain Nafsu's confession and that Shin Bet officers had presented false testimony to the military tribunal that had convicted him. A judicial commission set up to report on the methods and practices of Shin Bet found that for the previous seventeen years it had been the accepted norm for Shin Bet interrogators to lie to the courts about their interrogation methods (see Judicial System, this ch.).

Lekem

Until officially disbanded in 1986, the Bureau of Scientific Relations (Leshkat Kesher Madao—Lekem) collected scientific and technical intelligence abroad from both open and covert sources. Lekem was dismantled following the scandal aroused in the United States by the arrest of Jonathan Jay Pollard for espionage on behalf of Israel. Pollard, a United States naval intelligence employee in Washington, received considerable sums for delivering vast quantities of classified documents to the scientific officers (Lekem agents) at the Israeli embassy. Pollard was sentenced to life imprisonment. Although the Israeli government asserted that the operation was an unauthorized deviation from its policy of not conducting espionage against the United States, statements by the Israeli participants and by Pollard himself cast doubt on these claims.

Criminal Justice

A three-tiered court system of magistrate courts, district courts, and Supreme Court applied Israeli law to all persons within Israel's borders. Municipal courts, with a more limited sentencing power than magistrate courts, enforced municipal ordinances and bylaws. Juvenile matters were heard by juvenile court judges assigned to magistrate and district courts. The judiciary was independent and the right to a hearing by an impartial tribunal, with representation by counsel, was guaranteed by law. All trials were open, with the exception of security cases.

A separate Palestinian court system operated in the occupied territories, supplemented by military courts that tried security cases. A mixture of military regulations and laws dating back to the Ottoman and the Mandate periods were applied. Israeli citizens and foreign visitors were not subject to the local courts of the occupied territories. The quality of judicial standards in the military courts and the absence of any appeal system from the verdicts of Israeli military judges were widely criticized in Israel and abroad. Some questionable practices regarding the treatment of Palestinians in such courts are mentioned in the country reports on human rights compiled by the United States Department of State.

Judicial System

Israeli law provided normal guarantees for its citizens against arbitrary arrest and imprisonment. Writs of habeas corpus and other safeguards against violations of due process existed. Confessions extracted by torture and other forms of duress were inadmissible as evidence in court. The Criminal Procedure Law of 1965 described general provisions with regard to application of law, pretrial and trial procedure, and appeal. It supplemented the Courts Law of 1957, which prescribed the composition, jurisdiction, and functioning of the court system and provided details of appellate remedies and procedures.

All secular courts in Israel dealt with criminal as well as civil matters. The magistrate courts decided about 150,000 criminal cases in 1985. The district courts decided about 12,500 criminal cases in the first instance and 3,700 as appeal cases. The Supreme Court decided approximately 2,000 criminal cases of all kinds. The average lapse of time between committing an offense and conviction was nineteen months in magistrate courts and eleven months in district courts.

Punishments for convicted criminals included suspended sentences, fines, a choice of imprisonment or fine, imprisonment and fine, or imprisonment. The death penalty could be imposed for treason or for conviction for Nazi war crimes but, as of 1988,

Eichmann was the only person to be executed as the result of a judicial process. Prison sentences were mandatory only for exceptional crimes, such as attacking a policeman. Only a small percentage of criminal convictions actually resulted in incarceration, and sentences were relatively short. In 1986 more than half of the prison terms were for one year or less and 96 percent were for fewer than five years. Sentences by military tribunals were more harsh; terms of fifteen years to life imprisonment were not unusual.

Warrants generally were required for arrests and searches, although a person could be arrested without a warrant if there were reason to suspect that he or she had committed a felony, was a fugitive from justice, or was apprehended in the act of committing an offense. A person so arrested had to be brought before a judge within forty-eight hours; the judge could order the prisoner's release, with or without bail, or could authorize further detention for a period up to fifteen days. Authorization for detention could be renewed for an additional fifteen-day period, but any further extension required the approval of the attorney general. Administrative detention could be used in security-related cases when formally charging a person would compromise sensitive sources of information.

Unless detained for an offense punishable by death or life imprisonment, an arrested person could be released on bail, which could take the form of personal recognizance, cash deposit, surety bond, or any combination thereof. A person held in custody must be released unconditionally if trial had not commenced within sixty days or if it had not ended within one year from the date on which a statement of charge had been filed. Only a judge of the Supreme Court could order an extension of these time limitations.

Any person arrested was entitled to communicate with a friend or relative and a lawyer as soon as possible. In felony cases, arrests could be kept secret for reasons of national security upon request of the minister of defense. Representation by counsel in such cases could be delayed up to seven days and up to fifteen days in terrorist-related cases. Offenses committed by civilians against emergency regulations (which had been in effect since the state of emergency in force at the founding of the nation in 1948) were tried by military courts composed of three commissioned officers. Until 1963 the judgments of such courts were final, but at that time the right of appeal was granted under an amendment to the Military Justice Law. Individuals charged with offenses against the Prevention of Infiltration Law were tried by a military court consisting of a single officer; appeals were heard by a court composed of three officers.

Magistrate court cases generally were tried before a single judge. Cases in the Supreme Court were heard by panels of three judges as were appeals cases in district courts and cases where the maximum sentence was ten years or more. There were no juries in Israeli courts. Persons accused of crimes punishable by imprisonment of ten years or more, juveniles, and persons unable to afford private counsel could be represented by a lawyer appointed by the court. In pleading, defendants could remain silent or could testify under oath in their own behalf, in which case they were subject to cross-examination. They could also make statements upon which they could not be examined.

A special judicial commission headed by the former president of the Supreme Court, Moshe Landau, reported in 1987 that, since 1971, internal security agents of Shin Bet had routinely used physical and psychological mistreatment to obtain confessions. The Landau Commission found that Shin Bet interrogators had, under orders, systematically perjured themselves when accused persons tried to retract their confessions. According to the United States Department of States's Country Reports on Human Rights Practices for 1987, the commission set out in a secret annex to the report what it regarded as acceptable physical and psychological pressures that might be exerted in the interrogation of terrorism suspects.

Criminal Justice in the Occupied Territories

Local law in the occupied territories combined Jordanian and Ottoman legislation and regulations from the Mandate period, greatly extended by Israeli military orders affecting a broad range of political and social activities. The law applied to most criminal and civil matters in the West Bank. In the Gaza Strip, local law was based mainly on British mandatory law, as modified by Israel. Palestinians accused of nonsecurity offenses were tried in the local Arab court system, which consisted of nine magistrate courts, three district courts, and the one Court of Appeal in Ram Allah in the West Bank. In 1985 the magistrate courts decided more than 36,000 cases, the district courts more than 1,300 cases, and the Court of Appeal 1,600 cases. Local courts had no power in cases involving land, and Israeli residents could not be brought to trial or sued in them. Any judicial proceeding could be halted and transferred to a military court by the military government. The local courts had low standing, lacking the means to execute court decisions, with the result that in many cases judgments were not implemented.

The Israeli court system was empowered, under emergency regulations enacted by the Knesset, to try offenses committed in the occupied territories by Israelis and foreign visitors. Israeli citizens were tried under Israeli law, and were immune from charges based on local law. Military courts were empowered to try residents of the occupied territories for criminal offenses based on local law and security offenses as defined in military government regulations. Military courts were generally composed of three judges, one of whom must be a lawyer. Occasionally, a single military judge tried cases in which the maximum sentence did not exceed five years. There was no appeal from judgments of the military courts. In early 1988, the Supreme Court urged that an appeal system be established, although it did not have the power to impose such a change. This recommendation was rejected by the government as a budgetary burden and a sign of weakness in the campaign against terrorism.

Persons held on security grounds were not granted bail and were denied access to counsel or other outside contacts for a period of eighteen days, during which they could be held in custody without formal charges. Access could be denied indefinitely if the authorities believed access would impede the investigation. Many security cases involved secret evidence, access to which was denied to the accused and to his attorney. Convictions often were based on confessions recorded in Hebrew, which most prisoners did not understand.

International human rights organizations complained of systematic mistreatment of prisoners held on security grounds. Amnesty International reported that agents of Shin Bet extracted confessions by beatings, extended solitary confinement, immersion in cold water, and ''hoodings.'' In most security cases, confessions were the only evidence leading to conviction.

The military authorities also could impose administrative detentions and deportations. Administrative detentions normally had required confirmation by a military judge, but this step was abolished in 1988. During 1987, 120 Palestinians were subjected to administrative detention and 9 were deported. As a result of the violence during 1988, however, these measures were applied on a large scale. During the first six months of 1988, at least 18,000 Palestinians were taken into custody at various times; of about 5,000 Palestinians being held at mid-year, nearly half were administrative detainees. A further thirty-five had been deported. It was often difficult for relatives or lawyers to obtain confirmation of the detention or learn where the detainee was being held. Detentions could be appealed before a military judge whose decision was final. The brief appeal hearing was described as little more than a ritual.

Penal System

The penal system of both Israel and the occupied territories was administered by the Israel Prison Service, a branch of the Ministry of Interior independent of the Israel Police. It was headed by the commissioner of prisons. The prison system was originally set up in 1926 as part of the British Mandate police force. Many of the prisons still in use in 1988 were built in the 1930s by the British authorities. Outside the authority of the Prison Service were police lockups located in every major town and military detention centers in Israel and the occupied territories.

As of January 1, 1987, the Prison Service operated thirteen prisons and detention centers in Israel and eight penitentiaries in the Gaza Strip and the West Bank. Palestinians of the occupied territories serving sentences of more than five years were incarcerated in maximum security prisons within Israel. The prison population in Israel was 3,837 and in the occupied territories was 4,527. Neve Tirza, the sole facility for women, had ninety-seven inmates.

These totals did not include the sizable numbers of Palestinians who were being held in military detention centers. As of mid-1988 about half of the detainees were confined at Ketziot, a tent camp in the Negev Desert close to the Egyptian border, which held at least 2,500 prisoners. A large number of rock-throwing juveniles were held at Ansar 2, a camp in the Gaza Strip. As described in the Israeli press and by visiting human rights officials, tension among the detainees at Ketziot—many of them business and professional people—was high owing to petty humiliations, boredom, severe climatic conditions, overcrowding, and isolation. No radios, watches, or books were permitted. Punishment included periods of exposure to the fierce desert sun, but beatings and brutality were said to be rare.

Israeli prisons were chronically overcrowded; violence and abuse on the part of the staff were common. As of the early 1980s, an American specialist described the available occupational and rehabilitation facilities as only nominal. An investigative commission appointed by the Supreme Court reported in 1981 that "the condition of the prisons is so serious, subhuman, and on the verge of explosion that it calls for a revolutionary change in the way prisons are run." Conditions were especially bad in two of the four maximum security penitentiaries, Beersheba, the largest prison in Israel, and Ram Allah. At Beersheba the commission found severe lack of sanitation, drug smuggling, and close confinement with almost no opportunity for exercise. The commission recommended the demolition of the Ram Allah penitentiary as unfit for human habitation.

Palestinian and international human rights groups have complained of widespread and systematic mistreatment of Arab prisoners. Periodic hunger strikes have been undertaken by

Palestinian prisoners demanding the same basic privileges as Jewish inmates.

A number of new prisons were completed during the early 1980s and, as of 1987, construction of a new prison hospital was underway, as were new wings at several existing prisons. The increased accommodation would, however, do little more than provide space for a rising prison population. During 1986 the total number of inmates had risen by 587 while new construction added 670 spaces in the prison system.

Supplementary courses to enable prisoners to complete elementary or secondary education were available and completed successfully by nearly 1,000 inmates in 1986. In some prisons, employment was available in small-scale enterprises operated by the prison service or by private entrepreneurs. About 2,700 prisoners were employed in some fashion. A total of 500 inmates participated in vocational training in 1986 in a variety of trades, including carpentry, bookbinding, printing, tailoring, and shoemaking.

Furloughs were granted for good behavior; 15,000 permits for home leave were issued in 1986. A temporary parole often was allowed non-security prisoners after serving one-third of their sentences. After completing two-thirds of their sentences, such prisoners could earn a permanent parole for good behavior. Although parole privileges were not extended to those convicted of security offenses, the president had the power to grant pardons and, on occasion, group amnesties were offered to security prisoners.

During 1986 about 40 percent of the prisoners in Israel were serving sentences for crimes against property and a further 19 percent for drug trafficking or possession. In the Gaza Strip and the West Bank, nearly 36 percent had been convicted of terrorist or hostile activity, although many others were serving sentences for related crimes, such as use of explosives and Molotov cocktails, armed infiltration, and endangering state security. Less than 6 percent had been convicted of property offenses.

*   *   *

Among general studies on the IDF, one important work is *The Israeli Army* by Edward Luttwak and Dan Horowitz, which provides both a historical and a contemporary perspective up to the mid-1970s. Additional material can be found in Zeev Schiff's *A History of the Israeli Army, 1874 to the Present,* published in 1985, and Reuven Gal's *A Portrait of the Israeli Soldier,* published in 1986.

A vast amount of writing on the Israeli national security establishment resulted from the 1982 invasion of Lebanon. Perhaps the work with the greatest impact was *Israel's Lebanon War* by Zeev Schiff and Ehud Yaari. This highly critical account, with considerable detail on the personal interaction among leading political and military figures, caused an uproar when it was published in Israel. *Flawed Victory,* by Trevor N. Dupuy and Paul Martell, recounts Israel's military involvement in Lebanon over a somewhat longer period and provides a detached appraisal of the performance of the IDF.

The Middle East Military Balance, 1986, by Aharon Levran and Zeev Eytan, includes country-by-country analyses of the competing forces in the region. The study assesses the growing external security threat to Israel posed by the Arab military build-up between the mid-1970s and the mid-1980s and the budget restrictions affecting the IDF beginning in 1984. The capabilities of the IDF vis-à-vis its Arab neighbors are also examined in briefer commentaries by Kenneth S. Brower and Drew Middleton.

Since limited data are available from official sources on the units, personnel strengths, and equipment of the IDF, much of the discussion in this chapter is based on estimates published in *The Military Balance, 1987–1988,* by the International Institute for Strategic Studies in London. Israel's links with many other countries in the form of military sales and training assistance are traced in Benjamin Beit-Hallahmi's *The Israeli Connection: Who Israel Arms and Why.* A fuller, more scholarly treatment of the same subject is *Israel's Global Reach: Arms Sales as Diplomacy* by Aaron S. Kleiman. One chapter of Bernard Reich's *The United States and Israel: Influence in the Special Relationship* is devoted to the military aspects of cooperation between the two countries. Mordechai Gazit's article, ''Israeli Military Procurement from the United States,'' provides additional details on the subject.

An overview of the first six months of the uprising that began in the occupied territories in December 1987 can be found in Don Peretz's ''Intifadeh: The Palestinian Uprising'' in the summer 1988 issue of *Foreign Affairs.* Israeli punishment and legal sanctions against the Arab population are assessed in the United States Department of State's annual *Country Reports on Human Rights Practices.* (For further information and complete citations, see Bibliography.)

Appendix A

Table 1. Metric Conversion Coefficients and Factors

When you know	Multiply by	To find
Millimeters	0.04	inches
Centimeters	0.39	inches
Meters	3.3	feet
Kilometers	0.62	miles
Hectares (10,000 m²)	2.47	acres
Square kilometers	0.39	square miles
Cubic meters	35.3	cubic feet
Liters	0.26	gallons
Kilograms	2.2	pounds
Metric tons	0.98	long tons
. . . .	1.1	short tons
. . . .	2,204	pounds
Degrees Celsius	9	degrees Fahrenheit
(Centigrade)	divide by 5 and add 32	

Table 2. Sources of Jewish Population Growth, 1948–86
(in thousands)

	1948–60	1961–71	1972–82	1983–86
Population at beginning of period	649.6	1,911.2	2,662.0	3,363.8
Natural increase	392.3	412.9	523.3	198.4
Immigration	869.3	337.9	178.5	13.4
Total population growth	1,261.6	750.8	701.8	211.8
Annual percentage increase . .	9.6	3.0	2.1	1.5
Immigration as percentage . . .	68.9	45.0	25.1	6.3

Source: Based on information from Israel, Central Bureau of Statistics, *Statistical Abstract of Israel, 1987,* No. 38, Jerusalem, 1987, 31.

Table 3. *Students in Education Institutions, Selected Years, 1948–87*

	1948–49	1969–70	1986–87
Hebrew education			
Kindergarten	25,406	107,668	260,500
Primary schools	91,133	375,534	468,545
Schools for handicapped	n.a.	18,820	12,071
Total primary education	91,133	394,354	480,616
Intermediate schools	n.a.	7,908	109,365
General academic	7,168	63,731	86,813
Continuation	1,048	8,508	8,303
Vocational	2,002	49,556	91,720
Agricultural	n.a.	7,641	4,683
Total secondary schools	10,218	129,436	191,519
Teacher colleges	713	4,994	11,006
Other post-secondary education	583	6,900	20,073
Universities	1,635	36,239	67,160
Other institutions	n.a.	26,300	40,500
TOTAL	129,688	713,799	1,180,739
Arab education			
Kindergarten	1,124	14,211	20,100
Primary schools	9,991	85,094	139,515
Schools for handicapped	n.a.	355	1,262
Total primary education	9,991	85,449	140,777
Intermediate schools	n.a.	2,457	23,393
General academic	14	6,198	29,469
Vocational	n.a.	1,462	5,696
Agricultural	n.a.	390	640
Total secondary schools	14	8,050	35,805
Teacher colleges	n.a.	370	451
Other post-secondary education	n.a.	—	131
TOTAL	11,129	110,537	220,657

—means negligible.
n.a.—not available.

Source: Based on information from Israel, Central Bureau of Statistics, *Statistical Abstract of Israel, 1987,* No. 38, Jerusalem, 1987, 582–83.

Table 4. Hospital Beds and Hospitals, 1986

	Hospitals	Beds
Type		
General care	44	11,927
Mental diseases	29	7,672
Chronic diseases	75	7,285
Rehabilitation	2	495
Tuberculosis	0	20
TOTAL	150	27,399
Ownership		
Government	29	9,649
Municipality	2	1,329
Kupat Holim (Histadrut Sick Fund)	14	5,006
Hadassah	1	869
Missions	7	636
Other nonprofit	37	3,574
Private hospitals	60	6,336
TOTAL	150	27,399

Source: Based on information from Israel, Central Bureau of Statistics, *Statistical Abstract
of Israel, 1987,* No. 38, Jerusalem, 1987, 653–54.

Table 5. Government Revenues, Fiscal Years (FY) 1983-86
(Value in new Israeli shekels) *

Revenue	FY 1983		FY 1984		FY 1985		FY 1986	
	Value	Percentages	Value	Percentages	Value	Percentages	Value	Percentages
Ordinary								
Income tax	732.0	16.0	3,581.7	17.7	3,577.9	23.2	7,454.7	25.8
Value added tax	380.7	8.3	1,655.2	8.2	1,650.2	10.7	3,958.5	13.7
Customs	114.2	2.5	532.5	2.6	401.0	2.6	780.1	2.7
Purchase tax	120.1	2.6	519.3	2.6	524.3	3.4	1,126.9	3.9
Excise	13.8	0.3	66.1	0.3	61.7	0.4	144.5	0.5
Employers tax	48.1	1.0	213.0	1.1	215.9	1.4	404.5	1.4
Transfer from development budget	879.1	19.2	3,146.5	15.6	3,130.7	20.3	5,027.6	17.4
All other	393.4	8.6	1,442.2	7.1	1,588.4	10.1	2,802.6	9.7
Total ordinary	2,681.4	58.5	11,156.5	55.2	11,150.1	72.3	21,699.4	75.1
Development budget and debt repayment								
Foreign sources	620.0	13.5	2,846.7	14.1	3,516.2	22.8	6,819.0	23.6
Internal loans	870.0	19.0	2,829.3	14.0	2,837.6	18.4	5,027.6	17.9
Transfer to ordinary budget ...	-879.1	-19.2	-3,146.5	-15.6	-3,130.7	-20.3	-5,027.6	-17.4
All other	1,290.7	28.2	1,742.4	32.3	1,048.8	6.8	375.6	.8
Total development budget and debt repayment	1,901.6	41.5	9,065.5	44.8	4,271.9	27.7	7,194.6	24.9
TOTAL	4,583.0	100.0	20,222.0	100.0	15,422.0	100.0	28,894.0	100.0

* For value of the new Israeli shekel—see Glossary.

Source: Based on information from Israel, Central Bureau of Statistics, *Statitical Abstract of Israel, 1987*, No. 38, Jerusalem, 1987, 528-34.

Table 6. Government Expenditures, Fiscal Years (FY) 1983–86
(Value in new Israeli shekels) *

Revenue	FY 1983 Value	FY 1983 Percentages	FY 1984 Value	FY 1984 Percentages	FY 1985 Value	FY 1985 Percentages	FY 1986 Value	FY 1986 Percentages
Expenditure								
Ordinary								
Defense	771.0	16.8	3,589.1	17.7	3,639.5	23.6	7,281.3	25.2
Health	60.0	1.3	208.0	1.0	200.5	1.3	433.4	1.5
Education	208.0	4.5	895.6	4.4	894.5	5.8	1,935.9	6.7
Agriculture	6.9	0.2	29.0	0.1	30.8	0.2	57.8	0.2
Commerce and industry	3.4	0.1	15.2	0.1	15.4	0.1	28.9	0.1
Construction-housing	4.5	0.1	20.6	0.1	18.8	0.1	18.0	0.1
Interest	974.5	21.3	4,511.0	22.3	2,868.5	18.6	5,576.5	19.3
Subsidies	290.4	6.3	908.0	4.5	909.8	5.9	1,184.6	4.1
All other	590.8	13.1	2,630.0	13.1	2,575.7	16.7	5,172.1	27.9
Total ordinary	2,909.5	63.5	12,806.5	63.3	11,150.1	72.3	21,699.4	75.1
Development and debt repayment								
Debt repayment	1,443.5	31.5	6,411.0	31.7	3,269.5	21.2	5,518.8	19.3
All other	230.0	5.0	1,004.5	5.0	1,002.4	6.5	1,675.8	5.6
Total development and debt repayment	1,673.5	36.5	7,415.5	36.7	4,271.9	27.7	7,194.6	24.9
TOTAL	4,583.0	100.0	20,222.0	100.0	15,422.0	100.0	28,894.0	100.0

* For value of the new Israeli shekel—see Glossary.

Source: Based on information from Israel, Central Bureau of Statistics, *Statistical Abstract of Israel, 1987*, No. 38, Jerusalem, 1987, 528–34; *Statistical Abstract of Israel, 1988*, No. 39, 547–64.

Table 7. United States Government Aid, 1982–86
(in millions of United States dollars) [1]

	1982	1983	1984	1985	1986
Aid					
Grants [1]	1,259	1,618	2,271	3,885	3,817
Long- and medium-term loans	1,081	1,092	950	0	405
Total gross aid	2,341 [2]	2,711 [2]	3,221	3,885	4,222
Payments					
Loan repayments					
Principal	177	155	174	109	135
Interest	569	750	873	946	946
Total loan repayments ...	746	905	1,047	1,055	1,081
Total net aid	1,595	1,805	2,174	2,830	3,141

[1] Includes military and some economic grants.
[2] Figures may not add because of rounding.

Source: Based on information from Bank of Israel, *Annual Report, 1986,* Jerusalem, May 1987, 126; *Annual Report, 1987,* Jerusalem, May 1988, 202.

Table 8. Structure of Industry, 1984–85

	1984				1985			
	Establish-ments	Persons Engaged [1]	Revenue [2]	Percentages of Total Revenue	Establish-ments	Persons Engaged [1]	Revenue [2]	Percentages of Total Revenue
Mining and quarrying	69	5	113.9	3.2	37	4	440.3	2.5
Food, beverages, and tobacco	1,027	45	742.1	20.8	977	44	3,662.8	20.8
Textiles	394	17	189.2	5.3	363	15	838.3	4.8
Clothing	1,282	30	130.6	3.7	1,160	31	707.9	4.0
Leather and products	281	4	25.7	0.7	285	4	158.5	0.9
Wood and products	1,534	14	102.8	2.9	1,373	14	511.9	2.9
Paper and products	209	6	104.5	2.9	202	7	520.1	3.0
Printing and publishing	971	14	115.2	3.2	987	13	536.9	3.1
Rubber and plastics	524	13	176.1	4.9	526	13	850.4	4.8
Chemicals and oil products	239	18	389.8	10.9	239	19	1,905.3	10.8
Nonmetallic minerals	486	11	148.9	4.2	447	9	659.7	3.8
Basic metals	158	6	101.0	2.8	144	6	467.3	2.7
Metal products	2,334	46	406.3	11.4	2,327	45	1,977.1	11.3
Machinery	299	11	103.7	2.9	274	10	524.1	3.0
Electrical and electronic equipment	497	36	450.6	12.6	460	37	2,261.1	12.9
Transport equipment	88	20	190.2	5.3	91	20	996.2	5.7
Miscellaneous	392	7	72.3	2.0	400	7	443.4	2.5
TOTAL [3]	10,784	303	3,562.7	100.0	10,292	298	17,452.3	100.0

[1] In thousands.

[2] In millions of new Israeli shekels; for value of the new Israeli shekel—see Glossary. June prices were used to estimate the industry's revenues.

[3] As published.

Source: Based on information from Israel, Central Bureau of Statistics, *Statistical Abstract of Israel, 1986*, No. 37, Jerusalem, 1986, 427–54.

Table 9. Agricultural Production, 1980–85
(in thousands of tons unless otherwise stated)

	1980–81	1981–82	1982–83	1983–84	1984–85
Citrus fruit	1,416	1,804	1,530	1,547	1,487
Apples and other fruit	227	201	239	181	161
Grapes	84	88	95	92	80
Bananas	66	73	67	68	81
Avocados	8	40	62	52	77
Wheat	215	147	335	130	128
Hay	112	115	120	95	100
Cotton fiber	92	88	93	88	99
Groundnuts	26	26	23	22	23
Vegetables	677	771	779	778	763
Potatoes	218	207	206	198	204
Olives	20	37	37	17	39
Melons and pumpkins	133	118	122	131	132
Cattle (beef)	56	56	58	58	61
Fish	23	24	22	23	25
Poultry	210	229	250	269	244
Eggs (in millions)	1,531	1,740	1,803	2,026	2,049
Milk (in million liters)	682	726	756	797	788

Source: Based on information from Israel, Central Bureau of Statistics, *Statistical Abstract of Israel, 1986*, No. 37, Jerusalem, 1986, 386–410.

Appendix A

Table 10. Major Trading Partners, Selected Years, 1970–86
(in millions of United States dollars)

Year	Belgium/ Luxembourg	Britain	France	Italy	Netherlands	United States	West Germany	World
Exports								
1970	40	82	39	15	46	149	67	782
1972	46	113	55	29	65	224	103	1,149
1974	92	157	91	67	136	306	135	1,824
1976	102	180	136	73	160	437	199	2,415
1978	200	282	183	94	222	688	331	3,911
1980	237	466	299	285	246	886	542	5,543
1982	228	404	304	202	199	1,119	355	5,287
1984	231	482	237	212	258	1,645	360	5,809
1986	266	512	313	275	309	2,347	373	7,168
Imports								
1970	62	223	61	76	71	323	173	2,079
1972	122	365	95	166	83	373	228	2,472
1974	142	543	154	225	223	754	687	5,440
1976	127	609	151	172	242	888	417	5,669
1978	259	542	264	283	482	1,126	594	7,403
1980	405	673	270	315	190	1,549	791	9,685
1982	367	619	365	442	248	1,542	895	9,025
1984	773	698	322	403	160	1,772	944	9,800
1986	1,265	985	386	560	302	1,789	1,214	10,736

Source: Based on information from International Monetary Fund, *Direction of Trade Statistics*, 1987.

Israel: A Country Study

Table 11. *Balance of Payments Indicators, 1982–86*
(in millions of United States dollars)

	1982	1983	1984	1985	1986
Exports, excluding capital services ..	8,792	8,901	9,629	10,195	11,188
Civilian imports, excluding					
capital services	10,896	11,634	11,209	10,575	12,341
Trade balance	-2,104	-2,733	-1,580	-380	-1,153
Current account					
Total goods and services (net) ...	-4,570	-4,861	-4,816	-3,945	-3,966
Total unilateral transfers	2,616	2,855	3,352	5,043	5,336
Current deficit(-) or surplus	-1,954	-2,006	-1,464	1,098	1,370
Net medium-term and long-term					
capital movements	1,133	2,349	1,276	-35	303
Basic account deficit(-)					
or surplus [1]	-821	343	-188	1,063	1,673
Additional balance of payments data					
Implied private capital imports	883	480	-588	-1,053	-201
Net foreign debt	15,641	18,270	19,686	19,315	18,998
Foreign reserves, end-of-year [2]	4,317	3,780	3,255	3,793	4,868

[1] Basic account = current account, plus medium-term and long-term capital movements.
[2] Held by central monetary authorities.

Source: Based on information from Bank of Israel, *Annual Report, 1986,* Jerusalem, May
1987, 96–102; and Table VII-17, *Annual Report, 1986* (in Hebrew), Jerusalem, May
1987, 202.

Table 12. *Major Israel Defense Forces*
Equipment, Ground Forces, 1988

Type and Description	Country of Origin	In Inventory
Tanks		
Centurion	Britain	1,080
M-48A5	United States	560
M-60A1/-A3	-do-	1,300
T-54/-55	Soviet Union	250
T-62	-do-	115
Merkava I/II	Israel	550
Armored fighting vehicles		
M-113 personnel carrier	United States	4,000
M-2/-3 halftrack	United States	
	(rebuilt)	4,400
BTR-5OP personnel carrier	Soviet Union	1,900
Ramta light armored car	Israel	400
Guns and howitzers		
M-101 105mm howitzer	United States	70
M-46 130mm gun	-do-	110
Soltam M-68/-71 and M-839P/-845P		
155mm howitzers	Israel	300
L-33 155mm howitzer self-propelled	France, United States	180
M-50 155mm howitzer self-propelled	United States	75
M-109 155mm howitzer self-propelled	-do-	530
M-107 175mm gun self-propelled	-do-	140
M-110 203mm howitzer self-propelled	-do-	36
Multiple rocket launchers		
BM-21 122mm	Soviet Union	n.a.
LAR 160mm light artillery rocket	Israel	n.a.
MB-24 240mm	Soviet Union	n.a.
MAR-290 290mm self-propelled medium		
artillery rocket	Israel	n.a.
Mortars		
120mm, 160mm, some self-propelled	various	n.a.
Surface-to-surface missiles		
MGM-52C Lance	United States	n.a.
Jericho I	Israel	n.a.
Zeev	-do-	n.a.
Antitank weapons		
106mm recoilless rifle	United States	250
Wire-guided weapons		
TOW	-do-	n.a.
M-47 Dragon	-do-	n.a.
Milan	France	n.a.
Sagger	Soviet Union	n.a.
Mapats (laser TOW)	Israel	n.a.

n.a.—not available.

Source: Based on information from International Institute for Strategic Studies, *The Military Balance, 1988–1989,* London, 1988, 103.

Table 13. *Major Israel Defense Forces Equipment, Navy, 1988*

Type and Description	Origin	Commissioned	In Inventory
Submarines			
IKL/Vickers type 540	Britain	1977	3
Dolphin class	West Germany	ordered	3
Corvettes			
Saar 5, 985 tons	United States	ordered	3
Fast-attack craft			
Saar 4.5 Aliya, 500 tons	Israel	1980–82	2
Saar 4 Reshef, 415 tons	-do-	1969	8
Saar 3, 250 tons	France	1969	6
Saar 2, 250 tons	-do-	1968	6
Hydrofoils			
Shimrit (Flagstaff 2)	United States, Israel	1982–85	3
Coastal patrol craft			
Dvora	Israel	1977	1
Super Dvora	Israel	1977	(5 ordered)
Dabur	Israel, United States	n.a.	31
Amphibious			
Landing craft (tank)	Israel	1966–67	6
Landing craft (personnel)	United States	1976	3
Aircraft			
Seascan 1124N	Israel	n.a.	7
Bell 212 helicopter	United States	n.a.	25

n.a.—not available.

Source: Based on information from *Jane's Fighting Ships, 1988-89*, London, 1988, 279–82.

Table 14. Major Israel Defense Forces
Equipment, Air Force, 1988

Type and Description	Country of Origin	In Inventory
Fighter-interceptors		
F-15 Eagle	United States	50
F-4E Phantom	–do–	113
Kfir C2/C7	Israel	95 (75 more stored)
F-16A/B/C/D Fighting Falcon	United States	145
Fighter, ground attack		
A-4H/N Skyhawk	–do–	121
Reconnaissance		
RF-4E Phantom	–do–	14
Airborne early warning		
E-2C Hawkeye	–do–	4
Electronic warfare/command post		
Boeing 707	–do–	6
Transports		
Boeing 707	–do–	2
Hercules C-130E/H	–do–	21
C-47	–do–	19
Boeing 707 (tankers)	–do–	5
KC-130H (tankers)	–do–	2
Arava	Israel	10
Training		
TA-4H/J Skyhawk	United States	27
Kfir TC2	Israel	10
F-4E	United States	16
CM-170 Magister/Tzugit	France, Israel	94
Attack helicopters		
Bell AH-1S Cobra	United States	40
Hughes 500 MD	–do–	40
Transport helicopters		
CH-53A/D (heavy)	United States	33
Super Frelon SA-321 (medium)	France	9
UH-1D (medium)	United States	17
Bell 206A, 212 (light)	–do–	104
Electronic warfare/sea-air rescue		
helicopters Bell 206, 212	United States	20

Source: Based on information from International Institute for Strategic Studies, *The Military Balance, 1988-89,* London 1988, 104 and Bill Gunston, *An Illustrated Guide to the Israeli Air Force,* Tel Aviv, 1982, *passim.*

Table 15. United States Military Aid to Israel, 1979–89
(in millions of United States dollars)

Year	Grants	Sales	Total
1979	1,300	2,700	4,000
1980	500	500	1,000
1981	500	900	1,400
1982	550	850	1,400
1983	750	950	1,700
1984	850	850	1,700
1985	1,400	0	1,400
1986	1,723	0	1,723
1987	1,800	0	1,800
1988	1,800	0	1,800
1989	1,800 (proposed)	0	1,800 (proposed)

Appendix B

Political Parties and Organizations

Agudat Israel (Society of Israel)—A clericalist political party of ultra-Orthodox Jews, founded in Poland in 1912 and established in Palestine in the early 1920s. In 1949 it formed part of the United Religious Front (q.v.); in 1955 and 1959 it joined Poalei Agudat Israel to form the Torah Religious Front (q.v.). Originally anti-Zionist and messianic, in the 1980s this non-Zionist party, together with its Council of Torah Sages, still favored a theocracy and increased state financial support for its religious institutions.

Ahdut HaAvoda (Unity of Labor)—The party, founded in 1919 as successor to Poalei Tziyyon (q.v.), had three separate existences: from 1919 to 1930, when it merged with HaPoel HaTzair (q.v.) to form Mapai (q.v.); in 1944 its name was taken over by Siah B (Bet—Faction B), a faction that split from Mapai and formed a new party with HaKibbutz HaMeuhad (United Kibbutz Movement); and the last beginning in 1954 when Ahdut HaAvoda was reconstituted by the HaKibbutz HaMeuhad faction when it broke off from Mapam (q.v.). Ahdut HaAvoda was aligned with Mapai from 1965 to 1968 when both were absorbed into the Labor Party.

Arab Democratic Party—An Israeli Arab party founded in 1988 by Abdel Wahab Daroushe, a former Labor Party Knesset member.

Betar—A Revisionist Zionist youth organization founded in 1923 in Riga, Latvia, under the influence of Jabotinsky; it later formed the nucleus for Herut.

Citizens' Rights Movement (CRM)—Founded in 1973 by Shulamit Aloni, a former Labor Party Knesset member, the CRM advocates strengthening civil rights in Israel and greater compromise on Israeli-Palestinian issues.

Degel HaTorah (Torah Flag)—Formed in 1988, the clericalist party is a Shas (q.v.)-led Ashkenazi spinoff among the ultra-Orthodox community.

Democratic Movement for Change (DMC)—Founded in 1976 by Yigal Yadin and several other groups, of which the principal one was Shinui (q.v.). It broke up in 1979 when Shinui left over the issue of continued participation in the Likud government.

Free Center—A faction that splintered from Herut (*q.v.*) in 1967. From 1967 to 1973, the Free Center was a party in its own right. It became a faction in Likud (*q.v.*) from 1973 to 1977 and joined the Democratic Movement for Change in 1977. Its principal leader was Shmuel Tamir.

Gahal (Acronym for Gush Herut-Liberalim, Freedom-Liberal Bloc; also known as Herut-Liberal Bloc)—A political coalition list created in 1965 by an electoral combination of the Liberal Party (*q.v.*) and Herut (*q.v.*) to compete against the 1965 and 1969 Mapai (*q.v.*)-led electoral alignments. In 1967 on the eve of the outbreak of the Arab-Israeli War, Gahal joined a National Unity Government; in 1973 Gahal became part of the Likud Bloc (*q.v.*).

Gush Emunim (Bloc of the Faithful)—A militant right-wing extremist religio-nationalist settlement movement that seeks to impose Israeli sovereignty on the West Bank.

HaPoel HaMizrahi (Spiritual Center Worker)—Orthodox religious workers' movement founded in Palestine in 1922 by a left-wing faction of Mizrahi (*q.v.*). In 1956 it joined Mizrahi to form the National Religious Party (*q.v.*).

HaPoel HaTzair (The Young Worker)—A Labor Zionist political party founded and active in Palestine from 1905 to 1930.

Herut (Abbreviation for Tnuat HaHerut, or Freedom Movement)—Right-wing political party founded by remnants of the Irgun (see Glossary), following its disbandment in 1948. It was led by former Irgun commander Menachem Begin and is the direct ideological descendant of Revisionist Zionism (*q.v.*). In the 1980s, Herut was the dominant component in the Likud Bloc (*q.v.*).

Laam (For the Nation)—A party established in 1968 by remnants of Rafi (*q.v.*), which allied itself with Gahal. In 1973 it combined with the State List and followers of the Movement for Greater Israel to become a faction in Likud (*q.v.*).

Labor Party—The Labor Party, founded in 1968, resulted from the merger of Mapai (*q.v.*), Ahdut HaAvoda (*q.v.*), and Rafi (*q.v.*). Representation in top Labor Party institutions was based on a proportion of 57.3 percent for Mapai and 21.3 percent for each of the other two. This factional system broke down following the ascension to power in June 1974 of the younger generation triumvirate of Yitzhak Rabin, Shimon Peres, and Yigal Allon, who were less tied to the former factions. Following the 1984 Knesset elections, the Labor Party assumed an independent existence upon the dissolution of the Maarakh (*q.v.*) when it went into the National Unity Government with Likud.

Labor Zionism—Zionist movements and parties committed to the development of a democratic-socialist political economy in Israel.

Liberal Party—The second major component in the Likud Bloc; a middle-class party formed in 1961 from the merger of the Progressives and General Zionists.

Likud or Likud Bloc (Union)—The Likud Bloc was founded in preparation for the 1973 elections when the Free Center (*q.v.*) and Laam (*q.v.*) joined Gahal (*q.v.*). In 1984 Likud formed the National Unity Government with the Labor Party (*q.v.*).

Maarakh (Alignment)—An electoral and parliamentary alignment on the national and municipal levels between the Labor Party and Mapam, from 1969 to 1984.

Maki (Acronym for Miflaga Kommunistit Yisraelit, or Communist Party of Israel)—The party was founded in 1949. In 1965 it broke into two factions: Maki and Rakah (*q.v.*). Maki continued to have as members primarily Jewish communists. The electoral list of Maki and Rakah, which joined in the 1973 elections, was called Moked (Focus). In 1977 Maki joined with several other groups to create Shelli (acronym for Peace for Israel and Equality for Israel), a party that disbanded before the 1984 elections.

Mapai (acronym for Mifleget Poalei Eretz Yisrael-Israel Workers' Party)—Mapai resulted from the 1930 merger between the main prestate Labor Zionist parties, Ahdut HaAvoda (*q.v.*) and HaPoel HaTzair (*q.v.*). In 1920 the two parties together had founded the Histadrut. In 1944 a small left-wing kibbutz-based faction seceded from Mapai and reconstituted itself as Ahdut HaAvoda-Poalei Tziyyon (Unity of Labor-Workers of Zion). Nevertheless, Mapai became the dominant party in the Yishuv and later in Israel; after 1968 it was the dominant faction in the Labor Party.

Mapam (Acronym for Mifleget Poalim Meuchedet-United Workers' Party)—Mapam resulted in January 1948 from the merger of two Labor Zionist kibbutz-based parties, HaShomer HaTzair (The Young Watchman, which had been founded in 1913 as a youth movement and became a political party in 1946) and Ahdut HaAvoda-Poalei Tziyyon. The party also contained remnants of the former Poalei Tziyyon (*q.v.*). Mapam split in 1954, with former members of HaShomer HaTzair remaining, while former members of Ahdut HaAvoda-Poalei Tziyyon left to form Ahdut HaAvoda (*q.v.*). The formation of the Labor

Party in 1968 caused Mapam to reverse its previous opposition to unity among Labor Zionist parties and to join an electoral alliance (Maarakh—Alignment) with the Labor Party in
1969. There was much criticism within Mapam that, as the
junior partner of the Alignment, the party seemed excessively
subservient to Labor's status-quo oriented policies, particularly
on the issue of the future of the West Bank and the Gaza Strip.
Mapam broke away from the Alignment and resumed its independent existence in the fall of 1984, when the Labor Party
decided to join Likud (*q.v.*) in forming the National Unity
Government.
Mizrahi (Spiritual Center)—Established in 1902 as an Orthodox
religious Zionist party. In 1949 Mizrahi became part of the
United Religious Front. In 1956 it joined HaPoel HaMizrahi
(*q.v.*) to form the National Religious Party (*q.v.*).
Moledet (Homeland)—An extremist right-wing ultranationalist
party founded in 1988 by a retired Israel Defense Forces (IDF)
general, Rehavam (Gandhi) Zeevi.
Morasha (Heritage)—A religio-nationalist party led by Rabbi
Chaim Druckman that broke away from the National Religious
Party (*q.v.*) in 1984. In 1986 it was reincorporated into the National Religious Party.
National Religious Party (NRP) (also known as Mafdal—acronym
for HaMiflagah HaDatit-Leumit)—The NRP was formed
in 1956 with the merger of two Orthodox parties: HaPoel
HaMizrahi (*q.v.*) and Mizrahi (*q.v.*). From the founding of the
state in 1948 to 1977, the NRP (or its predecessors) was the
ally of the Labor Party (or its predecessors) in forming Labor-
led coalition governments; in return the NRP was awarded control of the Ministry of Religious Affairs. In 1981 the NRP's
electoral support declined from its traditional twelve seats to
six as a result of the formation of Tami (*q.v.*) and Tehiya (*q.v.*).
In 1984 the NRP suffered a further decline of two seats with
the formation of Morasha (*q.v.*) by a former NRP faction.
Peace Now—A movement established after the October 1973 War,
advocating territorial compromise over the West Bank and the
Gaza Strip in order to achieve peaceful relations with the Palestinian Arabs and the Arab states.
Poalei Tziyyon (Workers of Zion)—A Marxist Labor Zionist party
founded in Palestine in 1906; in 1919 it was incorporated into
the original Ahdut HaAvoda.
Progressive National Movement (also known as Progressive List
for Peace)—The joint Arab-Jewish party was established in 1984

and advocated the establishment of a Palestinian state alongside Israel.

Rafi (Israel Labor List)—The party was created in 1965 when David Ben-Gurion and some of his supporters broke away from Mapai. In 1968 most of the party's activists (except for Ben-Gurion) returned, and together with Mapai and Ahdut HaAvoda, formed the Labor Party.

Rakah (New Communist List)—The communist party created by a faction that broke off in 1965 from Maki (*q.v.*) (Communist Party of Israel). In the 1973 elections Rakah and Maki created a joint electoral list called Moked (Focus). Rakah consisted primarily of Arab communists and participated in the 1988 elections.

Revisionist Zionism—A right-wing Zionist party and movement founded in 1925 by Vladimir Jabotinsky; it demanded a revision of the conciliatory policy by the Zionist Executive toward the British mandatory government.

Shas (Sephardic Torah Guardians)—A clericalist and theocratic party formed in 1984 by former Agudat Israel (*q.v.*) members to represent the interests of the ultra-Orthodox Sephardim.

Shelli (Acronym for Peace for Israel and Equality for Israel)—A party created in 1977 by Maki (*q.v.*) and several other groups. It disbanded before the 1984 elections.

Shinui (Change)—Founded by Amnon Rubenstein in 1973 as a protest movement against the October 1973 War. In 1976, in preparation for the May 1977 elections, Shinui joined with other groups to create the Democratic Movement for Change (DMC), led by Yigal Yadin. In 1979 Shinui broke away from the DMC and created its own political party. In the 1988 elections its Knesset representation declined from three to two seats.

Tami (Traditional Movement of Israel)—Established in 1981 by an Oriental faction within the National Religious Party (*q.v.*) led by former Minister of Religious Affairs Aharon Abuhatzeira to represent the interests of Sephardim. In 1988 Tami became a faction in the Likud Bloc (*q.v.*).

Tehiya (Renaissance)—A right-wing religio-nationalist group that broke away from the National Religious Party (*q.v.*) in 1981. The party advocates the eventual imposition of Israeli sovereignty over the West Bank, accompanied by the transfer to the Arab countries of its Palestinian Arab inhabitants.

Torah Religious Front—Formed by Agudat Israel (*q.v.*) and Poalei Agudat Israel (Workers' Society of Israel) to campaign in the 1955 and 1959 elections. The front excluded the two Mizrahi religious parties, claiming they were insufficiently committed to the concept of a Torah state. The Torah Religious Front was dissolved prior to the 1961 elections.

United Religious Front—Electoral alliance created in 1949 composed of the four religious parties: Mizrahi (*q.v.*), HaPoel HaMizrahi (*q.v.*), Poalei Agudat Israel (Workers' Society of Israel), and Agudat Israel (*q.v.*). As of 1951 the four parties campaigned separately.

Yahad (Together)—An electoral list formed by Ezer Weizman in 1981; in 1984 it joined the Labor Party as a faction.

Bibliography

Chapter 1

Abu Lughod, Ibrahim (ed.). *The Transformation of Palestine.* Evanston, Illinois: Northwestern University Press, 1971.

Allon, Yigal. "Israel: The Case for Defensible Borders," *Foreign Affairs,* 55, No. 1, 1976, 38–53.

Alpher, Joseph. "Why Begin Should Invite Arafat to Jerusalem," *Foreign Affairs,* 60, No. 5, 1982, 1110–23.

Antonius, George. *The Arab Awakening.* London: Hamish Hamilton, 1955.

Arendt, Hannah. *Antisemitism.* New York: Harcourt Brace Jovanovich, 1951.

Aronoff, Myron. "The Decline of the Israeli Labor Party: Causes and Significance." Pages 115–47 in Howard Penniman (ed.), *Israel at the Polls, 1977.* Washington: American Enterprise Institute, 1979.

Aronson, Geoffrey. "Israel's Policy of Military Occupation," *Journal of Palestine Studies,* 7, No. 4, 1978, 79–98.

Avineri, Shlomo. "Beyond Camp David," *Foreign Policy,* 46, 1982, 19–36.

_____. *The Making of Modern Zionism: The Intellectual Origins of the Jewish State.* New York: Basic Books, 1981.

_____. "Peacemaking: The Arab-Israel Conflict," *Foreign Affairs,* 57, No. 1, 1978, 51–69.

Avishai, Bernard. *The Tragedy of Zionism: Revolution and Democracy in the Land of Israel.* New York: Farrer Straus Giroux, 1985.

Ball, George W. "The Coming Crisis in Israeli-American Relations," *Foreign Affairs,* 58, No. 2, 1979–80, 231–56.

Baron, S. *A Social and Religious History of the Jews.* (18 Vols.) New York: Columbia University Press, 1952–1983.

Bar-Simon Tov, Yaacov. *The Israeli-Egyptian War of Attrition, 1969–70.* New York: Columbia University Press, 1980.

Begin, Menachem. *The Revolt: The Dramatic Inside Story of the Irgun.* Los Angeles: Nash, 1972.

Ben-Gurion, David. *Israel: A Personal History.* New York: Funk and Wagnalls, 1971.

Ben-Sasson, H. H. (ed.). *A History of the Jewish People.* Cambridge: Harvard University Press, 1976.

Benvenisti, Meron. *The West Bank and Gaza Data Base Project: Interim Report, No. 1.* Washington: American Enterprise Institute, 1982.

_____. *The West Bank Data Project: A Survey of Israel's Policies.* Washington: American Enterprise Institute, 1984.

Brookings Institution. *Toward Peace in the Middle East: Report of a Study Group.* Washington: Brookings Institution, 1975.

Bullocks, John. *The Making of a War: The Middle East from 1967 to 1973.* London: Longman, 1974.

Cohen, Michael J. *The Origins and Evolution of the Arab-Zionist Conflict.* Berkeley and Los Angeles: University of California Press, 1987.

_____. *Palestine: Retreat from the Mandate: The Making of British Policy, 1936–1945.* New York: Holmes and Meier, 1978.

_____. "Sir Arthur Wanchope, the Army, and the Rebellion in Palestine, 1936," *Middle Eastern Studies,* 9, No. 1, January 1973, 19–34.

Dawidowicz, Lucy. "Toward a History of the Holocaust," *Commentary,* 47, No. 4, 1969, 51–58.

Dayan, Moshe. *Breakthrough: A Personal Account of the Egypt-Israel Peace Negotiations.* New York: Knopf, 1981.

Dubnow, Simon. *History of the Jews in Russia and Poland,* III. Philadelphia: Jewish Publication Society, 1946.

Eban, Abba. *Abba Eban: An Autobiography.* London: Weidenfeld and Nicholson, 1978.

_____. "Camp David: the Unfinished Business," *Foreign Affairs,* 57, No. 2, 1978–79, 343–54.

Elazar, Daniel J. (ed.). *Judea, Samaria, and Gaza: Views on the Future.* Washington: American Enterprise Institute, 1981.

Elon, Amos. *Herzl.* London: Weidenfeld and Nicholson, 1976.

_____. *The Israelis: Founders and Sons.* New York: Penguin, 1983.

Encyclopaedia Judaica. Jerusalem and New York: Macmillan, 1971–72.

Eytan, Walter. *The First Ten Years: A Diplomatic History of Israel.* New York: Simon and Schuster, 1958.

Fackenheim, Emil. *The Jewish Return into History: Reflections in the Age of Auschwitz.* New York: Schocken Books, 1978.

Fein, Leonard. *Israel: Politics and People.* Boston: Little, Brown, 1968.

Flapan, Simha. *The Birth of Israel: Myths and Realities.* New York: Pantheon Books, 1987.

Freedman, Robert (ed.). *Israel in the Begin Era.* New York: Praeger, 1982.

Goldman, Nahum. "Zionist Ideology and the Reality of Israel," *Foreign Affairs,* 57, No. 1, 1978, 70–82.

Halabi, Rafik. *West Bank Story.* New York: Harcourt Brace Jovanovich, 1982.

Halpern, Ben. *The Idea of a Jewish State.* (2d ed.). Cambridge: Harvard University Press, 1976.

Harkabi, Yehoshafat. *Palestine and Israel.* New York: Halsted Press, 1974.

Heller, Mark. "Begin's False Autonomy," *Foreign Policy,* 37, 1979-80, 111-32.

Hertzberg, Arthur. *The Zionist Idea: A Historical Analysis and Reader.* New York: Atheneum, 1969.

Herzog, Chaim. *The Arab-Israeli Wars.* London: Arms and Armour Press, 1982.

Horowitz, Dan and Moshe Lissak. *Origins of the Israeli Polity: Palestine under the Mandate.* Chicago: University of Chicago Press, 1978.

Hurewitz, J.C. *The Struggle for Palestine.* New York: Norton, 1950.

Israel Pocket Library. Jerusalem: Keter Books, 1973-74.

Jiryis, Sabri. *The Arabs in Israel.* (Trans., Inea Bushnaq.) New York: Monthly Review Press, 1976.

_____. "Secrets of State: An Analysis of the Diaries of Moshe Sharett," *Journal of Palestine Studies,* 10, No. 1, 1980, 35-57.

Johnson, Paul. *A History of the Jews.* New York: Harper and Row, 1987.

Kedourie, Elie. "Sir Herbert Samuel and the Government of Palestine," *Middle Eastern Studies* [London], 5, No. 1, 1969, 44-68.

_____. "Sir Mark Sykes and Palestine, 1915-1916," *Middle Eastern Studies* [London], 6, No. 3, 1970, 340-45.

_____. *Zionism and Arabism in Palestine and Israel.* London: Cass, 1982.

Kedourie, Elie, and Sylvia Haim (eds.). *Palestine and Israel in the 19th and 20th Centuries.* London: Cass, 1982.

Khalidi, Walid (ed.). *From Haven to Conquest.* Beirut: Institute of Palestine Studies, 1971.

Khouri, Fred J. *The Arab-Israeli Dilemma.* (2d ed.) Syracuse, New York: Syracuse University Press, 1976.

Kimche, David. *The Sandstorm: The Arab-Israeli Wars of 1967.* New York: Stein and Day, 1968.

Klieman, Aaron S. *Statecraft in the Dark.* Boulder, Colorado: Westview Press, 1988.

Laqueur, Walter. *A History of Zionism.* New York: Holt, Rinehart, and Winston, 1972.

Lesch, Ann Mosley. *Arab Politics in Palestine, 1917-1939: The Frustration of a Nationalist Movement.* Ithaca: Cornell University Press, 1979.

Lewis, Bernard. "The Arab-Israeli War: The Consequences of Defeat," *Foreign Affairs,* 46, No. 2, 1968, 321-35.

Israel: A Country Study

_____. "The Emergence of Modern Israel," *Middle Eastern Studies* [London], 8, No. 3, 1972, 421–27.
Louis, William Roger. *The British Empire in the Middle East, 1945–51.* Oxford: Oxford University Press, 1984.
Lucas, Noah. *The Modern History of Israel.* London: Weidenfeld and Nicholson, 1974.
Lustick, Ian. *Arabs in the Jewish State.* Austin: University of Texas Press, 1980.
_____. *For the Land and the Lord: Jewish Fundamentalism in Israel.* New York: Council on Foreign Relations, 1988.
_____. "Kill the Autonomy Talks," *Foreign Policy,* 41, 1980–81, 21–43.
Mandel, Neville J. *The Arabs and Zionism Before World War I.* Berkeley and Los Angeles: University of California Press, 1976.
Monroe, Elizabeth. *Britain's Moment in the Middle East.* London: Chatto and Windus, 1981.
Morris, Benny. *Birth of the Palestinian Refugee Problem.* Cambridge: Cambridge University Press, 1987.
O'Brien, Connor Cruise. *The Siege: The Saga of Israel and Zionism.* New York: Simon and Schuster, 1986.
Patai, Raphael (ed.). *Encyclopedia of Zionism and Israel.* New York: Herzl Press, 1971.
Peretz, Don. "The Arab Minority of Israel," *Middle East Journal,* 8, No. 2, 1954, 139–54.
_____. "The Earthquake: Israel's 9th Knesset Election," *Middle East Journal,* 31, No. 3, 1977, 251–66.
_____. "The War Election and Israel's 8th Knesset," *Middle East Journal,* 28, No. 2, 1974, 111–25.
Peretz, Don, and Sammy Smooha. "Israel's 10th Knesset Elections: Ethnic Upsurgence and Decline of Ideology," *Middle East Journal,* 35, No. 4, 1981, 506–26.
Peri, Yoram. *Between Battles and Ballots: Israeli Military in Politics.* New York: Cambridge University Press, 1983.
Perlmutter, Amos. "Begin's Rhetoric and Sharon's Tactics," *Foreign Affairs,* 61, No. 1, 1982, 67–83.
_____. "Begin's Strategy and Dayan's Tactics: The Conduct of Israeli Foreign Policy," *Foreign Affairs,* 56, No. 4, 1978, 357–72.
_____. "Cleavage in Israel," *Foreign Policy,* 27, 1977, 136–57.
_____. "A Race Against time: The Egyptian-Israeli Negotiations over the Future of Palestine," *Foreign Affairs,* 57, No. 5, 1979, 987–1004.
Porath, Yehoshua. *The Emergence of the Palestine-Arab Nationalist Movement, 1918–1929.* London: Cass, 1974.

Quandt, William B. *Decade of Decision: American Policy Toward the Arab-Israeli Conflict.* Berkeley and Los Angeles: University of California Press, 1977.

Quandt, William B., Fuad Jabber, and Ann Lesch. *Politics of Palestinian Nationalism.* Berkeley and Los Angeles: University of California Press, 1973.

Rabinovich, Itamar. *The War for Lebanon: 1970–1983.* Ithaca: Cornell University Press, 1984.

Rafael, Gideon. *Destination Peace: Three Decades of Israeli Foreign Policy.* New York: Stein and Day, 1981.

Randal, Jonathan C. *Going All the Way: Christian Warlords, Israeli Adventurers, and the War in Lebanon.* New York: Vintage Books, 1983.

Reich, Bernard. "Israel Between War and Peace," *Current History*, 66, No. 390, 1974, 49–52.

Rodinson, Maxine. *Israel and the Arabs.* (2d ed.) London: Penguin, 1982.

Roth, Stephen J. (ed.). *The Impact of the Six-Day War.* New York: St. Martin's Press and Institute of Jewish Affairs, 1988.

Sachar, Howard M. *The Course of Modern Jewish History.* New York: World, 1958Ł.

_____. *A History of Israel, I: From the Rise of Zionism to Our Time.* New York: Alfred A. Knopf, 1986.

_____. *A History of Israel, II: From the Aftermath of the Yom Kippur War.* Oxford: Oxford University Press, 1987.

Sadat, Anwar. *In Search of Identity: An Autobiography.* New York: Harper and Row, 1978.

Safran, Nadav. *The Embattled Ally.* Cambridge: Harvard University Press, 1978.

_____. *From War to War: The Arab-Israeli Confrontation, 1948–1967.* New York: Pegasus, 1969.

Said, Edward W. *The Question of Palestine.* London: Routledge and Kegan Paul, 1981.

Sanders, Ronald. *The High Walls of Jerusalem.* New York: Holt, Rinehart, and Winston, 1983.

Schiff, Zeev, and Ehud Ya'ari. *Israel's Lebanon War.* New York: Simon and Schuster, 1984.

Segev, Tom. *1949: The First Israelis.* New York: Free Press, 1986.

Shapiro, Yonathan. *The Formative Years of the Israeli Labor Party.* Los Angeles: Sage, 1976.

Shimoni, Yaacov, and Evyatar Levine (eds.). *Political Dictionary of the Middle East in the 20th Century.* New York: Quadrangle, 1974.

Shlaim, Avi. *Collusion Across the Jordan: King Abdullah, the Zionists, and the Partition of Palestine.* New York: Columbia University Press, 1988.

Smooha, Sammy. *Israel: Pluralism and Conflict.* Berkeley and Los Angeles: University of California Press, 1978.

Stein, Kenneth W. *The Land Question in Palestine, 1917–1939.* Chapel Hill: University of North Carolina Press, 1984.

Sykes, Christopher. *Crossroads to Israel.* Bloomington: Indiana University Press, 1973.

Teveth, Shabtai. *Ben-Gurion and the Palestinian Arabs: From Peace to War.* Oxford: Oxford University Press, 1985.

Tillman, Seth P. *The United States in the Middle East: Interests and Obstacles.* Bloomington: Indiana University Press, 1982.

Vital, David. *The Origins of Zionism.* Oxford: Oxford University Press, 1975.

_____. *Zionism, The Formative Years.* Oxford: Oxford University Press, 1982.

Weizman, Ezer. *The Battle for Peace.* New York: Bantam Books, 1981.

Chapter 2

Abramov, S. Zalman. *Perpetual Dilemma: Jewish Religion in the Jewish State.* Rutherford, New Jersey: Fairleigh Dickinson University Press, 1976.

Al-Haj, Majid. "Ethnic Relations in an Arab Town in Israel." Pages 105–32 in Alex Weingrod (ed.), *Studies in Israel's Ethnicity: After the Ingathering.* New York: Gordon and Breach, 1985.

Aronoff, Myron J. *Frontiertown: The Politics of Community Building in Israel.* Manchester (United Kingdom): Manchester University Press, 1973.

_____. "Political Polarization: Contradictory Interpretation of Israeli Reality." Pages 53–77 in Steven Heydemann (ed.), *Issues in Contemporary Israel: The Begin Era.* Boulder, Colorado: Westview Press, 1984.

Aviad, Janet. *Return to Jordan: Religious Renewal in Israel.* Chicago: University of Chicago Press, 1983.

Avruch, Kevin. *American Immigrants in Israel: Social Identities and Change.* Chicago: University of Chicago Press, 1981.

_____. "Gush Emunim: Politics, Religion, and Ideology in Israel," *Middle East Review,* 11, No. 2, 1978, 26–31.

_____. "The Emergence of Ethnicity in Israel," *American Ethnologist,* 14, No. 2, 1987, 327–39.

_____. "Traditionalizing Israel's Nationalism: The Development of Gush Emunim," *Political Psychology,* 1, No. 1, 1979, 47–57.

Ben-Dor, Gabriel. *The Druzes in Israel: A Political Study.* Jerusalem: Hebrew University Press, 1979.

Ben-Rafael, Eliezer. "Social Mobility and Ethnic Awareness: The Israeli Case." Pages 57-79 in Alex Weingrod (ed.), *Studies in Israeli Ethnicity: After the Ingathering.* New York: Gordon and Breach, 1985.

Ben-Zadok, Efraim. "The Limits of the Politics of Planning." Pages 141-52 in David Newman (ed.), *The Impact of Gush Emunim: Politics and Settlement in the West Bank.* New York: St. Martin's Press, 1985.

Benvenisti, Meron. *The West Bank Data Project: A Survey of Israel's Policies.* Washington: American Enterprise Institute, 1984.

———. *West Bank Data Project, 1986 Report: Demographic, Economic, Legal, Social, and Political Develolpments in the West Bank.* Washington: American Enterprise Institute, 1986.

Bradley, C. Paul. *Parliamentary Elections in Israel: Three Case Studies.* Grantham, New Hampshire: Tompson and Rutter, 1985.

Cohen, Erik. "The Black Panthers and Israeli Society," *Jewish Journal of Sociology,* 14, No. 1, 1972, 93-109.

———. "Ethnicity and Legitimation in Contemporary Israel," *Jerusalem Quarterly* [Jerusalem], 28, 1983, 11-124.

Deshen, Shlomo. "Israeli Judaism: Introduction to the Major Patterns," *International Journal of Middle East Studies,* 9, 1978, 141-69.

Deshen, Shlomo, and Moshe Shokeid. *The Predicament of Homecoming: Cultural and Social Life of North African Immigrants in Israel.* Ithaca: Cornell University Press, 1974.

Divine, Donna R. "Political Legitimacy in Israel: How Important is the State?" *International Journal of Middle East Studies,* 10, No. 2, 1979, 205-24.

Don-Yehiya, Eliezer. "The Resolution of Religious Conflicts in Israel." Pages 203-18 in Stuart A. Cohen and Eliezer Don-Yehiya (eds.), *Conflict and Consensus in Jewish Public Life.* Ramat Gan, Israel: Bar-Ilan University Press, 1986.

Eisenstadt, S. N. *Israeli Society.* New York: Basic Books, 1967.

———. *The Transformation of Israeli Society.* Boulder, Colorado: Westview Press, 1985.

Elazar, Daniel J. *Israel: Building a New Society.* Bloomington: Indiana University Press, 1986.

Elon, Amos. *The Israelis: Founders and Sons.* New York: Penguin, 1983.

Friedman, Menachem. "The NRP in Transition—Behind the Party's Electoral Decline." Pages 141-68 in D. Caspi, A. Diskin, and E. Guttman (eds.), *The Roots of Begin's Success.* London: Croom-Helm, 1983.

Gitelman, Zvi. *Becoming Israelis: Political Resocialization of Soviet and American Immigrants.* New York: Praeger, 1982.

Goldberg, Harvey E. *Cave Dwellers and Citrus Growers: A Jewish Community in Libya and Israel.* Cambridge: Cambridge University Press, 1972.

_____. "Historical and Cultural Dimensions of Ethnic Phenomena in Israel." Pages 179–200 in Alex Weingrod (ed.), *Studies in Israeli Ethnicity: After the Ingathering.* New York: Gordon and Breach, 1985.

Goldstein, Judith L. "Iranian Ethnicity in Israel: The Performance of Identity." Pages 237–57 in Alex Weingrod (ed.), *Studies in Israeli Ethnicity: After the Ingathering.* New York: Gordon and Breach, 1985.

Grose, Peter. *A Changing Israel.* New York: Vintage Books, 1985.

Halpern, Ben. *The Idea of the Jewish State.* (2d ed.) Cambridge: Harvard University Press, 1969.

Heller, Mark. "Politics and Social Change in the West Bank since 1967." Pages 185–211 in Joel S. Migdal (ed.), *Palestinian Society and Politics.* Princeton: Princeton University Press, 1980.

Hodgson, Marshall G.J. *The Venture of Islam: The Gunpowder Empires and Modern Times.* (3 Vols.) Chicago: University of Chicago Press, 1974.

Horowitz, Dan, and Moshe Lissak. *Origins of the Israeli Polity: Palestine under the Mandate.* Chicago: University of Chicago Press, 1978.

Israel. Central Bureau of Statistics. *Monthly Bulletin of Statistics,* 38. Jerusalem: 1987, 12.

_____. Central Bureau of Statistics. *Statistical Abstract of Israel, 1987.* Jerusalem: 1987.

Kushner, Gilbert. *Immigrants from India in Israel.* Tucson: University of Arizona Press, 1973.

Lewis, Arnold. "Phantom Ethnicity: 'Oriental Jews' in Israeli Society." Pages 133–57 in Alex Weingrod (ed.), *Studies in Israeli Ethnicity: After the Ingathering.* New York: Gordon and Breach, 1985.

_____. *Power, Poverty, and Education: An Ethnography of Schooling in an Israeli Town.* Ramat Gan, Israel: Turtledove Publishing, 1979.

Lewis, Herbert S. "Ethnicity, Culture, and Adaptation Among Yemenites in a Heterogenous Community." Pages 217–36 in Alex Weingrod (ed.), *Studies in Israeli Ethnicity: After the Ingathering.* New York: Gordon and Breach, 1985.

Liebman, Charles S. "The 'Who is a Jew?' Controversy—Political and Anthropological Perspectives." Pages 194–202 in Stuart A. Cohen and Eliezer Don-Yehiya (eds.), *Conflict and Consensus in*

Jewish Public Life. Ramat Gan, Israel: Bar-Ilan University Press, 1986.

Liebman, Charles S., and Eliezer Don-Yehiya. *Civil Religion in Israel.* Berkeley and Los Angeles: University of California Press, 1983.

————. *Religion and Politics in Israel.* Bloomington: Indiana University Press, 1984.

Loeb, Lawrence D. "Folk Models of Habbani Ethnic Identity." Pages 201–15 in Alex Weingrod (ed.), *Studies in Israeli Ethnicity: After the Ingathering.* New York: Gordon and Breach, 1985.

Lotan, Givra. "Social Security and Welfare." Pages 218–22 in *Israel Pocket Library: Society.* Jerusalem: Keter Books, 1974.

Lustick, Ian. *Arabs in the Jewish State.* Austin: University of Texas Press, 1980.

————. "The West Bank and Gaza in Israeli Politics." Pages 79–98 in Steven Heydemann (ed.), *Issues in Contemporary Israel: The Begin Era.* Boulder, Colorado: Westview Press, 1984.

Marx, Emmanuel. *The Social Context of Violent Behavior: A Social Anthropological Study in an Israeli Immigrant Town.* London: Routledge and Kegan Paul, 1976.

Matras, Judah. "International Social Mobility and Ethnic Organization in the Jewish Population of Israel." Pages 1–23 in Alex Weingrod (ed.), *Studies in Israeli Ethnicity: After the Ingathering.* New York: Gordon and Breach, 1985.

Middle East Research Institute. *The MERI Report: Israel.* London: Croom-Helm, 1985.

Migdal, Joel S. (ed.). *Palestinian Society and Politics.* Princeton: Princeton University Press, 1980.

Newman, David (ed.). *The Impact of Gush Emunim: Politics and Settlement in the West Bank.* New York: St. Martin's Press, 1985.

"1987 Year-end Worldwide Reported AIDS Cases Top 74,000," *AIDS Record,* 2, No. 2, December 31, 1987, 9.

Oppenheimer, Jonathan. "The Druze in Israel as Arabs and Non-Arabs." Pages 259–79 in Alex Weingrod (ed.), *Studies in Israeli Ethnicity: After the Ingathering.* New York: Gordon and Breach, 1985.

Orni, Efraim. "Human Geography." Pages 228–74 in *Israel Pocket Library: Society.* Jerusalem: Keter Books, 1974.

Oz, Amos. *In the Land of Israel.* San Diego: Harcourt Brace Jovanovitch, 1983.

Reich, Bernard. *Israel: Land of Tradition and Conflict.* Boulder, Colorado: Westview Press, 1985.

Rolef, Susan Hattis (ed.). *Political Dictionary of the State of Israel.* New York: Macmillan, 1987.

Rosenfeld, Henry. "The Class Situation of the Arab Minority in Israel," *Comparative Studies in Society and History*, 20, 1978, 374–407.

Sachar, Howard M. *A History of Israel, I: From the Rise of Zionism to Our Time.* New York: Alfred A. Knopf, 1981.

Schiff, Gary S. "The Politics of Fertility Policy in Israel." Pages 255–78 in Paul Ritterbrand (ed.), *Modern Jewish Fertility.* Leiden, Netherlands: E.J. Brill, 1981.

Shokeid, Moshe. "Aggression and Social Relationships Among Moroccan Immigrants." Pages 281–96 in Alex Weingrod (ed.), *Studies in Israeli Ethnicity: After the Ingathering.* New York: Gordon and Breach, 1985.

———. *The Dual Heritage: Immigrants from the Atlas Mountains in an Israeli Village.* Manchester (United Kingdom): Manchester University Press, 1971.

Shulewitz, M.H. "Health Services." Pages 199–217 in *Israel Pocket Library: Society.* Jerusalem: Keter Books, 1974.

Smooha, Sammy. "Existing and Alternative Policy Towards the Arabs in Israel," *Ethnic and Racial Studies*, 5, No. 1, 1982, 72–98.

———. *Israel: Pluralism and Conflict.* Berkeley and Los Angeles: University of California Press, 1978.

———. *The Orientation and Politicization of the Arab Minority in Israel.* Haifa, Israel: Institute of Middle East Studies, 1980.

Sobel, Zvi. *Migrants from the Promised Land.* New Brunswick, New Jersey: Transaction Books, 1986.

Spilerman, Seymour, and Jack Habib. "Development Towns in Israel: The Role of Community in Creating Ethnic Disparities in Labor Force Characteristics," *American Journal of Sociology*, 81, No. 4, 1976, 781–812.

Spiro, Melford E. *Kibbutz: Venture in Utopia.* (Augmented edition.) New York: Schocken Books, 1970.

Sprinzak, Ehud. *Fundamentalism, Terrorism, and Democracy: The Case of Gush Emunim Underground.* Washington: Woodrow Wilson Institute, 1986.

———. "Gush Emunim—The Iceberg Model of Political Extremism," *State, Government, and International Relations* [Israel], 14, 25–52.

Tabory, Ephraim. "Pluralism in the Jewish State: Reform and Conservative Judaism in Israel." Pages 170–93 in Stuart A. Cohen and Eliezer Don-Yehiya (eds.), *Conflict and Consensus in Jewish Political Life.* Ramat Gan, Israel: Bar-Ilan University Press, 1986.

Talmon, Yonina. *Family and Community in the Kibbutz.* Cambridge: Harvard University Press, 1972.

Weingrod, Alex. "Recent Trends in Israeli Ethnicity," *Ethnic and Racial Studies*, 2, No. 1, 1979, 55–65.

_____. *Reluctant Pioneers: Village Development in Israel*. Ithaca: Cornell University Press, 1966.

Weingrod, Alex (ed.). *Studies in Israeli Ethnicity: After the Ingathering*. New York: Gordon and Breach, 1985.

Willner, Dorothy. *Nation-Building and Community in Israel*. Princeton: Princeton University Press, 1969.

Wolffsohn, Michael. *Israel: Polity, Society, and Economy, 1882–1986*. Atlantic Highlands, New Jersey: Humanities Press, 1987.

Zucker, Norman I. *The Coming Crisis in Israel: Private Faith and Public Policy*. Cambridge: MIT Press, 1973.

Zureik, Elia. "Transformation of Class Structure Among Arabs in Israel: From Peasantry to Proletariat," *Journal of Palestine Studies*, 6, No. 1, 1976, 39–66.

Chapter 3

Ablin, Richard. "Forecasting Israel's Capital Flows—Some Econometric First Steps," *Bank of Israel Economic Review* [Jerusalem], 43, June 1976, 3–17.

_____. "Israel's Foreign Trade—Demand and Prices: A Regression Analysis of the Short Run," *Bank of Israel Economic Review* [Jerusalem], 45–46, February 1979, 23–62.

_____. "A Last Decade of Israeli Growth? Economic Policy Since 1973," *Bank of Israel Economic Review* [Jerusalem], 48–49, May 1980, 45–83.

Amir, Shmuel. "Changes in the Wage Function for Israeli Jewish Male Employees Between 1968–69 and 1975–76," *Bank of Israel Economic Review* [Jerusalem], 52, August 1981, 5–29.

_____. "Educational Structure and Wage Differentials of the Labor Force in the 1970s." Pages 137–52 in Yoram Ben-Porath (ed.), *The Israeli Economy: Maturing Through Crisis*. Cambridge: Harvard University Press, 1986.

_____. "The Effects of the Children's Allowance in Israel's Labor Supply," *Bank of Israel Economic Review* [Jerusalem], 47, October 1979, 1–45.

Arian, A. (ed.). *Israel: A Developing Society*. Assen, Netherlands: Van Gorcum, 1980.

Auerbach, Zvi. "The Income and Price Effects on the Computation of Private Consumption, 1956–77," *Bank of Israel Economic Review* [Jerusalem], 52, August 1981, 30–45.

Israel: A Country Study

————. "Private Consumption Prices in Israel in 1964–77 by Main Cost Components," *Bank of Israel Economic Review* [Jerusalem], 50, February 1981, 33–63.

Bank of Israel. *Annual Report, 1983.* Jerusalem, Israel: Ahva Printing, 1984.

————. *Annual Report, 1984.* Jerusalem, Israel: Ahva Printing, 1985.

————. *Annual Report, 1985.* Jerusalem, Israel: Ahva Printing, 1986.

————. *Annual Report, 1986.* Jerusalem, Israel: Ahva Printing, 1987.

————. *Annual Report, 1987.* Jerusalem, Israel: Ahva Printing, 1988.

Bar-El, Raphael, and Ariela Nesher (eds.). *Rural Industrialization in Israel.* Boulder, Colorado: Westview Press, 1987.

Barkai, Haim. "Defense Costs in Retrospect," *Research Paper, No. 115* [Jerusalem], Hebrew University, 1980.

————. "The Energy Sector in the 1960s and 1970s." Pages 245–75 in Yoram Ben-Porath (ed.), *The Israeli Economy: Maturing Through Crisis.* Cambridge: Harvard University Press, 1986.

Bar-Nathan, Moshe. "The Declining Productivity of Israel's Construction Industry," *Bank of Israel Economic Review* [Jerusalem], 58, September 1986, 68–82.

————. "Effect of Rising Raw Materials Prices on the Productivity and Profitability of Israeli Industry, 1965–80," *Bank of Israel Economic Review* [Jerusalem], 57, May 1985, 53–79.

Baron, Malka. "Changes in the Age Structure of Israel's Population and Their Effect on the Labor Market, 1965–82," *Bank of Israel Economic Review* [Jerusalem], 58, September 1986, 1–28.

Baruch, Joseph. "The New Economic Policy and Protection Levels on Industrial Import Substitutes and Exports," *Bank of Israel Economic Review* [Jerusalem], 48–49, May 1980, 84–91.

————. "Protection Levels in Israel, 1968 and 1972–74," *Bank of Israel Economic Review* [Jerusalem], 45–46, February 1979, 1–22.

Ben-Bassat, A. "An Evaluation of Israel's Reserve Portfolio Performance," *Bank of Israel Economic Review* [Jerusalem], 51, May 1981, 5–35.

————. "Industrial Investment Behavior in Israel, 1955–68," *Bank of Israel Economic Review* [Jerusalem], 42, June 1975, 72–106.

Ben-Porath, Yoram. "Diversity in Population and in Labor Force." Pages 153–70 in Yoram Ben-Porath (ed.), *The Israeli Economy: Maturing Through Crisis.* Cambridge: Harvard University Press, 1986.

————. "The Entwined Growth of Population and Production, 1922–1982." Pages 27–41 in Yoram Ben-Porath (ed.), *The Israeli Economy: Maturing Through Crisis.* Cambridge: Harvard University Press, 1986.

Ben-Porath, Yoram (ed.). *The Israeli Economy: Maturing Through Crisis.* Cambridge: Harvard University Press, 1986.

Berglas, Eitan. "Defense and the Economy." Pages 173–91 in Yoram Ben-Porath (ed.), *The Israeli Economy: Maturing Through Crisis.* Cambridge: Harvard University Press, 1986.

————. "Taxes and Transfers in an Inflationary Decade." Pages 221–38 in Yoram Ben-Porath (ed.), *The Israeli Economy: Maturing Through Crisis.* Cambridge: Harvard University Press, 1986.

Bergman, Arie. "The Slowdown of Industrial Productivity— Causes, Explanations, and Surprises," *Bank of Israel Economic Review* [Jerusalem], 56, April 1985, 1–24.

Bloom, Liora. "Israel's Demand Function for Imports of Goods, 1968–1976," *Bank of Israel Economic Review* [Jerusalem], 55, November 1983, 77–93.

Brenner, Menahem, and Dan Gabai. "The Effect of Inflation on Stock Yields: 1965–1974," *Bank of Israel Economic Review* [Jerusalem], 48–49, May 1980, 99–102.

————. "The Effect of Inflation on Stock Yields 1965–1979," *Bank of Israel Economic Review* [Jerusalem], 53, May 1982, 81–86.

Brezis, Elise A., Leo Leiderman, and Rafi Melnick. "The Interaction Between Inflation and Monetary Aggregates in Israel," *Bank of Israel Economic Review* [Jerusalem], 55, November 1983, 46–60.

Bronfeld, Saul. "The Banking System in a Monetary Model of the Israeli Economy," *Bank of Israel Economic Review* [Jerusalem], 51, May 1981, 36–57.

Bronfeld, Saul, and Reuven Brenner. "Inflation and the Liquidity of Index-Linked Bonds," *Bank of Israel Economic Review* [Jerusalem], 44, November 1977, 1–28.

Bruno, Michael. "External Shocks and Domestic Response: Macroeconomics Performance, 1965–82." Pages 276–301 in Yoram Ben-Porath (ed.), *The Israeli Economy: Maturing Through Crisis.* Cambridge: Harvard University Press, 1986.

Bruno, Michael, and Stanley Fischer. "The Inflationary Process, Shocks and Accommodation." Pages 347–74 in Yoram Ben-Porath (ed.), *The Israeli Economy: Maturing Through Crisis.* Cambridge: Harvard University Press, 1986.

Cukierman, A., E.A. Pazner, and A. Razin. "A Macroeconomic Model of the Israeli Economy, 1956–1974," *Bank of Israel Economic Review* [Jerusalem], 44, November 1977, 29–64.

Cukierman, Alex, and Joseph Cohen. "The Free Credit Market in Israel," *Bank of Israel Economic Review* [Jerusalem], 50, February 1981, 64-101.

Economist Intelligence Unit. *Country Profile: Israel: 1986-87.* London: 1986.

_____. *Country Profile: Israel: 1987-88.* London: 1987.

Elkayam, David. "Incorporation of Liquid Assets in a Dynamic Consumption Function for the 1970s," *Bank of Israel Economic Review* [Jerusalem], 58, September 1986, 29-52.

Elkayam, David, and Rafi Melnick. "An Annual Model of the Consumption Function," *Bank of Israel Economic Review* [Jerusalem], 56, April 1985, 25-54.

Fischer, Stanley. "Inflation and Indexation: Israel." Pages 57-84 in John Williamson (ed.), *Inflation and Indexation: Argentina, Brazil, and Israel.* Cambridge: MIT Press, 1985.

_____. "Monetary Policy in Israel," *Bank of Israel Economic Review* [Jerusalem], 53, May 1982, 5-30.

Flanders, June M., and Assaf Razin (eds.). *Development in an Inflationary World.* New York: Academic Press, 1981.

Flink, Salomon J. *Israel, Chaos and Challenge: Politics vs. Economics.* Ramat Gan, Israel and Forest Grove, Oregon: Turtledove, 1979.

Friedman, Benjamin M. "The Roles of Money and Credit in Macroeconomic Analysis," *Bank of Israel Economic Review* [Jerusalem], 55, November 1983, 1-7.

Gaathon, A.L. *Economic Productivity in Israel.* New York: Praeger, 1971.

Geva, Yehuda, and Jack Habib. "The Development of the Transfer System and the Redistribution of Income." Pages 209-20 in Yoram Ben-Porath (ed.), *The Israeli Economy: Maturing Through Crisis.* Cambridge: Harvard University Press, 1986.

Ginor, Fanny. *Socio-Economic Disparities in Israel.* Tel Aviv: Transaction Books, 1979.

Gottlieb, Daniel, and Sylvia Piterman. "Inflationary Expectation in Israel," *Bank of Israel Economic Review* [Jerusalem], 57, May 1985, 1-25.

Greenwald, Carol Schwartz. *Recession as a Policy Instrument: Israel, 1965-69.* Rutherford, New Jersey: Fairleigh Dickinson University Press, 1973.

Gronau, Reuben, and Zvi Weiss. "Road User Charges and Automobile Taxation in Israel," *Bank of Israel Economic Review* [Jerusalem], 55, November 1983, 8-47.

Gross, Ephraim. "An Analysis of Family Expenditure by Consumption Category," *Bank of Israel Economic Review* [Jerusalem], 56, April 1985, 55-96.

Halevi, Nadav. "Perspectives on the Balance of Payments." Pages 241–63 in Yoram Ben-Porath (ed.), *The Israeli Economy: Maturing Through Crisis.* Cambridge: Harvard University Press, 1986.

Halevi, Nadav, and Ruth Klinov-Malul. *The Economic Development of Israel.* New York: Praeger, 1968.

Heth, Meir. *Banking Institutions in Israel.* Jerusalem: Maurice Falk Institute for Economic Research in Israel, 1966.

_____. *The Flow of Funds in Israel.* New York: Praeger, 1970.

_____. *The Legal Framework of Economic Activity in Israel.* New York: Praeger, 1967.

Horowitz, David. *Enigma of Economic Growth: A Case Study of Israel.* New York: Praeger, 1972.

Israel, Central Bureau of Statistics. *Statistical Abstract of Israel, 1983.* Jerusalem: 1983.

_____. *Statistical Abstract of Israel, 1984.* Jerusalem: 1984.

_____. *Statistical Abstract of Israel, 1985.* Jerusalem: 1985.

_____. *Statistical Abstract of Israel, 1986.* Jerusalem: 1986.

_____. *Statistical Abstract of Israel, 1987.* Jerusalem: 1987.

Israel, Ministry of Finance. *Budget in Brief.* (Annuals, 1979–87.) Jerusalem: 1980–88.

Justman, Moshe, and Morris Teubal. "Towards the Formulation and Implementation of an Explicit Industrial and Technological Policy for Israel," (unpublished paper), 1987.

Kleiman, Ephraim. "Indexation in the Labor Market." Pages 302–19 in Yoram Ben-Porath (ed.), *The Israeli Economy: Maturing Through Crisis.* Cambridge: Harvard University Press, 1986.

Kleiman, Ephraim, and T. Ophir. "The Effects of Changes in the Quantity of Money on Prices in Israel, 1955–1965," *Bank of Israel Economic Review* [Jerusalem], 42, January 1975, 15–45.

_____. "Inflation in Israel, 1955–1965: The Wage Push on Prices," *Bank of Israel Economic Review* [Jerusalem], 43, June 1976, 18–28.

Klinov, Ruth. "Changes in the Industrial Structure." Pages 119–36 in Yoram Ben-Porath (ed.), *The Israeli Economy: Maturing Through Crisis.* Cambridge: Harvard University Press, 1986.

Landau, Philip. *Israel to 1991: Reform or Relapse?* London: Economist Publications, 1987.

Lavie, Yaakov. "Wage Dynamics in Israel 1963–1971," *Bank of Israel Economic Review* [Jerusalem], 44, November 1977, 65–99.

Lerner, Abba, and Haim Ben-Shahar. *The Economics of Efficiency and Growth.* Cambridge, Massachusetts: Ballinger Publishing, 1975.

Lev, Nachum. "Gasoline Demand in Israel, 1960–1975," *Bank of Israel Economic Review* [Jerusalem], 52, August 1981, 46–71.

Israel: A Country Study

Levinson, Pinchas, and Pinchas Landau. *Israel Economic and Business Review, 1985.* Jerusalem: Israeli Economist, 1985.

Levy, Haim. "Capital Structure, Inflation, and the Cost of Capital in Israeli Industry, 1964-1978," *Bank of Israel Economic Review* [Jerusalem], 53, May 1982, 31-63.

Levy, Haim and Marshall Sarnat. "Risk, Diversification, and the Composition of the Market Portfolio: An Analysis of the Tel Aviv Stock Exchange," *Bank of Israel Economic Review* [Jerusalem], 42, June 1975, 46-71.

Litvin, Uri, and Leora Meridor. "The Grant Equivalent of Subsidized Investment in Israel," *Bank of Israel Economic Review* [Jerusalem], 54, April 1983, 5-30.

Liviatan, Nissan, and Sylvia Piterman. "Accelerating Inflation and Balance-of-Payments Crises, 1973-84." Pages 320-46 in Yoram Ben-Porath (ed.), *The Israeli Economy: Maturing Through Crisis.* Cambridge: Harvard University Press, 1986.

Liviatan, Oded. "Frequency of Wage Indexation Adjustments," *Bank of Israel Economic Review* [Jerusalem], 57, May 1985, 37-52.

_____. "Israeli External Debt," *Bank of Israel Economic Review* [Jerusalem], 48-49, May 1980, 1-44.

Mayshar, Joram. "Investment Patterns." Pages 101-18 in Yoram Ben-Porath (ed.), *The Israeli Economy: Maturing Through Crisis.* Cambridge: Harvard University Press, 1986.

Menzly, Yehuda. "Interest Rates on Nondirected Bank Credit, 1965-1972," *Bank of Israel Economic Review* [Jerusalem], 45-46, February 1979, 86-126.

Meridor, Leora. "Deficit Neutrality: The Israeli Case," *Bank of Israel Economic Review* [Jerusalem], 57, May 1985, 26-36.

Meron, Raphael. *Economic Development in Judea-Samaria and the Gaza District: Economic Growth and Structural Change, 1970-80.* Jerusalem: Bank of Israel, Ahva Press, 1983.

Metzer, Jacob. "The Slowdown of Economic Growth: A Passing Phase or the End of the Big Spurt." Pages 75-100 in Yoram Ben-Porath (ed.), *The Israeli Economy: Maturing Through Crisis.* Cambridge: Harvard University Press, 1986.

Michaely, Michael. *Foreign Trade Regimes and Economic Development: Israel.* New York: Columbia University Press, 1975.

_____. *Israel's Foreign Exchange Rate System.* Jerusalem: Maurice Falk Institute for Economic Research in Israel, 1971.

Nachmany, Doron. "Price Equations for Israeli Manufacturing Industries, 1964-1977," *Bank of Israel Economic Review* [Jerusalem], 53, May 1982, 64-80.

Ofer, Gur. "A Cross-Country Comparison of Industrial Structure." Chapter in Nadav Halevi and Y. Kop (eds.), *Ikarot*

Bakalkala HaYisraelit (Issues in the Economy of Israel). Jerusalem: Maurice Falk Institute for Economic Research in Israel, 1976.

_____. "Public Spending on Civilian Services." Pages 192-208 in Yoram Ben-Porath (ed.), *The Israeli Economy: Maturing Through Crisis.* Cambridge: Harvard University Press, 1986.

Pack, Howard. *Structural Change and Economic Policy in Israel.* New Haven: Yale University Press, 1971.

Paroush, Jacob, and Malka Baron. "Employment Pressure in Israel, 1967-75," *Bank of Israel Economic Review* [Jerusalem], 45-46, February 1979, 63-85.

Patinkin, Don. *The Israeli Economy.* Jerusalem: Maurice Falk Project for Economic Research in Israel, 1959.

Pelzman, Joseph. "The Effect of the U.S.-Israel Free Trade Area Agreement on Israeli Trade and Employment." Pages 140-75 in Bernard Reich and Gershon R. Kieval (eds.), *Israel Faces the Future.* New York: Praeger, 1986.

_____. "The Impact of the U.S.-Israel Free Trade Area Agreement on Israeli Trade and Employment." Jerusalem: Maurice Falk Institute for Economic Research in Israel, 1985.

_____. "The U.S.-Israel Free Trade Area Agreement and Israeli Textile Exports to the United States." (Paper presented at Israel-American Trade Week, 1986.) Tel Aviv: 1986.

Pines, David, Efraim Sadka, and Eytan Sheshinski. "Discriminatory Taxation of Owner-Occupied Housing: Its Effects on Resource Allocation and Income Distribution," *Bank of Israel Economic Review* [Jerusalem], 58, September 1986, 83-110.

Piterman, Sylvia, and Ben-Zion Zilberfarb. "Financial Savings of the Private Sector in Israel, 1972-1977," *Bank of Israel Economic Review* [Jerusalem], 54, April 1983, 31-54.

Sanbar, Marsh. "Israel's Major Goals and Problems," *Bank of Israel Economic Review* [Jerusalem], 44, November 1977, 134-42.

Sharkansky, Ira. *What Makes Israel Tick: How Domestic Policy-Makers Cope With Constraints.* Chicago: Nelson-Hall, 1985.

Sussman, Zvi. *Israel's Economy: Performance, Problems, and Policies.* Tel Aviv: Jacob Levinson Center of the Israel-Diaspora Institute, 1986.

Syrquin, Moshe. "Economic Growth and Structural Change: An International Perspective." Pages 42-74 in Yoram Ben-Porath (ed.), *The Israeli Economy: Maturing Through Crisis.* Cambridge: Harvard University Press, 1986.

Tamari, Meir. "Equity, Financing, and Gearing in the U.K., U.S.A., Japan, and Israel," *Bank of Israel Economic Review* [Jerusalem], 43, June 1976, 29-54.

_____. "Monetary Policy and the Individual Firm. An Analysis
of Company Accounts in Israel, U.K., U.S.A., and Japan,"
Bank of Israel Economic Review [Jerusalem], 45-46, February 1979,
127-43.

Tamari, Meir, and Emanuel Gabai. "Some Effects of Differential Income Tax Rates on the Behavior of Israel's Industrial Companies," *Bank of Israel Economic Review* [Jerusalem], 42, January
1975, 3-14.

Tarab, Shlomo. "Some Aspects of Efficiency of Investment in
Mutual Funds Investing in Shares, 1965-72," *Bank of Israel Economic Review* [Jerusalem], 48-49, May 1980, 103-19.

Weiss, Zvi. "Allocation and Financing of Motor Transport Infrastructure Costs in Israel," *Bank of Israel Economic Review* [Jerusa-
lem], 50, February 1981, 5-32.

Williamson, John. *Inflation and Indexation: Argentina, Brazil, and Israel.*
Cambridge: MIT Press, 1985.

Wolffsohn, Michael. *Israel: Polity, Society, and Economy, 1882-1986.*
Atlantic Highlands, New Jersey: Humanities Press International,
1987.

Yitzhai, Shlomo, and Haim Shalit. "Efficient Portfolio Selection:
Application to the Tel Aviv Stock Exchange," *Bank of Israel Economic Review* [Jerusalem], 58, September 1986, 53-67.

Zilberfarb, Ben-Zion. "Topics in the Demand for Money in
Israel," *Bank of Israel Economic Review* [Jerusalem], 55, November 1983, 61-76.

(Various issues of the following publications were also used in
the preparation of this chapter: *Bank of Israel Economic Review* [Jerusa-
lem]; *Bank of Israel Recent Economic Developments* [Jerusalem]; *Israel
Economist* [Jerusalem]; *Monthly Bulletin of Statistics* [Jerusalem].)

Chapter 4

Abramov, S. Zalman. *Perpetual Dilemma: Jewish Religion in the Jewish State.* Rutherford, New Jersey: Fairleigh Dickinson University Press, 1976.

"Africa-Israel: Improved Relations Hinge on Peace Talks," *Africa
Research Bulletin* (Political Series), 25, No. 3, April 15, 1988,
8824-25.

Arian, Asher. *Politics in Israel: The Second Generation.* Chatham, New
Jersey: Chatham House Publishers, 1985.

Arian, Asher (ed.). *The Elections in Israel: 1969.* Jerusalem: Jerusalem Academic Press, 1972.

_____. *The Elections in Israel: 1973.* New Brunswick, New Jersey: Transaction Books, 1975.

_____. *The Elections in Israel: 1977.* Jerusalem: Jerusalem Academic Press, 1980.

_____. *The Elections in Israel: 1981.* New Brunswick, New Jersey: Transaction Books, 1984.

Arian, Asher, and Michal Shamir (eds.). *The Elections in Israel: 1984.* New Brunswick, New Jersey: Transaction Books, 1986.

Aronoff, Myron J. *Power and Ritual in the Israel Labor Party: A Study in Political Anthropology.* Assen, Netherlands: Van Gorcum, 1977.

Aronson, Shlomo. *Conflict and Bargaining in the Middle East: An Israeli Perspective.* Baltimore: Johns Hopkins University Press, 1979.

Avishai, Bernard. *The Tragedy of Zionism: Revolution and Democracy in the Land of Israel.* New York: Farrar Straus Giroux, 1985.

Ben-Meir, Dov. *HaHistadrut.* Jerusalem: Carta, 1978.

Brecher, Michael. *Decisions in Crisis: Israel, 1967 and 1973.* Berkeley and Los Angeles: University of California Press, 1980.

_____. *Decisions in Israel's Foreign Policy.* New Haven: Yale University Press, 1975.

_____. *The Foreign Policy System of Israel: Setting, Images, Process.* New Haven: Yale University Press, 1972.

Brooke, James. "In African Diplomacy, Israel Gains a Toehold," *New York Times,* July 27, 1987, A2.

Brookings Institution. *Toward Arab-Israeli Peace: Report of a Study Group.* Washington: 1988.

Caspi, Dan, Abraham Diskin, and Emanuel Gutmann (eds.). *The Roots of Begin's Success: The 1981 Israeli Elections.* New York: St. Martin's Press, 1984.

Cohen, Mitchell. *Zion and State: Nation, Class, and the Shaping of Modern Israel.* New York: Basil Blackwell, 1987.

Elazar, Daniel J., and Alysa M. Dortot (eds.). *Understanding the Jewish Agency: A Handbook.* Jerusalem: Jerusalem Center for Public Affairs, November 1985.

Elazar, Daniel J., and Chaim Kalchheim (eds.). *Local Government in Israel.* Lanham, Maryland: University Press of America, 1988.

Elizur, Yuval and Eliahu Salpeter. *Who Rules Israel?* New York: Harper and Row, 1973.

Frankel, Glenn. "Israel Imposes Sanctions on South Africa," *Washington Post,* September 17, 1987, A46.

_____. Israel Pledges to Reduce Military Ties to South Africa," *Washington Post,* March 20, 1987, A1, A26.

Frankel, William. *Israel Observed: An Anatomy of the State.* New York: Thames and Hudson, 1981.

Freedman, Robert O. (ed.). *Israel in the Begin Era.* New York: Praeger, 1982.

Friedman, Thomas L. "Israel Approves Curbs on Pretoria," *New York Times,* September 17, 1987, A4.

_____. "Israel Parliament Hears Plan on Pretoria," *New York Times,* March 20, 1987, A3.

Horowitz, Dan, and Moshe Lissak. *Origins of the Israeli Polity: Palestine under the Mandate.* Chicago: University of Chicago Press, 1978.

Hurewitz, J.C. *Middle East Politics: The Military Dimension.* New York: Octagon Books, 1974.

Kieval, Gershon R. *Party Politics in Israel and the Occupied Territories.* Westport, Connecticut: Greenwood Press, 1983.

Kifner, John. "Some Dismay on the Road to Morocco," *New York Times,* July 27, 1986, E3.

Klieman, Aaron S. *Israel's Global Reach: Arms Sales as Diplomacy.* Washington: Pergamon-Brassey's, 1985.

_____. *Statecraft in the Dark: Israel's Practice of Quiet Diplomacy.* Boulder, Colorado: Westview Press, 1988.

Laipson, Ellen B. "Israeli-American Relations," (Library of Congress Congressional Research Service, Issue Brief IB82008.) December 15, 1988.

Lapidoth, Ruth. "The Taba Controversy," *Jerusalem Quarterly* [Jerusalem], No. 37, 1986, 29-39.

Little, Tom. "Israel." Pages 452-64 in *The Middle East and North Africa, 1988.* London: Europa Publications, 1987.

Lukacs, Yehuda, and Abdalla M. Battah (eds.). *The Arab-Israeli Conflict: Two Decades of Change.* Boulder, Colorado: Westview Press, 1988.

Lustick, Ian S. *For the Land and the Lord: Jewish Fundamentalism in Israel.* New York: Council on Foreign Relations, 1988.

Lustick, Ian S. (ed.). *Books on Israel.* Albany: State University of New York Press, 1988.

Mahler, Gregory S. *Bibliography of Israeli Politics.* Boulder, Colorado: Westview Press, 1985.

Medding, Peter Y. *Mapai in Israel: Political Organization and Government in a New Society.* New York: Cambridge University Press, 1972.

Melman, Yossi, and Dan Raviv. *Shutafut Ivunit: Haksharim Hasodiim Bein Yisrael le Yerden* (Hostile Partners: The Secret Ties Between Israel and Jordan). Tel Aviv: Mitam, 1987.

Murphy, Richard W. "An American Vision of Peace in the Middle East," *Department of State Bulletin,* 88, No. 2135, June 1988, 37-38.

Oded, Arye. *Africa and the Middle East Conflict.* Boulder, Colorado: Lynne Rienner, 1987.

Patai, Raphael (ed.). *Encyclopedia of Zionism and Israel.* (2 Vols.) New York: McGraw-Hill, 1971.

Penniman, Howard R., (ed.). *Israel at the Polls: The Knesset Elections of 1977.* Washington: American Enterprise Institute, 1979.

Penniman, Howard R., and Daniel J. Elazar (eds.). *Israel at the Polls, 1981: A Study of the Knesset Elections.* Bloomington: Indiana University Press, 1986.

Peri, Yoram. *Between Battles and Ballots: Israeli Military in Politics.* New York: Cambridge University Press, 1983.

Phillips, James A. "America's Security Stake in Israel," *Heritage Foundation Backgrounder,* No. 521, July 7, 1986.

⸺. "Next Step in the Special Relationship: A U.S.-Israel Defense Council," *Heritage Foundation Backgrounder Update,* No. 76, June 5, 1988.

Quandt, William B. *Camp David: Peacemaking and Politics.* Washington: Brookings Institution, 1986.

Raphael, Gideon. *Destination Peace: Three Decades of Israeli Foreign Policy.* New York: Stein and Day, 1981.

Raviv, Dan, and Yossi Melman. "Hussein's Covert Israeli Connection," *Washington Post,* September 27, 1987, D1, D4.

Reich, Bernard. *Israel: Land of Tradition and Conflict.* Boulder, Colorado: Westview Press, 1985.

⸺. *Quest For Peace: United States-Israel Relations and the Arab-Israeli Conflict.* New Brunswick, New Jersey: Transaction Books, 1977.

⸺. *The United States and Israel: The Dynamics of Influence.* New York: Praeger, 1984.

Reich, Bernard, and Gershon R. Kieval (eds.). *Israeli National Security Policy: Political Actors and Perspectives.* New York: Greenwood Press, 1988.

Ro'i, Yaacov. "A New Soviet Policy Towards Israel?" *Jerusalem Quarterly* [Jerusalem], No. 44, Fall 1987, 3–17.

Rubenberg, Cheryl A. *Israel and the American National Interest: A Critical Examination.* Urbana and Chicago: University of Illinois Press, 1986.

Rubenstein, Sondra Miller. *The Communist Movement in Palestine and Israel, 1919–1984.* Boulder, Colorado: Westview Press, 1985.

Sachar, Howard M. *A History of Israel, I: From the Rise of Zionism to Our Time.* New York: Alfred A. Knopf, 1986.

Sager, Samuel. *The Parliamentary System of Israel.* Syracuse, New York: Syracuse University Press, 1985.

Saunders, Harold H. *The Other Walls: The Politics of the Arab-Israeli Peace Process.* Washington: American Enterprise Institute, 1985.

Schiff, Gary S. *Tradition and Politics: The Religious Parties of Israel.* Detroit: Wayne State University Press, 1977.

Schreiber, Jacob. "Does Israel Need a Constitution?" *Israel Economist* [Jerusalem], 43, April 1988, 18-20.

Segev, Tom. *1949: The First Israelis.* New York: Free Press, 1986.

Shapiro, Yonathan. *HaDemokratia Be Yisrael* (Democracy in Israel). Ramat Gan, Israel: Massada Publishing, 1977.

Sheffer, Gabriel (ed.). *Dynamics of Dependence: U.S.-Israeli Relations.* Boulder, Colorado: Westview Press, 1987.

Shinar, Dov. "The West Bank Press and Palestinian Nation-Building," *Jerusalem Quarterly* [Jerusalem], No. 43, Summer 1987, 37-48.

Shipler, David K. "For Israel and U.S., a Growing Military Partnership," *New York Times,* March 15, 1987, Week in Review, 1.

Sicherman, Harvey. *Changing the Balance of Risks: U.S. Policy Toward the Arab-Israeli Conflict.* (Policy Papers No. 11). Washington Institute for Near East Policy, 1988.

Sinai, Joshua. "A Bibliographical Review of the Modern History of Israel," *Middle East Review,* 10, No. 1, Fall 1977, 66-72.

Smith, Hanoch. *The 1988 Knesset Elections: III. A Victory for the Right and Religious Parties.* (American Jewish Committee Papers). New York: November 1988.

Spiegel, Steven. *The Other Arab-Israeli Conflict: Making America's Middle East Policy from Truman to Reagan.* Chicago: University of Chicago Press, 1985.

Tessler, Mark. "Moroccan-Israeli Relations and the Reasons for Moroccan Receptivity to Contact with Israel," *Jerusalem Journal of International Relations* [Jerusalem], 10, No. 2, June 1988, 76-108.

United States. Department of State. *Country Reports on Human Rights Practices for 1987.* (Report Submitted to the Committee on Foreign Affairs, House of Representatives, and the Committee on Foreign Relations, United States Senate.) Washington: GPO, 1988.

Washington Institute for Near East Policy. *Building for Peace: An American Strategy for the Middle East.* Washington: Washington Institute for Near East Policy, 1988.

Weiss, Shevach. *HaMahapach: Mai 1977—November 1978* (The Revolution: May 1977-November 1978). Tel Aviv: Am Oved, 1979.

Wolffsohn, Michael. *Israel: Polity, Society, and Economy, 1882-1986.* Atlantic Highlands, New Jersey: Humanities Press International, 1987.

Yanai, Nathan. *Party Leadership in Israel: Maintenance and Change.* Ramat Gan, Israel: Turtledove Publishing, 1981.

Zisar, Baruch (ed.). *The Israeli Political System: Proposals for Change.* Tel Aviv: Experimental Edition, May 1987.

Zucker, Norman L. *The Coming Crisis in Israel: Private Faith and Public Policy.* Cambridge: MIT Press, 1973.

Chapter 5

"Air War Over Israel," *Defense Update* [Hod Hasharon, Israel], No. 88, June 1988, 1–57.

Bar-Natan, Yaacov. "Arabs in the IDF," *Spectrum* [Tel Aviv], 6, No. 1, February 1988, 20–23.

Beit-Hallahmi, Benjamin. *The Israeli Connection: Who Israel Arms and Why.* New York: Pantheon, 1987.

Bensinger, Gad J. "Criminal Justice in Israel: A Research Note," *Journal of Criminal Justice,* 10, 1982, 393–401.

_____. "The Israel Police in Transition: An Organizational Study," *Police Studies* [Henley-on-Thames, United Kingdom], 4, No. 2, Summer 1981, 3–8.

Benvenisti, Meron. *West Bank Data Project, 1986 Report: Demographic, Economic, Legal, Social, and Political Developments in the West Bank.* Washington: American Enterprise Institute, 1986.

Bloom, James J. "The Six-Days-Plus-Ten-Weeks-War: Aspects of Israel's Summer Campaign in Lebanon, 1982," *Middle East Insight,* 2, No. 5, January–February 1983, 45–55.

Brower, Kenneth S. "The Middle East Military Balance: Israel Versus the Rest," *International Defense Review* [Geneva], 19, No. 7, 1986, 907–13.

Chen, Oz. "Reflections on Israeli Deterrence," *Jerusalem Quarterly* [Jerusalem], No. 24, Summer 1982, 26–40.

Chesnoff, Richard Z., and James Wallace. "The Twilight War," *U.S. News and World Report,* 104, No. 17, May 2, 1988, 30–34.

Dunn, Michael Collins. "Israel: New Priorities for a New Era," *Defense and Foreign Affairs,* 16, No. 7, July 1988, 8–14.

Dupuy, Trevor N., and Paul Martell. *Flawed Victory: The Arab-Israeli Conflict and the 1982 War in Lebanon.* Fairfax, Virginia: Hero Books, 1986.

Engel, Shimon. "The Long Road from Molotov Cocktails to Missiles, Tanks, and Lasers: A Technological History of the IDF," *IDF Journal* [Jerusalem], No. 15, Summer 1988, 22–31.

Eshel, David. "The Israeli Armed Forces: Part I: The Israeli Army," *Journal of Defense and Diplomacy,* 6, No. 6, 1988, 20–24.

Flume, Wolfgang. "Israeli Defence Industry—Peacetime Link in the Economic Chain," *Military Technology* [Bonn], February 1987, 93–100.

Friedman, Thomas L. "Israel's Development of a Major Arms Industry," *New York Times,* December 7, 1986, Section 3, 1.

_____. "Living with a Dirty War: Israel's Dilemma," *New York Times Magazine,* January 20, 1985, 32–51.

Gal, Reuven. *A Portrait of the Israeli Soldier.* Westport, Connecticut: Greenwood Press, 1986.

Gazit, Mordechai. "Israeli Military Procurement from the United States." Pages 83–124 in Gabriel Sheffer (ed.), *Dynamics of Dependence: U.S.-Israeli Relations.* Boulder, Colorado: Westview Press, 1987.

Gold, Dore. "Ground-to-Ground Missiles: The Threat Facing Israel," *IDF Journal* [Jerusalem], 4, No. 3, Fall 1987, 31–34, 62–63.

Gunston, Bill. *An Illustrated Guide to the Israeli Air Force.* Tel Aviv: Steinmatzky, 1982.

Hovav, Meir, and Menachem Amir. "Israel Police: History and Analysis," *Police Studies* [Henley-on-Thames, United Kingdom], 2, No. 2, Summer 1979, 5–31.

Hunter, Jane. "Israel and South Africa: Sidestepping Sanctions," *Middle East International* [London], No. 319, February 20, 1988, 16–17.

Inbar, Efraim. "Israeli Strategic Thinking After 1973," *Journal of Strategic Studies* [London], 6, March 1983, 36–55.

"Israel." Pages 468–82 in George R. Copley (ed.), *Defense and Foreign Affairs Handbook.* Washington: Perth Corporation, 1987.

"Israel." Pages 279–82 in Richard Sharpe (ed.), *Jane's Fighting Ships, 1988–89.* London: Jane's, 1988.

Israel. Ministry of Immigrant Absorption. *Military Service.* Jerusalem: Publications Department, Ministry of Immigrant Absorption, 1987.

Israel Prison Service: Annual Report 1986. Jerusalem: Israel Prison Service, 1987.

Katsiaficas, George. "Behind Bars in Israel," *Mideast Monitor,* 5, No. 1, 1988, 1–4.

Katzenell, Jack. "Minorities in the IDF," *IDF Journal* [Jerusalem], 4, No. 3, Fall 1987, 40–45.

Keegan, John. "Israel." Pages 301–12 in John Keegan (ed.), *World Armies.* (2d ed.) Detroit: Gale Research, 1983.

King, Barry B. "Crisis Facing Israeli Arms Industry," *Jane's Defence Weekly* [London], January 9, 1988, 17–18.

Kleiman, Aaron S. *Israel's Global Reach: Arms Sales as Diplomacy.* Washington: Pergamon-Brassey's, 1985.

Levin, Marlin, and David Halevy. "Israel." Pages 3–25 in Richard A. Gabriel (ed.), *Fighting Armies: Antagonists in the Middle East.* Westport, Connecticut: Greenwood Press, 1983.

Levran, Aharon, and Zeev Eytan. *The Middle East Military Balance, 1986.* Jerusalem: Jerusalem Post and Westview Press, 1987.

Lissak, Moshe (ed.). *Israeli Society and its Defense Establishment: The Social and Political Impact of a Protracted Violent Conflict.* London: Frank Cass, 1984.

Luttwak, Edward, and Dan Horowitz. *The Israeli Army.* New York: Harper and Row, 1975.

Michelson, Benny. "Born in Battle: A History of the IDF Through Four Decades," *IDF Journal* [Jerusalem], No. 15, Summer 1988, 8–21.

Middleton, Drew. "Israel's Defenses: As Good as Ever?" *New York Times Magazine,* May 19, 1985, 60–65, 95–97.

The Military Balance, 1988–1989. London: International Institute for Strategic Studies, 1988.

Milton, T.R. "Israel's First Line of Defense," *Air Force Magazine,* 69, No. 5, May 1986, 62–67.

Moss, Norman. "Vanunu, Israel's Bombs, and U.S. Aid," *Bulletin of the Atomic Scientists,* 44, No. 4, May 1988, 7–8.

Neff, Donald. "Israel Recycles US Arms Technology," *Middle East International* [London], No. 324, April 30, 1988, 18–19.

O'Brien, William V. "Counterterrorism: Lessons from Israel," *Strategic Review,* 13, No. 4, Fall 1985, 32–44.

Owan, Clyde. "The Arab-Israeli Naval Imbalance," *Proceedings, United States Naval Institute,* 109, No. 3, March 1983, 101–9.

Peretz, Don. "Intifadeh: The Palestinian Uprising," *Foreign Affairs,* 66, No. 5, Summer 1988, 964–80.

Peri, Yoram. *Between Battles and Ballots: Israeli Military in Politics.* New York: Cambridge University Press, 1983.

Reich, Bernard. *The United States and Israel: The Dynamics of Influence.* New York: Praeger, 1984.

Reiser, Stewart. "The Israeli Police: Politics and Priorities," *Police Studies* [Henley-on-Thames, United Kingdom], 6, No. 1, Spring 1983, 27–35.

Richelson, Jeffrey T. *Foreign Intelligence Organizations.* Cambridge, Massachusetts: Ballinger, 1988.

Schiff, Zeev. "The Government-Armed Forces Relationship." Pages 33–40 in Steven Heydemann (ed.), *The Begin Era: Issues in Contemporary Israel.* Boulder, Colorado: Westview Press, 1984.

_____. *A History of the Israeli Army: 1874 to the Present.* New York: Macmillan, 1985.

Schiff, Zeev, and Ehud Ya'ari. *Israel's Lebanon War.* New York: Simon and Schuster, 1984.

Shamir, Yitzhak. "Israel at 40: Looking Back, Looking Ahead," *Foreign Affairs,* 66, No. 3, 1987–1988, 574–90.

Sheffer, Gabriel (ed.). *Dynamics of Dependence: U.S.-Israel Relations.* Boulder, Colorado: Westview Press, 1987.

United Nations. Center for Disarmament. *Study on Israeli Nuclear Armament.* New York: United Nations, 1982.

United States. Arms Control and Disarmament Agency. *World Military Expenditures and Arms Transfers, 1987.* (Ed., Daniel Gallik.) Washington: GPO, 1988.

United States. Department of Defense. *Congressional Presentation for Security Assistance Programs, Fiscal Year 1989.* Washington: Department of Defense, 1988.

United States. Department of State. *Country Reports on Human Rights Practices for 1987.* (Report Submitted to the Committee on Foreign Affairs, House of Representatives, and the Committee on Foreign Relations, United States Senate.) Washington: GPO, 1988.

_____. *Patterns of Global Terrorism, 1986.* Washington: Department of State, 1988.

Yaniv, Avner. "The Study of Israel's National Security." Pages 63–82 in Ian S. Lustick (ed.), *Books on Israel, I.* Albany: State University of New York Press, 1988.

Yishal, Yael. "The Jewish Terror Organization: Past or Future Danger?" *Conflict,* 6, No. 4, 1986, 307–32.

Glossary

agora (pl., agorot)—An Israeli coin. One hundred agorot equal one new Israeli shekel—NIS (*q.v.*).

aliyah (pl., aliyot)—Literally, going up. The immigration of Jews to Eretz Yisrael, or the Land of Israel. Historians have classified five major periods of immigration to Israel, as follows: First Aliyah (1882–1903); Second Aliyah (1904–14); Third Aliyah (1919–23); Fourth Aliyah (1924–31); and Fifth Aliyah (1932–39).

Asefat Hanivharim (Constituent Assembly)—The Yishuv's parliamentary body and the Knesset's predecessor.

Ashkenazim (sing., Ashkenazi)—Jews of European origin.

bar—Son of; frequently used in personal names, as Bar-Lev.

ben—Son of; frequently used in personal names, as Ben-Gurion.

Bund—A political labor organization of Jewish workers founded in Vilna, Lithuania in 1897. The name is an abbreviation in Yiddish for The General Union of Jewish Workers in Russia, Lithuania, and Poland. The Bund opposed Zionism and viewed Yiddish as the only secular Jewish language.

Conservative Jews—Accept the primacy of halakah (*q.v.*) but have introduced modifications in liturgy and ritual.

Diaspora—Refers to the Jews living in scattered communities outside Eretz Yisrael (the Land of Israel) during and after the Babylonian Captivity (sixth century B.C.) and, especially, after the dispersion of the Jews from the region after the destruction of the Temple by the Romans in A.D. 70 and the Bar-Kokhba War in A.D. 132–35. In modern times the word refers to the Jews living outside Palestine or present-day Israel. When the word is applied—usually lowercased—to non-Jews, such as the Palestinian Arab refugees, the word describes the situation of the people of one country dispersed into other countries.

Druze(s)—Member of a religious community that constitutes a minority among Arabic-speaking Palestinians in Israel. Druze beliefs contain elements of Shia (*q.v.*) Islam, Christianity, and paganism.

fiscal year (FY)—Begins April 1 and ends March 31; FY 1988, for example, began April 1, 1988, and ended March 31, 1989.

Gaza Strip—former Egyptian territory occupied by Israel in the June 1967 War.

GDP (gross domestic product)—A value measure of the flow of domestic goods and services produced by an economy over a period of time, such as a year. Only output values of goods for final consumption and intermediate production are assumed to be included in final prices. GDP is sometimes aggregated and shown at market prices, meaning that indirect taxes and subsidies are included; when these have been eliminated, the result is GDP at factor cost. The word *gross* indicates that deductions for depreciation of physical assets have not been made. *See also* GNP.

GNP (gross national product)—GDP (*q.v.*) plus the net income or loss stemming from transactions with foreign countries. GNP is the broadest measurement of the output of goods and services by an economy. It can be calculated at market prices, which include indirect taxes and subsidies. Because indirect taxes and subsidies are only transfer payments, GNP is often calculated at factor cost, removing indirect taxes and subsidies.

Golan Heights—former Syrian territory occupied by Israel in the June 1967 War and formally annexed by Israel in 1981.

Greater Syria—Term used by historians and others to designate the region that includes approximately the present-day states of Jordan, Israel, Lebanon, and Syria as well as the West Bank.

Green Line—name given to the 1949 Armistice lines that constituted the de facto borders of pre-1967 Israel.

Haganah—Literally, defense. Abbreviation for Irgun HaHaganah, the Jewish defense organization formed in 1919–20 by volunteers in early Jewish communities as home guards for protection against hostile bands. It became the military arm of the Jewish Agency (*q.v.*) and went underground during the British Palestine Mandate period (1922–48) when it was declared illegal. Along with the Jewish Brigade, which fought with the Allied forces in World War II, it formed the nucleus of the Israel Defense Forces (IDF) established in 1948.

HaHistadrut HaKlalit shel HaOvdim B'Eretz Yisrael (General Federation of Laborers in the Land of Israel)—Commonly known as Histadrut. Founded in 1920, this national-level organization was also the nation's largest single employer after the government. Histadrut performs many economic and welfare services in addition to trade union activities; leadership of Histadrut has generally been drawn from the Labor Party and its predecessors.

halakah—Either those parts of the Talmud that concern legal matters or an accepted decision in rabbinical law. Sometimes translated as religious law.

Hasid (pl., Hasidim)—Member of a religious movement, known
as Hasidism, founded in the eighteenth century by Israel Ben-
Eliezer Baal Shem Tov in Eastern Europe. The movement,
still active in the 1980s, stresses the importance of serving God
in ecstasy and has strong mystical elements.
Irgun—An abbreviation for Irgun Zvai Leumi (National Military
Organization). Established in 1937 as an underground Jewish
extremist organization, also known as Etzel, derived from the
pronounced initials of its Hebrew name. A more extreme group,
known as the Stern Gang (*q.v.*), broke away from it in 1939.
Both groups were especially active during and after World War
II against the British authorities in Palestine. Both maintained
several thousand armed men until all Israeli forces were integrated after Israel declared its independence.
Israeli pound—see new Israeli shekel.
Jewish Agency—Representing the World Zionist Organization as
its executive body, the Jewish Agency works in close cooperation with the government of Israel, encourages and organizes
immigration of Jews into the country, and assists in their social and economic integration.
Keren HaYesod—Literally, Israel Foundation Fund. The central
fiscal institution of the World Zionist Organization that finances
its activities in Israel.
kibbutz (pl., kibbutzim)—An Israeli collective farm or settlement,
cooperatively owned and operated by its members and organized on a communal basis.
Knesset—Israel's parliament, a unicameral legislature of 120 members elected by universal suffrage for four-year terms; the Knesset may, through legislative procedures, call for elections before
the end of the regular term or postpone elections in time of war.
Ladino—Language based on medieval Castilian but with Hebrew
suffixes and written in Hebrew alphabet; developed and used
by Sephardim (*q.v.*).
Law of Return—Passed by Knesset in July 1950 stating that "Every
Jew has the right to come to (Israel) as an *olah* (new immigrant)."
Lehi—Acronym for Lohamei Herut Israel, literally, Fighters for
Israel's Freedom, a former resistance and political organization, created in 1939 and disbanded under pressure in 1948.
Commonly known as the Stern Gang. *See also* Irgun.
moshav (pl., moshavim)—A cooperative smallholders' settlement
of individual farms in Israel. Individuals own their farms and
personal property. Work is organized collectively, equipment
is used cooperatively, and produce is marketed jointly. There

are several variants including the moshav *ovdim,* a workers' cooperative settlement, and the moshav *shitufi,* a collective small-holders' settlement that combines the economic features of a kibbutz (*q.v.*) with the social features of a moshav. Farming is done collectively, and profits are shared equally.

new Israeli shekel (NIS)—In September 1985, the new Israeli shekel (NIS) went into circulation, replacing the Israeli shekel that had existed since 1980. (Before 1980 the Israeli currency was called the Israeli pound or lira.) The NIS is equivalent to 1,000 old Israeli shekels and is divided into 100 agorot. The require-ment for the NIS stemmed from the very rapid inflation rate of the preceding years, which also resulted in dramatic devalu-ation of the old shekel against foreign currencies; for example, from 1980 to 1985 the old shekel lost value against the United States dollar by 25,000 percent. As of August 1986, the NIS was no longer pegged to the United States dollar but rather to a trade-weighted basket of foreign currencies: 60 percent United States dollar, 20 percent West German deutschmark, 10 percent British pound, 5 percent French franc, and 5 per-cent Japanese yen. The currency notes in circulation are 5, 10, 50, and 100 NIS. The approximate exchange rate for the new Israeli shekel and the United States dollar in 1988 was NIS 1.6 = US$1.00.

Oriental Jews—*See* Sephardim.

Orthodox Jews—Adherents of that branch of Judaism that insists on a rigid and strict observance of halakah (*q.v.*) and an em-phasis on national ritual conformity.

Pale of Settlement—Area of twenty-five provinces of tsarist Rus-sia within which Jews were allowed to live, outside of which they could reside only with specific permission.

Palmach—Abbreviation for Pelugot Mahatz, shock forces. In British Palestine and until late 1948, it was a commando sec-tion of the Jewish military forces. Organized in 1941 to pro-vide the Haganah (*q.v.*) with a mobile force, it consisted of young men mostly from kibbutzim, who took military train-ing while working part-time at farming, serving in coopera-tion with the British army, without pay or uniforms.

Reform Jews (sometimes called Progressive or Liberal Jews)—Emphasize rationalism and ethical behavior, reject the abso-lute authority of halakah, and assert the private religious na-ture of Judaism.

sabra (pl., sabras)—From Hebrew word meaning "a prickly pear," but adapted to mean a native-born Israeli Jew.

Sephardim (sing., Sephardi; adj., Sephardic)—Basically Jews whose families were of Spanish or Portuguese origin, wherever resident; historically, they tended to speak Ladino (*q.v.*) or Arabic. The term is often applied to those Jews who are not Ashkenazim. Since the 1960s, Sephardim have often been called Oriental Jews.

Shabbat—Sabbath, observed from Friday sunset to Saturday sunset.

Shia (or Shiite, from Shiat Ali, the Party of Ali)—A member of the smaller of the two great divisions of Islam. The Shias supported the claims of Ali and his line to presumptive right to the caliphate and leadership of the Muslim community, and on this issue they divided from the Sunnis (*q.v.*). Shias revere Twelve Imams, the last of whom is believed to be hidden from view.

Stern Gang—*See* Lehi.

Sunni (from sunna, meaning orthodox)—A member of the larger of the two great divisions of Islam. The Sunnis supported the traditional method of election to the caliphate and accepted the Umayyad line. On this issue they divided from the Shias (*q.v.*) in the first great schism within Islam.

Talmud—Literally, teaching. Compendium of discussions on the Mishnah (the earliest codification of Jewish religious law, largely complete by 200 A.D.), by generations of scholars and jurists in many academies over a period of several centuries. The Jerusalem (or Palestinian) Talmud mainly contains the discussion of the Palestinian sages. The Babylonian Talmud incorporates the parallel discussions in the Babylonian academies.

Torah—The first five books of the Bible: Genesis, Exodus, Leviticus, Numbers, and Deuteronomy; often called the Pentateuch or the Law of Moses. In a broader sense, the entire body of traditional religious teaching and study.

ulpan (pl., *ulpanim*)—center for study, particularly for the study of Hebrew by adult immigrants to Israel.

West Bank—The area of Palestine west of the Jordan River seized from Jordan by Israel in the June 1967 War. In 1988 it remained Israeli-occupied territory and was not recognized by the United States government as part of Israel. Israelis refer to this area as Judea and Samaria.

World Zionist Organization (WZO)—Founded in August 1897 at the First Zionist Congress called by Theodor Herzl at Basel, Switzerland. The movement, named after Mount Zion in Jerusalem, was designed to establish in Palestine a national home for Jews scattered throughout the world. Since 1948 its efforts have been devoted primarily to promoting unity of the Jewish people and raising funds. In 1929 it established the Jewish Agency (*q.v.*). Until 1960 its formal name was Zionist Organization, but word *World* added in new constitution.

yeshiva (pl., yeshivot)—Traditional rabbinical school for the study of Talmud (*q.v.*).

Yiddish—A language based on medieval Rhineland German used by Jews in eastern, northern, and central Europe and in areas to which Jews from these regions migrated. It also contains elements of Hebrew, Russian, and Polish, and it is commonly written in Hebrew characters.

Yishuv—The Jewish community in Palestine before statehood. Also used in referring to the period between 1900 and 1948.

Index

Abbasids, 16
Abdul Aziz ibn Saud (king of Saudi Arabia), 45
Abdul Hamid (sultan), 30
Abdullah (king of Transjordan) (*see also* Amir Abdullah), 57, 232, 235
Abraham, 6, 8, 252
Abu Musa faction, 278
Abu Nidal organization, 78, 263, 277, 278
Acre, 16
administrative agencies (*see also* Chief Rabbinical Council), 102
administrative districts. *See* districts, administrative
Aelia Capitolina, 14
Afghanistan, 78
African countries, 203, 243, 320
Agranat Commission, 66, 67, 299
agreements, xxiv, 33-34, 35, 52, 67-68, 72, 158, 172, 235, 236, 255-56, 322
agreements for the preservation of the status quo, 105-6
agricultural sector, xvii, 161-62
Agudat Israel, xxvii-xxviii, 96, 99, 105-6, 212, 220, 355; founding and role of, 222-23; Hasidic factions of, 223; religious schools of, 131
Ahad HaAm. *See* Ginsberg, Asher (Ahad HaAm)
Ahdut HaAvodah (Unity of Labor), 40, 41, 213, 355
air force. *See* Air Corps (Hel Avir)
airline, 167
airports, xviii, 167
Al Ahd (The Covenant Society), 32
Al Aqsa Mosque, 16
Alexander II (tsar of Russia), 4, 20-21
Alexander III (tsar of Russia), 21
Alexander the Great, 11
Al Fatah (Movement for the Liberation of Palestine) (*see also* Black September group), 62, 258, 260, 275, 277-78; activity and factions of, 276, 279
Al Fatat (The Young Arabs), 32
Algeria: Al Fatah guerrillas in, 278
Al Haq (Law in the Service of Man), xxxi
Aliyah: First (1882-1903), 24, 28; Second

(1904-14), 29, 30, 57, 204; Third (1919-23), 37-38; Fourth (1924-31), 42
aliyah (aliyot): defined, 89
Alkalai, Judah (rabbi), 22
Allenby, Edmund, 35
Allon, Yigal, 74, 208, 216, 229
Al Mutawakkil, 16
Aloni, Shulamit, 217
Al Qunaytirah, 67
Altalena affair, 53, 255
Aman. *See* Intelligence Branch of general staff (Agaf Modiin: Aman)
Amana, 93, 225-26
Ames-Yissum, 155
Amir Abdullah, 32-33, 36, 45
Amir Faysal, 33, 35, 36
Amit, Meir, 229
Amital, Yehuda (rabbi), 224
Ammon, 10
Am Oved, 127
Anglicans, 120
Anglo-American Committee of Inquiry (1946), 50
Anglo-French Joint Declaration, 37
Anti-Lebanon Mountains, 87
Antiochus IV, 11
anti-Semitism, 3, 17, 20-21; in French society, 25; in Germany, 44, 48-49; of Russian tsars, 20-21
Anzar 2, 335
Arab Democratic Party, 227, 355
Arab forces: invade Israel (1948), xxiv, 51
Arab Higher Committee (AHC), xxiv, 44, 45; rejects UN resolution for partition, 51; rejects White Paper provisions, 47
Arabian Desert, 7, 15
Arab independence: geographic area for settlement, 33
Arab-Israeli conflict (*see also* Palestinian-Israeli conflict); United States position on, 320; in Yishuv (Palestine), 42-43
Arab Journalists' Association, 247
Arab League (League of Arab States): position on UN resolution regarding partition, 50-51
Arab Legion, xxiv, 52

393

Central African Republic, 243
central bank. *See* Bank of Israel (central bank)
Central Bureau of Statistics, 189
central hills or highlands, 85, 86
Central Institute for Intelligence and Special Missions (Mossad Merkazi Le Modiin Uletafkidim Meyuhadim: Mossad), xx, 327-28
Central Religious Camp, 224
chemical industry, 156-57
Chen. *See* Women's Army Corps (Chen)
Chief Rabbinate, 220
Chief Rabbinical Council, 102, 104, 220
Children of Israel, 8
China, People's Republic of, 244; military equipment sales to, 269, 318
Christianity, 13, 17; official religion of Roman Empire, 15
Christians: in Israel, xxvi, 84, 88; religious courts and councils for, 104, 195; responsibility for military service, 294
Churchill, Winston, 36, 47
Ciskei homeland, 320
Citizens' Rights Movement (CRM), 212, 355; ideological position of, 217
Civil Defense Corps, xx, 310
Civil Guard, xx, 324-25
civilian authority, 229
civil rights: court system to safeguard, 183-84; groups promoting, 228
Civil Rights in Israel, 228
Civil Servants' Union, 190
civil service (*see also* Local Authorities' Order (Employment Service) (1963)), 189-90
Civil Service Board, 190
Civil Service Law (1959), 189
climate, 87-88
clothing industry, 157-58
coalitions, political: Likud Bloc coalition, 70; National Unity Government as, xix, xxviii; of religious groups, 220-21
coastal plain, 85
Cohen, Eli, 328
Cohen, Geula, 224
Cohen, Ran, 217
Combat Engineering Corps, 310
Command and Staff School, 293
Committee of Union and Progress, 30
communications. *See* telecommunications
communism, 212, 227
Communist Party of Palestine, 227

Comprehensive Anti-Apartheid Act (1986), United States, 319
comptroller, state, 192-93, 198
conferences, 36
conscription, xxx, 288-90
Constantine (emperor of Rome), 15
Constantinople, 15, 16
constitution (*see also* Proclamation of Independence); argument over, xxvii, 53, 181-84; Basic Laws as representation of, xviii, xxvii, 182-83
construction industry, 158
cooperatives: affiliated with Histadrut, 142
Corfu, Chaim, 233
Côte d'Ivoire, 243
Council for Peace and Security, xxxii-xxxiii
Council of Settlements in Judea and Samaria (Yesha), 226
Council of Torah Sages, 104, 223, 355
councils, regional, 199
Courts Law (1957), 183, 194, 331
courts-martial, 300, 305
court system (*see also* High Court of Justice; National Labor Court; Supreme Court); civilian, 193, 331-33; Civil Service Disciplinary Court, 190; district courts in, 196, 331; Hasidic, 223; military, 193, 196, 198, 300, 331, 332; Palestinian, 331; religious, 193, 194, 195; to safeguard civil rights, 183-84; specialized courts in, 193-94; structure of, 194-98
Criminal Procedure Law (1965), 331
Crusaders, 16
currency, xvii, 163, 173
customary law, Arab: derivation of legal codes from, 194
Cyrus the Great (emperor of Persia), 11
Czechoslovakia: arms to Egypt (1955), 256, 315, 320; Yishuv receives arms from (1948), 51

Damascus, 65
Damascus (Aram-Damascus), 10, 16
Dan River, 87
Dardanelles, 33
Dari, Arieh (rabbi), 223
Daroushe, Abdul Wahab, 227
David (king of Israelites): unification and expansion by, 9-10; as warrior, 252

Israel: A Country Study

Israel Labor Party. *See* Labor Party
Israel Military Industries (IMI), 143, 316
Israel Police, xx, 189; Border Police as
subsidiary of, xx, 324; in Gaza Strip
and West Bank, 301, 323–24; organization and law enforcement responsibilities of, 323–26; reform for, 326–27
Israel Precious Stones and Diamonds Exchange, 156
Israel Prison Service, 334–36
Italy, 47

Jabotinsky, Vladimir, xxiii, 29–30,
41–42, 48, 70, 211, 218; establishes
Irgun Zvai Leumi (Etzel), 254
Jacob-Israel (son of Isaac), 8
Jaffa (Yafo), 37
Jaffee Center for Strategic Studies (Tel
Aviv University), xxxiii
Japan, 244
Jeremiah, 11
Jericho missile, 317–18
Jerusalem: as administrative division, 16;
as capital, xv; captured from Turks, 35;
as City of David, 10; Crusaders in, 16;
division in 1948 of, 52; fund-raising
program of, 199; Great Sanhedrin in,
13–14; as Islamic holy city, 16; re-
named, 14; reunification after June
1967 War, 5; siege of (A.D.66), 14
Jerusalem, East: occupation and annex-
ation of (1967), xvi, xxxvii, 5, 85, 300;
uprising among Arabs in, 303–6
Jew (definition), 106–8
Jewish Agency (*see also* Haganah; Israel
Foundation Fund (Keren HaYesod);
United Jewish Appeal (UJA); World
Zionist Organization (WZO)), 36, 37,
40, 48, 105; financing for Haganah by,
253; as national institution, 200–202;
Oriental Jews' interest in, 69; quasi-
governmental nature of, 142; rejects
British White Paper provisions, 47;
work to integrate immigrants of, 130
Jewish Agency (Status) Law (1952), 201
Jewish Brigade, 48, 254
Jewish Legion, 253
Jewish National Fund (Keren Kayemet),
26, 40, 57, 201, 202
Jewish National Home, 36
Jewish Settlement Police (Notrim), 253
Jewish state, 27

Jewish Terror Organization. *See* Gush
Emunim Underground (Jewish Terror
Organization)
Jews: Arab attack on, 42; in Eastern
Europe, 20; emancipation in Western
Europe for, 17; in Israel, 88; Nazi
persecution of, 48
Jews, Ashkenazic, 54, 88–89; differen-
tiated from Oriental Jews, 84; domi-
nance in Israeli society, xxv; dominant
group on kibbutzim, 128–29; as ethnic
group, 113–14; role in development of
Zionism, 22, 24
Jews, Oriental. *See* Jews, Sephardic
Jews, Orthodox (*see also* Agudat Israel
Party; Council of Torah Sages; Torah
Religious Front), 17, 91; arguments
with secular Jews of, xxv; importance
of religion in politics for, 220; power
of, 220–24
Jews, Sephardic (*see also* Black Panthers),
xxv, 22, 54, 89; changing political position of, 68–70; decrease in immigration of, 146; defection from Labor
Party of, 69–70; in development towns,
91; differentiated from Ashkenazic
Jews, 84, 88–89; dominance in Pales-
tine of, xxv; education in IDF for,
308–10; effect of influx of, 5–6; as eth-
nic group, 113–14; geographic and cul-
tural orientation of, 206; religious
beliefs of, 95; representation in military
support services of, 309–10
Jews in Ethiopia, 243
Jews in Iran, 234
Jews in Morocco, 232
Jews in South Africa, 243
Jiryis, Sabri, 56
Johnson-Lodge Immigration Act, 42
Johnston Plan, 235
Joint Economic Development Group
(United States-Israeli), 235
Joint Political-Military Group (JPMG),
1983, 234, 321–22
Joint Security Assistance Group (United
States-Israeli), 235
joint ventures, 316
Jonathan, 9
Jordan (*see also* Transjordan), 52; aircraft
destruction (1967), 259; Al Fatah guer-
rillas in, 278; arms from Britain and
United States for, 258; attempt to dis-
lodge PLO by, 63; border with, 85;

Index

Published Country Studies

(Area Handbook Series)

550-65	Afghanistan		550-153	Ghana
550-98	Albania		550-87	Greece
550-44	Algeria		550-78	Guatemala
550-59	Angola		550-174	Guinea
550-73	Argentina		550-82	Guyana
550-169	Australia		550-151	Honduras
550-176	Austria		550-165	Hungary
550-175	Bangladesh		550-21	India
550-170	Belgium		550-154	Indian Ocean
550-66	Bolivia		550-39	Indonesia
550-20	Brazil		550-68	Iran
550-168	Bulgaria		550-31	Iraq
550-61	Burma		550-25	Israel
550-37	Burundi/Rwanda		550-182	Italy
550-50	Cambodia		550-30	Japan
550-166	Cameroon		550-34	Jordan
550-159	Chad		550-56	Kenya
550-77	Chile		550-81	Korea, North
550-60	China		550-41	Korea, South
550-26	Colombia		550-58	Laos
550-33	Commonwealth Caribbean, Islands of the		550-24	Lebanon
550-91	Congo		550-38	Liberia
550-90	Costa Rica		550-85	Libya
550-69	Côte d'Ivoire (Ivory Coast)		550-172	Malawi
550-152	Cuba		550-45	Malaysia
550-22	Cyprus		550-161	Mauritania
550-158	Czechoslovakia		550-79	Mexico
550-36	Dominican Republic/Haiti		550-76	Mongolia
550-52	Ecuador		550-49	Morocco
550-43	Egypt		550-64	Mozambique
550-150	El Salvador		550-88	Nicaragua
550-28	Ethiopia		550-157	Nigeria
550-167	Finland		550-94	Oceania
550-155	Germany, East		550-48	Pakistan
550-173	Germany, Fed. Rep. of		550-46	Panama

550-156	Paraguay	550-89	Tunisia
550-185	Persian Gulf States	550-80	Turkey
550-42	Peru	550-74	Uganda
550-72	Philippines	550-97	Uruguay
550-162	Poland	550-71	Venezuela
550-181	Portugal	550-32	Vietnam
550-160	Romania	550-183	Yemens, The
550-51	Saudi Arabia	550-99	Yugoslavia
550-70	Senegal	550-67	Zaire
550-180	Sierra Leone	550-75	Zambia
550-184	Singapore	550-171	Zimbabwe
550-86	Somalia		
550-93	South Africa		
550-95	Soviet Union		
550-179	Spain		
550-96	Sri Lanka		
550-27	Sudan		
550-47	Syria		
550-62	Tanzania		
550-53	Thailand